Created and Directed by Hans Höfer

INSIGHT GUIDES
Japan

Edited by Malcolm B. Davis
Photography by Gorazd Vilhar, Jean Kugler
Updated by Scott Rutherford

Editorial Director: Brian Bell

APA PUBLICATIONS

Japan

Second Edition
© 1995 APA PUBLICATIONS (HK) LTD
All Rights Reserved
Printed in Singapore by Höfer Press Pte Ltd

Distributed in the United States by:	Distributed in Canada by:	Distributed in the UK & Ireland by:	Worldwide distribution enquiries:
Houghton Mifflin Company	**Thomas Allen & Son**	**GeoCenter International UK Ltd**	**Höfer Communications Pte Ltd**
222 Berkeley Street	390 Steelcase Road East	The Viables Center, Harrow Way	38 Joo Koon Road
Boston, Massachusetts 02116-3764	Markham, Ontario L3R 1G2	Basingstoke, Hampshire RG22 4BJ	Singapore 2262
ISBN: 0-395-66433-0	ISBN: 0-395-66433-0	ISBN: 9-62421-149-3	ISBN: 9-62421-149-3

ABOUT THIS BOOK

a country as culturally complex as Japan lends itself especially well to the approach taken by the 190-title *Insight Guides* series. Each book encourages readers to celebrate the essence of a place rather than try to shape it to their expectations and is edited in the belief that, without insight into a people's character and culture, travel can narrow the mind rather than broaden it.

Insight Guide: Japan is carefully structured: the first section covers the country's history and culture in a series of lively essays. The main Places section provides a comprehensive run-down on the places worth seeing – and not worth seeing. Finally, a fact-packed listings section contains all the information you'll need on travel, hotels, restaurants, shops and opening times. Complementing the text, remarkable photography sets out to communicate directly and provocatively life as it is lived by the locals.

The Expert Team

The book turned out to be one of Apa Publications' heftiest titles – and, needless to say, demanded a budget to match. But it quickly became a notable success, both with critics and with readers, and this current edition has been thoroughly updated by **Scott Rutherford** to take account of recent developments. In addition, Apa has produced a companion volume, *Insight Guide: Tokyo*, which examines Japan's capital in equal detail.

The original edition was masterminded by project editor **Malcolm B. Davis** of McDavis Associates, Inc. Having written for and edited travel and other books and magazines in Japan for 27 years, including the highly successful *ANA WINGSPAN* inflight monthly for All Nippon Airways and the quarterly *The Fountains* for Japan Airlines' Nikko Hotels, he was in a unique position to pull together the writing team for this project. He assembled no fewer than 18 top "Japan Hands," plus a remarkable galaxy of talented photographers who shared their experience with us. Actually, what Mac did was yell "help!" and hope for the best, he admits.

Fortunately, the best were not slow in answering. One of the first was author, book editor and craft specialist **Kim Schuefftan**, who contributed the extensively researched and insightful sections on history, festivals, architecture and gardens, traditional performing arts and Japanese crafts.

Next was **Alex Kerr**, bringing with him a number of Yale-Oxford degrees in things Oriental, and a deep love for and knowledge of Kyoto and Nara.

Also armed with some impressive academic credentials (USC, Waseda, University of Hawaii, Doshisha University) came **John Carroll**, pitching in to handle the sections on Okinawa, Yokohama, Kamakura, Narita and Chiba as well as a knowledgeable essay on Japanese religion.

Almost by accident, **Steve Usdin** became the next to heed the call, having dropped by the *WINGSPAN* editorial offices pitching a series of travel stories on southern Japan on the very day Mac was looking for someone with fresh eyes to cover that part of the country for this book. Usdin, a Washington, DC-based technical writer, was the only contributor who wasn't resident in Japan.

Thanks, too, to two seasoned Japan Hands: **Davis Barrager** (20 years), our dining/wining guru, and **Mark Schreiber** (24 years),

Davis

Kerr

Carroll

Usdin

Barrager

linguist, consumer analyst and consummate wit; to former editor (*Tokyo Journal*), author (*The Joy of Sumo*) and graduate of Beloit College ("the Yale of the Midwest") **David Benjamin**; to veteran journalist and inveterate *bushido* fanatic **Anthony J. Bryant**; to neo-novelist, *Japan Times* satirist and Sendai resident **Bruce Leigh**; to Kansai's most famous copywriter-cum-TV personality **Rich Blumm**; to tea maven and Kobeite **Peter Ujlaki**; to **Peter Hadfield**, best-selling author (*60 Seconds That Will Change the World – The Coming Tokyo Earthquake*) and former diamond- and oil-sleuth; to art expert **Arturo Silva**, author of the unique handmade book *Philosophy of the Shirt*, now a collector's item; to poet, teacher and Nagoya expert **Gail Feldman**, whose life goal is "to become a child prodigy"; to our friends from the long-loved *Tokyo Weekender*, associate editor **Evelyn Corbett** and sports editor **Wayne Graczyk**; and finally to the one woman in Tokyo who has already forgotten more about Japanese cinema than most people would ever want to know, **Jeanette Amano.**

The Photographers

Nothing gets done in Japan without consensus, of course, and the unanimous consensus among the staff in Tokyo as to how to maintain the high standards of photography set by Apa Publications was to dump the whole thing in the lap of **Robert McLeod**. He not only had eminent qualifications as a journalistic and editorial photogra-

pher, he also was a formidable commercial "stock" shooter, with fine collections in some of the world's leading stock photo houses. His tireless efforts to secure not only the most visually interesting but also the freshest and most revealing photography for this book greatly enhanced the book.

The distinction of having the Most Pictures Picked goes to Japan-based **Gorazd Vilhar**, whose discerning photographic eye and unique perspective on Japanese culture and people first came to our attention in *Cityguide: Tokyo*. Vilhar's work in *Japan* confirms our earlier suspicions: the guy knows how to take a great photo.

Jean Kugler lives in Kyoto but spends much of his time traveling in Japan and around the world, in search of the decisive moment. Proof of his success can be found in this book. His ability to come up with the photographic goods time after time has led to a long association with Apa Publications.

Carol Jopp of the Globe Press Agency in Hong Kong demonstrates the fine art of landscape photography. Featured here are many outstanding images of the Japanese countryside (and people, too).

Arigato also to **Miguel Rivas-Micoud** and his *Cityguide: Tokyo* team of photographers, who proved to be a natural resource for photos of the Kanto region.

Finally, special thanks to master photographer **Ken Straiton**; to McDavis staffers **Yumi Hirano** and **Ken Takashima**, who updated the listings for the Travel Tips section; and especially to **Hiromi Uchida Davis**, who said (and we quote): "I *told* you so."

Schreiber

Hadfield

McLeod

Vilhar

Kugler

CONTENTS

History

Features

Places

Maps

TRAVEL TIPS

**For detailed Information
See Page 373**

TOWARD A MORE SCRUTABLE JAPAN

A wanderer among the thousands of islands that make up the great Pacific nation of Japan usually seeks the exotic, the wondrous, the unconventional. First impressions, of cherry trees, temples, and snowy mountains, will not be disappointing. Inevitably, however, the traveler recognizes more and more familiarities, until it starts to seem that, apart from language and faces, Japan is quite Occidental. The thought then begins to occur to the traveler that Japan has become like the West.

Japan has always taken foreign things that are of use – or simply of interest – and made them, somehow, completely Japanese. Japan has adopted Chinese writing, Korean art and ceramics, and Western technology, clothes and fast-food. It is estimated that 10 percent of daily conversation involves English loan words. To the Japanese, there is nothing especially foreign about baseball, Valentine's Day or *tempura* (originally from Portugal).

Although Japan derives most of its culture from Asian neighbors, and most of its modernity from the West, the Japanese continue to cultivate a self-image of divine uniqueness, referring to things in Japan – including themselves – as "special" and thus beyond an outsider's understanding. Its special kind of snow did not suit imported skis, and the special Japanese digestive system has kept out imported beef.

Of course, Japan *is* special. It has become the world's second-largest economy while evenly, and uniquely, distributing the country's wealth – and without generating an economic lower class. But having done so, it has made itself into an extraordinarily expensive place, with rural land prices more expensive than the best Beverly Hills property.

Japan radiates an international image of technical sophistication and manufacturing efficiency, yet it is oddly behind the times. Just two-thirds of Japanese dwellings are connected to a modern sewage system, and less than 30 percent of elementary schools have access to a computer for teaching, compared with more than 90 percent in Western countries

There are those, Japanese and foreigners alike, who sustain an image of a Japan in a Zen-like serenity draped beneath cherry blossoms. It is a wistful image, a nostalgic retreat into one's dreams, or at best, amidst Kyoto's temples and shrines. The novelist and nationalist Mishima Yukio commented that, "Japan will disappear, it will become inorganic, empty, neutral-tinted; it will be wealthy and astute." Cultures and societies by nature change, shift, disappear and this applies to Japan too. But what does it matter? Japan suits the Japanese, it seems, and that's what counts.

(*Note: the names of all Japanese mentioned in this book are written in Asian style, that is, family name first, given name last.*)

Preceding pages: portrait of a *maiko* (apprentice geisha) pair; wedding day; the Emperor's birthday is a flag-waving occasion; punks mug for the camera in Harajuku. **Left,** juicy fruit.

THE LAND: TAME TO TORMENTED

The Japanese islands were formed from the tears of a goddess. Where each tear fell into the waters of the Pacific, there arose an island in its place.

So goes the legend. But no less poetic – and dramatic – is the scientific view of the origins of this huge archipelago, stretching from the subtropical waters of Okinawa to the frozen wastes of northern Hokkaido. The islands were born of massive crustal forces acting deep underground, and shaped by volcanos spitting out mountains of lava.

The results we see today are spectacular. Japan has long been regarded as one of the most scenic places on the planet, with towering, snow-capped mountain ranges and 27,000 kilometers (16,800 miles) of indented coastline ranging from tame to tormented.

Four Main Islands: The archipelago consists of four main islands – Kyushu, Shikoku, Honshu and Hokkaido (Honshu being by far the largest and most populous of the four) – and about 3,900 smaller islands. Together they stretch from southwest to northeast over a distance of 3,800 kilometers (2,365 miles) off the east coast of Asia, roughly the equivalent of a line reaching from northern Chad to southern Austria. All the main islands of Japan are noted for their rugged terrain, with 70–80 percent of the country being extremely mountainous.

Most of the mountains were uplifted over millions of years as the oceanic crust of the Pacific collided with the continental crust of Asia. The oceanic crust submerged beneath the thicker continental crust, buckling the edge of it and forcing up the mountain chains that form the backbone of the Japanese archipelago.

Other mountains in Japan – including Mt. Fuji, the highest – are volcanic in origin. They were formed from molten lava that originated far below the Earth's surface, as the oceanic crust sank into the superheated depths of the upper mantle. The molten rock was forced up through fissures and faults, exploding onto the surface.

Ice, wind, rain and glacial action did the

Left, white on blue: ice forest on the slopes of Mount Shirane.

rest, sculpting the mountains and sending the eroded debris down towards the coast to form the familiar plains of today.

Volcanoes and Earthquakes: One of the attractions of a visit to Japan is the possibility of seeing these forces in action. About 60 of Japan's 186 volcanos are still "active" in geological terms, and occasionally they make their presence felt. Mt. Mihara on Oshima, one of the Seven Isles of Izu, near Tokyo, is one example. It exploded as recently as 1986, forcing thousands of residents to evacuate the island. A few years earlier, the central peak of another Izu island, Miyakejima, erupted to bury the island's largest village under several meters of lava. Mt. Sakurajima, near Kagoshima in Kyushu, regularly spews ash – so much so that local people have resigned themselves to constantly having to wash their cars – and faces!

Earthquakes are a far more frequent occurrence than volcanic eruptions, especially around the more seismically active areas near Tokyo. They are also a more serious threat and the Japanese government currently spends billions of yen a year on one of the most sophisticated earthquake early warning system in the world – not that it works particularly well.

Most Japanese, however, tend not to dwell on the more morbid aspects of geological activity, preferring to enjoy its pleasures instead. *Onsen*, or hot springs, are a direct result of the massive quantities of heat released underground, and for centuries have occupied a special place in Japanese culture.

Climate: Another popular Japanese pastime, as the visitor will soon discover, is talking about the weather. Japanese people, as a matter of routine, nearly always greet each other by commenting on the weather, and the changing seasons still attract an unwarranted amount of attention from what is, after all, a largely urban society.

Using our earlier comparison, just as the climate in Chad is greatly different to that of Austria, so the two extremities of Japan, from the coral reefs of Okinawa to the ice floes of northern Hokkaido, are in very dissimilar climatic zones. Because of the high mountain ranges running the spine of Honshu island, there are also major climatic differences between the Japan Sea coast and the Pacific Ocean coast of Honshu.

Winter and Spring: Being a Northern Hemisphere country, the seasons are, of course, similar to those of Europe and North America. The coldest months are December through February, when the Japan Sea side of Hokkaido and Honshu experience heavy falls of snow.

The Pacific Ocean side, by contrast, is very dry during the winter months. This is accentuated in Tokyo by urban growth, which has tended to reduce evaporation and therefore is the cause of a further drop in winter rainfall. Winter water shortages are

Alas, the burst of spring that follows is all too short. Soon after the cherry blossoms have fallen they are blown around by strong, southerly winds which bring with them occasional rain and precede the start of *tsuyu*, the rainy season. Temperatures rise quickly, and continuous rains begin to fall about two months after the end of the cherry blossom season. (The Japanese are very definitive about their seasons. One weather forecaster once announced on television: "The rain you are now experiencing is not the rainy season rain – the rainy season will start as soon as this rain finishes.")

Summer and Fall: Once again, the central mountains of Japan define the boundaries of

now becoming a serious annual problem in the capital.

The southern areas of Kyushu and the Nansei islands have a relatively mild winter, and are the first to experience the coming of spring. This manifests itself with the flowering of the cherry blossom, an event which the Japanese like to celebrate with a festival called *hanami*.

The cherry trees flower in Kyushu towards the end of March, and the phenomenon moves slowly northwards, finally reaching Hokkaido about the second week in May. The cherry blossom season is one of the best times to visit Japan.

the rain fronts. On the Pacific Ocean coast of Honshu the rain is soft and drizzly. Further south and on the Japan Sea coast it is hard and much more tropical in nature, and in the southern areas especially the rain is often accompanied by typhoons. Hokkaido has a very indistinct rainy season.

The rains ease around late June on the Pacific Ocean side and make way for the hot, humid summer. Temperatures reach a peak in August, when many city dwellers escape to the cool comfort of the mountains. It is easy to forget that Tokyo is on the same latitude as Athens, and, with the exception of Hokkaido, all areas of Japan suffer from a very uncomfortable summer season. The city of Yamagata, for example, which is buried under one meter of snow in the winter, once recorded Japan's highest-ever summertime temperature: 40.8°C (105.4°F).

The warm body of water around Japan causes the heat of summer to linger into September, with occasional balmy days in October. But as the warm air mass moves south, the rains return, this time on the backs of devastating typhoons.

Typhoons: Generally three or four typhoons hit Japan during this season, smaller ones in August building up to larger ones in September. The southern, Pacific Ocean side of Japan bears the brunt of these ferocious

winds, which are quite capable of knocking down houses and wrecking ships, but they have generally blown themselves out by the time they reach the more populated centers of the Kanto Plain.

When the typhoon season ends, the Japanese islands once again relax to a relatively placid autumn. October and early November are the best times to visit Japan, not only because of the mild weather, but also because the changing autumn foliage turn the mountains into a spectacular blaze of color.

Left, autumnal colors blanketed by a sudden snow storm. **Above**, volcanic coastline.

A Land Divided: Despite the dominance of mountains in these islands, the Japanese are not a mountain people, preferring instead to concentrate all activities on the coastal plains, or squeeze them into the valleys of the interior. Being thus separated from each other by mountains, once taking days to traverse, the populated areas tended to develop independently, their dialects and other social peculiarities quite distinct; at the same time, the isolation and challenge of making maximum practical use of available land meant that quite advanced farming, land management and even communications techniques evolved early in the country's history.

The highest peaks occur in the Japan Alps of central Honshu, which are divided into the ranges of the Northern, Central and Southern Alps. Many of the landforms in these mountain ranges were sculpted by glaciers during an ice age, more than 27,000 years ago. "Cirques," or depressions, left where the glaciers formed, are still a common site on some higher slopes. Debris brought down by melting ice can also be seen lower down.

By far the largest of these flatlands is the Kanto Plain, an area centered on Tokyo Bay that was formed by a build up of sediments due to Ice Age-induced changes in sea level. Other extensive areas of flat land occur in the Tohoku region of northern Honshu, in Hokkaido, and along the Nagoya-Osaka industrial belt.

Such is the concentration of resources in these plains that factories, farmland, housing and public facilities are all crowded into approximately 20 percent of Japan's land area, and compete fiercely for space.

Thus very little of what one might call "countryside" exists on the plains. Cities, towns and villages tend to merge into an indistinct urban blur that stretches endlessly across the flat land, with fields and farms dotted in between.

The main industrial regions are the Kanto and Kansai areas, centering on Tokyo and Osaka respectively. The Kanto area alone produces nearly a third of Japan's entire gross domestic product. If it were an independent nation it would produce more goods and services than the whole of Great Britain.

Once again, it is the Kanto region, and Tokyo in particular, which has benefited from the recent rise in services. Metropolitan Tokyo now has a nominal population of over

8 million, but in fact the city spreads beyond its political boundaries and the Tokyo-Yokohama conurbation forms a massive urban complex that stretches across the South Kanto Plain. The actual population of this megalopolis could conservatively be estimated at around 20 million, and is sometimes stated as 25 million.

Metropolitan Tokyo and Yokohama are the first and second cities of Japan, respectively. Third in size comes Osaka, with a population of 3.2 million, followed by Nagoya with a little over 2 million.

Garden-Sized Farms: These cities have experienced phenomenal growth in the postwar years, as Japan's urban industrialization

and rural mechanization drew people off the farms and into the cities. Many rural communities are now suffering from an increasingly aged population, and some have become virtual ghost towns. Farming on the garden-size Japanese farms is only made profitable by heavy subsidies from the government, and sons and daughters are becoming less interested in taking over the family farm than in gaining an easy office job in the city.

This demographic problem is not one that will in future be restricted to the countryside. Japan as a whole has one of the slowest population growth rates in the world (0.7 percent), and many analysts believe that the

problem of an aging population will, more than anything else, eventually lead to Japan's demise as a world economic leader.

The reasons for this low growth rate are not hard to find. The average Japanese enjoys the longest life expectancy in the world (75.61 for men, 81.39 for women). At the other end of the scale, the overcrowded condition of the cities, which forces couples to live in cramped two- or three-room apartments, is not conducive to large families, and one child per family is the norm.

Too Few Resources: The concentration of employment opportunities in the cities is mirrored by a lack of job prospects in the countryside. Unlike most other modern, industrial nations, Japan has few natural resources and has depended heavily on its manufacturing industry as a source of wealth and employment.

There are coal mines in Hokkaido and Kyushu, but coal production peaked in 1941, and many coal mining communities are now in serious decline. Nearly all of Japan's other raw materials, such as oil, minerals and metal ores, are imported.

Timber is one resource Japan has in abundance, as most of the country's mountains are covered in natural or plantation forest. The natural cover varies from sub-arctic conifers in Hokkaido to deciduous and evergreen temperate broad-leafed trees throughout the other three main islands. Yet despite a soaring demand for timber, used in the construction industry and for paper-making, domestic production has actually been falling in recent years. The Japanese prefer to buy cheap, imported timber from the tropical rain forests of Southeast Asia, a practice which is causing considerable concern among many environmentalists.

Fishing is another rural occupation that has declined in activity, mainly because of a decline in fish stocks as a result of over-exploitation. Japanese fleets now operate in international waters far away, and home ports that once supported domestic fishing fleets are turning towards other occupations.

One of the most lucrative of these is tourism. As the urban Japanese become more affluent and seek recreation outside the cities, ports and harbors are being turned into leisure marinas, hotels and resorts are springing up all over the countryside, and mountains are being leveled in order to make way for golf courses. This has effected a retreat of the natural environment and an increase in pollution.

Ah, Nature!: Here it is worth noting a paradox. It has always been one of the proud boasts of the Japanese that they live close to and in harmony with nature. Nature is always a strong theme in Japanese poetry, and, as already noted, the Japanese are preoccupied with the weather and the changing of the seasons.

To the Japanese, man is a part of nature, and therefore anything man constructs can be considered part of the environment. A Japanese can look upon a garden – moulded, cut, sculptured and trimmed to perfect proportions – and still see it as a perfect expression of "nature."

The result of this philosophy has been disastrous for the indigenous wildlife of Japan. The crested ibis, for example, once considered to be a representative bird of Japan, and common throughout the archipelago 100 years ago, is reduced today to less than a dozen individuals, and the species is on the verge of extinction.

The Japanese crane (*tancho*) is also close to extinction, though the bird was once common in Hokkaido. Fish, such as salmon and trout, are no longer able to survive in Japan's polluted rivers and lakes. Brown bears have been hunted almost to extinction, and only recently have hunting laws been amended and the animal recognized as an endangered species. A few hundred remain on Hokkaido.

Of the other land mammals, the Japanese monkey, or *macaca*, is by far the most common in Japan. Originally a creature of the tropical rain forests, the *macaca* has adapted to the more temperate climates of these islands and can now be found throughout Kyushu, Shikoku and Honshu, although its numbers have been sharply reduced since the 1950s. During the winter months, *macaca* in one district of Nagano prefecture take to bathing in the local hot springs in order to keep warm.

In the far south of Japan, the Nansei Islands have a distinctive fauna and flora of their own. Here the natural forests are subtropical, but many of the indigenous species of fauna have now become rare or

even extinct. The most spectacular characteristic of these islands is the marine life. Most of the Nansei Islands (Okinawa, among others) are surrounded by coral, home to a rich and colorful variety of warm water fish. Yet here again, the rapid growth of the tourist and leisure industry – especially that of SCUBA diving – has led to the destruction of much of this natural coral.

Needless to say, nearly all the natural fauna and flora of the valleys and flat lands of Japan have been driven out in the intense competition for space. A quilt pattern of small rice paddy fields now dominates the areas outside the main urban conurbations, and Japanese farmers have become adept at

intensive cultivation of fruit and vegetables in large greenhouses.

In Hokkaido, the greater availability of space and natural moorland vegetation have led to the growth of a cattle and dairy industry. Meat is gradually becoming a more important part of the Japanese diet, just as rice is declining in popularity. In a sense, this is symptomatic of the way Japanse culture is changing over the years. The new generations are gradually turning away from the traditional fish-and-rice diet to eat more meat and bread, as Japan becomes more affluent, more urbanized, and, one suspects, increasingly more "advanced" in outlook.

Left, quintessentially Japan: cherry blossoms and Mt. Fuji. **Above**, rice field near Kyoto.

The lands that are now the Japanese archipelago were first inhabited by human beings between 100,000 and 200,000 years ago, during the Paleolithic Period. Archaeology of Paleolithic sites in Japan only began in the 1960s, so a clear picture of the earliest human habitation has yet to emerge. The shallow seas separating Japan from the Asian mainland were incomplete when people first settled on the terrain. However it is certain that the formation of islands took place after people arrived.

Whether or not these settlers are the ancestors of the present Japanese remains a controversy. It is generally agreed that Japan was settled by waves of people coming from the islands of South Asia and the northern regions of the Asian continent, and that these waves of migration very likely occurred over a long period.

Jomon Period (ca 10,000–300 BC): Japan's earliest pottery has been dated at about 10,000 BC, the oldest known in the world. Whether the pottery from this earliest period should be classified as belonging to a Mesolithic culture or as part of the subsequent Neolithic Jomon Period has not been resolved, but scholars generally refer to this ware as belonging to the earliest Jomon culture.

The earliest millennia of Neolithic culture saw a warm age in worldwide climate, reaching peak temperature levels between 8000 and 4000 BC. In Japan, this phenomenon led to rising sea levels, which cut any remaining land bridges to the Asian mainland.

At the same time, the local waters produced more abundant numbers and species of fish and shellfish. New types of forest sprang up and thrived in both northeastern and southwestern Japan. These natural developments in the environment set the stage for the Early Jomon Period.

The Early Jomon people were mostly coastal-living, food-gathering nomads. Dietary reliance on coastal fish, shellfish, and

Preceding pages, a picture from *Tale of the Genji* by Lady Murasaki Shikibu, Heian Period. **Left**, a clay figure doll, Jomon Period. (These items and those on pages 32–47 belong to the Tokyo National Museum.)

sea mammals gave rise to the community refuse heaps known as shellmounds, the archaeologist's primary source of information about these people. The Early Jomon people also hunted deer and wild pig. Typical artifacts include stone blade tools and the first cord-marked (*jomon* means "cord-marked") pottery, the type of pottery decoration that gives this culture its name. In addition, numerous stone implements show that wild seeds and other plant foods were gathered and eaten.

In the Middle Jomon Period (from about 3500 to 2500 or 2000 BC), the locus of life shifted away from coastal settlements toward inland areas. Fish and shellfish, by this time, may have been depleted by lower sea levels. Or more reliance may have been placed on plant foods as dietary staple. Grinding stones, capped storage jars, and other Middle Jomon artifacts indicate a much more intense involvement with plant food processing. Some evidence seems to point to actual cultivation of garden-plot crops.

At this time, pottery developed the wild, flamboyant rim projections and sinuous relief decoration often associated with the Jomon Period. The Middle Jomon pots are the ones that television documentaries highlight to illustrate the Jomon culture. Although most of the major pieces discovered to date from this era have become very famous and are without doubt unsurpassed examples of ceramic surface decoration and design, they are not typical of Jomon pottery as a whole, which was produced over a period estimated at 10,000 years.

Middle Jomon came to an end when tree crops in inland hilly areas failed to provide sufficient sustenance. Late Jomon, from about 2000 BC, is marked by a conspicuous resurgence of coastal fishing along the Pacific seaboard. Fishermen even risked the open sea with newly developed fishing tools and techniques.

Pottery during the Late and Final Jomon Periods (from about 1000 BC) became increasingly refined, using finer clays and smaller decoration. Pottery figurines, mainly female figures, also appear during the Late Jomon.

Yayoi Period (ca 300 BC–AD 300): Southwestern Japan received no influence from peoples living to the east and the north during this period. Instead, the people living in Kyushu and western Honshu received considerable influence from more advanced peoples residing on the Korean Peninsula. Probably the most dramatic impact of all was the practice of wet-rice cultivation – introduced in Kyushu about 300 BC – which basically changed the culture of the Japanese archipelago. (In northern Japan, the Jomon culture persisted well into Japan's early historic periods.)

The Yayoi Period (named after an archaeological site near Tokyo University in the Hongo area of Tokyo), which followed the Final Jomon Period, was a time of major

cultural transition, ushered in by peoples who migrated from rice-growing areas of the Asian mainland into northern Kyushu via Korea and, most likely, the Ryukyu Islands. Their permanent-settlement culture, with its wheel-turned pottery, was based on irrigated rice agriculture.

In a brief 600 years, Japan was transformed from a land of nomadic hunting-gathering communities into one of stationary farming villages. These communities formed the basis for the small-scale "kingdoms" characteristic of the Tumulus Period, which followed Yayoi. The Yayoi rice culture gave rise to the intense attention to the

cycle of the four seasons, the essential ethics and mores, and the fundamental social patterns that dominated life in Japan for the next two millennia, right up to the present.

The first rice culture communities developed in northern Kyushu, and their influence spread rapidly throughout the entire Inland Sea region. The new rice-farming techniques, along with cultivation tools and bronze weaponry brought in by mainland immigrants, were merged into a vigorous cultural mix, which included polished stone tools persisting from the prior Jomon Period. Shellmounds were still made by early Yayoi peoples, who continued to live in pit-house settlements.

In the Middle Yayoi Period, new tools and water control systems appeared. Some of these tools were probably made of iron, which followed the appearance of bronze working by only a brief century or two. The growth of tight-knit, autonomous rice-farming settlements was so rapid in Kyushu and western Honshu that, by AD 100, such settlements were found in most parts of the country, except for the extreme northern region of Honshu and Hokkaido.

In the Late Yayoi Period, distinct political units had developed, with individual communities forming close interdependent ties and evolving into small "countries."

Tumulus Period (ca AD 300–552): The Protohistoric Age begins with this period when – with bronze, then iron, technology to rely on – political and social institutions developed rapidly. The break with Yayoi culture is represented by the construction of huge earth and stone tomb mounds in coastal areas of Kyushu and along the shores of the Inland Sea. The first of these tombs, which included ceramic vessels, armor, weapons, and other grave furniture, were probably built between AD 250 and 300.

Hollow clay human and animal figures and models of houses called *haniwa* decorated the perimeters of these tombs. These were made, so it is said, as substitutes for the living retainers and possessions of the departed noble or leader. The largest number of Tumuli is found in the Yamato Plain, the area where the first imperial capitals were established (modern Osaka and Nara prefectures). The tomb, reputed to be that of the Emperor Nintoku (early 5th century), is one of the world's largest burial mounds.

Each of the Tumulus-period clusters of

communities that defined themselves as a "country" or "kingdom" had a hierarchical social structure; the tumuli were built to house the remains of the rulers. As this period continued, these independent "kingdoms" were subjected to increasing influence by a burgeoning central government based in the Yamato Plain. In general, it seems that the line of the most powerful chieftains of the Yamato Plain area increasingly claimed and consolidated rule over the whole of Tumulus culture in Japan in the later years of that period, largely by forming alliances with regional chieftains. Military force may have been a factor, but spiritual pedigree may have been of equal or even greater importance.

The imperial line, the so-called Yamato Sun Line, was most likely formed from one of a number of powerful *uji* (family-clan communities), which developed in the Late Yayoi Period. An uji community comprised a central family and its relatives as well as numbers of subjects – in short a clan, not unlike those of Scotland. The head of an uji wielded power as high priest, political administrator, labor manager, and distributor of community resources. The Yamato uji that became the imperial line claimed direct descent from Amaterasu Omikami, the Sun Goddess. Today, this claim is still made by a few Japanese (notably those of the right wing) but has been officially denied both by the government and – more importantly – by the Imperial Household Agency.

The 4th and 5th centuries comprise an age of contest and contention among restless, power-hungry clans. By the 6th century, the Yamato Sun Line had firmly established itself at the top of the hierarchy of local, loosely allied clans.

In time, the Sun Line obliged these lesser communities heads to organize hereditary vocational groups to provide products and work services for the central Yamato court. Each of the clans was given a specific work role and social ranking, with honorary titles bestowed by the imperial court.

Imperial rule was transmitted in the fraternal line within the Yamato uji. The earliest emperors were selected and confirmed by a process of consensus among uji leaders. But

Left, earthenware pot, Jomon Period. **Above**, bell-shaped bronze vessel, Yayoi Period.

in the latter half of the 6th century, the reigning emperor gained the power to select his own successor. About this same time, the three symbols of imperial rule – sword, mirror, and curved jewel – were passed on to each new emperor at his investiture.

Asuka Period (550–710): Buddhism came to Japan in the 6th century (the traditional date given is 552) from the Korean kingdom of Paekche. Though it is said that writing accompanied the religion, it seems that Chinese writing techniques preceded the religion by as much as 100 years to 150 years. It was literacy that made the imported religion accessible to the nobility and also exposed them to the thought of the Chinese classics

and writings of sages such as Confucius and Mencius. Such exposure also resulted in social and political change.

With the advent of Buddhism, the aggressive Soga clan strove to establish the faith as the official state religion. Their efforts met with some success. Emperor Yomei (reigned 585–587) and all succeeding emperors adopted the Buddhist faith.

The power of the Soga clan was enhanced by exclusive control of the imperial treasury and granaries and by the clan's monopolistic role as sponsor for new learning brought in from the Asian mainland. Their consolidation of political power culminated with Soga daughters being chosen exclusively as the consorts of emperors and with Soga clansmen filling important court positions. The same phenomenon occurred many centuries later with the Fujiwara clan in the Heian court.

The great figure of Shotoku Taishi (regent 593–622), who was appointed regent for his aunt, Empress Suiko, is associated with the first significant moves away from the native political system and in the direction of a system of central government based on Chinese models.

The event in question was his Seventeen-Article Constitution, which was promulgated in 604. After the death of Shotoku, a period of political unrest followed, which set the

stage for moving the capital and for the political changes embodied in the Taika Reforms of 646, promulgated by Emperor Kotoku. The series of imperial edicts that make up the Taika Reforms were aimed primarily at strengthening the central government and reducing the power of the clans at the imperial court. The Reforms were radical and far-reaching, including changes in social structure, economic system, legal system, provincial boundaries, bureaucracy, and taxes.

Yet another and equally sweeping political and social reform happened again in 689, with the promulgation of the Kiyomihara

Code by Emperor Tenmu. The capital changed location twice more before the end of the century, and the year 701 saw the completion of the vast Taiho Codes (*Taiho Ritsuryo*), which were to set the scene for the government of the subsequent Nara Period.

While the 6th century was one in which Japan encountered the intellectual developments of the Asian mainland head on, the 7th century saw the profound effects of this meeting, particularly in the areas of society and government.

Nara Period (710–794): Empress Gemmei (reigned 707–715) again constructed a new capital, this one in the northwest of the Yamato Plain and named Heijokyo, on the site of present Nara City. The court moved there in 710. The century that comprises the Nara Period saw the full enforcement of the system of centralized imperial rule based on Chinese concepts (the *ritsuryo* system) as well as a flourishing of art and culture.

It had become accepted practice to construct imperial capitals on the Chinese grid plan. Heijokyo was no exception. Streets were aligned in a strict north-south, east-west grid, with the focal point being the imperial palace situated north of center. Buddhist temples and monasteries lined the avenues, as did the residences and palaces of courtiers and aristocrats.

With the enforcement of the *ritsuryo* system, the imperial government achieved tight control during the early part of the period. This system placed administrative control in the powerful Grand Council of State (Dajokan), which was in charge of eight subordinate ministries. Government officials, including those of local government, were theoretically appointed by the emperor and were his direct representatives.

Political division included provinces, districts, villages and hamlets. One official document dating from the early Nara recognizes 67 provinces, 555 districts, 4,012 villages, and 12,036 hamlets. All land used for rice cultivation was claimed to be under imperial ownership, which later led to heavy taxation of farmers and subsequently to the weakening of the ritsuryo system in the Heian Period, which followed Nara. Also, the effective range of influence of the imperial court remained limited.

The year 712 saw the completion of the *Kojiki* and 720, that of the *Nihon Shoki,* the first great historical chronicles of Japan. These books combine myth, legend and event and recount the history of the imperial line and of episodes involving the country's leading families and personalities in the early centuries.

The reign of Emperor Shomu (r. 724–749) saw the high point of the Nara Period, the fabled Tempyo era. This era is best known for its cultural and artistic achievements, spectacularly represented by the Great Buddha of Nara and the vast (the world's largest) wooden building of the Todaiji temple, which houses the figure. Ample evidence of the accomplishments of this time have been preserved in the Shosoin Repository of the Todaiji. This is the building that has housed

year Heian Period; it remained the imperial capital until 1868 and is the hub around which the city of Kyoto developed.

The strength of the central government continued for several decades, but later in the 9th century the ritsuryo system gradually began to crumble. With the central government interested in expanding the area of its influence farther and farther from the capital, provincial government became harder to manage under the bureaucratic ritsuryo system.

This was modified so that aristocrats and powerful temple guardians could own large estates (*shoen*). Farmers working imperial lands were faced with oppressive taxation and were forced to flee to these estates in large

the collection of Emperor Shomu, given to the temple on his death by the empress, some thousands of objects of the 8th century and earlier, ranging from things of everyday use to the most resplendent and precious things.

Heian Period (794–1185): In the last decade of the 8th century, the capital was relocated again by Emperor Kammu. As usual, the city was built on the Chinese model, and was named Heiankyo. Its completion in 795 marked the beginning of the glorious 400-

numbers. Thus the estate holders gradually began to gain political and eventually military power in the provinces.

Such a leading family was the Fujiwara, who came to control the reigns of government by adroit placing of family members in high position and by marrying the Fujiwara daughters to emperors generation after generation. The Fujiwara were also blessed with producing highly gifted and capable leaders over a long time span.

The 9th century also saw the breaking of ties with China, which had been ongoing continually since the 6th century. The result was that the Heian Period saw the develop-

Left, Prince Shotoku Taishi with two princely escorts. **Above left**, a bodhisattva, Asuka Period. **Above right**, a standing bodhisattva, Nara Period.

ment of a culture in which native Japanese character and proclivities were no longer eclipsed entirely by foreign fashion and imported traditions.

One often cited example is the creation of a writing system to meet the needs of the Japanese language. Chinese is totally uninflected, while Japanese is a highly inflected language; Chinese characters were perhaps the worst possible system in which to write the Japanese language. To meet the urgent linguistic need, two syllabic systems (*kana*) were devised in the Heian Period by stylizing and abbreviating certain Chinese characters. Though the result is by no means simple, the system is flexible and fits the native language.

is the most famous example of this literature.

While the imperial court continued to patronize the arts and culture and engage in increasingly refined amusements in the capital, the situation in the provinces was inevitably bringing change to Kyoto. Provincial areas were neglected by the Fujiwara and the imperial court. Banditry became widespread, and local administrators were more interested in personal gain than in enforcing law and order. The result was that the lords of great estates continued to develop their own military power and engaged in power struggles among themselves. Two cadet branches of the Fujiwara, the Minamoto (also known as the Genji) and the Taira (the Heike), in

The more fluid and graceful appearing of the two kana systems, *hiragana*, is used for words of native origin; the other, *katakana*, which is harder and more angular in appearance, is used for emphasis and for words imported from other languages.

One result of this linguistic breakthrough was the appearance of a native literature, primarily written by women. Part of the accomplishment of a man of the imperial court was erudition in Chinese. This freed the women of the court to write diaries and novels in their native language using the *kana* syllabary. The world's first great novel, Lady Murasaki Shikibu's *Tale of the Genji*,

particular, had developed much power and become bitter rivals. Their struggle ended the Heian Period dramatically and decisively.

In the Heiji War of 1167, Taira no Kiyomori triumphed and became chief minister, marrying his daughter to the emperor. He was a provincial warrior with aspirations, and his rough handling of government made him many enemies. Not the least of these were the exiled sons of Minamoto no Yoshitomo, who had been defeated in the Heiji conflict. The Minamoto and their allies under the leadership of Minamoto no Yoritomo again confronted Taira power and defeated it at the battle of Dan-no-Ura in 1185.

Kamakura Period (1185–1333): Minamoto no Yoritomo had established his base at Kamakura, far to the east of Kyoto. There he established an administrative structure as well as military headquarters, creating ministries or offices to take care of (that is, govern) the warriors under his control. He had, in effect, just conquered the country. He remained in Kamakura, refusing to go to the imperial capital.

Besides the administrative foundation mentioned, he convinced the emperor to sanction officials called *shugo* (military governors) and *jito* (stewards) in each province. The former were responsible for policing (that is, military control) the provinces and the latter for supervising the land plus collecting taxes. Both posts were chosen by and answerable directly to the shogun. Thus, at one swoop, government by the warrior class located at a distance from the imperial capital was created. This was based on a system of obligation and dependency superficially not unlike that of medieval Europe, and thus can be called a true feudal system. This form of government is known as *bakufu* in Japanese, referring to the quarters of the officer commanding the imperial guard at court. The English word "shogunate" is used as well, referring to the court title of Seii Tai-Shogun (Barbarian-Quelling Generalissimo) given to Yoritomo and his successors. The shogunate form of government and the strict feudal system accompanying it lasted for 676 years.

The imperial court was in effect shoved into a corner and told to play there and not bother the people who were running the country. An attempt was made by Emperor Gotoba in 1221 to return power to the imperial line, but this coup ended in failure. Another, somewhat more successful attempt marked the end of this period. The imperial

court remained alive, though subsequent centuries saw its impoverishment. Still, it kept an important function in ritual and symbol as the embodiment of the Japanese nation until 1868, when the emperor again became the acting head of state.

Yoritomo died in 1199, after which his ally and father-in-law Hojo Tokimasa and his wife Hojo Masako both played Byzantine games with the Minamoto succession, establishing Tokimasa as regent (*shikken*), a position that held the real power in the shogunate. As a result of Hojo connivings, the Minamoto line was wiped out in 1219, an infant relative was set up as puppet shogun,

Left, print on a folding screen, *Battle between the Genji and the Heike*, Heian Period. **Above**, scene from Heiji Civil War, Kamakura Period.

and the Hojo line continued to hold the post of regent and rule the country.

Though the Kamakura Period was relatively brief, it saw events and developments that profoundly affected the country. A revolutionary advance of agricultural techniques occurred, allowing greater production of food, increase in population and economic growth, more intense settlement of the land, increase in commerce and trade, the growth of local markets, and the beginning of a currency system.

Contact with China resumed, but on a private basis. Zen Buddhism was brought over from the mainland and found a wide following in the warrior class. Strong Buddhist leaders arose, preaching doctrines that

introduced and flourished, and a kind of oral epic, sung to the accompaniment of the Japanese lute (*biwa*) developed.

After the coup attempt of Emperor Gotoba, the shogunate started to exert control over the imperial succession. Things became quite complicated when the imperial line split in two in 1259, somewhat previous to which the position of shogun was filled by imperial princes (starting in 1252), and the post of imperial regent was filled by rotation within five branches of the Fujiwara family (also from 1252).

The complexities of civil rule became top-heavy, added to which the system of military governors and stewards started to crumble.

appealed to the warriors and the common people, and Buddhism became a popular religion, whereas in the past it had been the monopoly of the aristocracy. The Amidaist Jodo and Jodo Shin sects and the mantric practices of Nichiren gradually spread throughout the country.

Clothing changed almost overnight. The warriors and their wives had no truck with the effete and gorgeous court costumes. Clothing that was light and in which one could move freely was favored by both men and women. This was a golden age of sculpture, unequaled in the remaining centuries of Japanese history. Song-style architecture was

More strain was added by the defense of the country against the two Mongol invasions in 1274 and 1281, both of which were unsuccessful due in great measure to the fortuitous occurrence of typhoons that destroyed the invading Mongol fleet.

Muromachi Period (1333–1568): The attempt of a strong-minded emperor to restore imperial power was the event that changed the nature of government and the name of the period. Emperor Godaigo's rather weak revolt of 1331 failed, but this gave him enough publicity to obtain the military support of disaffected leaders, and the uprising of 1333 in which he was supported by Ashikaga

Takauji and Nitta Yoshisada saw Kyoto captured, Kamakura destroyed and the Hojo family wiped out, and Godaigo restored as acting head of state. His favoritist policies shortly alienated the military men, however, and in 1336 Ashikaga Takauji recaptured Kyoto, enthroned an emperor from the other succession, and was made shogun.

Emperor Godaigo fled to the mountain vastness of Yoshino, where he set up a rival imperial court. This existence of the "Northern and Southern Dynasties" lasted for 60 years. Because of the friction in having two rival imperial lines and the difficulty of controlling that institutional infrastructure, which gave the military government the smell

of legitimacy, the Ashikaga shogunate did not obtain any kind of stability until the time of the third shogun, Yoshimitsu.

Ashikaga Takauji had moved his capital to Kyoto, which brought the shogunate nose to nose with the court and effectively eclipsed any power, political and economic, that the court may have retained. At the same time, the Ashikaga shogun and their vassals, in the age-old pattern of conquering warriors any-

Left, satirical picture scroll personifying noble people and priests of the Heian Period as animals. **Above**, portrait of Minamoto no Yorimoto, Kamakura Period.

where, caught aristocratitis and actively delved into such effete pursuits as connoisseurship and cultural patronage after the manner of the old aristocracy.

Yet, because of the collapse of imperial initiative, the Ashikaga had to rely directly on the system of feudal obligation and alliance and on the military might such compacts gave them to keep the country together. This was always a delicate road, for the military vassals were provincial lords of no small power and were jealous of each other as well as ambitious for more power. This situation ultimately led to the century of internal strife known as the Age of Civil Wars.

The name of the period, Muromachi, comes from the area of Kyoto in which Ashikaga Yoshimitsu built his residence. His life (1358–1408) represents perhaps the high point of the Ashikaga shogunate. This is certainly true in a cultural sense. Yoshimitsu took an active role in court politics as well as being effective in his military duties as shogun and subdued stubborn provincial lords. The year 1392 saw the start of a half century of peace under the Ashikaga, lasting through the rules of the next two shogun. It was then that the Japanese feudal system and the shogunate functioned in their most effective form.

Yoshimitsu had cultural aspirations and well as a head for statesmanship. He also reopened trade with China, which, though infrequent, brought large profits to the shogunate. His tastes were lavish, as witnessed by his construction of the Golden Pavilion (Kinkakuji), and he had a fine sense of pomp. He was an avid collector or art objects, and was known for his flamboyant parties. Yet he never descended to the vulgar. The glowing Golden Pavilion was small and meant to harmonize with its setting next to a pond in a park.

Yoshimitsu also was patron of the great Kan'ami and his son Seami, who are responsible for the *noh* drama. The influence of Zen is seen throughout his court, epitomized as "splendor with restraint."

The 6th Ashikaga shogun, Yoshinori, was assassinated in 1441, which started the decline of the shogunate. By the time of the eighth shogun, Yoshimasa (r. 1443–73), the situation had greatly degenerated, and the relationship between the shogun and the military governors of the provinces had broken down. This was manifest in the Onin

War, which lasted a decade (1467–77) and in which provincial military governors fought each other and destroyed Kyoto on several occasions. This conflict marked the total erosion of centralized authority and a general dissolution of society. It ushered in the Age of Civil Wars. Still, the imperial court and the shogunate continued existence as formal institutions.

Ashikaga Yoshimasa's rule, despite the desperate instability of the power structure, saw a glorious flowering of culture, one in which the basic aesthetic values that have characterized much of Japanese art as admired today were manifested. Yoshimasa was the patron of this creative period, particularly during the period from his retirement as shogun in 1473 to his death in 1490. He has been criticized by historians as leading a life of luxury while the country went down the drain.

Certainly this interpretation is possible. But apparently he was not by nature given to charismatic display. Even the Silver Pavilion (Ginkakuji) that he built reflects his inner-looking, contemplative nature, heavily influenced by Zen Buddhism. His delight in tea as an aesthetic pastime held in a quiet retreat made it a vehicle for connoisseurship. The Zen aesthetic promulgated under his patronage imbued all aspects of art. The contemplative gardens of Kyoto and the heights of monochrome ink painting occurred at that time.

Some historians have expressed wonder that this high point of culture should have occurred while the country was in such turmoil. Perhaps the cultural events happened because of rather than in spite of the conflict. Whatever the reason, the same phenomenon happened again about 100 years later, in late 16th century and early 17th century.

In general, the Muromachi Period saw the basic changes that set the scene for the economic growth and stability of the long Edo Period (1603–1868). Agricultural techniques developed, new crops were introduced, irrigation and commercial farming expanded. Guilds of specialized craftsmen appeared, a money economy spread, and trade increased markedly. Most important, towns and cities arose and grew, and such development is accompanied by the appearance and flourishing of merchants and a service class.

The almost total decentralization of government that occurred in the Age of Civil Wars saw the development of what might be called a true type of feudal lord, the *daimyo*. The need to defend territory by military might meant that the political unit became contiguous with its military potential, geographic and demographic. Up to this time, the provinces and land holdings generally were based on decisions made by a central bureaucracy. No longer. The daimyo became what he was by right of conquest and might. His position was backed up not by a gang of roughneck warriors, but by vast armies.

During this century of warfare, with its ethic of ambition and expansion by force of arms, it is not surprising that the idea of

unifying the entire country occurred to a few leaders of vision and ability. In the 1540s, European missionaries and traders arrived on the shores of Japan.

Momoyama Period (1568–1600): This short period is somewhat of a historian's artifact; it is really the climaxing portion of the Muromachi Period, but has been accorded a special name perhaps due to the embarrassing fact that the Ashikaga shogunate ended in 1573 (the Muromachi Period is when the Ashikaga shogun ruled), when Oda Nobunaga (1534–82), the first of three leaders to go about the business of unifying the country, overran Kyoto. The other leaders were

Toyo-tomi Hideyoshi (1536–98) and Toku-gawa Ieyasu (1542–1616).

Nobunaga conquered the home provinces in a rigorous manner. He eliminated rivals in the usual military fashion, and is known particularly for razing the temples of the militant Buddhist sects that opposed him. He had a flair for culture, and also put much effort into developing the lands under his control. He was assassinated by a treacherous general in 1582. Though he had only brought about one-third of the country under his control, Nobunaga laid the foundation for the unification that followed.

Hideyoshi, Nobunaga's chief general, did away with Nobunaga's murderer, and set top of a complex network of feudal relationships. Hideyoshi's hold on the country was slippery at best, based on oaths of fealty. Though he could and did act as head of state, the administration of the land, resources and population was in the hands of the various daimyo. Still, he effected sweeping domestic reforms and even tried to make his ambitions felt on the Asian mainland with two attempts to conquer Korea (in 1592 and 1597) and with the aim of taking over China thereafter. His death in 1598 brought this megalomanic effort to a swift end.

The cultural achievements of this tiny slice of Japanese history – a mere three decades – are astonishing. The country was in political

himself up as Nobunaga's successor. With military brilliance, statesmanship and brass, he proceeded vigorously with the job of unifying Japan. By 1590, all territories of the country were either his by right of conquest or after he had held the feudal lords, the daimyo as vassals.

But though the country was unified – under the power of one man – the government was still decentralized. Hideyoshi was not the king of Japan, he was just the guy at the ferment, war was rife, the society was in transition, and the most glorious textiles, ceramics, lacquer ware, screen paintings and tea utensils were produced. Such artistic achievement has never happened again in Japan.

The presence of Europeans and their exotic artifacts certainly acted as a leaven on the aesthetic and intellectual sensibilities of the Japanese, but it is doubtful that this influence was profound. It appears that Japan emerged from those decades of European contact with hardly a scratch. More important was the growth of the economy, the expansion of trade domestically and abroad, and the lifestyles of the daimyo and

Left, *sumi-e* (ink painting) by Sesshu, Muromachi Period. **Above**, Taisho Period Kinkakuji (Golden Pavilion) built in the Muromachi Period.

the national leaders. Nobunaga and Hideyoshi were cultural swashbucklers, and the great regional lords emulated them to some extent. Hideyoshi, in particular, seems to have had a penchant for gold and glitter and ostentatious splendor. Castle architecture encouraged the use of large areas of gold, in part to relieve the gloom of these mainly military structures, it is said, and the standing screen with opulent paintings on a gold leaf ground became a standard feature of the residences and castles of the mighty, as was the opulent use of decorated lacquer.

The tea ceremony, as it is known today, underwent its fundamental formation under Hideyoshi's tea master, Sen no Rikyu, and the aesthetics he espoused resulted, both directly and indirectly, in the production of ceramics and tea utensils that have never been surpassed, much less successfully copied, since. The textiles of the Momoyama Period are harder to explain. The gentle yet very vigorous design produced by a combination of stitched resist and hand painting of dyes (the textiles known as *tsujigahana*) also has never been emulated since, though the techniques themselves are not difficult. In the areas of both fine art (painting) and craft (textiles, ceramics), the Momoyama Period was special.

Edo Period (1600–1868): Toyotomi Hideyoshi, whose career had paralleled that of Oda Nobunaga, had waited patiently. The death of Hideyoshi was naturally an opportunity for the ambitions of the lords to surface. Ieyasu had about half of the lords immediately allied to Toyotomi sign pledges to him within a year. In 1600, however, he was challenged by a military coalition of lords from western Japan. He won that encounter, the famous battle of Sekigahara, and became the *de facto* ruler of the country.

In 1603, he was given the title of shogun, which he handed on to his son in 1605. He established his capital in the city of Edo (now Tokyo) and retired to a life of intrigue aimed at consolidating the position of his family and heirs. This meant primarily getting rid of Hideyoshi's heirs, which occurred in 1615 with the raising of Osaka Castle. Ieyasu died in 1616.

There is some question as to what date should indicate the start of the Edo Period. The battle of Sekigahara (1600) gave Ieyasu full hegemony; he became shogun in 1603,

and died in 1616. All have been used as starting dates for the period, as has 1635, when Japanese were prohibited from traveling abroad and when the country was effectively isolated.

The primary problem facing Ieyasu while and after consolidating his power was how to make a viable system out of the rather strange situation of having a strong, central power and a totally decentralized administration structure. Working with what he had at hand and with what to him was natural (he would hardly come up with a European monarchical system), a complex system that combined feudal authority and bureaucratic administration.

The Tokugawa shoguns were the supreme authority, from whom the various lords or daimyo received their domains, and to whom they allied themselves by oath as well as adopting a code of regulations that applied to all daimyo. The military nature of the domain was curtailed, but each daimyo had a great deal of autonomy in the administration of his domain, which he governed through a hierarchy of retainers. This system was perfected by the middle of the 17th century, by the end of the rule of Tokugawa Yoshimitsu, the third shogun. It sufficed to maintain the country in peace and a growing prosperity for somewhat over two centuries – no mean

42

feat. Its flaws were in its inability to adapt well to social and political change. Whether this fragile conservatism was inherent in the system or in the people who ran the system can be argued endlessly.

Why and how the Tokugawa's isolationist policy became ferocious has not been completely answered. Hideyoshi issued edicts banning missionaries in 1587, but this had no teeth and was generally overlooked. Ieyasu took a generally genial stance toward Europeans, both missionaries and traders, but then something changed. Christianity became a threat, and the shogunate began to react strongly.

As with today's Japan, there seems to have

Korea effected through the daimyo of the island of Tsushima, lying between Japan and Korea. Information has the quality of seeping through the tightest barriers. This is exactly what happened in the later half of the Edo Period. European learning trickled into Japan and began to create some intellectual excitement in limited circles.

The political, economic, social, religious, and intellectual aspects of the Edo Period are exceedingly complex. One often-cited general characteristic of this time is the arising of an increasingly prosperous merchant class. This went hand in hand with the development of urban centers and with the flourishing culture of the townspeople who lived in

been a predisposition towards xenophobia somehow coupled with a definite attraction toward things foreign. The xenophobia won, and the result was brutal and bloody.

The shutters of the country slammed down between 1635 and 1640, with only a chink or two left open. These were the Dutch trading factor on the island of Dejima in Nagasaki harbor, the Chinese trade quarter in Nagasaki (though there might have been some illicit trade with China) and the limited trade with

Left, *Mikaeri-Bijin* by Hishikawa Moronobu, Edo Period. **Above**, Commodore Perry's visit to Uragawa, Kanagawa, early Edo Period.

the cities. Edo itself was one of the world's great cities and is thought to have had a population of about one million at the beginning of the 18th century, greater than London or Paris.

The Tokugawa shogunate has been called repressive, a dictatorship, and other names, and the people in a daimyo's domain had little recourse if their lord was autocratic and arbitrary. In their attempt to make a functioning government out of the only reality they knew, the shogunate came up with the idea that their way was somehow the "Natural Order of Things." They set up a rigid class hierarchy – warriors, farmers, artisans, merchants – and adopted a school of Neo-Confucianism as the theoretical basis for social and political policy. The long years of sleepy peace resulted in the function of the warrior disappearing and the prosperity of the merchant increasing. The standard of living of all classes increased greatly, and the shogunate felt compelled to issue sumptuary laws at various times to quell the conspicuous consumption of, in particular, wealthy merchants who, officials felt, were presuming beyond their station.

The urban dweller became a confirmed consumer. In Edo, entire districts were given over to craftsmen of various specializations. This means that there was a thriving market

Period pleasure in the material world and in a kind of high consumerism. Today's Japan is hardly much different.

Aesthetically, in the area of fine art, the Edo Period never approached the qualities of objects produced in previous times. But the pop art phenomenon, of which *ukiyo-e* prints are one of the most famous examples, involved a very different kind of aesthetic than the high art and one just as lasting. In the later part of the Edo Period, it could be said that cleverness and novelty tended to supplant concerns with quality and beauty. In the area of folk art, however, the Edo Period produced some of the finest objects the world has to offer, from farmhouses to iron kettles

for the objects made, and objects were made in large quantities. The citizen of Edo obtained a reputation for a kind of happy-go-lucky, garrulous disposition.

These *Edokko* (Children of Edo) took delight in delight, and this sense of pleasure is grandly reflected in the popular culture of the time. The color and splash of *kabuki*, the *bunraku* puppet drama; *ukiyo-e* prints; the world of actors, sumo stars, courtesans and geisha; the pleasure quarters, both licensed and unlicensed; the vigorous publishing world, which published scholarship as well as cookbooks, guides to proper comportment, poetry, trashy novels – all show the Edo

to sheets of paper to fishermen's coats.

Japan in the first decades of the 1800s was a very different country indeed from Japan of 1600. Now a nation of prosperity, with well-developed domestic commerce, an incipient manufacturing potential, flourishing cities and towns, but with outdated, rigid social and governmental systems, internal pressures alone were demanding change.

And the world itself was not about to allow Japan to continue its exclusionism. The industrial revolution was gaining momentum in Europe, and expansion was the theme of a vigorous capitalism. The Western powers were casting about, looking for countries to put in their pockets. They could hardly leave Japan alone.

As early as 1792, Russia came knocking at Japan's door, and the shogunate told the envoys what to do with their nation's offer. Ships of other European nations, specifically Holland, England and France, thereafter started nosing around in Japanese waters. But it was the United States that took the initiative in 1853 with a show of might and a demand that Japan open up. This was Commodore Perry's visit to Uraga Harbor with the United States' East India Squadron – the famous Black Ships. He appeared the following year to back up the demand, and was successful. In 1858 a treaty of friendship and

without – that is, the sense of Japan afloat in a sea of hostile powers who possessed more technology and had voracious ambitions – may have acted to direct domestic energies away from internal wrangling and civil war. The *sonno joi* ("revere the emperor" and "expel the barbarian") movement was not the hate club that its name seems to imply, but rather, a rallying force that attracted young, often intellectual, hotheads who sensed the need for action. It produced many of the most forward-looking men who were to lead Japan in the Meiji Period.

Meiji Period (1868–1912): In a few decades, Japan effectively restructured itself as a polity. In retrospect, this seems astonishingly

trade was signed with the United States, followed shortly by treaties with other Western powers. This triggered the internal pressures for reform and resulted, in 1868, in the dissolution of the shogunate and, in the restoration of the emperor as acting head of state, a forward-looking, young government ready to tackle the needs of the times.

The turmoil and tumult of those 15 years from 1853 to 1868 have been documented well in many books. The sense of threat from

Left, *Kanagawa-Oki-Nami-Ura* ukiyo-e by Hokusai, Edo Period. Above, *53 Stations of the Tokaido* ukiyo-e by Hiroshige, Edo Period.

radical. Yet this did not happen overnight, but by a series of incremental and moderate modifications of the political system.

Because the office of emperor at the end of the Edo Period no longer was tied to a political system, his "restoration" could be used as a symbol and as a vehicle for picking and choosing from a wide range of governmental structures. The quality of the new leadership of the nation, the choices they made, and the political, economic, and cultural courses which they chose can be seen as nothing less than spectacular.

There are many theories concerning the processes of the Meiji Restoration. Scholars and historians seem somewhat baffled about the whole thing – at least there is yet no clear-cut consensus about the motivation and forces that determined events.

The first new government structure was a compromise between old and new. It cleverly borrowed names from archaic imperial institutions and government to give an aura of tradition to what was hardly traditional.

Meeting the rest of the world (that is, the West) as an equal was one of the guiding concerns of the Meiji years. This meant, first of all, positive Westernization – assimilating, using, adapting whatever the West had in order to bring Japan to a position as an equal. For Meiji Japan, this meant anything

wide range of fields and from countries thought to have lead in various areas. (Though, in fact, this recruiting from abroad had been started by the shogunate.) Thus, Italians were recruited as art instructors; Germans in the fields of scholarship and law; British experts advised on naval matters; an American helped set up the elementary school system, and the French helped adapt their legal code system to Japanese reality.

It did not take long for the Japanese to learn that the outlooks and views of the various Western nationalities and cultures were neither consistent nor parallel. But the essences of the West were squeezed in this manner only up to a point. The employment

and everything Western, from railroads to ballroom dancing.

The pendulum first swung to extremes, from a total rejection of all native things (which included even a mindless urge to abandon the Japanese language) to an emotional nationalism after the excesses of the first enthusiasm for foreign imports, to a relatively enlightened moderation and intelligent assessment of what both Japan and the West could offer.

This process of the nation pulling itself up with its own bootstraps by means of modernization is illustrated by the official policy of hiring foreign advisors and experts in a

of the numerous advisors (a figure of 3,000 hired by the government up to 1890 has been cited) was ended as soon as the Japanese sensed that they could continue perfectly well on their own.

Another urgent need of the Meiji leaders was modification of the unequal treaties with the West, which had been signed with the shogunate. This issue alone was not resolved until the 1890s and saw the fall of a number of highly competent leaders over failure to change the treaties.

After going through a number of unsuccessful drafts over the years, the new constitution of the country was promulgated in

1889. This Meiji Constitution was one of the major steps towards success in having Japan recognized as an advanced nation. The next was Japan's success in the Sino-Japanese War of 1894–95, which proved the country's ability to wage modern warfare as well as the fact that Japan was now a major power in the Orient.

In 1902, Japan signed a treaty of alliance with Britain, the first such between a Western and an Asian nation. And the clincher in making Japan a true world power was winning the Russo-Japanese War of 1904-06, the first time that an Asian nation defeated a European power. To this day, the Japanese are popular in Turkey because of this military victory.

Emperor Meiji died in 1912. By then, Japan had consolidated its economy, defined a political system, changed its social structure, and become one of the world's advanced nations, recognized as such (though not exactly understood) by the governments of the West.

Taisho Period (1912–26): The next reign period was that of Emperor Taisho, which saw the 20th century catch Japan in its grasp

Far left, *Woman Blowing A Glass Toy* ukiyo-e by Kitagawa Utamaro, Edo Period. Left, helmet and armor, Edo Period. Above, exposition in Tokyo's Ueno Park, Meiji Period.

and carry the country off on a strange and sometimes unpleasant odyssey.

During the Taisho Period, Japan began to fume and bubble intellectually. The growing prosperity, with the accompanying problems, the shrinking size of the world, and the relative youth of Japan in comparison with the West and as a world power all contributed to the "Taisho Democracy." This is little more than a time of good, healthy intellectual ferment, when ideas of all kinds were available for flitting and playing with and developing. It is important both as a precursor to Japan's plunge into the dark period of militarism and war and as a foundation for the country's emergence from the darkness.

Showa Period (1926–89): With the death of the Taisho emperor in 1926, Hirohito succeeded to the throne, the beginning of the Showa Period. Within a decade, Japan would be sliding into world war. Japan's isolation from direct military experience of in World War I kept the nation free from the cynicism of its aftermath in Europe and from the direct experience of the horrors of such war. As the toughest boy in the Asian neighborhood, there was no experiential precedent for Japan to do anything other than show its strength.

This is the time also during which Japan followed the Western advanced nations in developing as a "mass culture." Widespread literacy, newspapers, labor unions and other large-membership organizations, the growth of population, and the advent of party politics are all part of this phenomenon.

As with any party politics, the establishment contained factions that waltzed about and contended for power, and the establishment was confronted with the interest blocs representing the consumer and worker and intellectual. At this time, the distribution of wealth was still very uneven. The establishment factions included big business (*zaibatsu*), the upper crust of government, and the military interests. The non-establishment interests never received adequate representation in government until after World War II.

Party politics also saw the disappearance of the aristocratic, idealistic political patriarches of Meiji times, the grand figures of unswerving honesty whose main concern was the welfare of the country. Such men existed. They were supplanted by the type of self-serving 20th-century party politician common in democratic-style countries – the figure who is supported but not exactly trusted.

Again, historians' analysis of why and how militarism developed in the 1930s has produced a rash of theories, some of which argue a conspiracy going back to Meiji days. Whatever the political, economic and social forces that produced the military government and the aggressive war effort, some observations can be made.

Political power within the country was balanced in favor of establishment interests; suffrage was not universal; non-establishment interests were weak because they had little recourse for expression other than through imported political concepts – that is, socialism and communism – which were

the civilian politicians and they finally acted to make the government their own.

The pivotal point was the Manchurian Incident of 1931, in which Japanese military forces occupied Manchuria and set up the state of Manchukuo in 1932. Protest over this action by the League of Nations resulted in Japan departing from the League and following a policy of isolation. Within the military itself, extremist factionalism grew, and the 1930s saw a number of plots of one kind or another to take over power. The most famous is the 26 February Incident of 1936, a bloody military uprising that might have been a coup had it not been based on vague, romantic ideas that did not include a practi-

distrusted and feared. The Western powers dealt with Japan, but, at least in part, through a filter of ignorance and a certain amount of what might be called Occi-centric narrowness. (Asia was not part of the real world.) Japan, sensitive to this, felt a distinct national insecurity and with muscle-flexing anger – the "I'll show you!" syndrome. This, and what were seen domestically as economic and demographic pressures, made the obtaining of military hegemony seem a viable alternative, at least by the military elements in the establishment. These elements were increasingly frustrated by what they saw as ineffectual and compromising policies by

cal plan of how to use power. This bolstered the civilian resistance to military involvement in politics. But in the summer of 1937, hot war erupted in China with the Marco Polo Bridge Incident, and thereafter the country plunged into darkness, pulling a good portion of the world with it.

Seeking to discourage Western intervention in Japan's Asian expansion – the war in Europe was hopefully keeping everyone busy – the Japanese military launched pre-emptive attacks not only on Pearl Harbor in December of 1941, but against European colonial holdings throughout Asia.

In less than a year, Japan possessed most

of East Asia and the western Pacific. Japanese occupation was savage and brutal. In 1943, fierce battles in the Pacific reversed Japan's position. By early 1945, Japan was on the defensive, its major cities (except Kyoto and Nara) leveled by bombing raids.

Despite Germany's defeat in May of 1945, Japanese leaders did not yield. The Allies and most Asians say it was necessary, the Japanese say not, but in mid-August of the same year, atomic bombs were dropped on Hiroshima and Nagasaki. A week later, the war was over.

Revived rising sun: On 15 August 1945, Emperor Hirohito spoke on the radio – the first time commoners had heard his voice –

ties, established a British-style parliamentary system, dismantled the pre-war industrial conglomerates, and renounced war as national policy. With the signing of the 1952 San Francisco Peace Treaty, the occupation ended. Japan was sovereign.

Three significant characteristics help define postwar Japan: government-coordinated industrialization and spectacular economic growth, the mocking of parliamentary democracy by politicians, and modern Japan's collective inability to recall any history between 1930 and 1945.

Economic Dazzler: The decades following the war were of well-coordinated corporate and bureaucratic efforts to revive both them-

and declared an unconditional surrender. Japan lost its empire, its right to independent foreign policy, its emperor's claim to divinity, and its army. War crime trials convicted several thousand Japanese; 920 were executed. Over six million soldiers and civilians returned home to Japan.

A new 1946 constitution issued under the mandate of Gen. MacArthur's occupation government guaranteed western-style liber-

<u>Left</u>, a sortie from Kagoshima base, 1945 (Mainichi Shimbun). <u>Above</u>, Japanese team at opening ceremony, Tokyo Olympics, 1964 (Mainichi Shimbun).

selves and the country. Protected by the American military umbrella, Japan funneled full resources into its economy.

Buoyed by government protectionism and "administrative guidance," Japan's corporate footing gained stability. After suffering early setbacks with low quality products and often ill-advised exports – *Made in Japan* was once synonymous with cheap and flimsy – Japan gained confidence to conquer new markets, and to redefine manufacturing quality and excellence.

In the 1950s, Japan perfected its light industry; the 1960s shifted to shipbuilding, steel, and chemicals; the 1970s transformed

Japan into an export-driven economy of automobiles and consumer electronics. Urban population doubled between 1950 and 1970; farming's importance dropped to a fraction of the nation's GNP. The new national wealth was evenly distributed, leaving almost no one in an economic lower class; unemployment never exceeded 3 percent. Industrial labor disputes and strikes were minimal. But with industrialization came a deadly spread of pollution-related diseases, forced to the public foreground by W. Eugene Smith's photographs of industrial-poisoning victims in Kyushu's city of Minamata.

During post-war reconstruction, government regulation served Japan's interests well.

But as Japan joined the advanced economies, the one-way nature of Japan's market strained relations with others, especially the US, its largest market, and Europe. Over-regulation and chummy business-government relationships saddled consumers with ridiculously high prices (¥70,000-plus to get a phone line) for nearly everything except umbrellas, unaccountably cheap.

The economy accelerated with uncanny momentum, surpassing every other country except the United States. Japan became the new global paradigm for success and potency. The stock market was on a trajectory that, in the late 1980s, momentarily exceeded

the New York Stock Exchange in volume and vigor. Real estate became the planet's most valuable and banks dished money ou.t

Japan's "bubble economy" superheated in the late 1980s, bursting in 1990. The stock market lost half its value in a matter of days, banks lost still-unspeakable amounts on loans secured by hyperinflated land values, and a blossoming Japanese self-righteousness as economic superpower took a cold shower.

But in politics, life at the very top remained very good.

Shady Deals Galore: For nearly four decades, one political party has dominated Japan – the dubiously-named Liberal Democratic Party, or LDP. Conservative, unprogressive, and decidedly undemocratic by western standards, the LDP seemingly serves only to make its leaders wealthy.

Most Japanese are urban, but political power rests with rural farmers, who through arcane electoral laws have double the voting weight of city dwellers. Agriculture accounts for just 15 percent of Japan's GNP, but the LDP has subsidized and coddled the farmers, ignoring the welfare of the urban majority. Nobody complained. Indeed, in the times of sword-swinging shoguns and samurai, a wayward opinion or complaint was lopped off along with the speaker's head. Best to remain obscure within one's group.

In fact, the group, not tedious philosophical principles or fear of hell, defines one's purpose and morality on pragmatic, Confucian grounds. Corporations became extended families, and company employees would do most anything to assure the company's – the group's – growth. Take care of the politicians, for example, and the company would thrive.

Institutionalized and often immune to legal redress, *seiji fuhai,* or political corruption, festered unimpeded at the highest corporate and governmental levels. By the 1980s, *The Economist* opined, the LDP was "choking on its own corruption." In 1992, the last of the LDP's omnipotent kingpins was caught not only in one of the scandals that surface regularly like the new rice crop, but prosecutors searching his house uncovered a stash of gold bullion worth millions.

The LDP fell from grace in 1993, replaced by a coalition government led by Hosokawa Morihiro. With a head of thick young hair , Hosokawa invigorated the nation with calls for substantial reform. Seven months later, he resigned because of scandal. His short-lived successors formed coalitions of little substance, though the world continued to marvel at such visible signs of continuing modernity as the astonishing Kansai International Airport, built off the coast with the several mountains' worth of landfill.

Who governs Japan? The bureaucrats do, probably the world's best educated, most dedicated and deeply entrenched. Even the prime minister – who's paid almost twice the salary of the American president – submits his foreign policy speeches to the foreign ministry for approval, if not for rewriting. Not because he must, but because the ministry's power is understatedly fearsome.

forgetting is increasingly difficult to do. What rankles its Asian neighbors most, however, is the regularity with which Japan's conservative politicians denounce factual history. In 1994, Japan's minister of justice publicly declared that the 1937 Rape of Nanking – when between 100,000 and 300,000 Chinese were slaughtered by an out-of-control Japanese army – was merely an unsubstantiated fabrication.

Recent prime ministers, especially Hosokawa and socialist Murayama Tomiichi, have made efforts to apologize for the past, despite the vociferous views of right-wing politicians, nationalists and university scholars to the contrary. Yet to this day, history

The Unforgotten: If the past is not flattering, it is best forgotten, think the Japanese. But Japan's neighbors – especially Korea and China – think differently. Other than fuzzy regrets referring to "unfortunate circumstances" in the past, collectively the Japanese seem unable to recall five decades of brute Japanese aggression capped by a Pacific war killing 20 million people. But with the Imperial army's own documents magically appearing from hiding, and as aging veterans publicly purge their nightmares,

Left, fortunes won and lost in the stock exchange.
Above, the off-shore Kansai International Airport.

books are censored by the ministry of education, and the media focus on Japanese suffering in the war, so much so that some believe the war claimed only Japanese victims.

Heisei Period (1989–): Emperor Hirohito died in 1989, the longest reigning emperor (62 years) in Japanese recorded history. His son, Akihito, took the throne and adopted the period name of *Heisei,* which means attainment of peace. He and his family have made sustained efforts to humanize the imperial family, and to tangentially deal with the past. But as a politically-neutralized figure head, the emperor is not permitted candidly to address history, nor his father's place in it.

Who are the Japanese? Well, archaeologically and anthropologically, the origin of the people still remains something of an enigma. In the last half-century or more, not a small amount of effort has gone into researching this question, but, though some generalities have been forthcoming, no clear indications of immigrations, their origins, and a clear time sequence have been determined.

There is ample evidence that the Japanese archipelago was attached to the Asian mainland until relatively recently as geological time goes. At the beginning of the Jomon Period (Japan's Neolithic; ca 10,000 BC–3rd century BC), it is likely that the seas separating Japan and the continent were shallower and not so broad, if, indeed, there was no land bridge then. Far earlier, Paleolithic remains have been found to indicate a substantial time depth of human habitation. The earliest immigrants probably arrived on foot.

But who were these people, and are they the same as the present population of Japan? The answer to the former is not known, and to the latter question, probably not.

Theory and Conjecture: Analysis of Jomon skeletons seems to indicate that the Jomon people(s) were of physical types different from the present population.

The Yayoi Period (3rd century BC–AD 3rd century) saw waves of migration from the Asian continent, accompanied by technology, such as rice agriculture (including tools), metallurgy (first bronze and, about 150 years later, iron), a type of potter's wheel, and a different social structure or structures. These migrations are now considered to have brought the ancestors of today's Japanese people, who displaced and pushed the resident population north or into less desirable areas.

The classic ideas regarding the origins of the Japanese cite the north and the south – Manchuria/Siberia and the South China or Indochina regions – as likely origins. These ideas have not changed much, but it seems that different students of the subject differ in

Preceding pages, a warm, shy country smile. **Left**, dressed in samurai style at festival time. **Above right**, father and sleepy child.

emotional bias as to which area of origin to favor. The southern physical type is, of course, the Malay – swarthy skin, thick eyebrows, large eyes, small bones; the northern type is the Mongolian – light skin, broad, high cheekbones, narrow eyes, thick bones. At one time, the idea of a southern origin was very unpopular in Japan, especially in the period of the country's expansionist ambitions, when Southeast Asia was a conquered realm and its peoples looked upon with little tolerance. The times have changed, and only the old

guard maintains such bias – seen as racist and unrealistic by the majority, at least for now.

Today, both north and south Asia are considered equally valid as likely origins of the Japanese "race." Still, the precise configuration of the migrations and the cultural traits associated with areas of origin are subject to argument. For example, even the question of the Ainu is still being bounced about. Although the Ainu cultural traits are undoubtedly circumpolar, some students maintain that since the Ainu are Caucasian, they came from the south and picked up the circumpolar, Siberian-type culture after their arrival. This runs counter to the conventional theory that th Ainu are directly related to Siberian groups.

Korean Antecedents: There was also much immigration from Korea, a point vehemently denied by nationalists and racial purists, but undeniable in view of the archaeological and anthropological evidence. It is with some glee that Western historians like to point out the close ties of early noble houses with immigrants from Korea, if for no other reason than to have the conservatives sputter and deny any such possibility.

There is also a school of thought that links the imperial line with antecedents on the Korean Peninsula. Still another set of theories holds that the Korean and Japanese languages were mutually understandable, if not

tral of disciplines, without political overtones of any kind and thus a sanctuary into which scholar can retreat in times of political unrest, in Japan it is rife with factions and hot-tempered rivalries. (One group of "experts" in Japan has steadfastly refuted and rejected carbon-14 dating, particularly when used to authenticate theories proposing a Japan-Korea connection).

All this is interesting, no doubt even charming; none of it, however, sheds any light on the *identity* of the Japanese today; nor does it seem that archaeological evidence is going to be helpful.

But what about sociology? Can it give us a clue as to the identity of a people whose

identical, some 2,000 years ago, and that a close affinity between the people living on at least parts of the Korean peninsula and the Japanese or proto-Japanese of the time existed, even to the point of approximating a common culture.

This is a fascinating topic and one that is being researched by both Japanese and Koreans, each with a certain amount of distaste about the possibility of finding the other is a cultural cousin and closer than emotional proclivities engendered by four centuries of distrust would like.

And so it goes. Whereas archaeology in many countries is considered the most neu-

physical origins are less than clearly explained? There are many scholars who feel that trying to make grandiose generalizations about an entire people is a futile if not incorrect effort. Still, that the Japanese, today, are not Norwegian or Navajo or Bengali or even Korean is a fact. We tend to take for granted the fact that most if not all peoples have something that is theirs alone, if nothing more than a unique combination of traits shared by any other number of other peoples. And such intangibles as essence may also apply, though bringing in considerations that cannot be quantified is still subject to censure by the "scientific" community.

Today, much of the world, particularly the West, seems to be trying to get some kind of handle on "the Japanese," and thus "understand" the phenomenon of the nation's affluence and power. Too often, this effort is reductionist and ends up with a handful – or less – of oversimplified cantrips and clichés that are supposed to mean something. These are usually attached to an emotional bias – sometimes grudgingly positive, sometimes openly negative and hostile, seldom if ever balanced and "true."

"Don't understand us too quickly," someone once warned a visiting pundit. This is good advice at any time, but particularly now, applied in Japan, where the question of

Japanese") and the implicit – often explicit – definition of what "we Japanese" are or aren't, do or don't, believe or not believe. The compulsion to define the identity even shows up in popular advertising: "the beer brewed exclusively for *Japanese* taste," and so on.

Indeed, it seems there is an undercurrent in Japanese thought that all things Japanese, including people, are "special" and even unique among the world's things. Maybe it's due to three centuries of isolation in recent times, when the world in fact didn't exist for most Japanese. Stay here long enough and it seems that only Japan has earthquakes, typhoons, tasty rice, misery, hot weather,

identity – physical, cultural, national, spiritual – is one that sparks such emotional reactions in so short a time. Whatever their proclivities or inclinations, most Japanese do not remain indifferent to the question of who they are.

Books on the subject of "the Japanese" abound, and those written by foreign authorities – translated into Japanese – are consumed with gusto. Seldom does a television or radio "talk show" air without some reference to *"ware-ware Nipponjin"* ("we

Left, the "rice bowl" look next to a festival float. **Above,** all different beneath the umbrellas.

trees that change color in autumn, snowfall and fast trains.

When French ski manufacturers first tried to export skis to Japan several decades ago, the Japanese government declared the skis unsuitable because of the "special" Japanese snow. Later, when American beef producers were trying to open the Japanese market, a high-ranking official in the agriculture ministry argued that only Japanese beef was suitable for the "special" Japanese digestive system.

Turning Japanese: Outsiders (i.e., foreigners, even those born and raised in Japan, or Japanese who have spent "too long" overseas) eventually and invariably find themselves running into the proverbial brick wall somewhere along the line when attempting to function effectively in Japanese society. Foreigners are often told, and quite bluntly so, "you don't understand Japan *because* you are not Japanese." The fallacy in this, of course, is that one needn't "understand" Japanese ways in the intellectual sense in order to function in the society. One must, however, *accept* them. It's easier than it sounds, and one doesn't have to "turn Japanese" to pull it off.

Take, for example, the much-debated question over the meaning of "yes" in Japan. The myth about the "slippery Japanese 'yes'" – e.g., the foreign businessman who swears he got a firm "yes" from a Japanese client, only

at such-and-such a price, to be delivered on so-and-so a date." Anything less than this means either "no" or "maybe," and that's where the problem lies.

First, there is the sense in Japan, pervading virtually all areas of social and commercial intercourse, that "time heals all wounds." Translated into the gizmo salesman's parlance, anything less than a definite "yes" then means "maybe," and "maybe" probably means "no." If he doesn't have the patience to wait and see, or if he doesn't have the wits or wherewithal to amend his proposal and ask for another try, he probably deserves the "no."

The explanation for all this is almost too obvious to state: Japanese simply don't like

to find out later that it really meant "no" – is just that: a myth. It's a waste of time analyzing linguistically whether "*hai*" can literally be translated as "yes" (or "*iie*" as "no"), for it is always the semantics of it, the context in which an answer is given, that determines the meaning. Besides which, short of outright fraud or prevarication (not unknown in Japan), no Japanese will ever answer a direct question (such as "Will you buy 10,000 gross of my gizmos?") with a naked "*hai,*" or an unadorned "*iie,*" for that matter. One can be sure that an affirmative to such a question would translate as "Yes, I will buy 10,000 gross of your gizmos,

to give, or get, bad news. You may ask, who does? Well, no one. But the Japanese, instead of simply avoiding it, or "bravely" meeting it head on, have evolved, even codified, means of cushioning it to the extreme.

In a country where physical crowding and complex interpersonal relationships have over centuries shaped the language and social manners, even the slightest chance of offending or disappointing or inconveniencing someone else is couched in a shower of soft words, in bows, in grave smiles and even in laughter (or worse, giggles!). Of *course* it is hypocritical! It is hypocrisy legitimatized and codified, and there may be something quite wise in that. In any case, to call it insincere or "slippery" is, to the Japanese, just plain dumb – and hurtful. Such behavior doesn't have to be "understood" or "approved"; however, if one is to be effective in Japan, it must be learned and applied with grace and skill.

What's in a Word? Elsewhere in this book is a section on the Japanese language itself, and another offering a few "useful words and phrases" for the traveler. Not to steal thunder from those sections, but to underscore the lengths to which Japanese will, and do go to avoid unpleasant situations, we can cite the observations of Soviet journalist B. Ovchinnikov in his study of Japan, *Cherry Blos-*

accurately and in a straight-line fashion," writes Ovchinnikov with marvelous understatement, "corresponds very little with the Japanese understanding of courtesy."

Strangely, the very word for "thank you" (*"arigato"*) literally means "you put me in a difficult position." *"Oki-no-doku,"* which is an expression of sympathy, means "poisonous feeling." And who but the Japanese would think of expressing regret or apology with a word (*"sumimasen"*) which, in strictly literal translation, means "this will never end"?

Then there is that virtually untranslatable word, *"giri."* To violate it, wrote Joya Mock in his *Things Japanese* as recently as 1960, is "the worst thing one can do and may make

soms: "from generation to generation, the Japanese have become accustomed to beating about the bush in order to avoid open conflicts of opinion and direct assertations that might hurt someone's feelings."

There is, for example, the often-used auxiliary verb, *kudasaru* (to give), by which one can form polite imperatives. Thus *"tabete kudasai,"* though adequately translated as "please eat," is more precisely "please give (me) eating."

"The ability to express thoughts clearly,

Happy couples pose in post-purchasing (left) and post-marital bliss (above).

him a social outcast." What is this inviolable social no-no? Joya says it's often expressed as a "sense of duty and honor," but then hedges his bet by saying that explanation is inadequate, preferring to offer examples, such as one's obligation to observe community customs, lend a hand to others in holding wedding feasts, funeral services, building houses, planting fields, or harvesting crops, even if it means putting aside their own work to do so.

"Those who fail to offer such services are said to lack *giri*, and are regarded as disturbers of the community life. Such are unwelcome persons, and are often ostracized by the villagers." Three decades after those words were written there remain precious few villages in Japan today, and the fear of ostracism is about as widespread as the fear of flying.

Giri is the theme of many *noh* tragedies, for example. A plot might turn on a daughter's obligation to put aside *ninjo* (human feeling) and marry someone of her parents' choosing. Joya writes, "often unable to decide [between *giri* and *ninjo*], a girl in such a situation commits suicide." Today, however, while the *"omiai"* or "arranged marriage" custom continues in Japan, it long since has lost the backing of the law, and seldom, if ever, drives one to suicide; cases of taking

one's own life over a breach of any sort of *giri*, for that matter, are relatively few today, compared with those resulting from a breach of the law, or of simple trust.

Nonetheless, various forms of formalized obligation still inform one's actions in, say, the matter of accepting responsibility, not to say shame, for an error or malfeasance committed, wilfully or inadvertently, by a distant relative, a co-worker, even a close neighbor, as well as for avoiding, at all costs, any implication that someone *else* is at fault.

In short, Japan today is not, and never was, a society in which every member looks out for every other, but the *mechanisms* which

were set out to achieve this ideal are still firmly in place.

All in the Family: Naturally, obligation, like charity, begins at home. It is still true, for example, that the eldest child (once only the male, but now the female as well) is obliged to care for his or her aged parent(s). Likewise, it is still true that the estate, if any, of a deceased parent automatically passes to that eldest child. Once, these mutual obligations were inviolable, and any disagreement or complication regarding them could be settled by only, in feudal days, the *daimyo* or, in more modern times, a high court. Today, however, disputes over care for the aged, and the flip side, inheritance of wealth and property, are relatively common – and often decided in favor not of the parents or children, but of the national government, which justifies its high inheritance taxes on the grounds that state-run nursing homes are breaking the budget.

So it goes, and with it goes the "extended family," often cited as the secret of Japan's social stability and strength. Urbanization, "corporatization" and the resulting squeeze in space and time mean that grandparents are no longer in the house. Extended family are often as far flung from the original homestead as education, job opportunities and jet planes can take them. And although nostalgia for the *furusato* (hometown) and simpler living has caught on lately, the nuclear family now has to make it on its own.

On the surface, the nuclear family is traditionally both "paternal," in the sense that the man is still the head of the household, and "maternal" as women still control the household budget and child rearing. Wider opportunities for women in business, however, along with increased affluence and broader appetites for the "good life", are slowly challenging this status quo.

Finally, it seems that the question of Japanese identity not only cannot be answered anthropologically or archaeologically but also sociologically. The classic sociological studies by Ruth Benedict and Chie Nakane and Doi Masaru are still the best, though other studies and commentaries – written by non-Japanese – have gems of insight. In the end, it can only be left to the Japanese to sort it all out individually.

Left, caught by the camera. **Right**, making a fashion statement in Tokyo.

Is the Japanese language hard to learn? Many Japanese like to think so, convinced that their native tongue, known as *Nihon-go,* is so full of grammatical contortions, so strewn with subtle nuances, so... unique that it is simply impossible, nay, unthinkable, that foreigners can master it. *Nonsensu!*

Fortunately, as Japan inches toward "internationalization," people all over the world are discovering that Japanese is a relatively "easy" language to learn (relative to, say, Hungarian) and, even in its written form, is

The popularity in learning Japanese is commensurate with the country's rise in economic power, but what makes the change noticeable is the fact that until the 1980s, not that many people – long-term foreign residents included – bothered to make an effort. The few who persisted to the point of fluency were rarities. A Japan scholar at a US Ivy League university once voiced his doubts that there were even 400 Americans of non-Japanese ancestry who could translate a technical paper from Japanese into English.

far simpler than Chinese – the "official" *kanji* (Chinese character) count of Japanese being just under 2,000 compared to the 20,000-plus of standard Chinese.

According to statistics from the Ministry of Education, more than 31,000 foreign students are currently enrolled in Japanese schools, and it can be assumed that most of them have at least a basic familiarity with Japanese. Tens of thousands more pursue Japanese as a part of their secondary or higher education overseas. If goals stated by the government are to be met, the number of foreigners studying in Japan is expected to triple over the coming decade.

If the criteria is modified to those with the ability to read a daily newspaper, however, the number is more encouraging. It has also been reported that the Japanese government intends to spend "billions of yen" over the next decade, supporting Japanese-language teaching programs in Europe, the Americas and elsewhere. If true, this could be a lot more effective in improving people-to-people relations than the pitifully limited "cultural exchange" programs now in place.

At this point, let's suspend the debate for a minute to take a look at the language itself.

The Spoken Language: *Nihon-go,* claims over 130 million speakers, making it the world's 10th most commonly spoken language after Mandarin Chinese, English, Spanish, Hindi, Russian, Arabic, Portuguese, Bengali, and German.

Japan's national standard of speech, as taught in the schools and spoken by TV announcers, is known as *koku-go,* literally, the national language. It is based on the dialect of the Tokyo region, Japan's *de facto* capital since the 1600s and official capital for more than 120 years.

One feature of Japanese is its many regional dialects, some of which depart considerably from Tokyo speech and which sound almost totally incomprehensible to the unpracticed ear. But dialects in Japan are

not the problem they are in China, for example, due in no small part to Japan's uniform educational system and blanket radio and television network coverage.

Nihon-go is not the sole language spoken within Japan, as Korean and Chinese can also be heard on the streets, especially in the Kansai and parts of Kyushu. But the only non-Japanese language considered native to the four main islands and still in use is Ainu, spoken by a dwindling number of aboriginals in Hokkaido. Ainu was once much more

Left, bold *kanji* for a *sushi* shop and **above**, writing *kanban* (signboards) for *kabuki*.

widespread, and its linguistic legacy can be found in many Hokkaido and eastern Honshu place names, such as Sapporo. Japanese is also spoken to varying degrees in the large emigrant Japanese communities in the United States, (especially Hawaii), in Brazil, and in many other South American nations. It is still widely spoken by the older generation in parts of Japan's former pre-war empire – in such countries and regions as Korea, Taiwan, northeast China (Manchuria), Saipan, Palau, and other Pacific islands.

The Chinese Connection: Although it uses Chinese ideographs in its writing, Japanese bears no linguistic relation whatsoever to Chinese. Neither have phonologists been able to establish satisfactory proof of its relation to any other languages, although its syntax bears many similarities to both Ainu and Korean.

It is generally agreed that the sentence structure and grammar of Japanese clearly places it in the family of Ural-Altaic languages, a family which is spread across north-central Asia and reaches into eastern Europe. This linguistic goup includes Korean, Manchu (now extinct), Mongol, Turkish, Hungarian, Finnish and Estonian.

The picture is confused by the hybrid nature of Japanese, as its vocabulary clearly bears strong influences of a second source from the south. So the "roots" of Japanese are also believed to include Polynesian-Malay and languages from southeast Asia.

No one is sure how this odd mixture came about. Professor Ono Susumu, an authority on the language concludes that it was successive waves of immigration from both the south and the west took place in prehistoric times, quite some time before Japan became unified under the Yamato tribes in the 7th century. In any case, the roots of Japanese go back a long way indeed.

No confusion exists over the history of written Japanese. As the dominant culture in East Asia, Chinese has played a major influence on the evolution of the Japanese language, providing both elements of the writing system and a huge vocabulary. Chinese was adopted wholesale, and for some time it was the sole means of written communication in Japan.

Contacts with Europe began from the 16th century, and continued over the past 400 years. Modern Japanese has adopted thousands of words of Portuguese, Dutch, French, German and English origin.

One thing is for certain: considering its nearly two millennia of evolution, from the ancient poetry of the *Manyoshu* (*Collection of 10,000 Leaves*) to the *Ichitaro* computer software program, Japanese has proved itself to be a versatile and adaptable tongue.

Talk of the Devil: What is it about the Japanese language that makes it difficult to learn? Is it, in fact, the terrible tongue which a Jesuit missionary once memorably termed as the "Devil's language"?

By virtue of having lived in Japan for more than half his life, this writer challenges the notion that Japanese is especially hard to

change a word's meaning; in fact, syllables are only lightly stressed.

In verb structure and grammar, Japanese is highly regular. Learners need not be concerned with distinctions in case (genitive-nominative, etc.); gender (masculine-feminine); or number (singular-plural). They simply do not exist. Like the other languages of East Asia, Japanese does not employ articles like "a," "an" or "the."

But There Are Quirks: So what's all the fuss about then? Aside from the quirks of the writing system, two aspects of the language – problems which are more socio-cultural than purely linguistic – are probably responsible for giving foreign learners the impres-

learn. Not because I learned it, or even because I have seen so many other successful examples, but because there is no evidence to suggest any reason why it should present any difficulties.

Firstly, along with Malay and Hawaiian, Japanese is indisputably one of the world's simplest languages to pronounce. It has only five vowels and 13 consonants. Consonants do not occur in clusters (as in "growl" or "strike"). Each consonant is always accompanied by a vowel, which is why the word "strike" (as in baseball) is pronounced "*sutoraiki.*" Unlike Chinese, Thai, or Vietnamese, Japanese does not alter tones to

sion of difficulty. These are 1) a seemingly complex range in levels of politeness, beginning at the top with extreme honorifics and then moving in stages to neutral, conversational, and very simplified construction; and 2) noticeable differences in speaking styles between men and women.

But let's not worry about these two points, because they are the sort of thing that you can add to your repertoire later, after you have picked up the fundamentals. The good news

Above, sport fishermen document their catches on ink rubbings, displayed at a seaside train station in Chiba.

– if you are in Japan – is that you'll find no shortage of opportunities to practice: on trains, in offices, and in restaurants, bars and coffee shops. You see, Japan is a country where people pride themselves on their conversational ability, and you'll find you have 120 million "teachers" to help you along.

Politeness first: Every language has its ways of dealing with different situations. The way people speak at a funeral wake is different from old school friends at a class reunion. Depending on the language, these distinctions may be a speaker's choice of words and phrases. If you went into a shop and the salesperson responded to your request with a snappy "Yes, sir!" your immediate impression would be that you could count on attentive service. Or, you might be greeted with a friendly, "Hi, can I help you?" If you were greeted with a slovenly, "Yeah, waddya want?" you would leave with quite a different impression altogether.

The Japanese *kei-go*, or "polite language," is a holdover from the structured class system of feudal times, which no longer exists. In the present century, kei-go has been preserved as a key element in the deeply rooted Japanese tradition of deference to one's superiors and courtesy to guests. (Incidentally, the Japanese word for "customer" or "guest" is *okyakusama*.)

Proper speech is a source of pride for most Japanese, and the use of wkei-go cannot be expected to become extinct any time soon. Fortunately, foreigners are not expected to learn these niceties at the beginning, and the younger generation appears keen dropping some of the more complicated constructions.

Boy Talk, Girl Talk: As mentioned above, Japanese grammar does not concern itself with gender. However, noticeable differences exist between conversational styles of males and females.

Take the pronoun "I." Men might use such terms as *watakushi, boku,* or *ore;* females sometimes address themselves as *atashi.*

In informal speech, women tend to drop the copula and substitute the particle "*wa*" to end a sentence, such as "*Shiranai wa*" (or "I don't know.") To get the same effect, a man might grunt "*Shiran na.*" Both expressions use the negative form of the verb "*shiru*" ("to know") but it comes out slightly different.

A neutral (Americans might call it "non-sexist") speaking style does exist. For example, "*Ashita ikimasu*" ("I'll go tomorrow.") could be used by males or females. But in common practice, a man talking to his wife would probably say something like "*Ashita iku'n da,*" in which only the diction, not the meaning, is changed.

Modulation and tone of voice also tend to vary between the sexes. Men try to affect a deep rumble. Japanese women, on the other hand, tend to have high and more nasalized voices and the overall effect can be both irritating and pleasant to the ear. But when talking among themselves, women can also effect a masculine growl.

Another point which foreigners find frustrating when learning Japanese is the way the language handles ordinal numbers. Although *ichi, ni, san* apply when counting with fingers, one, two and three become *hitotsu, futatsu* and *mittsu* for objects in general. When counting people, *hitori, futari* and *sannin* are normally used; for animals, *ippiki, nihiki, sanbiki*; for elongated objects like pens, *ippon, nihon, sanbon* and so on.

The usage of a classifier to suffix numbers is another borrowing from the Chinese language, although, strangely, few of them correspond anymore.

Japanese Writing: While the combination of Sino-Japanese ideographs and two syllabaries used to write Japanese is admittedly difficult, those who make a sincere effort to study the written language find the effort rewarding. It is surely be one of the most fascinating writing systems ever developed.

The single most significant influence on the Japanese language was the introduction of the Chinese ideographs – known as the Han characters – in the 7th century.

The ideographs are much older, however, having been developed over several millennia by the Chinese. The oldest known examples of these characters were found etched on tortoise shell and bone fragments and are believed to date back to 1700 BC. They demonstrate that this system used to write modern Chinese and Japanese is at least 3,700 years old. In way of analogy, imagine if the same hieroglyphics used in ancient Egypt were still being taught to schoolchildren, used in daily newspapers, and in personal computers – and not only Egyptian, but Greek schoolchildren as well!

What Are Ideographs?: Originally, they were words represented in the simplest characters that are stylized representations of the subject. Then, a long time ago, a system was developed by which the pictures could represent more abstract ideas.

To make "bright," for example, combine the characters for sun and moon, the two most important sources of light to ancient people (Figure 1). Another example might be "safe," which shows a woman sitting under a roof (Figure 2). Reflecting ancient wisdom, the same character followed by the sound "*i*" to make it an adjective, has the meaning "cheap"!

Kanji continued to evolve into a highly sophisticated system that presently makes use of 214 abbreviated symbols, or radicals,

immediately evident, regardless of how the word is pronounced.

The graphic representation of such a concept is a great advantage, and once the concept is mastered, the ingenuity of kanji becomes apparent and their comprehension becomes quite intuitive.

Since a single word can occupy the space of two letters of the alphabet, text written in kanji is also highly concentrated; editors usually expect the volume of Japanese text to increase by about 20 percent when translated into English.

Written Japanese underwent considerable reform in the post-war era, with many archaic features dropped from usage after 1945.

Figure 1

bird (*tori*)

moon (*tsuki*)

turtle (*kame*)

hand (*te*)

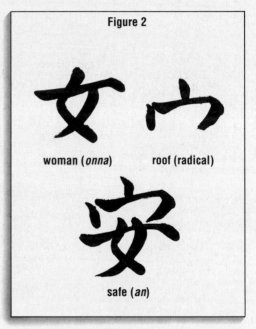

Figure 2

woman (*onna*)

roof (radical)

safe (*an*)

which are combined with phonetic elements to indicate the pronunciation.

Thus, while far more memorization is required at the initial learning stage than the 26 letters of the English alphabet, there are nonetheless advantages to the use of kanji as a means of communication.

Instant Recognition: When a non-English speaker encounters the word he doesn't recognize – take "diabetes" as an example – the word is just a jumble of letters and there is no way to gain understanding without the aid of a dictionary. When the same word is expressed in Chinese characters – "sugar-urine sickness" – the meaning (usually) becomes

The number of kanji required for children to learn was also reduced and the characters themselves were simplified.

Today the Ministry of Education specifies which kanji are to be learned in each grade, and a high school graduate is expected to be able to know the entire "*Toyo*" or "formal" kanji list, which contains about 2,000 separate entries. (Japan's "literacy rate" of nearly 99 percent indicates that these expectations are being met; in truth, however, this percentage applies only to reading, while the actual requirement includes writing as well – something quite a few high-school graduates, especially those who depend on modern kanji word processors, don't do well.)

The average university-educated Japanese might know several thousand more, including geographic names, family and personal names, and specialized vocabulary in their own fields of study.

Clever Combinations: In practice, learning to recognize and reproduce the kanji ideographs is not particularly difficult. Most kanji are formed of two or more simpler elements (the "radicals" mentioned earlier); a classic example is the tree – woods – forest progression (Figure 3).

The difficulty for any student of the Japanese language comes, however, when he or she takes into account the different pronun-

Figure 3

tree (*ki*)

woods (*hayashi*)

forest (*mori*)

ciations of the kanji – as many as 10 – depending on the context.

For example, the "*on*", or "original" pronunciation of the ideograph for "tree" is "*moku*," as in "*mokuyobi*" ("tree-day" – Thursday). The *kun*, or "normal" pronunciation, however, is "*ki*" (or "*gi*" when it is preceded by other phonetic combinations), as in "*Kinoshita*" ("under the tree," a family name) or "*Roppongi*" ("six trees"). Another example is the kanji for "mountain," sometimes pronounced "*yama*" as in "*Karasuyama*" ("Crow Mountain"), sometimes "*san*" (or "*zan*"), as in Fujisan.

Scholars maintain there is some sort of

"system" behind this, but in practice, the only way to master it is… well, practice.

Spelling It Out: Besides kanji, Japanese makes use of two other sets of characters, called *kana* (*gana*). The general method of writing Japanese is to use the *kanji* to express proper nouns and the roots of all verbs. The endings of verbs, of particles such as prepositions, and other inflections or endings, such as the interrogative "*ka?*" which converts a statement into a question, are written with hira**gana**.

The other set, *katakana*, is used for words of foreign origin, words for which the writer doesn't know the kanji, and other specialized uses, such as onomatopoeia.

All kana signify syllables, not separate letters. The sounds (fewer than 50) including the five vowels, the sound "*n*" (or "*gn*"), the "*ya*," "*yi*" and "*yu*" sounds, and only these consonants, each followed by a vowel: *k, r, h, t* (except "*ti*" is "*chi*" and "*tu*" is "*tsu*"), *s* ("*si*" becomes "*shi*"), *m, w* (but there is no "*wi*") and *n*. Using diacritical marks, the "*g*" sound is modified from "*k*", the "*d*" sound is modified from "*t*," and the "*b*" and "*p*" sounds are modified from the "*h*" root, which also substitutes for the missing "*f*." Note that there is no "*c*" ("*k*" usually serves), no "*l*" ("*r*" is substituted), no "*th*" (usually, "*su*" is substituted), and no "*v*" (it is replaced either by a plain "*b*" or a modified "*u*").

Finally, in addition to all its other drawbacks, this ancient and ethnocentric syllabary simply cannot deal with the "*er*" or "*aw*" sounds, common in Western languages, making the word "lawyer," for example, sound as "*raayaa*."

Both kana forms were derived from kanji shapes, but the two can be easily distinguished visually: hiragana (the older of the two) is more rounded and cursive; katakana is sharp and angular (and, as it happens, ideal for computer screens).

Here is a sentence written first in hiragana, then in katakana:

にほんごはそんなにむずかしくない。
ニホンゴハソンナニムズカシクナイ。

What does this mean? They look completely different but in both cases, it reads "*Nihon-go wa sonnani muzukashiku nai*." Which, in plain English translates as, "Japanese isn't all that difficult."

At a temple called Zenrinji in the Tokyo suburb of Mitaka you can find the grave of the brilliant bohemian novelist Dazai Osamu, author of *The Setting Sun* and *No Longer Human*. In 1947, Dazai finally managed to commit suicide after several unsuccessful attempts. Inevitably in front of his tombstone there is at least one cup of cheap *sake*, left by adoring fans who want to indulge Dazai's well-known thirst for booze and maintain some kind of communion with his departed spirit. Come back in a few days and the level of the *sake* will most likely have gone down considerably. You can attribute it to evaporation, or…

The Japanese are among the most religious or least religious people on earth, depending on whom you talk to or how you define "religious." Ask a Japanese how many gods there are and you might get "one" or "800 million" for an answer. Ask about the nature of the *kami-sama* (deities) worshiped and you might get confused silence.

The average Japanese thinks nothing of marrying at a Shinto shrine, burying loved ones in a Buddhist cemetery or boisterously celebrating Christmas. Although the devout Christian or Muslim – whose jealous monotheistic God demands unswerving fidelity – might find this religious promiscuity a bit hard to fathom and at least slightly sinful, your typical Japanese is blithely unaware of any contradiction in his or her behavior.

Polls asking Japanese which religion they adhere to consistently yield results that total well over 100 percent. That's because most of those who reply say they are followers of both Shinto and Buddhism. Furthermore, there is no Japanese equivalent of the Bible, unless you count the *Kojiki*, and even the most ardent ultranationalist does not accept the 8th-century chronicle as divine writ.

Conversely, many of those Japanese embracing Christianity – a figure usually given as roughly 1 percent of the population – tend to be very pious, and see the Bible, first

translated into Japanese by Portuguese monks, as quite literally "true."

Although few church bells ring on Sunday mornings, until recently nearly every home was equipped with a *kamidana* godshelf with Shinto symbols, or a *butsudan* Buddhist household altar containing worship vessels and memorial tablets for the family's ancestors, before which offerings of flowers, food, drink or incense were made daily. People passing by any of the thousands of Shinto shrines throughout the country still tend to

drop in for a brief devotion before going on their busy way again.

It is hard to attribute all this to simple custom; the Japanese definitely seem to have a sense of religious piety and spiritual yearning, although it is far different from that in the West. The main difference seems to be that the line between the sacred and the profane is much less clearly drawn in Japan. In many ways, community life and religion are one and the same.

For example, only a few decades ago, head craftsmen or shipbuilders as a rule performed purification rites in the robes of a Shinto priest. They were considered involved in a

Preceding pages, ceremony to honor 47 samurai, held each December in Tokyo. **Left**, priests watch the procession at Kyoto's Aoi Matsuri. **Right**, Buddhist beneath a sacred waterfall.

kind of priestcraft capable of controlling the nature gods.

First-time visitors to Japan are apt to overlook the important role that religion continues to play in the daily lives of the Japanese. In rushing from one ancient temple to the next, they more often than not miss that little Shinto shrine perched on the top of a department store, the purification-cum-exorcism being conducted by a Shinto priest at a ridgepole-placing ceremony for a new Seven-11 Store, or the amulet (it could be Shinto, or Buddhist, or a combination of both) hanging down from the mirror of the taxi they are riding in.

The often cited tolerance and eclecticism of Japanese religion (and Japanese ways of thinking in general) can probably be explained by the fact that foreign imports have been adapted to the indigenous world view. Likewise, the well-deserved reputation of the Japanese for hard work is partly anchored in their religious consciousness. For example, traditionally skilled workmen – swordsmiths, lacquer and mask makers, carpenters, even barbers and cooks – have kept godshelves in front of them while they work. To these they direct thanks for the skills they consider gifts from their patron deity.

A basic understanding of the Japanese religious sensibility, then, must begin with Shinto – not a "national religion" in any current official sense, but one that influences virtually every aspect of Japanese culture and society, even today.

Shinto Defined: It is hard to give any simple definition of Shinto, since it is not really a national religion or even a systematized set of beliefs. The term "Shinto" was not even invented until after the introduction of Buddhism, a date traditionally given as AD 552, as a way of contrasting the native beliefs with that universal faith. One of the problems is that many of the things that are called "Shinto" are really not the original Shinto at all.

In general, however, it can be said that it shares, with many other primitive faiths of the world, the belief that all natural objects and phenomena possess a spiritual side. It is this animism, mixed with ancestor worship, that characterizes Shinto, then. A tree, for example, was revered by the ancient Japanese as a source of food (nuts and fruit), of energy (firewood), of shelter and even of clothing. For that reason, when a great tree

was felled to provide wood for the (Buddhist) temple complexes at Nara or Kyoto, it was not used for several years, to give the spirit within time to safely depart. Mountains, forests and even the oceans were also similarly revered.

As for ancestor worship, the Yamato "race" always believed that it had descended from Heaven, and worshiped Amaterasu Omikami – she who ruled the heavens – as the ancestress of the imperial family, if not all the people. Thus the *Kojiki* is basically a justification for their conquest of the "Middle Land Where Reeds Grow Luxuriously" and their rule over other apparently related groups, such as the inhabitants of Izumo on the Japan Sea, who were said to be descendants of Amaterasu's brother, the rowdy Storm God, Susanoo no Mikoto.

Shinto Concepts: It should be recognized that the term *kami*, although usually translated as "god," is quite different from the Western concept of divinity. The classic definition, as originally understood in Japan, was made by the 18th-century scholar Motoori Norinaga: "Anything whatsoever which was outside the ordinary, which possessed superior power, or which was awe-inspiring, was called *kami*."

That goes for people, too. So, today, we often hear expressions like "the god of baseball," or "the god of management." These expressions are not intended to be taken entirely tongue-in-cheek. The Japanese at least subconsciously still believe that their land and its air is filled with the presence of kami-sama of all kinds.

In ancient Shinto there was also a belief in a kind of soul – *tamashii* – that lived on after death. An unrefined form of ancestor worship also existed, remnants of which can be seen in the *Higan* observances of the spring and autumn equinoxes. It can also be seen in in the *Obon* which, although primarily Buddhist in other parts of Asia, has distinct Shinto overtones in Japan.

Primitive Shinto had concepts of heaven and hell, as well, although they were hazily conceived at best. To use electricity as an analogy, you might say this world is "plus," while the afterworld is "minus." There was no concept of sin, or divine retribution, or absolution for offenses committed. Just about

Right, the Itsukushima Shrine *torii* at Miyajima.

SHINTO SHRINES

The thousands of Shinto shrines, known as *jinja* (or *jingu* when they are national shrines) and other names, vary in size from tiny roadside boxes to large compounds such as the primevally simple Grand Shrines at Ise and the opulent-verging-on-decadent Toshogu Shrine at Nikko. But nearly all share certain features.

First, there is at least one *torii*, shaped somewhat like the Greek letter . This gateway may have evolved from a bird's perch – a certain kind of bird having been a religious symbol in many animistic cults – and it may be made of wood, stone or metal, or even concrete. Like the *shimenawa*, or sacred straw festoon, zigzag cuts of paper, mounts of salt and cleanly swept gravel, the torii serves to mark off areas considered sacred from those thought profane.

Often the largest building of the shrine is the inner sanctum called the *honden*. This is the main dwelling of the deity. It is usually elevated above the other buildings and reached by a staircase. Unfortunately it is likely to be off-limits to visitors, but other than a mirror or, on rare occasions, an image, there is little to see inside. These objects, by the way, are the *mitama-shiro* or *go-shintai*, serving as spirit substitutes for the kami being worshiped.

Also inside are a few green twigs, changed daily, an earthen vessel for offerings, and a grass mat for the head priest who administers these rituals. Naturally, everything is kept scrupulously clean in accordance with Shinto's fixation on ritual purity.

In front of the honden is the often quite spacious *haiden* or worship hall, used for ritual ceremonies. Usually, this structure is merely a roof supported by pillars, open on all sides, and is used only by the priests and special guests.

Various subsidiary buildings can also often be found in shrine precincts, such as a *noh* stage or *masha* which are subordinate shrines that encourage private devotion such as the Roman Catholic shrines to the various saints. Stone lanterns and extensive greenery frequently lend an air of mystery to the grounds.

There are no elaborate rituals or prescribed procedure involved in worshiping at a shrine. On entering the grounds you see a stone wash-basin, often with wooden, bamboo or tin ladles balanced across it. Here you rinse your mouth and hands in preparation for approaching the deity. Water, like salt, such as you see tossed at sumo matches, or the shreds of paper ties to the duster known as the *obarai*, are used extensively for purification.

It is customary to toss a small offering into the cashbox at the foot of the haiden, before sounding the *piñata*-like shaker to attract the attention of the god. Most devout worshipers also clap their hands twice, making doubly sure the god is listening. Then, with or without the hands held together, a deep bow is performed, and held, while the prayer is offered. Two more sharp claps of the hand, another light bow, and the simple ritual is done, the worshiper backing slowly away a few steps before going on about his or her business.

Often, that business is conducted at the shrine office, or in a nearby kiosk, where there is usually an array of amulets of all kinds, "guaranteed" to ensure everything from safety from bering run down in traffic and success in schoolk or university exams to recovery from serious illness. They can make fine souvenirs, but they are not always inexpensive.

Although shrines are usually delightfully serene and provide a much appreciated haven from the hurly-burly of everyday life in Japan, they undergo a complete transformation at festival time, especially the mid-autumn harvest *matsuri*.

On such occasions, the gods are taken out for rollicking rides through the streets in *mikoshi* (portable shrines) by tipsy bearers, so as to bring the blessings of the *kami-sama* to all the community. This one of the few times when Japanese collectively shed social inhibitions. In some areas, they are still housed in temporary structures known as *otabishio*, throughout the matsuri.

This regular communion between local residents and the kami preserves ancient traditions and helps maintain cohesion in the community during periods of rapid social change.

the worst thing that could happen was the pollution of a ritual. Otherwise, as far as the afterlife was concerned, it was commonly thought that the dead would eventually be reborn into this world, just as spring returns after winter.

Shinto Origins: The aforementioned "plus/minus" concept in Shinto suggests an affinity with Taoism, and indicate that the basis of the religion arose in China and/or Korea. In fact, however, not much is known of the origins of Shinto; elements in it seem also to have come from as far afield as Southeast Asia and Polynesia.

Some experts feel that prehistoric beliefs from as far back as the Jomon culture also

World War II that the government took any direct part in Shinto.

It was during the Restoration, however, that the government introduced *Kokka* (National) Shinto as a political tool for controlling the people through the policy of *saisei it'chi* – the "unity of rites and politics." Although the Emperor was said in the Meiji Constitution to be "sacred and inviolable," the nature of his sacredness was never officially defined; the most common interpretation, though, was that through prayer he became one with his divine ancestor Amaterasu and the other gods, and could therefore interceded on behalf of his people.

The Yasukuni Jinga, a Shinto shrine on

have survived in Shinto. They look to remnants of the original Ainu beliefs, and to the still-surviving Okinawan religion, for evidence of this. Specifically, the Ainu creation myth, as well as that found in Okinawa's *Omoro Soshi*, which was compiled in the mid-16th century, has some interesting parallels to the ostensibly "Shinto" tale of Izanami and Izanagi told in the *Kojiki*.

"National" Shinto: There are 13 mainstream Shinto sects and numerous sub-sects in Japan today, but since the Occupation, they have not been controlled by the government. In fact, it was only during the period from the Meiji Restoration of 1868 through the end of

Kudan Hill in central Tokyo, near the Budokan, is an example (a particularly notorious one) of the national shrines set up by the authorities. Because it is here that the spirits of every soldier who died in the name of the Emperor since 1853 are enshrined (including war criminals executed by the Allies after World War II), visits made here – official or not – by the prime minister and other members of government are often violently opposed by those who believe the Constitution now supports the separation of church and state. Another national shrine is the impressive Meiji Jingu, not far away, whose majestic architecture reminds one that

Emperor Meiji, enshrined therein, was thought of as both royal and divine.

In fact, none of the national shrines – state inventions all – has much to do with traditional beliefs. Dismissing them as unimportant in the modern scheme of things, however, would be a sociological, if not religious, mistake. Excepting the radicals, even those Japanese who claim they are "not religious at all" often do not accept the Constitution's apparent "denial" of Shinto's role.

The "Middle Way" of Buddhism: We have mentioned that the traditional date for Buddhism to have "arrived" in Japan is AD 552. While this may be true, technically, it wasn't until centuries later that it ceased to be the

be ended and the "self" totally done away with through entry into the blissful state of *Nirvana* (Buddhahood).

Buddha's followers came to believe that one who really knows the truth lives the life of truth, and becomes truth itself. By overcoming the conflicts of the ego, then, one can attain a vision of universal, cosmic harmony.

Mahayana, meaning "Greater Vehicle," was the form of Buddhism that became established through most of East Asia. It holds that every being, sentient or non-sentient, shares a basic spiritual communion, and that all are destined for Buddhahood. Although all beings are separate in appearance, they are one and the same in reality. Every per-

exclusive province of aristocrats and the professional priests drawn from their ranks. This is somewhat ironic in view of the basic beliefs of the religion's founder, Sakyamuni (or Siddharta), born a prince in eastern India (now a part of Nepal) around 500 BC, who advocated a "Middle Way" between self-indulgence and asceticism.

The Buddha, as he came to be known (though this is a misnomer), blamed all pain and discontent in the world on desire, and claimed that through right living, desire could

Left, praying at Yasaka Shrine in Kyoto. **Above**, shrine dance at Yasukuni Shrine, Tokyo.

son's present situation is determined by past deeds, Buddhists believe; this is the principle of *karma*.

Since the main Mahayana sutras only appeared around 100 BC, it is not known how closely they reflect the original thoughts of the Buddha.

Buddhism is "Japanified": By the time it reached Japan's shores via China, Buddhism had already changed tremendously from the simple message that Sakyamuni had preached. It was to undergo even more radical change when it encountered the beliefs already held in the "Land of the Gods."

As early as the 6th century, for example,

Ryobu Shinto began to emerge as a syncretic compromise with Buddhism. In this hybrid belief system, kami-sama were regarded as temporary manifestations of the Buddhist deities. In time, Buddhist thought became so influenced by the indigenous beliefs, deviating so far from the original, that some scholars of religion doubt whether Japanese version really deserves to be called Buddhism.

Buddhist "Afterlife": For example, although the goal of Nirvana is to break the cycle of reincarnation, most Japanese Buddhists seem to believe that the souls of the dead are eventually reborn. As the famed folklorist Yanagida Kunio once pointed out, if you ask a typical Japanese where people go after they die, he will usually answer *"Gokuraku,"* which translates as "Paradise." Contrast this with the more "orthodox" Buddhist belief in death as a "permanent state"; in fact, a euphuism expressing someone's death is *"Hotoke ni natta"* (which means "He became a Buddha").

In practice, however, Japanese who can continue to return to their *furosato*, or ancestral home, for the two Higan equinoxes as well as during the mid-summer Obon or "Feast of the Dead" observances – an equivalent of the Christian "All Souls' Day" and historically linked to a story in Buddhist tradition about how an unhappy ghost was consoled and saved. In Japan, though, the purpose of attending Obon is to be present when the family's ranking male ceremoniously offers food to the spirits of departed ancestors – spirits which supposedly return to earth for the occasion.

Where do they return from? Yanagida says most people will answer "the mountains." This may derive from the special place mountains have always held in Japanese religious lore. Certain peaks, such as Mt. Omine near Nara, and of course Mt. Fuji, are especially sacred; each year, thousands of pilgrims dressed in white ascend them. Such considerations also lay behind the choice of Mt. Koya and Mt. Hiei as the sites for the headquarters of the Shingon and Tendai sects, respectively.

The Japanese concept of an after-life, then, appears to be quite similar to that held before Buddhism arrived. Excepting those Japanese Buddhists whose particular sect specifically countermands such a concept, most seem to believe that the life force passed on from one generation to the next continues eternally, though little energy is spent in explaining exactly how.

Early Buddhist Disagreements: Shingon, one of the earliest Buddhist sects in Japan, was founded by Kukai (also known as Kobo Daishi), who, returning from China in 806, brought back to his homeland knowledge of esoteric Lamaistic rituals and symbolic art. Shingon's great rival was Tendai Buddhism, imported by Saicho only two years earlier.

Tendai took Sakyamuni's teachings – originally limited, it seems, to the concept that only the elimination of one's own passion could lead to Buddhahood – and transformed them into the belief that all men, even

the evil, could enter that state by relying on the strength of another. This became the mainstream of Japanese Buddhist thought.

Another sharp distinction between Kukai and Saicho was that while the former believed that all nature, including the mountains and the rivers, could share Buddhahood, and in fact thought of himself as a Buddha, Saicho and his Tendai followers believed otherwise.

Both of these sects flourished during the Nara and subsequent periods, with relatively

Above, religious traditions still count with the new breed. **Right**, offerings to Kamakura's Daibutsu.

THE TEMPLE TRAIL

Temple hopping in Japan can be a bewildering experience, particularly if you have no idea of What You Are Looking At (WYALA). Not simplifying matters is the abundance of eras, sects and religious terms involved. Then there is the purely secular matter of removing your shoes – and searching for them later. But be not dismayed, all ye who enter here. A temple visit almost always is worth the effort, Therefore, beginning at the end, so to speak, you might put the cemetery at the top of your WYALA list.

Under the Tokugawa Shogunate, Japanese Buddhism lost much of its vigor, leading cynics to charge that priests were good for nothing but buying people. An exaggeration, no doubt, but cemeteries still provide a good part of the income for most temples and those attached to the great old temples of Kyoto, Kiyomizu-dera, for example, are marvelous places to explore. And no, the departed are not buried "standing up" to save space in land-scarce Japan, as more than one visiting foreigner has quipped; cremation being the Buddhist burial method of choice, not so much space is needed for the urns of ashes.

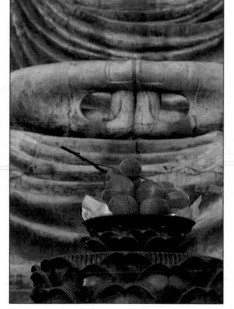

Look out for those impressive gravemarkers with five tiers, as they generally mark the resting places of important samurai and other high-ranking individuals.

The main building (*hondo*), library (*bunko*), bell tower (*shoro*) and other buildings of a temple complex can be exquisite architectural creations. But the one most easily admired is the pagoda, or *to*. The form seen in Japan is the culmination of a long evolution from the dome-shaped stupa (thought to represent an upside-down rice bowl) in which the bones of the Buddha and Buddhist saints were buried in India.

Entire books could be (and have been!) written on temple art, as opposed to architecture and landscaping. It's impossible, in a few words, to sort it all out, but we could begin by eliminating the paintings, sketches and calligraphy you will encounter – not because they are unworthy of notice, but because they generally relate to the temple's own history (portraits and sayings of former priests, etc.). This narrows it down to the statuary, alone inviting many lifetimes of study to encompass. Nevertheless, the following are among the statues you may see:

● Nyorai (Tathagata) Buddhas: Like Sakyamuni after Enlightenment, these seek to assist others to realize the truth; the lump on their foreheads (a reminder of Buddhism's roots in Hinduism) is a sign of wisdom.

● Maitreya (Miroku) or "Future Buddhas" can be distinguished by a pose with one leg crossed over the other.

As the power of the samurai grew and Buddhism filtered down to the lower classes, aristocratic restrain in religious art gave way to more dynamic styles. Here are some examples:

● Nio: This fierce-looking, muscle-bound pair, flanking the gates to many temples, are kinds of Deva Kings, derived from the Hindu gods Brahma and Indra.

● Shi-Tenno also are Deva Kings, often standing nonchalantly on the heads of demons at the four cardinal points, are examples of *ten*, or heavenly beings who are not yet perfect but superior to human beings.

● Myo-o: Also in the *ten* category are these five, fiery faced fellows. One of them is Fudo, who sits cross-legged with burning flames around him.

● Oni, *et al*: Then, below us on the karmic ladder are perpetually hungry ghosts known as *gaki*, furious spirits (*ashura*) with bird-like beaks and small wings, and netherworld spirits (*naraka*) like the *oni*.

Far less intimidating are the representations of a benevolent Buddha, such as the following two examples:

● Amida, beckoning to the Western Paradise, with its ambrosia pond filled with lotuses and hosts of angels. The hands are often on his (her) lap, the forefinger touching the thumb to form a near-perfect circle.

● Kannon, the Goddess of Mercy, began as a manifestation of Amida, but is now worshiped in his (he only looks feminine) own right. There is always supposed to be a tiny statue of Amida in his crown.

Incidentally, good luck with finding your shoes.

few challengers until the Kamakura Period. It was then that a number of popular new sects were founded, and before long, many Buddhist priests in Japan were taking wives, eating meat and, in general, carrying on in ways Sakyamuni, the prince who had turned his back on such things, might have found very hard to comprehend.

Amida Buddhism: There are today an estimated 56 main divisions, and 170 subdivisions, in Japanese Buddhism. The single most popular sect is Jodo Shinshu, founded by Shinran (1173–1262), who preached an "easy road to salvation" by means of the *nembutsu* prayer to the Amida, a boddhisatva who made a vow eons ago to save all who

siderations of good and evil. This, no doubt, helps account for its popularity.

Buddhist Calvinists: Back in the Kamakura Period, when religion was a much more vital social force than it is today, the Amidaists directly contended for converts with the followers of the obstinate reformer Nichiren (1222–82). He claimed that he was the man selected to spread the "True Word" that would lead men to the "Primeval Gateway" opened by the "Lord of the Universe" (Sakyamuni) to the "Ultimate Reality." Nichiren gloried in street preaching, and neither exile nor the threat of execution could faze him.

His highly nationalistic thinking is well-

placed faith in him/her, and guide them to the "Blissful Land of Purity" in the West.

About half of the Japanese Buddhists belong to either Jodo Shinshu, or to Jodo, another form of Amidaism established by Honen (1133–1212). True believers of Jodo Shinshu think that it is not even necessary to be "good" to be reborn into the Western Paradise, and that the laity can become Buddhas as easily as priests, even without the faith that Honen claimed was essential.

Amidaism is perhaps the form of Buddhism closest to the core Japanese beliefs, as in its slight concern for moral judgement and exaltation of natural inclinations beyond con-

known; he predicted the Mongul thrust at Japan and noted that Buddhism had constantly been spreading eastward toward the land where it would achieve its ultimate maturity: Japan.

Nichiren's followers have been called "Buddhist Calvinists," and are usually to be found among the *petite bourgeoisie* and lower classes. During the 14th century, they often engaged in pitched battles with Shinran's followers, who were usually farmers or townspeople.

Today, many of Nichiren's followers in Japan belong to the Soka Gakkai, a controversial organization whose political arm, the

Komei-to or "Clean-Government Party" has considerable strength in the National Diet.

Zen "Emptiness": The impact of that particularly eclectic form of Buddhism called Zen on Japanese culture is considerable, reaching far beyond the temple and entering into cultural and social areas of all kinds, including interior decoration, gardening, ink painting, calligraphy, the tea ceremony, the cuisine, and even military strategies and the martial arts.

Two Buddhist priests in the 12th and 13th centuries, Eisai, founder of the Rinzai Zen sect, and his disciple Dogen, who established the Soto Zen sect, are given the lion's share of the credit for bringing the principle

tion is to stimulate (or perhaps divert) the mind into a similar state.

Zen was influenced by both Taoism and the Wang Yangming school of neo-Confucianism that stressed the "prime conscience" and the importance of action. They would describe the "Great Ultimate" as being akin to the hub of a well – empty but the point from which all action flows. For various reasons, Zen sects proved better able than the others to satisfy the spiritual needs of the samurai.

The Zen Leap: Whether through zazen or the use of koan posed by the Zen master, the goal is for the disciple to be provoked, excited or irritated to the point where one

of "emptiness" into Japanese Buddhism.

Soto-sect followers rely almost solely on *zazen*, or sitting meditation; they reject scripture and seek to emulate Sakyamuni, who reached the state of enlightenment while meditating without conscious thought in such a position. In contrast, the Rinzai sect also utilizes *koan* riddles – such as the famous "What is the sound of one hand clapping?" Koan must be tackled with something beyond "logic" and "non-logic," and their func-

Left, shrine maidens at the Heian Shrine in Kyoto. **Above**, *sake* rice wine and fruit offerings at an altar in a snow-house.

makes a non-intellectual leap into the void and experiences reality and the unity of all things directly. If successful, one will then view everything anew with a light from within, and there will no longer be any contradictions or duality.

As Alan Watts put it, "Zen discipline is one of activity and of order; its doctrine the invalidity of doctrine; its end an illumination by immediate experience." D.T. Suzuki pointed to an explanation made by numerous Zen teachers: Don't look for the donkey, since you're on it. Don't look for your head, since it's on your shoulders. The donkey, you and the universe are one in the same.

One of the great thrills of traveling in Japan, for first-time visitor, foreign resident, and Japanese alike, is running across, suddenly and without warning, a local festival. This is not as impossible or as rare as it may seem, especially in the warm months of the year. The first excitement, the palpable attraction that draws one into the crowd to mill about and observe whatever is happening and become part of the color and energy of the event, is irresistible. One's heart beats faster and one becomes excited. Festivals are like that, period.

Japan's explosive transformation from a primarily agricultural nation to a post-industrial economy has been so rapid and intense that many traditional customs and institutions have had to sprint to keep up or be forgotten quickly. Change is so rapid that tradition is sometimes sucked along with it, only to be rediscovered with surprise at the doorstep when the Japanese had thought that it was long gone and blown away. Both these phenomena are noticeable in the case of traditional festivals and observances, of which Japan has an astonishing number.

Daily events: Almost every day of spring, summer and autumn, a festival – however small and humble – takes place somewhere in Japan. There is a distinction between annual observances (*nenchu gyoji*) and festivals (*matsuri*). The former are part of the national culture and are observed throughout the country by everyone. The latter are usually more local, being associated with an area or place, and may be the purely local celebration of a specific event or the specific way in which an annual observance is carried out in a place or region. (There are local annual observances as well, but the working definition here classes them with the matsuri.) There are also categories of festivals, such as spring and autumn festivals. The dividing line between annual observance and festival is hard to pinpoint, so, since both are generally celebratory and happy occasions – that is, they are feasts and

are festive – they will all be called festivals.

There are a number of simple ways that Japanese festivals have been categorized, the most common being by season and by origin. Seasonal differences are the basis for almost the whole system of Japanese festivals, the exception being observances of specific historic events, foundings, birthdays, etc. Yet even the way in which events are feted may partake of the nature of a seasonal observance, especially if the festival is old. A case in point is the national holiday called Culture Day (November 3), which is the birthday of the Emperor Meiji (r. 1868–1912). If the seasons in Japan are seen in terms of their psychological influences, of the emotional effects and temperamental rhythms produced, then the soft, gentle melancholy of autumn and early winter is the ideal time to read books and sop up culture, the time that the appetite for such activities is keenest. Thus, Emperor Meiji's birthday did not become Family Day or Pet Day or Yodle-in-the-Bathtub Day, but, with great psychological precision, Culture Day.

The Japanese sensitivity to the characters and changes of the seasons has been touted beyond triteness, especially by the Japanese themselves, but it is true. The Japanese (and Koreans) are acutely and unconsciously in tune or in rhythm with how the seasons behave and affect people. The festivals of Japan, some of which indeed have roots that are quite ancient, reflect this sensitivity in both subtle and obvious ways.

Though Japan has gone through periods of internal strife and civil war (particularly from 1467 to 1600), the islands were never conquered and there has never been any type of sudden social or political revolution. In many parts of the country the continuity of residence goes back very far indeed. Cultural traditions are cumulative or agglutinative (like the Japanese language), and in such areas where the continuity of residence is long, there has been no clearing away process. Festivals and observances often have the deposits of ages all mixed about in varying amounts and intensities. Trying to analyze Japanese festivals in terms of origin is very interesting, but without a great deal of

Preceding pages, jostling through the streets with a portable shrine. **Left**, female archer at the Procession of the Ages.

scholarly information and powerful analytical tools, it would be like trying to chart the ancestries by sight alone of all the dogs in the dog pounds of a large metropolis during, say, a year. Some are obviously not, but…

Unfortunately, no in-depth study of the world of Japanese festivals is available; it is a wide-open and fascinating field that is calling for further study.

The Calendar: Though Japan today uses the standard Gregorian calendar, which is solar, it was adopted only in 1872. Before that, the Chinese lunar calendar had been in use for a millennium and a half or so. And before that the Japanese presumably had some system or traditional means of calendric reckoning.

There are two major observances in the year – *Oshogatsu* (New Year) and *Obon*, the Japanese "All Souls." These occur quite naturally at roughly antipodal points of the year, in midwinter and late summer, respectively. Both are basically celebratory and bring together the extended family. At the same time, there is a kind of joyful solemnity, a pleasant dignity and seriousness in the proceedings of both events.

The New Year: The Japanese New Year is a whole series of rituals and observances, not just a one-shot frivolity as in the West, and it lasts many days. There are, in fact, two New Years – a Greater New Year and a Lesser one. It seems that the native Japanese time

The Western solar calendar that became the official system in 1872 had little to do with the agricultural cycle and with the round of rituals and observances and festivals of the year. As a result, the lunar calendar is still used in some instances to determine festival dates, and sometimes a festival is celebrated twice, by the solar calendar in the city, and by lunar calendar in the country. In fact, New Year may be celebrated three times. In some areas, the solar calendar is used for certain observances and the lunar for others. A date on the lunar calendar, say the 3rd day of the 2nd month, comes about a month after the same date on the solar calendar.

reckoning used before the introduction of the Chinese lunar calendar favored a full moon as the beginning of things, while the Chinese system used the new moon as the beginning. Thus, the Greater New Year starts at the new moon, and the Lesser New Year is observed 15 days later. The whole thing is made more complex by the fact that the Japanese New Year was originally associated with spring or the last days of winter. This timing was distorted by the use of the solar calendar, which displaced the entire affair back into winter. Today, urban dwellers observe only a fraction of the Greater New Year, and the Lesser New Year rituals are seen only in the countryside and are becoming increasingly weaker and fewer.

The ending of one year and the beginning of the next is a time of starting fresh – that is, of purification. It is basically a religious event, but centered around the individual and the family, not a church. The pervading mood is one of calm and optimism and joy. Relaxation and pleasure are integral parts of this observance. Rocking the boat is not only considered gauche, but is harmful and unseemly for the New Year.

The New Year starts with a thorough cleaning of the house at the end of December, in which *shoji* screens are repapered and broken and worn things are replaced, and

planted by fashionable things to eat, including "French" cooking, but such adventures are passing symptoms of the times and not lasting parts of the Japanese New Year.

The Lesser New Year involves numerous ancient practices, especially those associated with agriculture and rice. These are practices as part of the yearly ritual cycle of the imperial household, and in the countryside have numerous local applications that are unique and colorful. As with the Greater New Year, purification is a major theme. These Lesser New Year practices tend to be clearly and directly religious.

February 3, Setsubun: This name means "dividing the seasons," and indicates that

ends either on the 3rd or 5th or 7th day of January. There are different things to do at various times of the New Year – special decorations to put up and take down at set times, and special foods. The decorations and foods all have symbolic value and felicitous meaning, containing references to longevity, prosperity, happiness, and the like. In recent years, many New Year foods have tended to become cloyingly sweet, and traditional dishes to some extent are being sup-

Left and **above**, children, dressed in colorful costumes, play a major role in many of the country's festivals.

this is a celebration of the end of winter and of the beginning of spring, which is when it occurs (February 3). Beans are scattered inside the home with the cry "*Oni wa soto, fuku wa uchi*" ("Out with demons, in with good fortune"). Eating the number of parched beans corresponding one's age is said to ensure health for the coming year. A number of large Buddhist temples hold – public Setsubun observances, at which popular personalities of sumo, sports and television scatter beans over crowds of people, who try to catch the beans thus thrown in the belief that they will be efficacious in bringing good luck.

March 3, Girls' Day (Doll Festival): The major Japanese festivals that fall on 3/3, 5/5, and 7/7 find their origin in China. This colorful observance, now a celebration of having daughters in the house, has changed over the centuries. Dolls representing the emperor and empress and imperial court are displayed on a tiered dais, and a "sweet *sake*" is served, along with a light meal, perhaps. Such doll sets can be very elaborate, including miniatures of vessels, kitchens, and other objects of daily life. The manner of display and types of dolls once varied greatly throughout the country. In certain areas, simple dolls were set afloat as a means of exorcising bad fortune.

costume of the Kamakura Period which dated from 1185–1333.

April 8, Flower Festival (Birthday of Buddha): Small statues of the infant Buddha are set up in an enclosure bedecked with flowers, and a hydrangea tea is ladled over the statue by worshipers, who may take the latter home. This observance is associated with children. At this time of the year there are many different observances held throughout the country, particularly those associated with mountain worship.

March and April (mainly), Cherry Blossom Viewing: The cherry blossom front moves from south to north during spring, and different types of cherry blossom at different

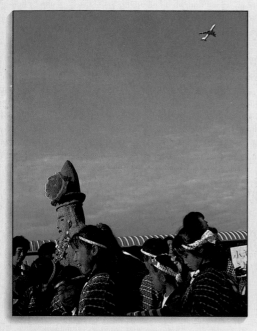

March 12, Water-Drawing Ceremony (Omizutori) of Todaiji, Nara: This is one of the most famous fire festivals of Japan, an observance of solemnity and drama and mystery. At midnight, great torches are wielded by priests to cast about showers of sparks, marking the drawing of sacred water from the Wakasa Well below the *Nigatsu do* (February Hall).

April 7–14, Spring Festival, Tsurugaoka Hachiman Shrine, Kamakura: This ancient shrine with the 800-year-old ginkgo tree guarding its steps, holds a series of events celebrating spring and the cherry blossom season. There are various processions in the

times. In Tokyo, the trees blossom about mid-April. The celebration of this event is a national mania, a time of letting go and simply enjoying, with food and drink, under the boughs of delicate blossoms against a blue sky with soft breezes. The ephemerality of the blossoms is important, and the observance of their beauty is the recognition that they are there for only a moment of the year. This recognition of sadness in ephemeral beauty, somewhat over-touted as a so-called

Above left, procession of Haniwa in rural Chiba. **Above**, the Great Lantern Festival at Suwa Shrine in Aichi. **Right**, Sanja Matsuri in Tokyo.

The *omikoshi* (*mikoshi* means portable shrine: and the "*o*" is an honorific) is a basic element in the typical Japanese festival. This is the vehicle in which the god manifests and in which the god-presence is carried about the village, town, or neighborhood. It is carried on the shoulders of the young bucks of the community, with ritual purification beforehand and often much partaking of *sake*. It is common to give the portable shrine rather rough treatment, jouncing it vigorously up and down and about. The exuberance of the god is manifest, and the amount of *sake*, which is another manifestation of the god – a kind of holy madness.

In some communities where nearby shrines

become symbolic women, with a hasty smear of lipstick and a woman's kimono worn over the festival attire. This is part of the holy madness and is quite common and traditional in the country. Midwinter sees the occurrence of naked festivals, in which the men of a community undergo purification and strip to a loincloth to test their strength and purity.

The festival of the agrarian community is an anachronism in many ways. It continues life often as a means of exposing kids to tradition. This is true especially of desultory little neighborhood city festivals, which seem to be held more for the satisfaction of the older merchants and as an

have festivals on the same day, the custom has developed of having mikoshi fights in which the youths carrying the mikoshi of their shrine try to jostle through or in some way "win" over the mikoshi of other shrines on the same road.

Festivals often have a heavy sexual content, implicit and explicit. The god of a small number of shrines scattered about the country manifests as a huge phallus, which is carried about the streets at festival time. A festival may involve the meeting and consummation of the union of male and female gods, expressed symbolically. The carrying of the mikoshi into the sea or river and then out again is one example. The holy madness often is expressed in a kind of sexual transformation; the young men carrying a mikoshi may

encounter with tradition for children who live in cramped flats and spend much time before the television set. Often tiny children appear, with a dutiful, young mother; older kids are more blasé and more difficult to tear away from televison or video games.

Even in farwaway village towns, the idea that festivals are largely something for children has grown, perhaps as a result of the growing worldliness of young parents. At the same time, some young Japanese have gone through this attitude and emerged from the other side, realizing that their festival is a source of identity and of continuity. Though its agrarian roots have vanished, the festival is a kind of barometer of themselves and it is a precious legacy, spiritual and material.

samurai code, is beloved by the Japanese, and may or may not be reflected in the mountains of garbage left after a day under the cherry blossoms in city parks.

April 14–15, Sanno Festival, Takayama, Gifu Prefecture: The mountain town of Takayama is one of the "little Kyotos" of the provinces. This festival is based on the Gion Festival of Kyoto, featuring massive floats decorated with rugs and tapestries. The town, its setting, and the floats are themselves spectacular, but the real feature is mechanical figures of astonishing cleverness and ingenuity that perform on the floats.

May 1–5, Giant Kite Battle, Suwa Shrine, Hamamatsu, Shizuoka Prefecture: This festi-

val has a venerable history (from 1550) and has gained an international reputation, largely as a result of the enthusiasm of the participants. It is a grand spectacle, with a large number of huge kites aloft, and the teams of kite flyers trying to cut the cords of other kites with their own. Novel kite designs are also now a feature of this event.

Late April, early May, Rice-Planting Festivals: One of the most important agricultural observances, one imbued with a sacredness, solemnity and mystery, yet full of joy and rejoicing, was the series of events that centered around the first planting of rice in the paddy fields. The climax of these observ-

ances is the planting rite commonly known as *Hana-Taue*. This is often a dance, with music, done in a paddy field or symbolically in a shrine. The planting is done by young women, who symbolize virgins and who have fasted and undergone purification in preparation for the rite. Today the planting of rice is done by tractor, and the festival has taken on more the nature of an entertainment and attachment to tradition rather than an offering to the god of rice.

In many shrines around Japan, the rice-planting observance is time when the *kagura* is performed. This is a sacred drama with musical accompaniment, often of great antiquity and often in mime and often comic, performed before the god as an invocation and an offering. The *kagura* are important aspects of Japan's Shinto heritage, and some of them have been designated as Important Cultural Assets by the government.

May 5, Children's Day (Boys' Day): This is a national holiday built around the older *Tango-no-Sekku* observance on the 5th day of the 5th month, which celebrated the boy offsprings of a family. In the countryside, a household flies colorful carp streamers, one for each son. Miniature sets of armor and model warrior's accoutrements are displayed in the home.

The iris, which blooms at this time, is associated with the observance, and iris leaves, thought to have restorative qualities, are put into the bath water on this day. Small cones of sweetened rice wrapped in bamboo or iris leaves are eaten on May 5, as are confections of rice and bean jam wrapped in aromatic oak leaves.

May 14–16, Kanda Myojin Festival, Kanda Myojin Shrine, Tokyo: This is one of the three great festivals of Tokyo, the other two being the Sanja Festival of Asakusa on May 17-18 and the Sanno Festival of Akasaka on June 15-17. All these festivals are large, brilliant and very colorful, capturing the atmosphere of the city of Edo (Tokyo before 1868), known for its garrulous and happy-go-lucky town citizens.

May 15, Hollyhock Festival (Aoi Matsuri), Kyoto: This traditional event is 1,400 years old and is more of a pageant-parade than anything else. It is very popular and seats may be purchased on grandstands along the parade route. This is one of Japan's most spectacular festivals, resplendent with costumes of the Heian period (794–1185) in which it was initiated.

Mid June, Dragon Boat Race (Peiron), Nagasaki: Basically a Chinese custom adopted by the Port of Nagasaki, which housed the Chinese trading missions during the Edo Period (1603–1868), the Nagasaki Dragon Boat race is similar to the Dragon Boat races in Hong Kong, Thailand and Okinawa. The long boats demand skill and strength, the competition is fierce, and the event is an exciting one.

July 3–7, Tanabata Festival: The festival is held on the 7th day of the 7th month. Though clearly of Chinese origin, and one which celebrates the romantic legend of the Oxherd

Some communities have bylaws that limit the decorations to paper, but most have graduated to plastic. Some hold contests for originality and novelty. The most famous of such street decorations are in Sendai, in Miyagi Prefecture, while the city of Hiratsuka on the coast south of Tokyo has a famous Tanabata display. Though this observance has become commercial and sometimes tacky, the better Tanabata decorations, like the Sendai effort, are great fun and worth a visit.

July 13–15 or August 13–15, Obon: This is the time when the souls of the deceased are said to return, briefly, to this plane. The origins of Obon are Buddhist, but many of the practices

and Weaver Maid (both of whom were fated to meet only once a year across the Milky Way), the festival and the origin of its observance in Japan, and even the meaning of the name Tanabata, are obscure.

The custom of attaching poems and small paper ornaments to long bamboo poles on this day has been expanded beyond recognition by local merchants' associations to create fantastic, elaborate (to put it mildly) street decorations of streamers and dripping and drooping festoons to mark the occasion.

Left, "Flower Hat" dance at Chiyoda's Rice Festival. **Above**, participants in the *Jidai Matsuri*.

are not. The former date relates only to the cities, where neighborhoods will hold a Bon dance in a school ground or park. People who have family living in the countryside usually celebrate Obon in the middle of the month of August, at which time many return to their towns and villages from the city to visit and tend the family grave plots as well as to partake in the Bon rites. The event is solemn, but the atmosphere is lively and joyful; the family dead are welcomed and feted, in effect.

The highlight of the festival is the Bon dance, which is a community gathering. A raised platform supports musicians and singers, while the dancers circle the platform. Although the music and the dance itself vary throughout the country; the Bon dance form is the basic style of traditional Japanese folk dancing.

As with New Year, the festival involves a series of rites and observances held over the three-day period. One of these is the lighting of candles or lanterns to guide the spirits. Obon occurs at the hottest time of summer, and is associated with cool, light cotton kimono (yukata), fans and mosquito coils.

July 16–24, Gion Festival, Kyoto: Started, it is said, as a thanksgiving for being spared from the ravages of the plague in AD 869, the Gion Festival is one of the largest and most spectacular in Japan.

There are many events associated with the festival, which occurs at the height of Kyoto's muggy and enervating summer. The most spectacular events are the processions of huge floats, for the passing of which the trolley lines (when there were trolleys) used to be taken down. The floats are gorgeous affairs, decorated with, among other things, Persian carpets and grand tapestries of venerable age and value. Each float has its own special theme. Gion festivals are organized by many communities throughout the country.

August 1-7, Nebuta Festival, Hirosaki, Aomori Prefecture: This is a variation of the summer lantern (that is, fire) festival, featuring great floats made of translucent paper formed into fantasy figures of warriors and legendary scenes, brightly painted and illuminated from within. This is night-time spectacle at its best.

August 23–25, Kiriko Festival, Wajima, Ishikawa Prefecture: The entire Noto Peninsula has kiriko festivals, which are held in various communities at various dates. A kiriko is a rectangular, vertical lantern carried on the shoulders of young men. It can be two or three stories tall. The procession of kiriko at Wajima is the climax of a series of rituals, which ends with a huge torch being set afire on the beach.

The festival symbolizes of the union of the female god from an offshore island with the male god of the town.

September 14–17, Hachiman Festival, Kamakura: The art of archery from the back of a galloping horse has been kept alive for more than 800 years and is skillfully demonstrated at this festival, taking place annually at the Hachiman Shrine, Kamakura, Kanagawa Prefecture.

September full moon, Moon Viewing: The pleasure taken in the change of seasons is again illustrated by this observance. Summer's heat has ended, the full moon of autumn has risen, impossibly big, and the air has begun to cool. There is a touch of melancholy and of longing. Special foods have been prepared, and the family gathers on the veranda of the home (or somewhere) to enjoy the bright moon and the sense of change and flow of nature.

Also around the same time of year is the **Grand Kagura of Ise Shrine, Ise, Mie Prefecture:** This kagura drama performed at one of Japan's two major Shinto shrines is a famous and important event.

Harvest Festivals: Autumn is the time of year when one is most likely to encounter a local festival while traveling or just passing through a city by taxi.

In urban areas, the traditional dates for neighborhood autumn or harvest festivals have been supplanted by some convenient Sunday in autumn. If the Sunday chosen turns out to be cold and rainy, the festival may be sodden and a little sad, but still, it is held! These little festivals announce themselves from a distance: there is always the boom of a large drum, often punctuated by the piercing sounds of a flute and of a brass instrument hit with a wooden mallet. In the city, local mer-chants will be ensconced with plenty of sake in an open storefront gaily decorated with bunting and displaying the altar to their god.

October 22, Festival of the Ages (Jidai Matsuri), Heian Shrine, Kyoto: This is a new festival, which features a grand and colorful costume parade displaying all the historical periods of Japanese history. Geared toward tourists, it occurs during one of Kyoto's loveliest seasons.

Finally, a recent granting of national funds under a "Hometown" promotion program has enabled towns and villages all over Japan to revive their own local festivals in hopes of attracting tourists.

With all these "new" events plus the ones mentioned above, practically every day in Japan is a matsuri!

Right, the demure look at Kyoto's Obi Festival.

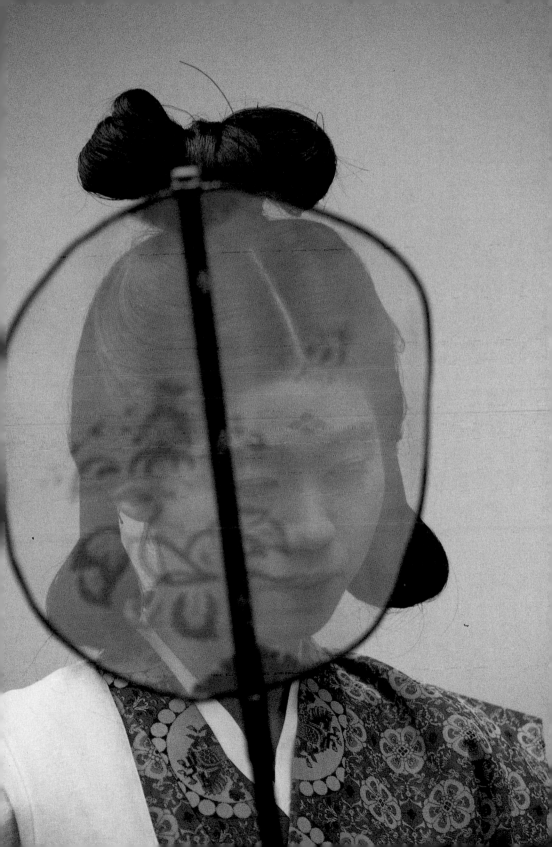

The earliest, distinctly Japanese art works preserved are those of the late Yayoi Period. These were small, tubular clay figurines called *haniwa*, some of which were set up like fences around imperial mausolea. Whatever their purpose may have been – substitutes for people buried alive in the tombs, magical instruments to ward off evil spirits or bandits – their immediate interest lies in their utter simplicity and charm.

Though many of them are only cylinders, some of the haniwa (and there are hundreds) are figures of men and women (dancers, warriors, singers, etc.), horses, monkeys and birds. Most are very simple, with only a few details of decoration, a sword or a necklace, perhaps. They have large hollow spaces for the mouth and eyes, which prevented them from cracking when being fired, and which adds much not only to their charm, but their mystery, too. Who are they? What are they saying? Some emotion or song seems to have been eternally suspended here, and while the will to know them may be strong, the recognition of the eternally human, of the eternally here and now, is more compelling.

Natural Aesthetic Impulses: The haniwa figures are also important for another reason. We find in them – at the very beginning of the culture – many of the salient characteristics of almost all Japanese art. The haniwa are, so to speak, decorative; they are very much in this world (regardless of how much they may evoke the next). They are narrational – we want to create stories for them; as still in time as they are, we imagine a time before and after their eyes and mouths opened. And, with their soft modelling and indolent lines, they are recognizably human. These figures are not gods or angels: they smile, they shout, they gaze. In fact, there is little that is abstract about them. This is an "art of the real" (which does not eliminate the fantastic or even the artificial).

It is easy to see that the haniwa possess a

Preceding pages, fan-shaped Buddhist scripture from the Heian Period, 12th century. **Left**, *Fugen Bosatsu*, Heian Period silk painting. **Above right**, *Maple Viewers*, by Kano Hideyori, from the Muromachi Period.

beauty that seems – almost uncannily – to come from a natural aesthetic impulse. They occur during a lull in Japanese absorption of outside influences, at a time when Japanese culture was developing its own native hues. It is possible to draw a parallel with another art: the haniwa are to later art what the slightly later poetry of the *Manyoshu* (compiled in AD 759) is in purity of diction and sentiment.

Recognizing the Conventions: Decorative, narrative, human. The decorative extends

from modest fence posts to elaborately gilded and painted screens and walls in palaces and castles to pin-ups in a swordsmith's shop. The narrational can range from rolls and rolls of scrolls illustrating one of the world's biggest (and greatest) novels to a single illustration of a young boy playing a flute before a warrior and that would set the viewer off on a reverie of related legends. As for the human: in Japanese art it embraces everything, from demons to gods, from animals to, well, people.

And by being so stubbornly sublunary and real, by taking so much elaborate and sophisticated pleasure in this world, this exceedingly human art at times also achieves and reveals the spiritual.

The viewer needs only a few moments to get used to looking at Japanese art. He or she will soon recognize the conventions – the raised roofs to reveal scenes (no perspective here), the hooks and slits for eyes, the seemingly abstract patterns that resolves themselves into a few variations on plants and birds and insects (the Japanese are great appreciators of insects).

Just look a little closer and the clothes and faces (brilliant kimono, endless streams of hair on the women) will soon take on individual qualities. There is no reason either to fear that cliché "open space". There is and isn't any great metaphysical principle at work here – the idea is simple enough: like European Symbolist poetry of a millennium later, the Japanese knew that art evokes, it does not depict.

But we have dwelt too long on ideas. Time to move on to the works themselves.

Nara and Kamakura Sculpture: Before the Nara Period there are some superb examples of sculpture (such as the Kuze Kannon and the Kudara Kannon, both at Horyuji in Nara). To recommend only one, mention must be made of the Miroku in Koryuji, in Kyoto. This is a delicately carved wooden statue of the Buddha of the Future. The young person (gender is blurred in Buddhist art, but one assumes the figure is of a boy) has one leg crossed over the other, his chin rests on a couple of extended fingers, and one detects the slightest hint of the most gracious, lyrical smile imaginable. The Miroku is a hint of the greatness to come.

In the Nara Period, with Japan's full-scale welcome of things Chinese, the native response to the real is fused with its spiritual aspirations without ever abandoning the former. Work is done in wood, clay, bronze or by using the curious technique of hollow lacquer. There are some fine early pieces to be seen in the Yakushiji in Nara, but visits must especially be made to the Kofukuji and the Todaiji to see some of the world's masterpieces of sculptures. There, one can see numerous sculptures of the Buddha, of guardian deities, and of monks. There is, for example, the somewhat awkwardly modelled, three-headed, six-armed Ashura, a young demon (demoness?) that has all the charms of a sensitive youth.

All of these sculptures – gods and humans alike – are spiritually powerful because they are so real (they probably had real models). And though it cannot now be seen, they were originally colored. The patinas of age may lend them a spiritual depth, but one should not forget their original splendor. While the Buddha and some of the deities are ruled by convention (the beatific smile, various hand gestures for the former; terrifying gazes for the latter), the portraits of the blind monk Ganjin (Toshodaiji) and of the Buddha's disciples (Kofukuji) are utterly remarkable for the realism of their portraiture.

It was also during this time that the 16-meter high, bronze Daibutsu (the Great Bud-

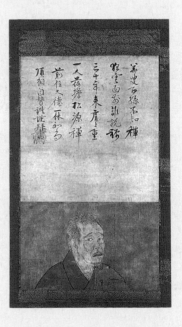

dha) was created. It is a sorry sight from what it must have originally looked like, housed as it is now in a much smaller hall and worn by age. It was originally gilded with bronze, and incised with designs that can now only be barely discerned on some of the lotus petals upon which the figure sits. This is the great tourist attraction at Todaiji in Nara, which should not be missed. The other Nara temples already mentioned are also worth visiting if you want to look at the true genius of Japanese sculpture.

The Nara Period ended with the moves of capital to Kyoto. With that, the beginning of the Heian Period, Japanese sculpture declined as other arts ascended, and did not revive until the Kamakura Period, several centuries later. While Nara Period sculpture was both human and ideal, that of the Kamakura Period was wholly human, passionate, personal and emotional.

For example, the Kamakura Period produced more portraits of monks and of demons (warriors, really) than of aloof gods. Many of these (of the priests Muchaku and Seshin, and of the Kongoo Rikishi, the Guardians of the Law), fortunately, can also be seen in Todaiji and Kofukuji in Nara. The Kamakura Period also produced its Daibutsu, which, though somewhat smaller than that in Nara, is equally affecting. Now sitting un-

not miss out on the many small, elegant Boddhisatva musicians floating around the statue of the Buddha.)

Japanese painting had long existed, but it had not flowered into great sophistication, particularly in the form of long, unfolding (and hand-held) scrolls. These paintings, called *Yamato-e*, might depict the changing seasons, famous beauty spots, or illustrate well-known stories.

The best Yamato-e were of the latter type, depicting popular legends, warrior tales, or works of great literature, such as the *Ise Monogatari* and the *Tale of the Genji*. The popular legends might include a satirical look at pompous officials turned into bat-

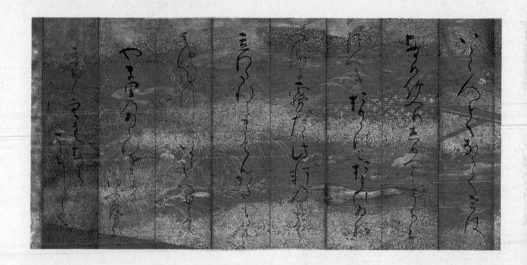

covered in the Kamakura hills, its impressiveness has been enhanced by time and exposure to the ocean air.

Painted Screens and Scrolls: In the Heian Period, life itself became an art, and works of art became its decorative attendant. Kyoto's Byodoin may have been meant as a model of the next world, but it only showed that life in this one was already exquisite. (One last note on sculpture: when visiting the Byodoin, do

Left, the priest Ikkyu, by Bokusai, Muromachi Period, 14th century. **Above**, *Excerpts from Tale of the Genji*, by Konoe Nobutada, Momoyama Period, 17th century.

tling frogs and rabbits, or a man who can't stop farting, or a look into the punishments that await evil-doers in hell. Post-Heian Period warrior tales drew on the many heroic or sentimental tales collected in the *Heike Monogatari* and other stories (just as Western artists drew theirs on Homer and Virgil).

The scrolls are easy to follow, and with their delicacy of line reveal the Japanese gift of design. With the Genji scroll are the conventions of the removed roof, the "dash for the eye and a hook for the nose," and the floating, golden clouds that rhythmically lead the eye from scene to scene. It is a splendid example of the great Japanese graphic sensibility that is still seen today in advertising and comic art.

In the Kamakura Period, war and religion came together. This was the great period of Zen art, when *suiboku* ("water-ink," painting with black *sumi* ink) comes to the fore. One of the world's masterpieces of the art can be seen in the National Museum in Tokyo: Sesshu's *Winter Landscape*, a bold landscape of a traveler dwarfed by nature, a lonely town and mountain all around, and a vertical streak of ink that cuts the sky. Because of his line, his sense of composition, and the moods he can evoke, Sesshu seems at times to be a contemporary artist, though he died in 1506 at the age of 86;

Muromachi Period, when the sober Zen hold was giving way to the splendors of Momoyama, we see the development of the schools of painting (Kano, Tosa, etc.), which would affiliate themselves with the court of the castles, and which, for all their occasional greatness, could also lead to an excessive formalism and mannerism. This conservatism is endemic to Japanese art, and often leads to simplistic sentimentalism, something that Japanese aesthetics in general, and Zen-inspired art and poetry in particular, go to great lengths to avoid.

The Momoyama Period is Japan's age of Baroque splendor, when, as one scholar says, "The simper of the late Ashikaga court went

another of his masterpieces, the *View of Amanohashi-Date*, can be seen in the National Museum in Kyoto.

In addition to calligraphy, *suiboku* includes portraiture and landscape. An example of the principal "the line is the man himself" in portraiture is the stark portrait of the priest Ikkyu in the National Museum in Tokyo. In *suiboku* landscapes ("open space") the emphasis is, again, on the real, on the visually pleasurable (hence, Japanese landscape is rarely as profoundly mystical as that of Chinese), and quite often, on the grotesque and the fantastic.

Around this time too, especially during the

down before the swagger of men like Nobunaga." It is the one of the high points of Japan's decorative genius. It is filled with gold and silver, with very bright, flat colors (no shading or outlining), with lush scenes painted on screens and walls of tea of flower-viewing parties, of lovely women and sightseeing spots.

This is not to imply that monochrome was abandoned during Momoyama. Far from it: there was a great deal of superb *sumi-e* (ink picture) screens and paintings done at this time. The overwhelming impression, however, is of gold, as one can see in the *Joodan-no-ma* and other ceremonial halls in the Nijo

Castle in Kyoto, with its painted walls and gilded ceilings, or at nearby Nishi Honganji in its expansive *taimensho* (audience hall) and *Koo-no-ma* (stork room).

Pictures from the Floating World: The Edo Period is the great age of popular art, even though much great decorative art was being made for the aristocracy or the military classes, especially by Koetsu, Sotatsu and Korin. The latter's gorgeous "Irises" – all violet and gold – is an excellent example and can be seen in the Nezu Museum in Tokyo. The merchant class, however, was developing its own pleasures in fiction, drama (kabuki) and art, and "mass appeal" soon became more important than ever before.

Though the names of hundreds of ukiyo-e artists are known, it should be remembered that the production of these prints was a cooperative effort between many highly skilled people. There was the artist who created the design and suggested colors, the carvers of the many blocks, the actual printers, and finally the publishers.

Early ukiyo-e, especially those by the first great master, Moronobu, are usually portraits of prostitutes from the Yoshiwara district of old Edo, or illustrations to books; with polychrome printing, ukiyo-e, a number of "genres" became established. There were, for example, portraits of prostitutes (*bijin ga*), kabuki actors in famous roles, the ever-

The art most associated with Edo is *ukiyo-e* (literally, "pictures of the floating world"). Once again, the sublunary, fleshy human existence was a key element.

Though woodblock printing had been used to reproduce sutras, for example, the technique first began to be used in a more popular vein in the early 18th century; at first the prints were either monochromatic or hand-colored with an orange-red. In time, two colors were used, then four, and so on.

Pictures from the floating world: *Oden, Snow-white Skin* (left), by Komura Settai, and *shunga* erotic woodblock print (above).

present scenes of renowned places, and of plant and animal life.

Most people are familiar with Hokusai's *Great Wave* or his *Fuji* (Hokusai is, with Sesshu, one of the prime exponents of that distinctly Japanese "nervous line"), with Hiroshige's *53 Stations on the Tokaido*, with the grotesquely amusing actor portraits of Sharaku, and with the many beautiful women of Utamaro. Ukiyo-e, suffice it to say, is one of the world's great graphic art forms, and in more ways than one. For example, the charmingly named *shunga* (literally, "spring pictures") represent pornographic art of stupendous imagination, and comprised a large part of every ukiyo-e artist's oeuvre. Unfortunately, *shunga* cannot be seen in Japan, but outside, most museums with an ukiyo-e collection is sure to have some examples.)

Ukiyo-e is always a visual delight; look closely and notice the delicacy of line, the complexity of color and printing, the occasional relief work or mica flecking.

Then Came the Black Ships: Japan did not look upon art as "art" until just over a century ago. Though we might have begun with this observation, it will just as well serve as an introduction to the so-called "modern" period of Japanese art, one which began almost simultaneously with the arrival of the "Black Ships" of America and other Western na-

(Taisho Period *bijin ga* prints are lovely, for example), the Japanese art of the Meiji, Taisho and early Showa Periods is not worthy of much consideration, so let's skip a few decades to look at more contemporary styles.

The School of Things: Economic recovery was not the only thing happening in the 1960s in Japan. Like elsewhere around the world, life changed, and the Information Age – or Post-Modernism, or other unfriendly terms – suddenly dawned. In art, ideas were big (Conceptualism), and some Japanese were thinking very hard about recovering their native traditions in a contemporary manner, and by acknowledging their locale, having international relevance.

tions in the early part of the second half of the 19th century.

It was at this point that, in its rush to "Westernize," Japan began to look down on its own arts. The "Western" ideal was that art has "meaning," beyond the decorative. It was a novel idea to the Japanese.

It was also in the early years of the Meiji Restoration that not a few museums and individuals abroad began to amass some very impressive collections of Japanese art. A few decades later, during the Taisho Period, several Japanese artists donned berets, went to Paris and turned out third-rate imitation academic art. With a few exceptions

The first indication came in 1968, when Sekine Nobuo dug a deep round hole in the ground, and placed the displaced dirt in the same shape alongside the hole. "Phase – Mother Earth" is not as silly as it sounds. Here was a traditionally Japanese confrontation with natural materials, a clearly Asian expression of *yin* and *yang*, and a statement that art was going back to its origin. ("Earthworks" were also happening in America and Europe at the time.) And thus *Mono-ha* (School of Things) was born.

Very soon, a number of other artists began making works with similar ideas in mind. For example, Lee U-Fan (a long-time Korean resident of Japan and a great painter) dropped a large stone on a plate of glass and calling the result "Relatum." Simple perhaps, but complex really. The act of dropping the stone was as sudden a move as that which compels a calligrapher; the cracks were the "writing"; the round stone on the flat glass not only contrasted shaped and materials, but seemed to reverberate into ideas and spaces far beyond the work itself; "Relatum" also seemed like an abstract garden. (Sekine, by the way, joined in the fun by laying a plate of black steel on a large, white pillar of sponge.)

Of course, this can be dismissed as avantgarde wisecracking and/or timewasting.

However, there are many works in which Suga Kishio would take disparate materials and combine them in ways that led to innumerable associations and relations, while humor and philosophy joined forces in demarcated spaces that took on almost sacred – Shinto – meaning.

Mono-ha was committed to letting materials speak for themselves; the artist's task – like the garden designer – was to arrange the materials so as to achieve the right effect, to

Left, *View on a Fine Breezy Day*, by Katsushika Hokusai, Edo Period. <u>Above</u>, Kyoto's Daisenin meditation garden.

point to the hitherto unnoticed, to open a space where the viewer could make his or her own discoveries.

These and other artists had a great effect on the Japanese art scene, and in time began to be recognized abroad. In recent years especially, the West has begun to appreciate what's happening here. Shows such as *Against Nature*, and *A Primal Spirit*, traveled around the U.S.A. in the early 1980s.

Gallery Hopping: For the traveler to Japan curious about what's going on in Japanese contemporary art, a walk through Tokyo's Ginza should be just the thing. (There are an estimated 500 galleries in Ginza alone.) The weekend newspapers usually have a listing of galleries and artists, but it is better to just take a chance on half a dozen galleries, and be surprised, shocked, bored, pleased, and interested by what you see.

Austere, abstract wood sculptures – but clearly derived from a garden and landscape tradition, as well as modern art – might be seen in one gallery; in another there might be a Japanese variation on Dada, a mishmash of industrial and household objects, and clearly derived simply from the fact of living in gaudy, gorgeous, maddening Tokyo. In another, you may see an abstract painting, clearly contemporary, but whose visual sensibility – the colors, the patterns, the composition – are as much within the Japanese decorative tradition as they are within the great modern tradition of abstraction. In yet another, an installation of flickering diodes that is as unsettling as it is meditative, may strike you as much an expression of today's techno-life as of the eternally Buddhist.

The list could go on and on. The important thing is that it be not seen as Japanese copycatism, but observed on its own terms first. Just keep in mind the principles outlined here, and the idea that landscape (in painting and gardening), Buddhism (gaudy esoteric or somber Zen), calligraphy (the instant!), and an acute sensitivity to line, materials, spatial arrangement, all have a far longer tradition in Japan than does the relatively quite young Western view of art. What future artists will make of these traditions will depend on how long the current, superficial fascination with "globalism" and "new-waveism" will last, and how deeply it will penetrate the society.

Japanese art is quite well – and very alive.

Toyota and Sony, Fujitsu and Nikon – such names evoke one of Japan's primary roles today, that of a supplier of practical, cleverly and attractively designed, and affordable devices to the world's consumers. This is nothing new; "made in Japan" sword blades, gold-decorated papers, and folding fans were in demand in China back in the 10th and 11th centuries, for example. The fact that many of the original techniques for producing such goods were, and still are, copied or imported is irrelevant; what Japanese

craftspersons did – and still do – with them is what cowunts.

It is not surprising that the Japanese public as a whole supports and appreciates a wide spectrum of traditional crafts. The magic word is "traditional." These are not crafts that have died under the onslaught of industry and then revived, but living, unbroken lines of tradition and technique that may go back as recent as a century ago or to as early as a millennium.

In the rigid society of the Edo Period, the artisan was the third of the four social classes, one step above the merchant, who was at the bottom (in theory). This was the age of the unknown craftsman, whose tools, hands, and skills were part of a tradition, and one who learned techniques as an apprentice from the bones out, not with the head. In some respects, apprenticeship in the main Japanese crafts – ceramics, textiles, lacquer, wood, metalwork, bamboo, paper and stone – still requires one to suffer this "osmotic" system. As for the artisan's place in today's society, however, the regime is less strict, and talent often *does* have its rewards.

Ceramics: Japan is a treasure house of ceramic techniques, a craft which has attracted many students from abroad over the years. There are famous wares, the names of which have a certain amount of currency in antique and crafts circles throughout the world. In general, pottery in Japan is stoneware or porcelain, that is, high-fired wares. Earthenware and low-fired pottery are found in small quantities, usually in the form of humble utensils, in Raku ware, and in some of the enameled wares of Kyoto and Satsuma.

There are a number of unglazed wares, of which the most famous is Bizen. Traditional glazes are mainly iron glazes (ash glazes), though feld spathic glazes are used in some wares. The palette of the traditional folk potter is thus usually browns and black. Green from copper and iron, and a milky, streaked blue glaze made with rice bran ash are also found. Saturated iron glaze in thick application results in the deep black *temmoku*; when thin, the same glaze fires a persimmon ocher. Stonewares also show iron and cobalt blue underglaze decoration.

Porcelains are decorated with underglaze cobalt and overglaze enamels. The decorated porcelains produced by numerous kilns in the Arita area of northern Kyushu and shipped from the port of Imari from the 17th to the 19th century are still avidly sought and collected by antique buffs, as is the Kutani porcelain of the Kanazawa area. The porcelain industry still thrives, and much of it is hand-painted, though modern transfer processes are able to capture all the shades and nuances of hand-painted wares.

Today the little potteries are not making just chicken feeders or grinding bowls for the kitchen, or anything artless and direct. Every potter is now an artist, and pots are sold by name value. Artlessness and spontaneity are calculated or cultivated. Handcrafted ceramics are sold by galleries and department stores, and by the occasional craft and "folkcraft" shop. Visits to kiln towns may turn up interesting work, even inexpensive pieces, but beware of "tourist traps."

The future devepoment of the craft is in the hands of the artist-potter. Though their pottery traditions are very much part of Japan, today's young potters are educated and motivated in pretty much the same way as their Western counterparts.

Textiles: This craft includes weaving and dyeing as well as braiding (*kumihimo*) and

quilting (*sashiko*) and the like. Japan is a vast storehouse of textile techniques, one Western craftspeople have yet to tap.

Of course, silks are the most famous and highly refined of Japanese textiles. The glorious brocades used in *noh* drama costumes and in the apparel of the aristocracy and high clergy in bygone ages are among the highest achievements of textile art anywhere, as are the more humble but lyrical *tsujigahana* "tie-dyed" silks of the 16th century.

Far left, hand-painted tiles in Arita. **Above left**, 16th-century silk *noh* costume; **right**, **designer** *kabuki* costumes on display.

The work of contemporary textile artists can be seen in the exhibitions of the nationwide craft societies and in the kimono salons of department stores. Kimono and *obi* companies in Kyoto often maintain lavish showrooms that are open to the public. The prices of contemporary handcrafted kimono and obi usually leave the visitor somewhat more than numb. The other side of that coin is that one of Japan's best bargains is used silk kimono and obi, which can be found at flea markets in large quantities in Tokyo and Kyoto. A little time spent digging through mountains or racks of old kimono will not only produce gifts (lightweight and easy to pack too) for just about everyone, but will reveal much about Japanese design and color sense and the answer to why Japanese fashion designers are at the top. (As in the case of pottery, however, shoppers should be wary of "real old" silk kimono, cotton *yukata* panels or embroidered obi that are neither "real" nor "old.")

Japanese folk textiles are a world unto themselves. Cotton and hemp and ramie are the most common fibers, but the bark fibers of the *shina* tree, *kuzu* (kudzu), paper mulberry, plantain (in Okinawa), and other fibers were used in remote mountain areas. There are even textiles woven from paper yarn. Indigo is the predominant color, and the *ikat* technique (known as *kasuri*) the most popular for country work clothes, quilt covers, and the like. These white-on-blue textiles are also found at flea markets and antique shops. Stencil-dyed, indigo quilt covers are also charming and available. One of the most spectacular types of folk textile are the large cloth panels (now used as hangings) with a picture dyed in many colors against an indigo ground. *Yuzen* (and, in Okinawa, *bingata*) are the resist-dyeing techniques for these and they use rice paste applied to the cloth with tubes, not unlike the kind used for applying cake icing.

Lacquer: Japanese lacquer (*urushi*) is the sap of a certain tree that has been refined and

gold, often in relief, the Japanese popular image of lacquerware is of food bowls and serving trays, simply decorated if at all. It is doubtful if there is a household in Japan that does not possess lacquer bowls (or their plastic copies). Lacquered vessels and trays, in sets or singly, are very available at reasonable prices in antique shops and flea markets. Besides food vessels, lacquer today is also used on the low tables in *tatami* Japanese rooms, and as a pigment with which to create pictures and decorative panels.

Contemporary lacquer work is done by a number of craftspeople who exhibit in craft society shows and department stores, but the visitor will be perplexed by the high prices.

which may or may not have pigment added. It is an organic, living substance, and has been used as a decorative coating on wood, leather, and cloth for 1,500 years. Actually, the earliest-known examples of lacquer in Japan – red and black lacquered earthenware pots – date back about 4,000 years, to the Neolithic Jomon culture.

Lacquer is a true community craft – no one person can do all of the 50 or so steps involved in just making a plain coating on a wooden bowl. Decoration techniques may involve another 30 steps. Whereas in the West, "Japanese lacquer" evokes images of objects and panels opulently decorated with

Most lacquer work today is conservative, but there are a few artists who try to stretch the limits of their craft. A visit to lacquer producing areas, such as Wajima on the Noto Peninsula, is worthwhile.

The care of lacquerware is simple enough – just be nice to it. Do not put it in automatic dishwashers but wash it with light detergent or soap and rinse it in warm water. If not in use for a while, give it a quick wipe with a soft cloth occasionally. And do not store it in direct sunlight or on high shelves.

Bamboo: Generally, bamboo is split and made into baskets, screens, and the like, but on Kyushu, where the best bamboo grows, it is used to make bottles and containers. Japanese basketry, bamboo and otherwise, is unsurpassed anywhere in refinement and skill. Contemporary craftspeople have explored the abstract and light-capturing qualities of fine bamboo basketry. This substance also forms the frameworks of fans, umbrellas, kites and lanterns.

Metalcrafts: There are a number of alloys, particularly alloys of copper and gold, that are unique to Japan. Japanese carbon steel used for swords and knives also has never-been surpassed. One of the best gifts a cook can receive is a set of fine Japanese kitchen knives – the vegetable knife (*nakiri-bocho*) and all-purpose knife (*deba-bocho*; really a fish knife) are sufficient, but a slicer (*yanagi-ba*) makes a complete set.

Though traditional work in metals is easily available in the antique market, contemporary work is somewhat limited and harder to come by. Japanese designers have been more active in jewelry design than in expanding the limits of the country's traditional metallurgy.

"Living Treasures": In 1955, the Japanese government inaugurated what has popularly become known as the "Living National Treasure" system, officially honoring (and, to some degree, funding) craftspersons of the highest capability. Actually, it is the skill, designated an "Intangible Cultural Asset," that receives recognition, not the person.

Another criterion is that the work cannot just repeat tired formulas but must be innovative and fresh. Unfortunately, however, many if not most of these "Living Treasures" today are in their 70s and 80s and they have few, if any, apprentices or students.

But is it Art?: The respect traditional crafts enjoy in Japan is considerable, but we must also point out that, in Japan's affluent society today, craftwares must nearly always be marketed as "works of art" (meaning the artisan has to be "famous" and the price sky-high) if they are to be commercially successful.

Ironically, this may, in part, be the result (if not the original intent) of a movement begun in the 1920s by Yanagi Soetsu, author (e.g. *In Praise of Shadows*) and all-around free spirit. He clearly foresaw the replacement of the artisan by the artist-craftsperson

and, with potter Hamada Shoji and others (including the Briton, Bernard Leach), founded the *mingei* (which simply means "folk art") movement.

The term mingei was meant as a concept, as a direction for artist-craftspeople and the public to follow and a source from which to derive nourishment and inspiration for creative work and aesthetic appreciation. Intellectuals the world over admired and adapted this concept throughout the 1930s while Yanagi himself created an international collection of such folkcraft and folk art he (and his successors) considered to represent the best of its kind. This collection is housed in the Japan Folkcraft Museum in Komaba,

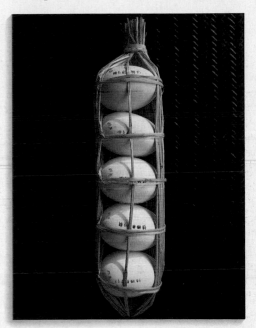

Tokyo, and is worth a visit.

One of the principles of mingei was anonymity. Hamada, like many others in the original group, refused till his dying day to sign his own work, intentionally "devaluing" it and thus denying "arty" pretention.

Mingei had a sizable revival in the 1970s (perhaps in response to the activities of the "love-generation" in the West) but fizzled out in the yuppie 1980s. The 1990s may see another resurgence: many young people are drawn to the satisfaction of making things with their hands (witness the so-called *tezukuri* revolution) and in the process, rediscover their heritage of excellence.

<u>**Left**</u>, printing an ukiyo-e by Hosokawa Kenjiro. <u>**Above right**</u>, traditional method of packaging eggs.

For many of the traditional Japanese performing arts, the distinction between dance and drama is tenuous in the extreme. All the traditional Japanese drama forms extant today (except perhaps *bunraku*, the puppet drama) developed out of some form of dance, and all, accordingly, employ musical accompaniment of one kind or another. *Noh* and *kyogen*, *bunraku* and *kabuki* also involve vocal disciplines to some extent, but not enough to qualify as opera.

Often, visitors confuse traditional and classical Japanese performing arts. This is an unfortunate error, because it potentially limits the enjoyment of bunraku and, especially, kabuki. There are five major traditional performing art forms or genres in Japan – *bugaku, noh, kyogen, bunraku,* and *kabuki*. (Pure dance forms, of which there are many, form another topic.)

Of these, only the first three could be called classical. Bugaku, noh and kyogen are all tightly contained and formal entertainments performed originally for the aristocracy. Both bunraku and kabuki are traditional stage arts, but welled up out of the vigorous pop culture of the Edo Period. *Kagura* needs to be mentioned here as well. Although it falls within what could be called folk drama, there is no one constant form of kagura. Rather, these offeratory dance/drama/story/religious performances, held on festival days before the deity, all differ greatly throughout the country, involving anything from religious mystery to heroic epics to bawdy buffoonery and overt sexual enactments (symbolic) or a combination of all these elements.

The 20th century has also seen the development of a number of uniquely Japanese performing arts, not the least of which are the sensitive development of the moving- picture idiom and *butoh*.

Bugaku: What the indigenous Japanese dance and drama forms were is not known. There certainly must have been some such

expression before the cultural imports from the Asian mainland, but whatever traces remain have not been reconstructed. Concentrated and intelligent study might turn up some interesting results. During the 7th and 8th centuries, mainland culture, from both Korea and China, dominated the life of the imperial court. In the year 702, the court established a Court Music Bureau to record, preserve, and perform the continental music forms (now known as *gagaku*) and dance (bugaku). These dances are so highly styl-

ized and abstract that there is little or no sense of story or dramatic event. The choreography is very rigid and is usually symmetrical, since the dances are most often performed by two pairs of dancers, though solos and a quintet are known to have guested. An almost identical music and dance form has been preserved in Korea as well.

The bugaku stage is a raised platform erected outdoors. It is independent of other structures and is ascended by steps at the front and back. The performance area is floored with green silk, the stairs are lacquered black, and the surrounding railings and posts are in cinnabar lacquer. Given that the bugaku repertoire has been preserved for almost 15 centuries, it is amazing to consider that about 60 different dances are known and performed today . These dances are categorized into "right" and "left," as was the custom in China. "Left" dances are slow, flowing and graceful, while "right" dances are relatively more humorous and spirited. The costumes for "left" dances are long and full, while those for "right" dances are far less voluminous.

Masks are often part of a bugaku dance. Those used for dances still performed, and many of those preserved in temples and other repositories though the dances associated with them are no longer performed, closely

stylization, lack of overt action, and monotonous seeming vocal declamation (a cross between chanting and dramatic narrative) makes it a distinctly acquired taste. It is admired by many in Japan, but its "hardcore" devotees are few. Still, it is performed, and a new, modern noh theater was completed in Tokyo in the 1980s.

Such terms as classic dignity, grace and symbolism are used to describe the noh drama. It is said to have been developed from a dance-drama form called *sarugaku*. Little is known about sarugaku. There is evidence that places it in the same category as kagura – a calling down into physical manifestation and also an offering to a deity or deities.

resemble some of the masks employed in religious performances in the Himalayas, particularly in Bhutan.

Bugaku is further classified into four categories: ceremonial, military, "running," and children's dances. The Imperial Household Agency maintains a bugaku section for the preservation and performance of this ancient form, and performances are held at certain times of year. Further, some shrines and temples have kept up bugaku performances as part of festival and other yearly observances.

Noh and Kyogen: What is called noh drama today dates from the early part of the 15th century. As an art form, its high degree of

Also, it seems there were wandering troupes who performed sarugaku. Considered part of the noh repertoire, the sprightly dance *sanbaso* is performed by tradition as part of the rituals to invoke a felicitous beginning, such as at the opening of New Year or the start of a new company, and is thought to be the closest in the noh-kyogen repertoire to any kind of ancestral form.

Whatever its origins, noh was perfected by Kan'ami Kiyotsugu (1333–84) and his son Zeami Motokiyo (1363–1443), who were playwrights, actors, and aesthetic theorists of the highest level. Between them they created about one-third of the 240 noh plays which are known today. Zeami's writings of the aesthetics of the the theater remains as some of the most profound thinking on the subject of its kind.

The "-ami" ending on Kan'ami and Zeami's names indicates that they were both part of a Buddhist calling. This religion had a profound influence on the content and dramatic structure of noh. The veil of "illusion" that we perceive as everyday "reality" is, in a sense, pierced momentarily by noh to expose something more basic, something that subsumes the senses – the bones of things, as it were.

Masks, highly stylized sets and props (when such things do appear), a tightly con-

form by themselves, one that ranks among the great arts of the world.

There are a number of schools of noh drama, namely Kanze, Komparu, Kongo, Hosho, Kita, and Umewaka.

As with Greek drama, the heavy and sober noh is performed in tandem with light farces, kyogen. Kyogen is thought to reflect more directly the sarugaku antecedents it shares with noh. Though the dramatic methods share something with noh, kyogen does not use masks and is more direct and active. Traditionally, it is performed during intermissions of a noh performance, but today it is often performed by itself. These farces are both part of and independent of noh. Their

trolled, contained style of movement, a voice style that projects and declaims but does not entice, and musical accompaniment of a few types of drum and a piercing fife mean that this form of play relies mostly on imagery and symbolism for its dramatic impact. In contrast to the sparse and uncluttered form of drama, the textiles used for noh costumes are the diametric opposite. The world's most opulent and gorgeous gold and silver and polychrome brocades are what the noh actor wears on stage. And noh masks are an art

Left, the exquisite experience of *noh* drama. **Above**, stage sets are kept to the bare minimum.

purpose is to be light-hearted, to deal with nonsense, and to be simple. By achieving this, they also say something about the human condition, thus presenting the other face of noh.

The main schools of kyogen are Okura and Izumi. An energetic American student of the art has been performing it in English for some years, and lately, several Europeans, including a Czech, have also immersed themselves deeply in the kyogen discipline.

Bunraku: Japan's glorious puppet drama is a combination of three elements, which, about 400 years ago, met and fused into a whole much greater than the combination of the parts. The three are: *samisen* music, puppetry techniques, and a form of narrative or epic chanting called *joruri*. The result is bunraku, the puppet drama which is considered to be an equal with live stage theater performance.

The samisen (the name of this banjo-like instrument is usually pronounced "shamisen") entered Japan from the Kingdom of the Ryukyus (Okinawa) sometime in the 16th century and, for whatever reason, was adapted and spread throughout the country very quickly. Though the instrument only has three strings, music produced by the samisen has great versatility and, in particular, lends itself well to dramatic emphasis, as

The narrative style derives from heroic epic chanted to accompaniment of the *biwa*, a form of lute that made its way to Japan from Central Asia at an early date. One such epic dealt with a Princess Joruri, and the narrative style took on the name joruri. Though there may be more than one samisen to give musical density to the accompaniment, there is only one chanter. He uses different tones of voice to project dialogue, distinguishing male from female characters, young from old, good from bad. Accent and intonation convey nuances of feeling and indicate shifts of scene.

At the end of the 17th century, a master joruri chanter named Takemoto Gidayu

a solo, in ensemble, and as accompaniment to narrative.

Though the bunraku puppet drama developed and matured in the two centuries after its creation, the origin of the puppetry techniques used is still shrouded in mystery. There are folk puppet dramas scattered throughout Japan, and a wonderful tradition of mechanical dolls, but no real study of their history has been done. Unlike marionettes, the puppets are manipulated directly by hand and are quite large. It takes three men to handle one of the major puppets in a play. The skills involved in this manipulation of bunraku puppets are awesome.

teamed up with playwright Chikamatsu Monzaemon (referred to as the Shakespeare of Japan) to produce a brilliant series of puppet dramas, some of which were later made part of the kabuki repertoire. The narrative chanting is sometimes called *gidayu* as well, honoring the skill and innovations of Takemoto.

The name bunraku appeared in the 19th century, after the impresario Uemura *bunrakuken*. The center of bunraku puppet drama is in Osaka.

It should be emphasized that while bunraku and kabuki share many traits and have some plays in common, bunraku is the older of the two, and it was kabuki that adopted elements of the puppet drama, not the other way around, as one might naturally think. In some of the plays taken from bunraku, kabuki actors even imitate the stiff movements of bunraku puppets at certain points in the drama.

The important point is that both bunraku and kabuki are popular theater. Bunraku was written and produced for the people of the towns (Osaka, in this case), not for aristocratic patronage. Its entire existence and content was as pop entertainment – not unlike the plays of Shakespeare in his own day.

Kabuki: Kabuki plays are still being written. Not many, granted, but the genre is still

part of the fun. Any visitor who goes expecting to see "classic theater" is in for a dull time, but if one goes knowing that this is high camp unsurpassed, then everything opens up. Even the tear-jerkers are the soggiest (and the longest) one could hope for. Catharsis right and left, even if one does not understand the language.

Kabuki originated in the early years of the 17th century with a troupe of women who performed what seems to have been a kind of dance, based on a dance performed at Buddhist festivals, and perhaps comic skits as well, on the riverbank at Kyoto. Whether there was anything untoward in this performance probably will never be known, but

alive, and like bunraku, it is not "classical." Kabuki is the equivalent of an MGM spectacular, soap opera, morality play, Ma and Pa on the farm, religious pageant, *I Love Lucy* and tear-jerker. It is music and dance and story and color and pathos and farce and everything any theatergoer could want.

The highly stylized language of kabuki, the poses and posturing and eye-crossing for dramatic emphasis, the swashbuckling and acrobatics and flashy exits, instant costume changes and magic transformations are all

Left, the Kabukiza in Ginza. Above, *bunraku* **showcases the artistry of the puppet masters.**

the shogunal authorities seemed to think there was and in 1629 banned women from appearing on stage. Male performers took their place. To this day, all kabuki performers are men, and the discipline of the actor who takes female parts (*onnagata*) is particularly rigorous.

The female troupes were supplanted in short order by itinerant troupes of young men, who too got into trouble with the authorities. These were disbanded, and the permanent theater companies developed in the cities of Kyoto, Osaka and Edo (now Tokyo) after the middle of the 17th century.

Kabuki became the Edo Period's most

popular entertainment. The production of a kabuki play involves strict conventions: gestures and movements, colors, props, costumes, wigs, makeup; even the types of textiles used for costumes are determined. (And there are places in a play left for ad-libs, as well.) Within this framework, an actor can bring a part to life and thrill the audience.

The audience directs much attention to the performer or performers. The story is secondary, and it will be well-known anyway. Kabuki devotees want to see favorite stars in familiar roles. Kabuki has been actor-centered since its beginning. The playwright is recognized, but their role is more of a supporter in which performers can showcase their talents and advance their prestige. There have also been some outstanding actor-playwrights, especially in the Danjuro lineage of star actors.

Kabuki actors belong to professional acting families, and each family may contain lineages of a given name. For example, the Ichikawa family contains the Danjuro lineage. A Danjuro will train his son (physical or adopted) to take on the Danjuro tradition, and the name will be passed on whenever it is felt that the son has matured into the role (and the father is no longer). The present Danjuro is the twelfth of his lineage.

Training of a kabuki actor starts at about the age of three, when actors leave their children backstage in order to do nothing other than internalize the ambience and also the music and rhythms. With this kind of training, kabuki literally becomes part of one's body at an early age. This facilitates but does not eliminate the long years of rigorous apprenticeship and training that every kabuki actor must undergo.

The kabuki stage has a number of unique features. The most striking one is the walkway that extends from the stage to the doors at the rear of the theater at stage level. Actors enter and exit at this stage extension (the *hanamichi*, or "flower path"), and it is sometimes used as a venue of action. Another is the classic draw curtain, which is in vertical stripes of black, green and persimmon and is opened from stage right to left with the percussive sound of wooden clappers. It is closed in a similar fashion. The kabuki theater also featured a revolving stage long before the concept arose in Europe.

Both noh and kabuki show no clearcut distinction between dance forms and stage movements. However, kabuki's grandiloquent gestures are a far cry from the austere containment of noh, though the latter had no small influence on the development of the kabuki genre. The kabuki technique called *mie* illustrates the formalized beauty of performance. A mie occurs at certain climactic moments, when the starring actor, projecting dramatic energy at top output, freezes into a statuesque pose with rigid stare and eyes crossed to emphasize a dramatic peak of intense emotional power. Glorious overkill. At such (and other) high points of a performance, shouts will ring out from the audience – the equivalent of "Do it, Charley!" or "Kill

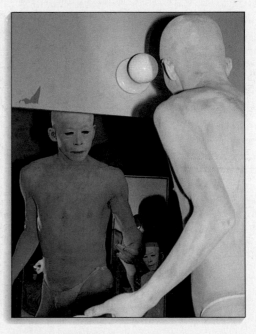

'em dead, Hank!" – the same kind of encouragement you might hear at a ball game or boxing match.

There are two categories of kabuki play: *jidai-mono* and *sewa-mono*. The former deals with historical events, legends, heros, magic, and bigger-than-life stuff. These tend to be flamboyant, colorful, sometimes with incredible costumes and makeup, and may have lots of flashy stage effects. *Sewa-mono* deal with the lives of the townspeople and include many of the tear-jerkers and soap operas. There are some 300 plays in the conventional kabuki repertoire, though by no means all are commonly performed. A kabuki performance usually is composed of famous scenes and pieces of longer plays. Both the morning and afternoon performances at the Kabukiza in Tokyo last about 4½ hours, but it is almost always possible to buy tickets for the "cheap seats" in the gallery. Performances are also held in Tokyo's National Theater, in Osaka and Kyoto and elsewhere in Japan.

Just Music: In addition to solo or small-ensemble musical forms, particularly those featuring the harp-like *koto,* the *shakuhachi* bamboo flute, and/or the samisen, and the numerous *taiko* (drum) and *minon* (folk singing) troupes, the most authentic (if not typical) form of Japanese music performed

single-stringed droners, for example – and this, together with a slow, "courtly" tempo, makes gagaku ideal for (and to most Japanese ears, synonymous with) funeral music. In fact, probably the first and only time the Japanese public has heard it recently was during the televised funeral of Emperor Showa (Hirohito) in 1989. True devotees, however, find tremendous excitement in gagaku's extended, soulful sounds and unrelieved tensions, and they may have a point. Fan or foe, however, one would agree that the ancient costumes worn by the musicians are interesting and colorful.

If you're a musicologist, a weird-sounds freak or simply a glutton for punishment,

apart from drama or dance is gagaku. It is a kind of orchestral music developed in the 9th century and little changed since. Quite unlike the popular entertainments described above, gagaku was strictly "court music," almost never performed in public before World War II and only occasionally now.

It employs esoteric instruments resembling (sometimes identical to) those used in India and China long before high-tech instruments such as the *koto* or the sitar were developed – drums, nose-flutes and bowed,

you should catch one of the three gagaku performances held in Tokyo's National Theater during the year. Or, you could seek out a recorded version (see the local Denon, Crown and Techiku labels).

Musicians who synthesise traditional forms and instruments with jazz (such as shakuhachi artist John Kaizan Neptune), rock (keyboardist Kitaro, et al.) and avant-garde or "contemporary" (Ishii Maki and many, many others) is resulting in some very exciting – and valid – new sounds being produced. These and new drama-dance forms, such as butoh, are enriching and refreshing the traditions.

<u>Left</u>, getting ready for a *butoh* performance. <u>Above</u>, *koto* ensemble.

He towered above Tokyo, smashing everything in his path, the epitome of really good *Baaaaad* over the mediocre and humdrum on the silver screen. Naturally, despite (or perhaps because of) its hokey special effects and far-fetched plot, the first Godzilla movie (1954) became a monster hit (pun intended), not only in Japan but throughout Southeast Asia, the U.S., Europe and elsewhere. The real significance of this was the fact that unlike Kurosawa Akira's classic *Rashomon* four years earlier, or the 1953 *Tokyo Story* by

Ozu Yasujiro and the handful of other Japanese productions to gain notice abroad, *Godzilla* was in no way an "art film." (It was to achieve "cult" status later on, of course, but that was many years later.)

In a sense, then, back there in the mid-1950s, *Godzilla* confirmed that the "Golden Age" of Japanese cinema, on both a domestic and an international scale, was no flash in the pan. If Japan could make movies like this and *Rashamon* as well… Hollywood had better watch out!

From the early 1950s, there were six so-called major film studios (Daiei, Nikkatsu, Shintoho, Shochiku, Toei and Toho) in Japan. Each, on the average, turned out two

feature films a week – yes, more than 600 features a year. It was in those years that such internationally acclaimed directors as Mizoguchi Kenji, Kobayashi Masaaki, Ichikawa Kon and the aforementioned Kurosawa and Ozu made their best films, almost entirely free of the need to be commercial; since the studios had to turn out so many, they could risk artistic or oddball films.

A mere decade later, however, the Japanese film industry was entering a steep and disastrous downslide – one from which it is only just now beginning to recover.

TV Games: Japanese cinema's unlucky streak began with the Tokyo Olympic Games in 1964. To watch the first Olympiad held in Japan in their own living rooms, millions of Japanese bought television sets. Once the games were over, however, there was precious little to watch. The market suddenly blossomed beyond the abilities (both creative and financial) of broadcasters to meet the new demand with homegrown shows. This, in turn, led to an explosive increase in the importation of American TV shows and theatrical films.

Perry Mason, *Bonanza*, *Route 66* and *77 Sunset Strip*. Not a day went by without an American TV series available on the tube, and because of this – and the airing of an average of five or six imported movies per day – box office sales at movie theaters suffered massively.

Official Indifference: Some observers feel strongly that the national government should have stepped in at this point and, like many countries in the West, provided funding (or at least tax breaks) for the film industry in its battle against TV. But despite Japan's rush into material affluence throughout the 1960s, slowed only slightly and briefly by the oil shocks of the early 1970s, no such assistance was – nor is today – forthcoming. Japanese cinema remained a second-class citizen compared to such traditional arts as *kabuki*, *bunraku* and *noh*, even classical (Western) and contemporary music and dance.

One ray of hope remained during this time in the form of the ATG – the Japan Art Theater Guild. This subsidiary of the Toho Studios began in the 1960s as a distributor of foreign "art films," but then began shifting its operation to financing films by young or art-oriented "next-generation" Japanese directors such as Oshima Nagisa, Shinoda Masahiro, Yoshida Kiju and Kuroki Kazuo. Sadly, however, the last ATG-financed film was made in the late 1980s, and in the face of Hollywood blockbusters, came and went almost without notice.

Meanwhile, the industry's mainstream studios stuck to safe merchandise – theatrical versions of hit TV series, comic films starring pop idols and tasteless war films with cameo appearances by big TV names. This further perpetuated the feeling that Japanese films lacked spectacular scenes, excitement

ing the past decade Oshima has made *Merry Christmas, Mr. Lawrence*, *Max Mon Amour* and *The Lovers*; Shinoda has turned out *MacArthur's Children*, *Gonza, the Spearman* and *Shonen Jidai*; Yoshida has not been as active, but he has *The Human Promise* and *Onimaru* to his credit; Kuroki's *Tomorrow* won high praise. Imamura Shohei won the Grand Prix at Cannes with his film *The Ballad of Narayama* and also much acclaim (as well as box office revenues) for his recent *Black Rain*.

Hot New Talent: Among the hottest Japanese directors to emerge internationally during the last decade are Oguri Kohei, Morita Yoshimitsu and Itami Juzo. Oguri's *Muddy*

and originality, and further discouraged meaningful support from the government and privately-funded patrons alike.

At present, only three major studios – Shochiku, Toei and Toho – remain in full operation. Shochiku remains a major mainly on the strength of its ever-popular *Otoko wa Tsuraiyo* series of full-length features (the so-called *Tora-san* films) of which no fewer than 42 sequels have come out since the first in 1969.

Among the next-generation directors, dur-

River, *Rikyu* and *Thorns of Death* all have taken awards at international film festivals. Morita's *Family Game* impressed the international audience with its offbeat humor, and *Sorekara* amazed many film critics with its innovative approach to the period-drama genre. Meanwhile, actor/director Itami has been even more sensational: as of this writing he has directed five films, including *The Funeral* and *Tanpopo*. Surprisingly, all have become box office hits.

Visitors have the chance to see many of the classic films mentioned above as they are often screened in art theater cinemas in and around Tokyo, particularly the Namikiza in the Ginza and, and other large cities.

Left, Godzilla battles Biorante for supremacy over Tokyo. **Above**, Mifune Toshiro ponders a problem in Yojimbo.

What kind of house would one build in Japan if one knew it might be blown away by winds or fall apart by movements of the earth? Besides typhoons and earthquakes, Japan also has severe rains, which often cause flooding and landslides. How would one make a palace or temple or hall, a farmhouse or gate to survive such destructive forces?

These questions had to be faced and solved by the builders of buildings in Japan's remote past and are still faced today. The fact that Japan has the world's oldest wooden buildings (the Golden Hall, Pagoda, and Inner Gate of Horyuji, built about AD 670) and the world's greatest wooden structure (the Great Buddha Hall of Todaiji, some 50-meters/165 ft high and said to have been rebuilt at only two-thirds its original size) seems to argue that the architectural system adopted by the Japanese was at least partially successful in creating structures to last.

But rather than wind, earth and water, it is fire that is the greatest destroyer of buildings in the long year. It is also no coincidence that Japanese architecture has influenced architectural design throughout the world. Its concepts of fluidity, modularity, utilization of limited space, and use of light and shadow have a great power and appeal, both aesthetically and as solutions to architectural problems of the 20th century.

Whatever the factors may be that determined how buildings were built and what they looked like in Japan – survival, tradition, aesthetic preference – there are some common characteristics that can be found, a bedrock of shared traits that define the tradition of Japanese architecture. Given the great range of climates, the complex topography of the archipelago, which has produced numerous local styles of building, and the long history of the islands, the persistence of such common architectural features is truly remarkable.

A Box with a Hat: The favored material of building construction is wood. Walls, foundations of castles, the podia of some structures, and a few novel experiments saw stone in limited use, usually without mortar. Yet, undoubtedly because it was plentiful, wood remained the material of preference, particularly the wood of conifers. This is reflected in the reforestation laws of the shogunate and various feudal lords. The disappearance of certain types of large trees due to lumbering can be seen today in certain historical changes in temple and shrine buildings.

This preference for wood is directly re-

lated to the fact that the basic structural system in Japanese architecture is post and lintel. It is basically a box, on which a hat – the roof – rests. This system allows great freedom in the design of the roof, and the Japanese seemed to prefer large ones, sometimes exceeding one-half of the total height of a structure. Roofs also became elaborate, with generous eaves, and often are very heavy. (Building codes in some Western countries do not recognize this type of top-heavy structure. Getting a building permit for a traditional Japanese house in the United States is not easy.) The spectacular complex brackets upholding the eaves are one of the

Preceding pages, inside is outside in the Japanese house and garden. **Left**, Kinkakuji, Kyoto's Golden Pavilion. **Above right**, the Great Buddha at Jorenji in Tokyo.

more arresting aspects of temple architecture. The preference for generous eaves has a chicken-and-egg relationship with the widespread use of veranda.

Straight lines dominate Japanese architecture, seemingly a natural result of using wood and the post and lintel system. There are few curves and no arches. Barrel vaulting is unheard of. Curves, when they appear as an integral part of a structure, are gentle and are used as aesthetic relief from the predominantly planar – that is, boxy – construction. The curves on gables and eaves are a good example. On the other hand, carved, non-structural embellishment, especially on temple and other buildings that go in for opulent walls and became more like movable partitions instead. (The main exceptions were buildings which were meant to have a protective or defensive function – storehouses, go–downs, and castles – which had thick walls of clay or wood.) This is the origin of perhaps the most noteworthy single aspect of Japanese buildings, their fluidity or modularity. Interior spaces were partitioned so that rooms could be expanded (combined, rather) or contracted. The former was accomplished through the use of sliding door panels, which could be easily removed. A room could be divided by decorative standing screens. The use of such screens, especially those with gold backgrounds to act as

display, often shows wild proliferation of scrolls, volutes, and curvilinear motifs of many kinds, perhaps to offset the effect of this basic boxiness of the structure.

Post and lintel boxes also may be combined and strung together in many ways to create fine aesthetic effects. The Katsura Detached Palace outside of Kyoto represents the height of such architecture.

Since posts or columns bear the weight of the roof, walls could be, and were, thin and non-supporting. This lightness of wall is another feature that makes traditional Japanese buildings top-heavy, and it was developed to the point that walls often ceased to be a reflective surface and bring light into gloomy castle/palace interiors, gave birth to an entire genre of artistic expression.

This fluidity of interior space went hand in hand with the modularity of room size. Room area were measured in the number of floor mats of standard size, and some combinations of mats became standard – specifically, three, four and one-half, six, eight, ten, twelve. Veranda and corridor width came to be standardized as just the width to allow two people carrying serving trays to pass.

Inside is Outside: Also in this approach, the distinction between wall and door often disappears. This applies to outside walls – the "boundary" between interior and exterior – as well. Outside walls are often nothing more than a series of sliding wooden panels that can be easily removed, thus eliminating the solid border between inside and outside, a feature very much welcomed in Japan's humid summer. The veranda thus becomes a transitional space connecting interior with exterior of the building.

Since the floors of traditional Japanese buildings are generally raised, house floor and ground surface are not contiguous (except in the case of the packed-earth *doma*, the work and implement storage area of a farmhouse). In effect this means that the indoor-outdoor fluidity is mainly visual and for

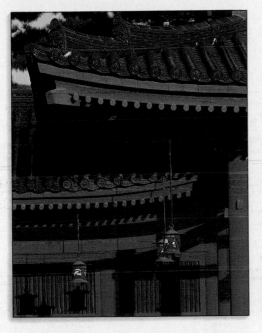

circulation of air, not for movement of people. In rural areas, the veranda, when open, becomes a place to sit and have a good gossip with a neighbor or friend.

The ability to open up a house interior completely to external vistas led to the development of a heightened sensitivity to such vistas and to their manipulation. Or perhaps it was a desire to view nature that led to the ability to remove the outer partitions of a house. Whatever the origin, the juxtaposition of building and nature without a clear

Left, Nara's impressive Todaiji. **Above**, roof lines at Kyoto's Heian Shrine.

dividing line is one origin of the Japanese garden – a manipulated or totally artificial vista, grand or miniature, "natural" or stylized and symbolic. The Japanese garden is an artifact open to the sun and rain but clearly made to be seen and appreciated from within a building. Gardens for walking exist, but are rather exceptional.

The materials used in traditional Japanese room interiors are few and limited, reflecting an ambivalence between interior and exterior or perhaps a pleasure in harmonizing rather than sharply demarking interior and exterior. Sliding door panels are either translucent *shoji* or the heavier, opaque *fusuma* paper screens or of wood. Walls are of clay (wattle and daub, with a surface of fine-quality clay). Floors are of thick, resilient straw mats surfaced with woven reed (tatami mats) or of plain wood. Supporting wooden posts remain exposed, and ceilings are generally of wood or of woven materials of various kinds. Wooden surfaces remain unpainted (a fact that received little understanding from the American Occupation forces housed in requisitioned Japanese homes). In the few areas of the country where wooden architectural surfaces are lacquered, the lacquer enhances the woodiness of the material, letting it speak; to cover it over would be seen as "cheap".

Because of the generous eaves of Japanese buildings, interiors tend to be dark and, often enough, may be gloomy. The use of translucent paper shoji screens to diffuse soft light helps, but the soft, natural colors of the room materials generally absorb rather than reflect light. The colors, lighting and textures of traditional Japanese rooms directly influenced the qualities of all objects that were made to be used in them, including clothing. A Japanese ceramic bowl and a kimono are very different when seen in a Japanese room and in a room with plaster walls and glass windows.

New Principles: The artistic unity or harmony of a building extends to its properties as well. Master carpenters, who were both the architects and the builders of traditional buildings, developed formulas of pleasing proportions that applied to all elements of a single structure as well as to individual buildings in a complex. There are special and very sophisticated traditional carpenter's measures that apply this system of aesthetic proportion to new buildings.

And finally, Japanese architecture is united in the display of an astonishing degree of contrast and variety. The earth's oldest wooden buildings exist not too far from the Ise Shrines, whose immortality is defined by it being ritually rebuilt exactly as the original every 20 years. The shrine is both ancient and new at the same time. Tiny teahouses and the world's biggest wooden building both show an equally awesome skill in building, but of varying scales and degrees. Gardens are contrived to draw in the vistas of distant mountains within their boundaries. Tiny "dry landscape" gardens may display such symbolic potency that they are both big

plation and quiet, while the latter's primary message is loud flaunting of skill, effort, money and power.

Historically, Japanese architecture shows a dialectic between imported, continental styles (mainly Chinese, with some Korean) and native Japanese styles. The former was constantly being modified, adapted, and made into something clearly Japanese in taste, a process that demarks Japan's entire cultural history.

A Historical Summary: The oldest Japanese dwellings are the pit houses of the Neolithic Jomon culture, but the oldest structure to which the term "architecture" might be applied is the Grand Shrines of Ise, mentioned

and small at the same time; or rather, they have no confines, and their size ceases to have meaning.

Some of the finest teahouses, whose total lack of surface ornament is itself a purely ornamental statement, were built at roughly the same time as the Toshogu Shrine at Nikko, whose detail- and color-crammed surfaces display a naive delight in complexity and brightness and that seems to go so far beyond mere clutter as to define a new set of principles. Both the teahouse and the ornate shrines, temples, and palaces shout out that they were built by skilled artists, the former emphasizing taste, but as a tool to contem-

above. First completed in the 5th century, it has been ritually rebuilt 60 times, every 20 years. Each rebuilding takes years to accomplish, starting with the cutting of special cypress trees deep in the mountains, and involves special carpenter's techniques as well as time-honored rituals. The disappearance of carpenters with the necessary skills and the enormous cost of the project have resulted in the prediction that the last rebuilding in 1993 will also be the final one.

The introduction of Buddhism to Japan in AD 552 brought with it in one sweep many cultural and technical features, not the least of which was architecture in the continental manner. It is said that Korean builders came over to Japan and either built or instructed to build the Horyuji (AD 607). The foundations of the vast temple that was the prototype of Horyuji can still be visited in Kyongju, South Korea.

In the 7th century at the capital in Nara, Chinese architectural influence became quite obvious, not only in the structures themselves, but in the adoption of the north-south grid plan of the capital, based on the plan of the Chinese capital. At this time, both secular and sacred architecture was essentially the same, and palaces were often rededicated as temples. Both displayed red-lacquered columns and green roofs with pro-

corridors. The layout of the Imperial Palace at Kyoto is similar, though it is a replica of this style.

When the imperial court at Kyoto lost the reins of power to the military government (shogunate) located far to the west in Kamakura, the open and vulnerable *shinden* style was supplanted by a type of residential building more easily defended. This warrior style (*bukke-zukuri*) placed a number of rooms under one roof or a series of conjoined roofs, and was surrounded by a defensive device such as a fence, wall, or moat, with guard towers and gates. Tiled roofs gave way to either shingled or thatched roofs.

This period also saw the importation of

nounced upswinging curves in the eaves. Roofs were tiled.

The mutability of residence and temple held true in the following Heian Period as well, as evidenced by the villa of the nobleman Fujiwara no Yorimichi (990–1074), which became the Phoenix Hall of Byodoin at Uji, near Kyoto. The graceful *shinden-zukuri* style of this structure, utilized for the residences of Heian Period court nobles, is characterized by rectangular structures in symmetrical arrangement linked by long

Left, temple roofs in Kyushu. **Above**, stunning ornamentation at Nikko's Toshogu Shrine.

Chinese Song dynasty architectural styles for temples, particularly the so-called Zen style, which is characterized by shingled roofs, pillars set on carved stone plinths, and the "hidden roof" system developed in Japan, among other features.

In the subsequent Muromachi Period, which saw the purest expression of feudal government and its breakup into the Age of Civil Wars, Buddhist influence, Zen in particular, transformed the "warrior style" into the *shoin* style.

This at first was little more than the addition of a small reading or waiting room (shoin), with a deep sill that could be used as a desk and decorative, built-in shelves to hold books or other objects. This room also displayed an alcove, the *toko-noma*, in which treasured objects could be effectively displayed. This shoin room eventually exerted its influence over the entire structure. Both the Golden Pavilion and the Silver Pavilion of Kyoto are examples of this early style.

The period also saw the development of the teahouse, which is said to be a stylization of traditional farmhouse architecture.

At the end of the Age of Civil Wars, firearms became common in warfare. In response to this, massive castles were built. Few remain today; Himeji Castle, with

white walls and soaring roof (it is nicknamed the "Heron") is the finest surviving example.

Political change brought the country into the Edo Period, and architecture saw a melding of the shoin style and teahouse concepts to produce the *sukiya* style, the grandest example of which is the Katsura Imperial Villa outside of Kyoto.

This residential architecture displays an overall lightness of members, a simplified roof, and restrained, subtle ornamentation. By the end of the 17th century, it had achieved its mold.

A Look at Gardens: The unique beauty of the Japanese garden, which has been imitated all over the world, comes from a sensitive attention to combinations of natural elements and compositional harmony. Clearly enough, it is derived from the Japanese landscape itself and well as from the sharply defined seasons of the archipelago.

Religion, particularly Zen, also plays a profound role in the design of the Japanese garden, especially the "dry landscape". It is said that viewing such a garden in the right conditions and with the appropriate mental preparation is a form of meditation and may lead to a spirtiual experience for which there are no words.

In the Heian Period, courtiers sought relief from oppressive humidity of summer by having their residences and grounds landscaped to include little streams, small waterfalls, and ponds. This type of garden was situated on the south of the residence and was often created as a simulation of the Buddhist Garden of Paradise. The garden of Byodoin at Uji is an example of this style still in existance.

The military ethic of the Kamakura Period saw a modification of the garden plan to fit the needs and tastes of the warrior class. This period also saw the oldest Japanese writing on garden design and composition, Tachibana Toshitsuna's *Sakateiki*.

In the Muromachi Period, a further development occurred, with gardens becoming fashionable as objects for tranquil contemplation and as miniature representations of nature to be savored and actively explored for their spiritual values. During this same period, considered the Golden Age of Japanese gardens, the tea garden developed in conjunction with the teahouse.

Elements that these prototype tea gardens introduced to the art of garden making include stepping stones, groves of trees, stone lanterns and washbasins, and rustic huts where tea is served. The splendid garden of the Katsura Detached Palace is, in essence, a series of individual tea gardens.

The Momoyama and Edo Periods saw numerous beautiful gardens built, and these must be included along with those of the Muromachi Period as being among Japan's supreme artistic achievements.

Above left, the majestic Karatsu Castle in northern Kyushu. Right, three-tiered temple pagoda in snowy Kyoto.

Whether you encounter it through one of the traditional crafts, through architecture, landscape gardening or even through an interest in social history or religion, it is hard to explore very deeply into Japanese culture without stumbling over the curious expression "tea ceremony."

Most foreigners marvel at the very words. What kind of ritual can it be? How can a society – even one as steeped in tradition and brimming over with precious refinement as the Japanese – formalize something as inherently unstructurable and lightweight as enjoying an afternoon beverage with a few friends? For some first-timers, images of spoons, sugar cubes and soggy tea bags may come to mind.

Mystification only increases when one delves further and hears that, far from being merely the kind of quaintly preserved pageant implied by its name, this "ceremony" has exerted a massive influence on Japan's sensibility, aesthetics and manners, and many of the glorious artifacts of the artisanal world are created with the tea room specifically in mind.

Finally, one may even be told that, at the higher levels of its mastery, the "ceremony" can impart all kinds of transcendent and spiritual rewards. Part of our initial surprise at the depth and seriousness of Tea could be avoided by a small change in vocabulary: in Japanese, the art is often called *sado* or even *chado*; the "*do*" in each case means "way," and the "*sa*" and "*cha*" both mean "tea." Translated into English the word means "The Way of Tea," which is far more accurate and informative.

The Soul of Japan: Dozens of international centers dedicated to the study and practice of Tea have opened over the past few years and thousands of Americans, Spaniards and Thais are whipping up bowls of tea – often in the painful kneeling position – as if it were the most natural practice imaginable. They do this not only to gain an appreciation for the soul of Japan, but also to follow a serious path of spiritual growth and, ultimately,

Left, light and shadow heighten the graphic effect of a cup of tea on a *tatami* mat.

some say, to make a small contribution to world peace.

It is amazing that all this can be derived from a discipline whose main activity (as expressed by a founding master) is simply to "boil water and make tea." (Speaking of semantics, this reminds us of another common term for the art, *chanoyu*, which simply means "the hot water of tea.")

Nevertheless, when viewed in a fancy hotel lobby or at a "taste-of-old-Japan" tourist extravaganza, the "tea ceremony" may seem nothing more than a chance for charming young ladies to dress in kimono and study some manners. This view represents the final obstacle of understanding the nature of Tea. Clearly, Tea stands for different things at different levels of practice.

Though some form of tea drinking was brought to Japan from China in the Heian Period, it was not until the end of the 12th century that the special strain of bush, and the technique for making the powdered green tea called *matcha,* were brought over by the founder of the Rinzai Zen sect, Eisai.

Eisai planted his first seeds on a hillside in Uji, near Kyoto – a region still boasting Japan's best buds – and then encouraged his monks to drink the frothy, bitter-tasting tea as a health potion, as a cure for hangovers (Rinzai monks are very worldly) and, most importantly, as a sleep inhibitor. Meditating monks need every possible aid to stay awake, and matcha – loaded with caffeine and vitamin C – provides more than an adequate jolt.

Porcelain parties: By the 15th century, matcha – in conjunction, of course, with traditional *sake* – had evolved into the party stimulant of choice for the rich merchant class, particularly the businessmen around the Port of Sakai, south of Osaka. These merchants were engaged in the lucrative China trade and they used these (often rather licentious) tea parties to show off their rare porcelains and other costly treasures.

The Zen connection was maintained, however, thanks to the nightly presence of eccentric monks such as Ikkyu (abbot of Daitokuji in Kyoto) and his disciple Murata Shuko (1422–1502). In a fateful conversation, Ikkyu told his student to forget Zen and concentrate only on making tea, thereby suggesting that the two disciplines were on the same level and in consequence had equal potential for spiritual development.

Two members of the Sakai merchant class, Takeno Jo-o (1504–55) and his student Sen no Rikyu(1522–91), are credited with elevating the tea party far above the category of rich pastimes. Theirs is not the only aesthetic in the tea world today but, in effect, they started a revolution by rejecting showy extravagance in favor of the uncontrived beauty in things simple, earthy, humble, uneven, sad, overlooked, rustic, old and imperfect. These words (and numerous oth-

everywhere. Nonetheless, the *wabi* principle did subvert this society's rigid class structure by making the practice of Tea accessible to those who possessed only found objects and a little imagination.

Rikyu helped liberalize thinking in other ways as well. "All people are equal in the tea room" is an importan axiom, a rule actually built into teahouse design. For example, the door is so small that all guests must bow equally low to enter. Also, participants rarely engage in small talk and they leave outside the room all symbols of class or status – samurai swords, watches, bags, even jewelry and wedding rings – in order to help create within the communion-like gathering

ers), are part of *wabi* and *sabi*, crucial Tea concepts that are reflected in the look of the implements, in the tea sweets and flower arrangement, in the design of the teahouse and garden, and even in the calligraphy scroll that is put out for the day.

Equality in the Tea Room: One of the several ironies of this famous "poverty" aesthetic of Tea (which cynics have labelled something only the extremely rich would dream of) is that Japanese craftsmen have learned to charge small fortunes for their best "imperfections." Only the wealthy and the affluent can afford them now and they are shown off just as brazenly as the Chinese porcelains

an atmosphere redolent of "harmony, respect, purity and tranquility."

Achieving this four-word dictum is what makes "true Tea" such an elusive pursuit. Merely to insure *physical* harmony in the tea room, for example, requires a certain command of architecture, gardening, calligraphy, flower arranging and ceramics.

Additional elements in the room test one's knowledge of lacquer, paper, incense and charcoal-making; bamboowork, confectionery, weaving and woodcarving; and lastly, bronze and iron casting.

Full-scale Tea events, moreover, further include food and *sake*, thereby opening the door to yet another complex field of study.

Seeking to create other kinds of harmony, not to mention fulfilling the remaining objectives, is part of the reason for Tea's painstakingly rehearsed movements with the cloths, the implements and the hot and cold water. These sometimes appear gratuitously mannered but, in addition to having symbolic importance, they are all designed to get the bowl of matcha made in the most natural, beautiful and economical way.

Also involved at the higher levels of the Tea experience are Zen concepts of the unique, fleeting moment and the impermanence of all things, Taoist notions of *yin* and *yang*, and perhaps even some Christian mystical influence. Jo-o and Rikyu seem to have been aware of a variety of profound teachings – recent research has suggested, for example, that Rikyu's design for the ideal tea room is intended as a paradigm of Buddha's Western Paradise. Over the centuries since the founding of Tea, the more evolved masters have refined and codified these profundities (sometimes to a degree so esoteric that it invites ridicule).

Attitude Adjustments: Ultimately, however, what makes Tea so hard to achieve (and define) is that "true Tea" is largely a state of mind. Making a bowl of tea is not the challenge; it is making it in the right spirit that consumes a lifetime of effort. As in Zen, implements, procedures and esoterica have value only as prods toward a higher objective, and in Tea that higher objective, quite simply, is the ability to show sublime hospitality. With a pure heart and loving intentions a host does everything in his or her power to provide comfort and consideration to the guest, and the latter graciously returns the respect.

In the Japanese frame of things, "comfort" means that there can be no awkwardness, hence the prescribed scenario. The years of training are to make the motions second nature so that the mind will be reeded for creative improvisation and the whole thing will appear casual and effortless. Only then will the guest not feel either beholden to the host or ill at ease.

Given this background, it perhaps be-

comes easier to see why Tea can attract practitioners interested in everything from social betterment to a spiritual-aesthetic discipline to the creation of kinder societies and better world relations.

In Japan today, the tea schools (three of them were started by grandsons of Rikyu, the largest being Urasenke and Omotesenke) prosper due to the first type of student – mostly young ladies who reluctantly take a year's worth of lessons to improve their bridal resumes.

Japanese males, many of whom once defined themselves in terms of the spirit of Tea, have all but abandoned it in favor of golf. This leaves the international community

who, in the vision of Urasenke's current grandmaster, have the potential to revitalize *chanoyu* and make it everybody's cup… er, bowl of tea.

Chanoyu Note: Visitors to Kyoto can find a relatively tasteful demonstration of Tea at a confectionery shop named Kano Shojuan on the Philosopher's Walk just north of Eikando (10am–4.30pm, closed Wednesdays; tel: 751-1077 in Japanese only).

Special presentations in English are held on Thursdays in the modern concrete building at Urasenke's headquarters; call 451-8516 before midday to reserve a space at one or three o'clock in the afternoon.

Left, graceful presentation at a tea ceremony. **Above right**, special water ladle used during the tea ceremony.

FOOD WITH A FLOURISH

With Houdinian dexterity, a white-smocked man twirls a huge roll of dough in mid-air until thick rings of it resolve themselves into thinner ones that finally, miraculously, become noodle-like strands. They are now ready to be chopped into a length manageable to eat with chopsticks. The Japanese specialist in *tezukuri-soba* (hand-made noodles) – the real thing – has worked his magic again.

Nearby, another performer takes the stage. With practiced aplomb he places a morsel of steamed rice in his palm, dabs a bit of Japanese green horseradish onto it, and deftly twists it into a small mound that he then tops with a slice of fresh raw fish. Voila! *Osushi*. He repeats the performance and sets his pair of delicacies before a customer serenely twitching with anticipation.

The scene shifts. In the kitchen of an elegant Japanese restaurant, the chef arranges artfully prepared pieces of individual foods into several small dishes, some of them ceramic works of art, setting each piece precisely in place as if fashioning a cut-glass mosaic. With a flourish he completes his masterpiece, the inimitable *kaiseki-ryori*.

Fresh Comes First: The artistry of all of these specialists is matched, and their concentration perhaps even exceeded, by yet another fastidious food preparer addressing his task as if its precise execution were no less than a matter of life and death. In fact, it is – for this is one of the relatively few cooks licensed to remove the sac of deadly poison from the *fugu*, or globefish – one of Japan's winter delicacies.

Japan's culinary world abounds with such performers. Not every type of food served in every type of establishment is attended by a diamond-cutter's passion for perfection, to be sure. But even the operator of a mite-sized shop serving regional specialties as simple as *nimono* (foods boiled in soy sauce) not uncommonly will take strong personal pride in their quality. Correct preparation and freshness – at all events freshness of the ingredients – are essential to the Japanese dining experience. The proliferation of hothouse cultivation has assured the Japanese a year-round fresh supply of many food products once available only in certain seasons. Despite this, though, the Japanese are taken with ingredients of the season. Fresh comes first.

Delicacies such as osushi, kaiseki-ryori and fugu can cost one a pretty penny in Japan, although in the better establishments they can be well worth the price. But banish the thought that the cost of dining out in

Japan will necessarily come high, as this is an outside misconception that should be persistently rectified.

Many of Japan's most enjoyable and popular dishes are commonly very reasonably priced. Among them are such everyday delights as *yakimono* (fried dishes), *nabemono* (pot dishes), *agemono* (deep fat fried dishes), nimono (boiled dishes) and a wide variety of noodle dishes. Here we will look at a few, starting with that perennial year-round favorite, noodles.

Slurp Up Some Lunch: Noodles are eaten in Japan throughout the year and nearly throughout the day, from lunchtime on into the wee

Preceding pages, food as art – delicate *kaiseki-ryori* spread. **Left**, this shop owner is in a pretty fine pickle. **Above right**, chopsticks at *bento* (lunchbox) time at school.

hours of morning. Most common are *soba*, made from buckwheat flour and particularly delicious if not overburdened with non-buckwheat flour extender. It is usually served with *wasabi* (Japanese green horseradish) and thinly sliced scallions and a dip made of *mirin* (sweet *sake*) and *katsuobushi* (shaved flakes of dried bonito). Soba noodles in this form, served on a *zaru* (bamboo tray), are called *zaru-soba*. Soba is not only delicious but extremely nutritious, the more so in proportion to its *sobako* (wheat flour) content, a rich source of vitamins B1 and C.

A hot weather favorite – as soba is, but entirely different – is the thin, off-white wheat noodle called *somen*, noted for its

a dip before being eaten. Udon, a real bodywarmer, is particularly appreciated for its excellent texture.

Not strictly a traditional dish, but one that is uniquely Japanese and that can be (one must admit) quite delicious is *kareudon*. As its name implies, it's *udon* served in the thick brown gravy that passes for curry. Yum.

As one travels about Tokyo and elsewhere in Japan, sooner or later the *tachigui-sobaya* hoves into view, usually near a train station and often right on the platform. Tachigui means stand and eat, and sobaya means soba shop ("*ya*" suffixed to a category of food denotes a shop, as in *sushiya, yakitoriya*, and *okashiya*, the latter being a shop selling Japa-

delicate flavor and adaptability to a variety of garnishes. Somen can be served *gomoku* ("five-flavor") style with strips of omelette, chicken, and vegetables, *gomadare* style with eggplant, fish, and *shiso* (beefsteak plant), with fruit and hard-boiled swallow eggs, or *hiyashi* style – cold, with nothing but soy sauce containing sesame oil. As a light, refreshing treat on a hot summer day, somen may have no rival.

One of Japan's great cold weather favorites is *udon*, a somewhat thick to very thick wheat noodle served in a hot soy-base broth with scallions, other vegetables, and an egg. Unlike soba and somen, udon is not placed in

nese-style cakes). When time is precious and hunger strikes, the tachigui-sobaya can be a blessing. Gourmet noodles aren't to be expected, but the best are passing fair, the price is always right, and the health standards are reliable. Japan's standards of hygiene in food preparation are very high, if not always rigidly heeded.

Something In the Pot: If pot dishes are your pleasure, Japan is your oyster. In fact, one of the more delicately flavored pot dishes is *kaki-no-dote-nabe* (oyster pot), a specialty of Hiroshima. Every part of Japan, without exception, has its own distinctive *nabe-ryori* (pot dishes). A few of many that deserve your warm consideration – they are winter dishes, essentially – are *ishikari-nabe* (Hokkaido Prefecture), containing salmon, onions, Chinese cabbage, *tofu*, *konnyaku* (a jelly made of root starch), and *shungiku* (spring chrysanthemum); *hoto* (Yamanashi), containing hand-made udon, *daikon* (white radish), *ninjin* (carrot), *gobo* (burdock), squash, onions, Chinese cabbage and chicken; *anko-nabe* (Ibaraki), containing lantern fish, *mitsuba* (trefoil), *shiitake* mushrooms, garden peas, gingko nuts, starch noodles and tofu; and *chiri-nabe* (Yamaguchi), containing bone-in fugu white meat, Chinese cabbage, button mushrooms, tofu and starch noodles.

To dare to suggest that these few nabe-individual taste); and Tokyo-style *oden nabe*, a potpourri containing potatoes, tofu, konnyaku, boiled eggs, octopus, carrots, daikon, kelp, and a wide variety of other ingredients. Make a note of *oden*, which is one of the better winter body-warmers and a hearty dish.

Fried dishes have a secure place in the Japanese cuisine and fried fish of all kinds are popular any time. At a traditional Japanese pub, the ubiquitous *izakaya*, try the likes of *saba* (mackerel), *sanma* (mackerel pike), *nijimasu* (rainbow trout), *nishin* (herring), *iwashi* (sardines) and *katei* (turbot). Try them *shioyaki-style* (salt broiled) with a good cold Japanese beer or a very dry *sake*.

ryori dishes should be considered to the exclusion of many others of equal merit from all over Japan would incur well-deserved local censure from regions far and wide. Three of the best-known *nabe* dishes originated in Tokyo.

Yanagawa-nabe, containing *dojo* (rice-paddy loaches), burdock and eggs, is an old Tokyo favorite. So are Tokyo-style *sukiyaki*, made by first preparing the sauce in the pan (as opposed to the Osaka method of omitting water and broth and adding seasoning to suit

Left, dried squid is a popular snack. **Above**, counter at a seafood restaurant on Okinawa.

Japanese ginger-fried pork and beef are other simple but satisfying fried dishes enormously popular in any season. In izakaya and *koryoriya*, traditional small Japanese eateries featuring regional foods, such dishes are invariably served with rice. Izakaya, essentially drinking places, serve a wide variety of Japanese snack foods but not meals, whereas koryoriya, being essentially eateries, serve light Japanese meals. Both types of establishments serve alcoholic beverages, invariably beer and *sake*, often *shochu* (a vodka-like spirit), and sometimes whisky.

The better izakaya and *taishu sakaba* (drinking halls), their outsized cousins, are

CHOPSTICKS ETIQUETTE

Chopsticks poised, you contemplate the next delicacy you'll savor from among those arrayed before you. The *nasu* pickle? The salmon? The burdock? Gently taking it in your chopsticks, you bring it to your mouth and enjoy the bite-sized morsel in one bite. Well done. But never wave your chopsticks indecisively over the food (*mayoi-bashi*). When dining Japanese style, that's bad manners, and so are a number of other pratices you should consciously avoid.

Never, for example, spear your food (*sashi-bashi*) with the tips of the chopsticks. Certain things may be a tad more difficult to pick up with chopsticks than certain others, but chopsticks are designed to pick food up, not to spear and stab it. Sashi-bashi is forbidden.

The same goes for *yose-bashi*, using your chopsticks to pull a dish toward you. For that, you use only your hands. To eat rice or drink soup, raise the bowl up to your breast.

For dishes that are dipped in sauce, such as *tempura* and *sashimi*, hold the sauce dish with one hand and dip the food into it with your chopsticks. Never lift large dishes or plates. Food in pot dishes should be placed in the small dish provided.

If food is in pieces too large to eat with proper dining decorum, separate it into bite-sized pieces with your chopsticks. This can require a bit of a knack, since some foods are reluctant to be separated very easily. Try to hold it against the dish with the bottom stick and gently push away part of it with the top stick. Practice it on your own.

Japanese-style soups (*suimono*) and other liquid dishes should be sipped straight from the bowl. Whereas it is altogether acceptable form in Japan to slurp noodle dishes, it is not required nor indeed is there any reason to slurp Japanese soups. Sip them, as this the best way to savor their delicate nuances of flavor.

Soy sauce should not be splashed on – avoid doing so even if you see it done. Pour into your small soy sauce dish only a little at a time and use it sparingly. When pickles are served in a large bowl, transfer them from it to your small dish. Eat all the rice in your bowl and when asking for more, only take what you are sure you can eat. Place fish bones neatly to the side of the plate they are served on, and replace the lid on bowls served with a lid.

Finally, when the meal is over, put your chopsticks back in their disposable paper sleeve and place them on the chopstick rest.

Whatever you do, do not jam your chopsticks down into your rice, and do not pass food back and forth with chopsticks (*hashiwatashi*).

If the other "don'ts" are socially gauche, hashiwatashi is unconsciably an athema – it is the way dishes are served to the dead!

Chopsticks – which you may have gathered by now are called *hashi*, or *bashi* – might be made of almost any stiff, hard and non-splintering material. In feudal days, silver hashi were used by aristocrats, both as an affectation symbolizing wealth and as a precaution against assassination: it was believed that any poison slipped into the food would cause the silver chopsticks to tarnish.

The wood most commonly used in making chopsticks is *sugi* (cryptomeria). Perhaps the second-most common is bamboo, either cured or fresh-cut. The latter (*aotake*, or "green bam–boo") closely resembles the earliest form of chopsticks, probably originating in southern China, except that the first hashi was a single, slender stick, curved at the end.

On formal occasions, such as New Year's Day, hashi made of *yagi* (willow) wood are called for. Often, these are in the shape known as *Rikyu-bashi*, named after the famous tea master: thick in the middle, tapering at both ends. But as a rule, Japanese *hashi* are blunt.

In most restaurants these days, you will inevitably be given *waribashi*. Japan has been the target of criticism from environmentalists about these disposable chopsticks and the "millions of trees wasted" to make them. The government, however, says the wood used is less than 1 percent of Japan's annual consumption, and that any other material (e.g. plastic) would pose even bigger environmental problems.

But speaking of threats to the environment and ecology, the use of ivory for making new chopsticks is now, finally, illegal in Japan.

good places to discover a wide range of simple, everyday Japanese snack dishes. The koryoriya are more focused on *kyodo-ryori* (regional cookery), a subject deserving a bit more of our attention.

Fruits of the Land and Sea: Many of the dishes already referred to – nabe-ryori, for example – fit the category of kyodo-ryori. For the most part they are simple dishes using a given region's *sachi*, or marine products (*umi no sachi*) and agricultural products (*yama no sachi*). Included in the repertoire are *nimono* (boiled foods), *mushimono* (steamed foods), *agemono* (deep fat fried foods), *sunomono* (dressed foods), *suimono* (soups), and *tsuke–mono* (pickles).

such great variety that you should try as many side dishes as you can. Best known among the agemono are *tempura* and *tonkatsu* (Japanese pork cutlet), but others such as deep-fried tofu and chicken balls with white sesame seeds are most enjoyable.

A Fine Pickle: Never is one served a Japanese meal without *tsukemono* (pickles) in some form or other. Pickles in history probably owe their origins to the practice of pickling foods in anticipation of the famines that decimated populations through the ages. So it was in Japan, where nearly every form of food was pickled long before agriculture became widespread. Literature of the Nara Era makes reference to the practice of pick-

By all means try such nimono as *kabocha* (squash) with ground beef, and a melange of *aburage* (fried tofu), boiled eggs carrots, potatoes, daikon, and *satoimo* (taro), – a very traditional nimono dish. Among *mushimono* the almost compulsory choice is *chawan mushi*, a custard containing chicken, mushrooms, gingko nuts, eggs, spinach, and peeled shrimps. *Sunomono* (vinegared dishes) and *aemono* (small salads) tend to be simple and "*sappari*" (clean and refreshing) and are of

Left, chopsticks have aesthetic as well as practical value. **Above**, *yakitori*, one of Japan's original fast foods.

ling as a means of food preservation, and in the Muromachi Era, pickling reached new heights of sophistication as a means of complementing and enhancing the flavors of other foods.

During the Edo Period, pickles came into their own in Japan, increasing in variety and popularity, and the *tsukemonoya* (pickle shop) emerged as a new type of business.

Ingredients used in Japanese pickles vary somewhat with the seasons and are of considerable variety. Common ingredients are Chinese cabbage, bamboo, turnips, *kyuri* (Japanese cucumbers), hackberry, daikon, ginger root, *nasu* (Japanese eggplant), *myoga*

(Zingiber Mioga), *udo* (a type of asparagus), *gobo* and many others…

Besides the obvious ones of taste and nutrition, tsukemono play several other roles in Japanese cuisine. They add color – very important in even the simplest meal; they offer a wide range of textures, from crunch to (if you'll pardon the expression) squish, often missing from the main dishes; and they can serve to clear the palate for new tastes – such as in a round of sushi, in which a bite of pickled ginger root rids the mouth of the aftertaste of an oily, white-skinned fish such as *aji* (Spanish mackerel), and prepares it for the delicate sweetness of, say, an *ebi* (prawn).

Japan is a nation of travelers who were

obsessed with domestic travel long before the Japanese tourist became a familiar figure abroad, and of all modes of domestic transportation the train is uncontestably the most popular. Thus some of Japan's most popular forms of food are those sold inside the stations of major terminals and on the platforms of those linking Japan's many cities on the major train routes. Trains often makes stops of just long enough duration to permit passengers to get off briefly and buy some of their favorite *meisanbutsu* (local specialties) or the ubiquitous *ekiben* (box lunches), and often the meisanbutsu will include a variety of box lunches featuring ingredients that are the pride of the city or the region. Actually speaking, ekiben may be thought of as another word for *bento*, the generic word for a Japanese-style box lunch. *Eki*, meaning station, simply points to the fact that the bento is sold at a railway station and contains local ingredients.

Limitless Lunch: Ekiben have been around for just over a century, increasing in variety and never waning in popularity. At train stations alone throughout Japan one could find upwards of 1,500 kinds and the possibilities may be considered limitless, for the Japanese box lunch, like the casserole, gives full play to the human imagination to create whatever it can with available, fresh, local ingredients.

Considering that the first ekiben were nothing more than *onigiri* (balls of steamed rice, usually wrapped in crispy *nori*), the variety today is remarkable – a result, no doubt, of the extensive expansion of Japan's excellent national train network and of the the rather reasonable price of ekiben. When given the opportunity to get off the train and buy one, grab it. Not all ekiben are created equal, but the odds are in favor of finding you'll enjoy. In concession stands where they are sold you can see samples of what they contain. Typical ingredients are bamboo stalks, konnyaku, kelp, shiitake, chestnuts, chicken, beef, gingko nuts, and fish and seafood. For the most part Japanese box lunch ingredients tend to be low in fat.

As a matter of fact, virtually all of the traditional Japanese diet is low in fat (especially the "bad" kind), high in fiber and higher still in vitamins and minerals. The emphasis in that statement, however, is on "traditional": with the increase in red-meat consumption, the boom in "instant" concoctions stuffed with preservatives, salt and little else, and the tendency to replace rice (very nutritious even without the husk) with bread made from bleached wheat flour – ugh! – there is a decided shift away from the traditional diet.

But don't you get caught in the trend. Stay away from the double-cheeseburgers and have a real Japanese meal or snack instead. You won't regret it.

<u>Above left</u>, *okonomiyaki* and many other types of tasty treats are available at all times. <u>Right</u>, soft drinks from one machine, rice from another.

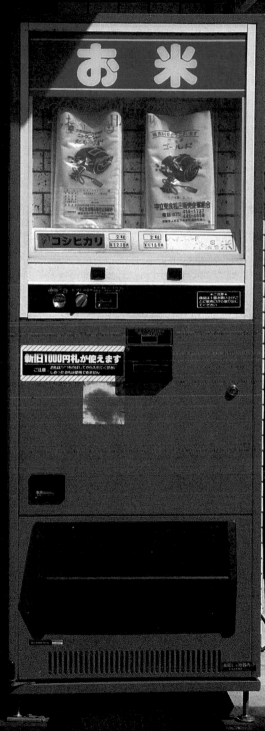

Imagine, if you will, the covers of such English-language publications for business executives as *Fortune*, *Business Week* or *Forbes* were festooned each issue with illustrations – not of entrepreneurial figures like Lee Iacocca – but with General Douglas MacArthur, the Duke of Wellington or William the Conqueror. And suppose that the articles were full of in-depth stories on the noble ideals and exceptional personal qualities of these military leaders of yore.

Well, that's what Japan's top businessmen read about each month in *President* magazine, a popular journal for business leaders published through a tie-up with America's *Fortune*. The cover of almost every issue of *President* depicts an inspiring illustration of some ancient or modern military hero.

Military heroes: If a poll were to be held among Japan's businessmen, the greatest inspiration would almost surely be Tokugawa Ieyasu, the man who united the country's warring domains in the 1590s and, as the Shogun, founded a 250-year old dynasty. The exploits of popular naval hero Admiral Yamamoto Isoroku, of more recent fame as the architect of the attack on Pearl Harbor, are given frequent media coverage (as a guidance in the sinking of business rivals, perhaps?). The Japanese Imperial Navy may be just a fond memory to its survivors, but the charismatic admiral is idolized by his countrymen even today as an imaginative and inspiring leader.

Wait, you think; isn't there a contradiction here? Isn't this idolization of the military mentality by business a bit puzzling? After all, peace has reigned supreme in Japan since 1945, and under its "Peace Constitution" the country maintains a military force confined to its borders (known, euphemistically, as the Self Defense Forces). Japanese defense industries aren't even allowed to export weapons.

What is it about the military mind that seems to capture the imagination of contemporary Japanese males in the business world?

Preceding pages, a relatively calm day on the Tokyo Stock Exchange. **Left**, new HQ for the Tokyo Metropolitan Government, designed by Tange Kenzo. **Above right**, "Commuter Squash."

An interesting anecdote sheds a bit more light on this phenomenon. It seems that not long after the end of World War II, a Japanese author named Kojima Jo paid a visit to the United States Military Academy at West Point. Having had precious few opportunities to talk with their former enemy, a pair of instructors at the school directed a stream of questions at their Japanese visitor.

"Tell us," one enquired, "what were considered to be the prime qualities expected of a Japanese general officer?"

As Mr. Kojima promptly replied, "I would say such attributes as lofty ideals; fairness of temperament; an infinite capacity for understanding; a firm, decisive will; superior discernment; and…an exceptional power of insight."

The Americans were astonished. "It sounds more like the qualities of a saint," the first said. "Having leadership with such magnificent personal qualities," another asked, somewhat cynically, "how did Japan manage to lose the war?"

Given today's situation, that same instructor might have well rephrased his question to something along the lines of, "How was the aggressive dynamism that once fueled Japan's military machine so promptly and effectively harnessed into qualities which turned a pacifist Japan into one of the world's top industrial and commercial giants?"

The Samurai Spirit: This analogy represents an oversimplified view of the real situation. It is true that Japan's top management is guided to some degree by samurai-like discipline, which functions to maintain the hierarchical structure of the organization and preserve internal harmony within the group. And it is also true that a key part of the samurai spirit involved a great deal of absorption in self-reflection and self-improvement.

But just as the duality of nature is explained by the twin metaphysical concepts of *yin* and *yang*, there is another, equally important attribute to Japanese business philosophy, and it is this attribute which is far more visible to those customers and clients dealing with Japan from the outside. This is the mood of *shokon*, loosely translated into English as "entrepreneurial spirit."

Looking back in history, the samurai – the feudal warrior class – had always held titular leadership to the country's domains. But once the Tokugawa clan ruled over a united and peaceful Japan, an urban merchant class began to develop, and eventually flourish. These men traded in silk, wool and cotton garments; distributed rice, soy sauce, tea and *sake*; sold home furnishings like lamps and *tansu* (storage chests); dealt in books, works of art, bedding, pottery and medicinal herbs. The energy these men poured into their trade became exemplified in the word shokon, whose philosophy can be refined to the single maxim "*O-kyaku wa kami*" ("Treat the customer like a god").

Here, then, is the combination that has sustained Japanese industry on its export drives to world markets. On the one hand, the samurai spirit, (the "*yang*"), to which can be attributed such standout qualities as tight group discipline, company loyalty through lifetime employment and a dedication to

quality control. Inseparable from this is the "*yin*" – the sense of shokon – that manifests itself through an exceptionally solicitous desire to keep the customer satisfied.

Chain of Command: One word that unfailingly pops up soon after one begins one's study of the structure of Japanese business is *keiretsu*, which might be translated as "corporate affiliation." This system is so entrenched that it has been targeted by the U.S. government as one of the "structural impediments" standing in the way of free trade.

Keiretsu ties have their origins in the days of the notorious *zaibatsu*, or family-owned industrial cliques, which held a near-pervasive influence over Japan's political, economic and social life before World War II. The biggest names should be familiar: Mitsubishi, Mitsui, Sumitomo, Nomura and Yasuda. Except for Mitsubishi, which was controlled by the Iwasaki family, the others bear the names of their original founders.

Although the zaibatsu were forcibly broken up during the postwar occupation, the ties gradually returned, albeit in a less threatening form. Today, the keiretsu maintain their status as giant conglomerates, with each one having its own banks, manufacturers, construction companies, real estate firms and large trading houses. The Mitsubishi "club," for example, includes the Mitsubishi

independently, and members on occasion even compete with other members.

It's confusing – unless you're Japanese.

Age-Rank Relations: The deferential treatment to one's elders clearly stems from Japan's Confucianistic social traditions, which place importance on maintenance of social order. Confucius may have said a lot of things, but his message was that society ran most smoothly by everyone's knowing, and keeping one's proper "place." And who is to say he was wrong?

So a policy of seniority tends to be upheld, but although the chairman and president of a Japanese company are usually the most senior staff, the real power in a company is not

Bank, Mitsubishi Trading, Mitsubishi Mining & Cement, Mitsubishi Heavy Industries, Mitsubishi Chemical, *ad infinitum*. But some of the keiretsu affiliations are less transparent: also under the Mitsubishi corporate umbrella are such diverse firms as Akai Electric, Kirin Brewery and Nikon Cameras.

Although it is obvious that this kind of financial integration gives a large business organization some amazing strengths, the Japanese insist that even within a given keiretsu, company management functions

Left, high-tech worker does some fine-tuning. Above, another long day at the office.

necessarily exercised from the top down. It is customary for top executives to concern themselves mainly with general policy and leave the decision making to department heads.

On a day-to-day basis, it is middle management that carries the lion's share of this burden. To be a *kacho*, or the chief of a section (*ka*) of a Japanese company places a great demand on one's ability to perform one's assigned tasks, demonstrate organizational skills, and communicate well with both one's superiors and subordinates.

A section head in a Japanese firm spends a great deal of time nurturing personal relationships, cultivating consensus and developing cooperative effort among the members of the group. And it is a very demanding role indeed, extending beyond normal working hours in the office to drinking or playing mahjong with co-workers in the evening, or golfing with clients on weekends.

It has been argued, nevertheless, that a manager in a Japanese company is not under the same degree of pressure that might be the case in a Western firm.

To explain things, it might help to dust off the old baseball-versus-sumo analogy: In baseball, the place rankings change dynamically, with each team moving up or down in the daily standings depending on their own record of wins and losses, as well as the

even make a few mistakes, and hope that he will listen to advice and get the hang of things before the end of the "tournament."

In any case, the seniority system remains well-entrenched in Japanese corporate life and there are few signs that this is changing. Impatient, strong-willed young men who feel they want to buck the system of promotion by "escalator" have always had the freedom to strike out on their own. Many have done so, and gone on to found their own business dynasties; men like Sony's Morita Akio, the late Honda Soichiro and the late Matsushita Konosuke of National Panasonic fame. All three were, above all, men who personally embodied the spirit of shokon.

performance of their opponents. In sumo, however, the ranks are fixed for the course of the tournament, so that even if a wrestler's final score is abysmal, he is allowed the dignity of holding his rank, not only through the current tournament, but until the rankings are released a few days before the *next* tournament takes place.

So in sumo, performance is not judged on the basis of daily ups and downs, and that means a little bit of pressure is off the athlete.

By the same token, top management – more secure in their own roles thanks to the security of the seniority system – is willing to let the kacho get a feel for the job, maybe

The Office: Moving past the uniformed guard at the door and the polite and smiling female receptionist, you at last find yourself in the inner sanctum of the Japanese corporation, the *honsha* or head office. At first encounter, the average Western visitor is invariably impressed by the beehive of activity: People are busy! On closer inspection, the place appears tacky, disorganized and uninspired. Although interior decorators have been struggling to get their foot in the door of the office market for years, the typical Japanese workplace does not boast much in the way of visual appeal.

Here are gray metal desks, jammed together in a long row; folders and documents piled in disarray; overflowing ashtrays; and a bank of lockers that often resemble the place where the high school football team changes into their uniforms.

One thing you can be sure about when you walk into a Japanese office is the hierarchy of the workers therein. The desks are arranged to reflect the order of the organizational chart. Look yonder, in the building's coziest corner; in that private room is sequestered the *shacho*, the company president. He is, as often as not, the only member of the organization accorded the honor of a private room.

The president's office, however, is invari-

Except in the case of advertising agencies or other firms engaged in creative work, the desk layout in the center of the room tends to resemble a game of dominoes, with rank-and-file members facing one another in a long double row of desks. The head of each section flanks them, almost always on the side of the building nearest the window. And behind him is the division head, closer yet to the window. Rank does have its privilege.

A seat near a window is not necessarily coveted, however. The term *"mado-giwa-zoku,"* or "window-gazing tribe," refers to those members of middle management who have reached the end of their usefulness to the company. These deadwood executives

ably equipped with sofa and chairs; a practical move that performs a dual purpose: The first is making visitors feel welcome, as the days are long gone that managers were forced to stand at attention while addressing him from behind his desk. The second is that in his absence from the office, the room can, in a pinch, be used for conferences. (While the president is treated with deference, the practical side of Japanese efficiency dictates that precious space should not go unused.)

Left, salarymen reserve space for a company party beneath the cherry trees. **Above left**, cubicle disguised as a garage and **right**, cars being blessed.

are promoted one notch above their level of competence, moved out of the mainstream to their semi-private windowside desks, there to spend the rest of their working days nodding off into nothingness.

For the majority of white-collar workers, however, privacy is of secondary importance. The general consensus appears to be that industriousness is contagious; in any event, things move around at a furious pace. Train a video camera on this scene for an 8-hour – no, better make that a 10-hour – day, and you would probably see that the Japanese office worker expends a great deal of physical motion. This may or may not reflect the actual amount of work being done, but appearance count for a lot, and nobody will accuse this section or that section of sitting on the job.

Meetings: Reams have been written on the subject of the great Japanese *kaigi*, or group discussion. A theorem in the Japanese scheme of holding kaigi is that the higher the ranking of the participants, the longer the meeting tends to last. This is partly because in a meeting of such gravity, it would be considered impolite to set an arbitrary time limit.

It is interesting to note that once the meeting starts, the demand not to be interrupted "under any circumstances" is seldom heard, and it would be an imposition by the visitor

while still in university and hired right after graduation, may indeed choose to ride the corporate escalator, remaining with the same company – or group of companies – throughout their entire career. Group psychology is an important factor here, as each year, a new "class" arrives at the company simultaneously on April 1. There is this trend to belong to a group of *doki-sei* (classmates) of the same age and background ready to commiserate when things don't go well.

There is no disputing the fact that the Japanese tend to place a high value on close loyalty to one's employer, and the commitment by the company in return is mutual. If times are hard and the company is having a

– no matter how important – to expect to be accorded this inflexible treatment. Thus the meeting room, invariably wreathed in clouds of cigarette smoke, seems to be in a constant of comings and goings, as participants are called out to check documents, sign papers or receive telephone calls. Interruptions aside, somehow everybody seems to be there at the moment when the key points are discussed.

The Company Man: A frequently asked question concerns the system of so-called "lifetime" employment: Does one, indeed, make a commitment to stay in a Japanese company for a lifetime, or does it only seem that way?

Students, recruited for white-collar jobs

difficult time getting the necessary funds to pay salaries, it is a common practice to offer its assets as collateral to a bank in order to obtain a loan.

But the notion of a monolithic lifetime employment system is a far cry from the reality. Like everywhere else, people in Japan quit their jobs every day. The reasons range from personal disputes with co-workers to refusing a transfer that would create economic hardship for the family.

Human beings being the fallible creatures they are, many small companies lead a marginal existence and have little to offer their workers in the way of fringe benefits. As soon as they get experience or find a better opportunity, these workers leave. The worker turnover rate among small manufacturers and service businesses is far higher than keiretsu-affiliated companies.

In the recent past, one reason why workers held onto their jobs come hell or high water was the strong perception that job-hoppers were "losers." But much has happened to alter this situation. The large influx of foreign firms in the banking and securities area has had little choice but to depend on mid-career hiring to fill up their ranks, and their heavy recruiting by headhunters has forced many Japanese firms to re-evaluate their hiring policies as well. Needless to say, job spe-

of thirty-something dropouts at top companies who quit within the first three months of service has actually become a serious concern among personnel managers.

With good jobs going wanting, Japanese workers today feel less insecure about taking the risk to move to a better paying or more appealing position. Workers, too, know that they can depend on a reasonably high degree of material comforts no matter where they work, so now a higher priority is being placed on psychological satisfaction – which naturally includes more satisfying work.

Payday and Bonuses: At one time, it used to be that the assembled workers waited to hear their name called by the division head and

cialization in such areas as computers – where a huge shortage of competent staff current exists – means that talented individuals can find better paying employment elsewhere with ease.

Another change has been evolutionary. The younger generation, having grown up knowing nothing but peace and prosperity, is regarded by older Japanese as having a lower boiling point and less willingness to endure intolerable situations. The growing number

Far left, *karaoke* relieves working-day tensions. **Left**, women are often employed on construction sites. **Above**, graduates recruited by Japan, Inc.

went forward to receive their bonus, in cash, one by one.

Today, the payment of twice-yearly bonuses to company employees (the term "*bonasu*" is commonly used) is virtually automatic, and the party-like atmosphere tied to their distribution has vanished from the scene, replaced by an automatic transfer to the worker's bank account.

Since it is paid out to one and all, a bonus can hardly be viewed as a reward for outstanding performance on the job. Rather, these twice-a-year remunerations on top of a worker's regular salary can best be understood as the withholding of a portion of the worker's salary for lump-sum payment every six months.

How much is in the bonus? The usual practice is to pay out the equivalent of two to four months of an employee's base pay. The amount might be boosted to a limited degree depending on business conditions, which means the bonus does incorporate elements of profit-sharing. On the other hand, the size of bonuses is announced publicly; the amounts paid out to workers in a given industry (such as automotive or electronics) tend to adhere closely to within certain norms, whether a particular company is enjoying high profits or not.

The bonus system has a major impact on

to receive a bonus, therefore, could spell possible disaster for the household budget.

The advantage to the Japanese system is that when the wife works out the family budget (as she invariably does), she adjusts household expenditures according to the monthly wage. The bonus, when it comes, is usually apportioned into savings, credit payments and outlays for any consumer durables the family plans to acquire. For younger salaried workers, especially women, bonuses represent a twice-yearly windfall that can be spent on high-ticket household items and overseas vacation travel.

Advertising – The Soft Hard-Sell: Given Japan's fascination with hierarchies, it should

household finances in three important areas: savings, credit and spending. Japanese workers have traditionally maintained a high sav-ings rate compared to workers in Western countries, and much of their bonuses go into such areas as bank or postal savings deposits, interest-bearing life insurance policies or securities.

When Japanese take out loans to purchase a house or car, the financing plan invariably incorporates two extra installments at the time of bonus. Thus in terms of consumer credit spending, the twice-a-year bonus is counted on to relieve what would otherwise be much heavier monthly payments. And not

not be surprising that the best-selling new products and services of the year are also accorded rankings. Each December, the *Nikkei Ryutsu Shimbun* newspaper's listing of top commercial "hits" is eagerly awaited in the form of a *banzuke*, or listing of sumo standings. The bestseller at the top of the list is given the rank of *yokozuna* – the title of a sumo grand champion.

Anything is eligible to be named to the hit list, but the one criteria is that it must not only sell well, but also be a product whose impact is felt on business and society alike.

An example is a success that has made the list for the several years: Asahi Brewery's

"Super Dry" beer. When it appeared that "Super Dry" was headed for hit status, the three other major breweries launched their own "dry" varieties, and soon, "dry" was about the only word you heard in a beer commercial. Out of virtually nowhere, dry beer (characterized by a fizzier texture and slightly higher alcoholic content), came to command over 30 percent of the domestic beer market.

Threatened by imitators on all sides, Asahi management launched an all-out advertising blitz of full-page newspaper advertisement. They did not try ploys like "ours tastes better" or "you'll have more fun if you drink Asahi." The message was simple: a sincere

"*Arigato gozaimasu*" (thank you) to its many customers. This refreshingly direct approach kept dry beer drinkers loyal to the Asahi brand (the fact that their beer tasted fine helped a lot too) and the firm has dominated the lucrative dry beer market ever since.

Why did Asahi take such a low-key approach? Why didn't they take off the kid gloves and come out fighting? Because hard-sell, comparative advertising is simply not

Left, namecards as offerings at Kyoto's Fushimi Inari Shrine, dedicated to commerce. **Above**, businessman with briefcase takes a breather by the Imperial Palace moat.

done in Japan. A powerful watchdog organization known as the Fair Trade Commission does not permit companies to run advertisements which target the prices or features of specific competitors, or to offer special premiums or buyer incentives that would "destabilize" the market.

Faced with such restrictions, the advertising agencies usually rely on three possible strategies:

1. Advertisements which promote a product on the basis or some new or unique feature. One of the most controversial advertisements of 1990 was for a Hitachi washing machine sporting two separate vats. The idea was that the woman of the house seemed to feel a bit uncomfortable washing her dainty underthings in the machine together with her husband's rank jockey shorts. Hence a two-vat washing machine that has everybody talking about it.

2. Advertisements which attempt to capture the viewer's attention either through the endorsement of some well-known foreign personality (such as Arnold Schwarzenegger plugging a vitamin tonic on TV) or through some other eccentric approach.

3. Advertisements which work to promote new products through "culture." Japan seems to have an inordinate share of such advertising. Marketers who pay close attention to social trends and popular concerns tend to emphasize such advertising.

One of the best known examples, and without a doubt one of Japan's most innovative advertisers, is Suntory Ltd. The firm's roots go back to an Osaka liquor shop, Torii Shoten. Mr. Torii, who founded the shop in 1899, had a flair for promotion, and instinctively understood the need to develop a social infrastructure in which consumers could enjoy his product.

Suntory's multivaried advertisements have been, by turn, humorous, surrealistic, oddball, cosmopolitan, and manic. Yet Suntory insists they are never aimed merely at selling the product; rather, they are always seeking out that elusive "something" that makes potential customers take notice.

Thanks to shokon, its founder's uncanny ability to exploit the essential points of advertising, Suntory, still a family business today and has become a global food and beverage empire with annual group sales of ¥1 trillion worldwide.

It is the rare visitor to Japan who does not eventually take a ride on a train or subway during their stay. But there's probably only one train with the distinction of actually convincing thousands, perhaps millions, of visitors to come to Japan to ride on it. And that's the Shinkansen, the bullet train.

In service now for over a quarter of a century, the Shinkansen (the "*sen*" means "line") continues to rack up new records. On more than one occasion in its history the network has moved one million people in a

areas – Tokyo and Osaka – by efficient rail transport. Steam locomotive service began in 1889, a time when the 515-kilometer (320-mile) trip between the two cities took 20 hours. Diesel service, introduced in 1930, reduced this to 8 hours, 20 minutes; full electrification, completed in the 1960s, carved off another 2 hours.

Privatized Profits: As the flagship line of the Japan National Railways (JNR), the Shinkansen was the organization's largest profit-maker and one of only six lines in the entire

single day; after three billion passengers, the Shinkansen has yet to lose a paying customer to a fatal accident.

The original Tokyo-Osaka segment, known in English as the New Tokaido Line, began service on October 1, 1964. The original line was extended to Okayama City in 1972 and to Hakata (Fukuoka), Kyushu, in 1975. Two new Shinkansen were put into service to Morioka, Iwate Prefecture in the Tohoku (Northeast) region and Niigata City on the Sea of Japan in June and November 1982, respectively.

The Shinkansen is part of an ongoing evolution to link Japan's two largest urban

country to operate in the black. Eventually the JNR was broken up and control of the Shinkansen transferred to private regional firms, such as JR Tokai, operating the To-kyo-Osaka route.

The businessmen who know it best take the safety and efficiency of the Shinkansen for granted, but the first encounter for children still carries the same thrill as a first airplane flight. It may have been designed and built 2½ decades ago, but the Hikari limited express is still an impressive sight, about as long as four football fields (400 meters/1,300 ft). Power is supplied by four electric motors per car, giving it a total of

16,000 horsepower. When full, each train carries a total of 1,340 passengers. Along the Tokaido between Tokyo and Osaka, it makes 230 runs a day, for a daily average of over 300,000 passengers.

Although flying time between the two cities is less than 60 minutes, the Shinkansen still handles 80 percent of Tokyo-Osaka traffic. It's simply more convenient.

As the older Shinkansen models are phased out of service, a new breed of deluxe cars is gradually being introduced. The new cars include double-decker first class cars with spacious seats, radio earphone jacks on the armrests, modernized lavatories, and even private compartments. The restaurant-

type dining car has been replaced by a brightly lit cafeteria with a wide variety of packaged foods that passengers purchase and carry back to their seats to eat. Speed has also been slightly boosted, and the journey between Tokyo and Osaka now takes close to 2½ hours.

The Shinkansen has made the Japanese great believers in railways technology, and they are not resting on their laurels. By the beginning of the 21st century, a 500 km/hr

Left, the Shinkansen shoots past Tokyo's Shimbashi Station. **Above**, the bullet-nosed train has brought Tokyo and Osaka closer together.

(310 mph) linear motor car that "floats" above its rails by magnetic levitation is expected to start service between Tokyo and Osaka.

It's (faster than) a Plane!: Almost everyone in Japan has a favorite bullet train story. This writer's favorite goes back to an old article he uncovered while doing research on the development of the Shinkansen prototype.

The tests were performed on a special test track near Odawara City, southwest of Tokyo, and after months of slow-speed runs, engineers finally got the go-ahead to turn on the juice and see what it could do. They did, and on March 3, 1963, the train set a new world speed record for rolling stock, as it soared past the timing device at the speed of 256 km/hr (160 mph).

The emotionally charged event set engineers and spectators cheering when they noticed that overhead, a light airplane sent by a newspaper to photograph the train's run actually fell behind.

Fancy that: There follows some little-known facts about the history and technology of the Japanese railway system:

● The first Shinkansen project was launched in March 1941, but the war forced a two-decade postponement. The present train, however, runs through three of the original tunnels started in 1941.

● There was much initial opposition to the building of the Shinkansen because its design demanded it be built as a wide-gauge (1435 mm/56½ inch) railway, and therefore unable to use track in the existing narrow gauge (1067 mm/42 inch) network. Today, the Shinkansen remain the only wide-gauge trains in Japan.

● The railway was built with a US$80 million loan from the World Bank negotiated in September 1959, paid back precisely on schedule in 1981.

● In the beginning, the Shinkansen was run at slow speeds to allow the rail bed to settle. Only 13 months after it began service, in November 1968, did it officially outstrip the French Mistral to become the world's fastest train at the time, with an average speed of 162.8 km/hr (101.2 mph). The French have since reclaimed the speed record.

● It takes 3 kilometers (1½ miles) to bring it to a halt from its top speed.

● Thousands of Japanese use the Shinkansen to commute to work each day, in spite of fares as high as ¥100,000 a month.

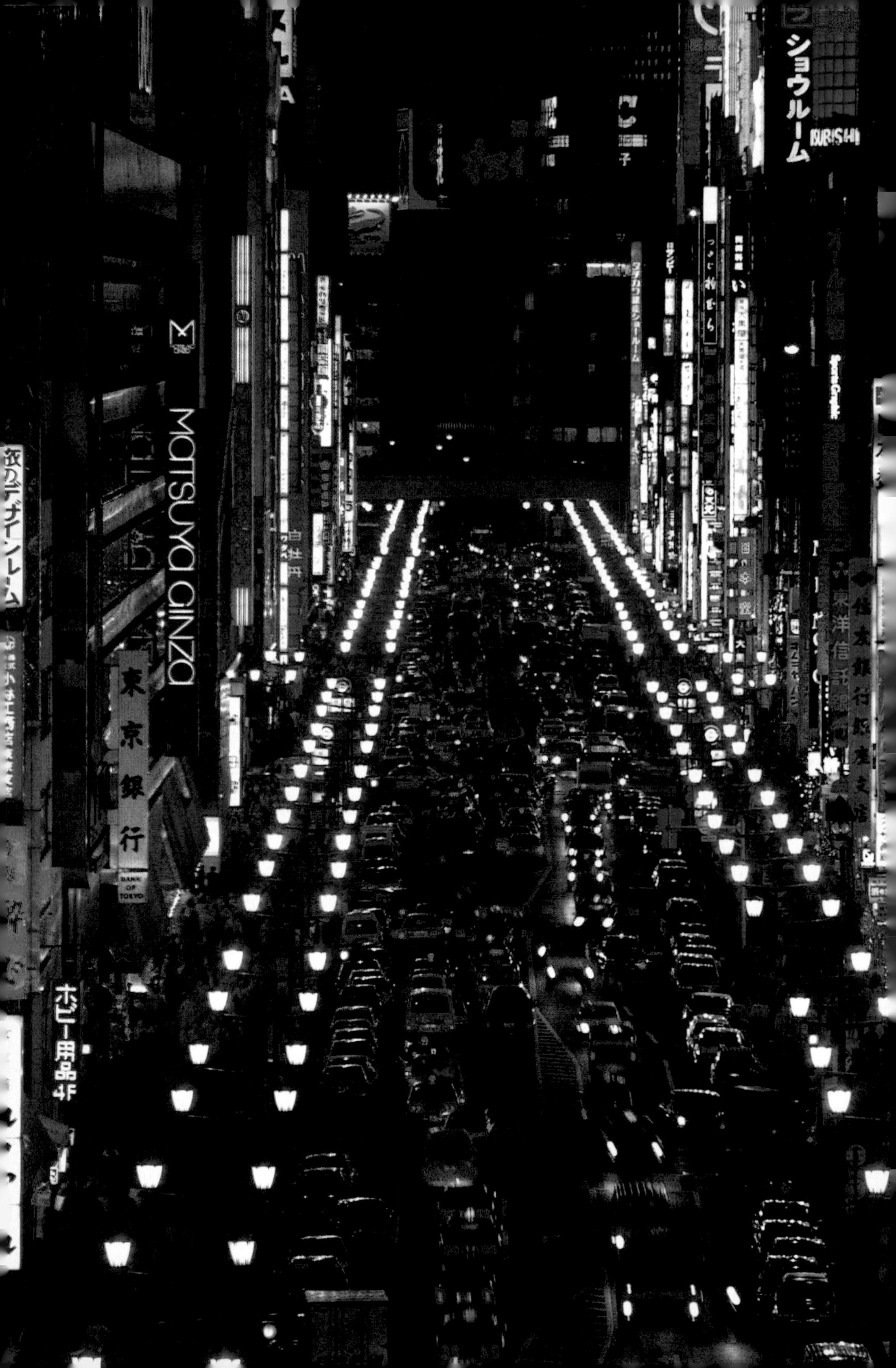
matsuya ginza
東京銀行
ショウルーム
ホビー用品

Newly arrived visitors to Japan who find themselves in an urban entertainment district (such as Tokyo's Ginza, Akasaka or Kanda, or Osaka's Dotombori) for the first time usually knit their brows and exclaim something such as "Good grief! How do all these places stay in business?" Hundreds – thousands! – of bars, pubs, tiny eateries, mammoth restaurants, mini-cabarets, cafes and "snacks" line the streets and alleys, hang out their shingles from every floor of buildings large and small, and generally give these districts the ambience of a high-class (and in some cases not so high-class) amusement park.

A peek inside any of these establishments between 6pm and 11.30pm will answer the question of how they stay in business: they are so jammed packed with patrons, they couldn't afford not to stay in business.

Starting with the middle item on the proverbial night-out list of "wine, women and song," what about them?

Geisha parties? Forget it. These days, such luxuries are the perks of the well-heeled businessman or politician, and outsiders (not just foreigners, but Japanese outsiders as well) are usually not welcome in the few remaining true geisha teahouses.

Houses of ill repute? Forget it. The world's oldest profession has been outlawed in Japan since the late 1950s.

Bar hostesses? Well, yes and no. That is, it's *no* if what you've got in mind involves the subject discussed in the previous paragraph. But it's yes if you mean the age-old Japanese tradition of providing the companionship of *onna* (women) in certain kinds of entertainment establishments, namely the "hostess bar" and the cabaret-style "night club," *and* if you have the money.

Speaking of money, it should be mentioned that, in Japan, companies can (and do) make use of tax write-offs on as much as 45 percent of their gross revenues for "entertainment expenses."

"Hostess bars" have been around for decades, and the "system" has changed very

Left, **Start of a busy evening on Chuo Dori, Ginza's dazzling main street.**

little – except to add zeros after the prices. Another change is that today, it's not at all unusual to find multilingual hostesses (many foreigners among them) working in these bars.

It's a different story for the nightclubs, however. In the 1950s, 1960s and even into the early 1970s there were numerous mammoth-size cabaret-style nightclubs (the Queen Bee and Ginbasha in the Ginza were world-famous, for example, as were Mama Cherry's Copa in Akasaka, where Dewi Sukarno once graced the tables). The dance orchestras were extremely good, the champagne and good Scotch flowed like, well, champagne and good Scotch, and the stage shows were nothing short of fabulous, outdoing Paris, Berlin and even Las Vegas for pomp, splendor and pulchritude. As many as 500 "lovely hostesses" lined up at the entrance to greet the patrons, each miniskirted, bright-eyed and wearing a large plastic disc with a number on her bosom.

Now many of the large cabarets have virtually disappeared. Huge payrolls, inflated land values and a perhaps more discriminating fun-hungry market have forced them out of business.

Join the hoi polloi: Also dwindling down to a precious few, for the same reasons but on the other end of the scale, are the grungy scrums of slummily lovable little eateries and drinkeries that once attracted everyone from delivery boys to board directors. A few of these alley haunts still exist in Tokyo (as in Osaka and other cities) and can be fun to explore; by the way, you need not worry about "street crime" in these dingy places (but neither should you walk about with ¥10,000 notes hanging out of your pockets), nor need you be too concerned with getting ptomaine poisoning (though you'd be well advised to stay away from the "fresh" oysters).

One typical "low-rent" area in Tokyo is Yūrakuchō (near Ginza), in the area along the sides of and behind the overhead train tracks between the Hankyu department store and the Imperial Hotel. Here you will find rows of stalls sitting literally in the street, where *yakitori*, other simple dishes, bottled beer, and other beverages are served at very reasonable prices. It's great fun, especially if it's not too cold, and an atmosphere where friendships blossom freely.

Different in that it has no outdoor atmosphere, but similar in its slummy camaraderie, is another low-rent area called Shonben Yokocho near the west exit of Shinjuku Station. Jostling together here, with a reed-like walkway between their tawdry ranks, are tiny shops that specialize in everything from eel parts, offbeat variety meats and noodle dishes to *yakitori* and other Japanese pub foods.

If the Shonben Yokocho clientele includes many of those you'd find by the train tracks in Yurakucho – company employees and shopworkers, for example – it also contains

a liberal sprinking of students, scholars, writers and even an occasional *yakuza*. None of these places has, of course, any sort of formal entertainment. But if people-watching is your thing, go for it.

O Solo You-o!: English-speaking foreigners usually mispronouce it as "carioca" or "care-a-OK" or some such mishmash, but actually the word *karaoke* (new Japanese shorthand for "empty orchestra") is pronounced *ka* (as in a crow's call), *ra* (as in a football cheer), *o* (as in orchestra) and *ke* (as in K-Mart).

What it *means* is a little better understood abroad – America, Australia, parts of Europe, Africa, Southeast Asia and South America and wherever else it has caught on as the latest in do-it-yourself entertainment, and that is, in short, sing-along.

The concept of *karaoke* has been around almost since the beginning of recorded music, or at least since multi-tracking: you make a recording of a song, with the instrumentation intact, but *sans* the singer's voice. But around 1965, enterprising record companies began pushing the idea of using these recordings – originally cut to help novice professional singers perfect their art – in bars, "snacks" and other drinking establishments too small or poor to offer live entertainment.

Operators of such places would then play the song over a P.A. system; and one of the patrons would grab a mike, wait for the downbeat, then sing the lyrics, reading them (if necessary) from a songbook provided by the record company. Today, in the more modern places, the lyrics are scrolled, bouncing-ball style, across the bottom of a TV screen whose picture, generated from a laserdisc player, provides visual accompaniment as well.

Will you be that sing-alone singer? If you're mike-shy, steer clear of *karaoke* bars, because regular patrons don't like party-poopers very much. On the other hand, if you want to take part in what has become Japan's most popular nightlife activity, drop in anywhere you see the sign of a cartoon parrot with a mike in his hand and the word "LaserDisc" in English. This is actually a trademark of the Pioneer Corporation. who make most of the laserdisc players (this is not a plug: Kenwood, Hitachi and other firms make them, too, while Toshiba EMI, CBS/Sony and virtually all other record labels provide the software for them), but it also serves as your guide to an evening of fun.

Many karaoke and laser-karaoke places stock "empty orchestra" tunes having foreign-language lyrics (and appropriate read-along lyric sources) and, even if the repertoire contains only *You Are My Sunshine* and *Yesterday*, your performance of one of the songs, will be insisted upon, loudly applauded and very, very much appreciated by all.

Also, by the way, in most karaoke spots a couple of hours, several drinks, a few snacks and enough singing to last you a while should run you about ¥5,000 per person, tops.

Eat, Drink and Eat: Having an exciting night out in Japan doesn't *have* to mean going out to drink, but the fact is that most of the nightlife involves at least the opportunity to drink alcoholic beverages. Particularly interesting, though, is that throughout Japan, "just-plain-bars" are almost non-existent (except, of course, in Western-style hotels). This is because there is an old, deeply rooted and still observed "taboo" against drinking alcoholic beverages without eating some kind of food along with them – and this doesn't mean just beer nuts and a Polish sausage or two, but an endless parade of delicious side dishes ranging from a couple of boiled "sugar-potatoes" in *miso* or a small plate of *tofu* to an entire salt-broiled mackerel, squid or octopus.

nese-style snack dishes and the wife looks after the customers. Clientele tend to be regulars (*otokui*) whose individual preferences the mama-san comes to know well. The beverage list invariably includes Japanese beer and *sake*, usually the owner's favorites, and usually whisky and *shochu* (a vodka-like spirit made from a wide range of ingredients).

The friendly, intimate, and sometimes bibulously boisterous atmosphere of izakaya makes them the ideal place to enjoy sake. Although they are altogether unaffected and unpretentious places, they do have a pecking order of sorts. Regulars may be seen seated closest to the master, who may even hold preferred seats (*kamiza*) for them,

One type of place that provides the best opportunity to sample this drinking style is the *izakaya*, a phenomenon that first appeared during the Edo Era. The original izakaya was the brainstorm of *sake* dealers who placed tables and benches in their shops to increase profits by selling laborers and other have-nots cheap *sake* served in *masu*, or small square wooden boxes.

Today's izakaya is small, intimate, and often a mom-and-pop business where typically the husband prepares the various Japa-

while other customers take seats farther away (*shimoza*) along the counter or at the small tables along the far wall.

One of the better traditional alternatives to the ordinary izakaya is the *taishu-sakaba*, (literally "mass *sake* house," a reference to its much greater floor area). Taishu-sakaba lack the intimacy of izakaya, but their prices are usually lower because they cater to a much larger number of customers at one time. What they lack in cozy ambience they more than make up for with their quite extensive menus and sense of energy. Both food and drink can be of considerable variety, and the presence of so many kinds of people

Left, the "pink" show area at Kabukicho. **Above**, Tokyo-style pub.

drinking and eating so many things so indulgently at one time, amidst a steady din, is curiously absorbing.

Then there is the so-called *nomiya* (drinking place), a traditional small bar, so to speak, but by no means a bar in the Western sense. It can be any type of small Japanese-style drinking establishment that also serves simple snacks, and the term itself is often used loosely to fit places of that general description. Typically it would not have *zashiki* (tatami rooms), whereas izakaya might have. Without exception it is cozy, pleasant and reasonably priced. Small shops serving yakitori and *oden*, the hodge-podge Japanese stew, are among the various types of nomiya.

steams and clinks away beneath a tattered awning while its master cooks *ramen* noodles, oden or yakitori and pours beer and cheap *sake* and *shochu*. Its customers are anyone who still happens to be around at a very late hour or someone who found its wares irresistible on the way home. Intimacy is the night stall's stock in trade. Four or five people sit on the short bench flanking it. All others stand. Inevitably, everyone gets to talking, and drinking, and it's all good fun.

Incidentally, this is as good a place as any to bring up one of the *musts* regarding drinking manners. Unless you are drinking alone (not a good idea anywhere), be *absolutely* sure to keep your eye on your companion's

Somewhere in between pure izakaya and nomiya are the raunchy *akachochin* (red lantern) holes in the wall, usually found on back alleys near suburban train stations and identified (hence the name) by red lanterns hanging in the doorway. Here, you can grab a bowl of hot noodles, maybe some oden or – at least – another "just-one-more" tote of booze before toddling off home.

Then, to really hit the bottom of the scale (but only in style, not necessarily in quality), consider the ubiquitous night stall. Tucked away against one side of a mall closed for the evening, or parked (illegally) at the not-too-well-lit curb of a major thoroughfare, it

glass, *sake* cup or *masu* (wooden *sake* box); if the level of liquid in it falls below the very brim, do not fail to grab the bottle, the jug or whatever and fill it back up.

Failing to observe this common courtesy – even if you have to come nearly to blows to do it – is a severe breach of etiquette, and obliges you to commit harikiri on the spot.

Well, that's an exaggeration. But, actually, fights over the bottle and who pours whose drink can be quite comical – and they do get rough, particularly when the drinkers have poured or been poured one too many. Likewise, a complicated routine is also often involved wherein the host *must* pour the first round, the senior guest the next, and so on down the line. If someone isn't drinking and their glass remains full to the top, it is polite to insist that they drink up.

So what do you do if you're the one who's had enough and don't feel like another? It's easy: let someone fill your glass, then, while they're watching, pretend to take a sip from it, and ostentatiously set it aside, smile widely, grab the bottle and turn the tables.

To put an even finer point on this arcane but important subject, it is also the obligation of the host to make sure his or her guests do not drink too much, or if they do, to see they get home safely. This cultural contradiction is just one of many in Japan.

Boogie Till the Cows Go Home: Granted, eating/drinking establishments – even karaoke places after a while – can leave a bit more to be desired in the way of entertainment. If live entertainment is what you want, the numerous "live houses" in Tokyo, Osaka and other major cities is where you'll find it. The Japanese term *raibu hausu* ("live house") is self-explanatory, if a little odd, and covers establishments ranging from simple, cozy little piano bars to large jazz

Left, live music at The Ink Stick. **Above, Morgan makes a pit-stop at a fast-food noodle shop in Akasaka.**

clubs, chanson bars, ethnic-music joints and beyond. For jazz, one of Tokyo's oldest and most famous (also most funky) is the jazz-oriented Pit Inn in a Shinjuku back-alley basement (there's an up-scale branch in Roppongi); one of Tokyo's newest (and least funky) is the *tres*-expensive Blue Note in Roppongi. What these two places – and the many in between – have in common is the live-house "system," usually involving a cover charge (varying by the clout of the featured performers) that includes two drinks, a small snack and the right to enjoy one "set" of musical performance.

Sometimes combined with the "live house" (i.e., offering live entertainment) is the "keep bar," (also rarely a "bar" in the Western sense) wherein patrons are allowed to become "members" by purchasing a bottle of whatever (at retail-plus price) from them, leaving it on the premises, and on each visit, paying an extra charge for setups of mix and ice. Most "keep bars" impose some sort of time limit on one's "membership" in the system, usually three months: if a bottle isn't emptied by then, its "owner" is obliged to buy another or seek his entertainment elsewhere.

Discotheques in Japan are somewhat identical to those in other countries – they range from the bare-bones basics to the most opulent imaginable, they all play the same music over the same sorts of ear-splitting sound systems you'd find elsewhere, nearly all levy a cover charge and/or a one-drink minimum, and most are patronized by an "in-crowd" that may take several visits to penetrate.

Japanese discos can, on the other hand, be very, different indeed from those you may be used to. For instance, if you are Japanese, you will rarely go to a disco unaccompanied – the Japanese "herd instinct" at work. There's also the curious habit of disco habituees in Japan of vanishing *en masse*, leaving the dance floor dismally empty, around 11.30pm to catch that last train.

This doesn't mean you can't drop by a disco alone and boogie till dawn if you want to: the number of all-night, all-comers places is increasing, particularly in the more "international" nightlife districts such as Tokyo's Roppongi. But on the other hand, if you want to experience typical, contemporary Japanese nightlife, you're better off giving the discos a pass and heading for an izakaya, "live house" or karaoke bar instead.

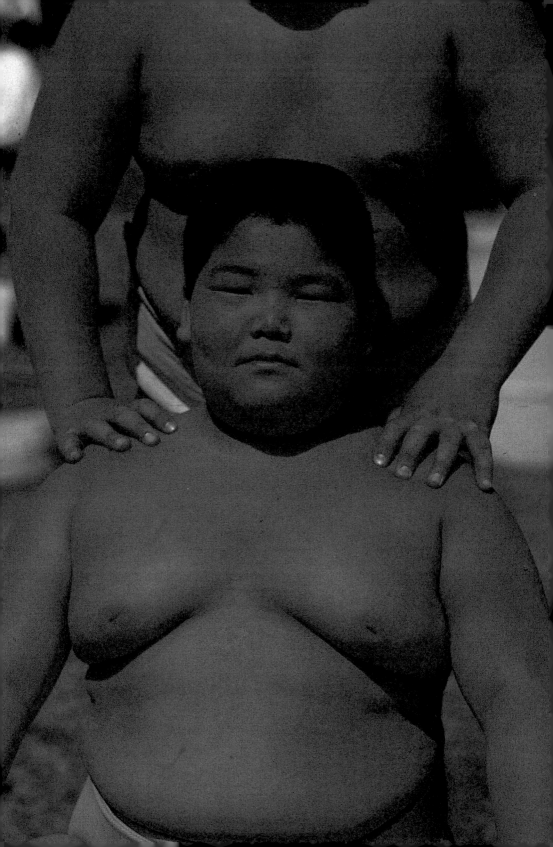

SUMO: WHEN WORLDS COLLIDE

Although baseball is truly the athletic obsession of Japan, occupying much more of the time and energy of the country's young athletes, sumo (pronounced "s'mo") remains the "official" national sport. This is fitting, partly because of its history, dating back as far as the third century, and its hoary, quasi-religious ritualism – but mostly because, in Japan, it's a more exciting sport.

History and culture are the reasons most visitors consider the sumo arena an obligatory stop in Japan. However, a warning: unless you really like sports – especially wrestling – you might find your sumo pilgrimage costly, somewhat uncomfortable and – after an hour or so – boring. The thrifty alternative is sumo on TV (NHK, 3pm–6pm during tournaments; a commercial channel also airs highlights later in the evening). The tube captures all the pageantry, from a better vantage point, and with instant replay.

Of course it is also possible to go in person. The most likely venue is the **Ryogoku Kokugikan**, Japan's national sumo arena, located at Ryogoku Station on the JR Sobu Line in Tokyo. Of the six annual *basho*, each 15 days long, three occur in Ryogoku, in January, May and September. Other basho are in Osaka in March, Nagoya in July and Fukuoka in November.

Tickets are usually available in Tokyo. Ringside and box seats require "connections," because they are permanently controlled by teahouses and corporations. Know someone? If not, queue up at the box office before 9am for tickets to the day's matches. Upper deck seats – with good sightlines in one of the world's best-designed, best-lit sports arenas – are ¥1,000 to ¥4,700.

The prestige seats, in which four persons occupy one standard tatami mat, cost, by comparison, at least ¥25,000 per person. The teahouse provides food, drinks and souvenirs, but no relief for the inevitable sore back and numbed legs.

Sumo, as court entertainment, dates back to the 8th century, when wrestlers drawn from army ranks fought to amuse the Imperial Court in Kyoto. It evolved over the years, mainly as gladiatorial entertainment. Sumo was formalized as a sport during the 17th century. The parades, costumes and rituals preserve a long tradition and nicely embellish the universal passion for man-to-man combat.

Crash Course: Before you visit the Ryogoku Kokugikan, a crash course in sumo history and terminology is helpful, though

optional. Books in English on sumo culture are abundant. The sounds and colors, the costumes of referees, ushers and wrestlers (*rikishi*), and the crowd are interesting, however, without any books. The spectacle of the wrestling itself, involving huge (yes, really fat), almost naked men, is simple, powerful and engaging.

The main features you need to know: the rikishi wrestle on a raised square of mud and sand, the *dohyo*. A circle within the square, the *tawara*, is made of rice-straw bales. The wrestler's goal is to force his opponent to touch the surface of the dohyo with some part of his body (other than the feet), or set

Preceding pages, when push comes to shove in the *sumo* ring. **Left**, budding star. **Above right**, the recently retired Grand Champion Chiyonofuji.

foot out of the ring. This happens very fast. The average sumo bout lasts no longer than six seconds.

A Good Belt Grip: Few holds are barred, but tradition frowns on the rikishi who grabs his opponent below the waist. The waist itself is wrapped in sumo's only garment, a belt called the *mawashi*. The most dignified (and probably dullest) winning technique – called *yorikiri* – requires a two-handed grip on the *mawashi*, which allows the winner to lift and push his opponent out. *Tsuridashi* is a more dramatic cousin of yorikiri, in which the winner literally carries his foe (kicking and helpless) over the edge.

Much of sumo lore concentrates on the

ily on a two-handed belt grip – or *morozashi*. A good belt grip creates a myriad of possibilities, the most artistic of which are the sudden twisting, one-armed belt throws (*uwatenage* and *shitanage*) that flip the loser, like an up-ended turtle, onto the sand.

It's possible – and spectacular! – to execute one of these powerful throws with no belt grip at all, but this requires a blend of superior upper-body strength, good leverage, and perfect timing.

Arm throws, as these are known, are preferred among smaller rikishi, who compensate for their lack of size with cleverness, muscle and technical virtuosity.

Not all sumo wrestlers are fat. Although

names and method of these winning "holds." In fact, a better way to enjoy your day of sumo is to watch each rikishi's style of attack, just after the *tachiai*, or "face-off." Most violent is the rikishi who prefers *tsuppari* (open-handed boxing) and *hikate* (head-slapping). This furious charge is risky but devastating and it works, usually ending in a "push-out" or *oshidashi* – as the loser lands among delighted spectators in the first row of "sand seats."

More conventional are rikishi who stay low and reach out quickly for a grip on the belt. Like baseball players, wrestlers are left- or right-handed, though some depend heav-

the biggest rikishi in history (a Hawaiian named Salevaa Atisanoe, whose sumo name is Konishiki) has reached 253 kg (557 lb), most grand champions have ranged in weight from 110–150 kg (220–330 lb). There are active rikishi in sumo's upper two divisions as small as 90 kg (198 lb). Sumo fans delight in seeing one of these mighty mites outmaneuver opponents sometimes twice their size.

Big or little, if you watch the rikishi's hands from the very moment of tachiai, you will learn quickly the nuances of what seems, at first glance, a brute sport. The other key is to watch the rikishi's feet. As in basketball, a wide stance is good defense. Cross your legs and in seconds you're beat.

Levels of the Game: The rikishi who consistently keeps his hands and feet in good position inevitably moves up the long, grinding path to sumo's upper divisions.

Just as they come in all sizes, rikishi come in a range of abilities. The top sumo rank is *yokozuna*, or Grand Champion, and there are rarely more than four active yokozuna at any time. Just below is the rank of *ozeki*. Both yokozuna and ozeki retain their rank, even after a losing record in a basho. After two straight losing basho, however, ozeki are demoted and yokozuna are pressured to retire. Very few have refused. ("Forced" re-

the ranks; *makekoshi* (eight or more losses) on the other hand means demotion.

Funny, Frantic and Surprising: During a basho, the action begins about 10 a.m., with lower-ranked wrestlers in the *makushita* (or below the curtain) divisions. These matches are brief, with little of the muscle-flexing, glaring, salt-throwing (to purify the dohyo) and gamesmanship that even a novice fan associates with sumo. At about 3 pm, matches in the *juryo* (second-highest) divsion begin. Only juryo and makunouchi wrestlers get to wear silk mawashi in bright colors, in contrast to the brown cotton of *makushita* wrestlers.

Makunouchi matches present sumo's full

tirement, by the way, is no disgrace; in many cases, yokozuna prepare themselves for such an eventuality well in advance, and even welcome it.)

The top division is called *makunouchi* (or inside the curtain). Here, the descending ranks below ozeki are *sekiwake*, *komusubi* and a large group of *maegashira*, the latter being the rank-and-file wrestlers. A rikishi who achieves *kachikoshi* – at least eight wins out of the 15 bouts he must fight during a given tournament – moves automatically up

suspense, with rikishi lumbering forth and sizing each other up as many as five times – each time throwing salt as they step out. Usually, makunouchi wrestlers are bigger, more mature, more skilful and earn more than their counterparts in juryo and maku–shita. This does not always, however, guarantee more entertainment: some of the lower-division matches can be funny, frantic and unpredictable.

At all levels, sumo is a grand entertainment and, if one watches carefully, an intricate, elegant and intensely dramatic sport. It's definitely more fun for the spectator than Japanese baseball.

Left, *tachiai*, **the start of a match. Above, flags decorate the outside of a sumo hall.**

To better appreciate Japan's martial arts, one might begin with a simple language lesson. One of the key words is "*do*," pronounced like "dough" but with a shorter vowel, and usually translated as "way" or "path." *Kendo* is thus "the way of the sword," and implies that the tenets of the sport should have an effect on the way one lives one's life. *Do* is also the root word in "*dojo*," which is the place one studies – and practices – a martial art, and in *budo*, the general term for all Japanese martial arts.

Then there is the most important "*do*" of all, as in *bushido*, or "the way of the samurai" – a code followed during the feudal eras, and to some extent even today, by Japan's elite "warrior" class – and one covering far more than merely one's behavior in battle.

Among the *budo* the samurai would have had to learn: *ba-jutsu* (literally, "horse art," *atemi waza* (a relative of karate), *bo-jutsu* (staff fighting – a little *outré* for the samurai), *hojo-jutsu* (binding the opponent), *jitte-jutsu* (techniques with the iron truncheon used as the badge – and weapon – of the Edo Era policeman), *kama-jutsu* (techniques with the scythe), *ken-jutsu* (both one- and two-sword schools existed), *kyu-jutsu, naginata-jutsu, shuriken-jutsu* (throwing knives and deadly ninja "throwing stars"), *so-jutsu* (spear work), and *teppo-jutsu* (matchlock gunnery).

It's a wonder some of the samurai found time to write poetry…

"Hard" versus "Soft": There is no clear-cut lexicon here. Some of the *budo* learned by the *samurai* have been modified into sports, and some of the things that qualify today as *budo* (e.g., *judo* and *aikido*) did not exist when the *samurai* were defining their defensive skills. As some do not use weapons, and no one gets hurt, they might not even qualify as "martial."

At any rate, "*jutsu*," as you may have guessed from the above, means "art." The *jutsu* may have been the more subtle parts of a holistic study; or perhaps the distinction is not but the imagination of modern martial arts historians trying to justify the terminological difference.

Some claim that one may adopt many "*jutsu*" but only one "*do*." This may have been true in the distant past, but today it's not uncommon to find people who are "black belts" in two or three completely different forms. In fact, most of what is called a "*do*" today was historically referred to as a "*jutsu*." At any rate, there are opinions and arguments (and evidence) for either side of the issue. Make your own choice.

It may be said, and not without some justification, that most Japanese martial arts have been diluted; that which was once practiced earnestly for survival – kill or be killed – have become a sport. Punches are pulled, form is emphasized, swords are blunt, padding is worn.

As an example, watching a *jidai-geki* or "period drama" on television and seeing a scene of an Edo kendo *dojo*, the difference between that and what goes on today at the *dojo* around the corner are surprising. In old *kenjutsu*, the hard, solid wooden swords called *bokken* are used, and there is no padding. Shots to the ribs hurt. Shoulder bones are fractured. Concussions suffered. Compare that with the kendo dojo of today; students wear fiberglass cuirasses, heavy fabric tassets and padded gloves, and bulky steel and fabric "helmets," and the swords are made sectional, to cause no injury.

There are also so-called "soft" forms (e.g., aikido) where the actual idea is to cause no injury, and then there are hard forms (e.g., karate), where any injury occuring to the opponent is just tough luck. Martial arts may likewise be divided into weaponless and weapon forms, but even in *karate* – which literally means "empty hand" – weapons can be used in advanced levels of study.

The following is a brief look at some of the better known (and undoubtedly more interesting) families of Japanese martial arts. In each family there are several – as many as a dozen or more – schools, each with their own

new form coalesced into what is now known as aikido.

One's principle energy, the "*ki*," meets with that of the opponent to bring about victory. The very name – the way of meeting "*ki*" – explains the whole basis of the sport.

Aikido is probably the best purely self-defensive form to have emerged from the great smorgasbord of Japanese unarmed combat. Although injuries may be inflicted, the idea is not to do so – it is merely to discourage or briefly disable (through pain) the opponent.

Karate, on the other hand (no pun intended), aims to actually cause damage, first and last, with the hands and feet, making it

lineage, teachings, traditions and objectives.

The Many Forms of Budo: Aikido is often compared to judo, as it is a "soft" form emphasizing throws and using the opponent's strength and attacks against him. It originated during the Kamakura Era, but like many martial arts, despite the veneer of antiquity, did not reach its present recognized form until fairly recently. During the 1920s and 1930s, Ueshiba Morihei took what he knew from various defensive schools and his

Left, foot for thought at a *karate* competition. **Above**, *kendo* practitioner demonstrates the proper stance.

more a truly offensive art than judo or aikido, which are more passively defensive. Perhaps the best known of all, karate is actually a relative newcomer to the world of the martial arts. True, it has a long history, but in many forms, and with many names. It came to Japan from Okinawa in the 1920s, though it first gained hold there in the 17th century. It had been developed as a form of self-defense for the unarmed (in an age when only certain classes were allowed to bear weapons) against a typically armed opponent. Its characteristics are sharp chops with the empty hand and kicks.

Its potential for injury – and original intention for inflicting same – also makes karate less likely to be considered a sport, although there are schools that practice so-called full contact karate with padded boots and gloves and protective gear, scoring with "points" for touches. Some, however, disdain this as not true karate.

While karate is most certainly of plebian origins, judo comes from samurai stock, where it could be, in addition to a great moral and physical conditioner, an excellent form of combat when accidentally disarmed in the field. It reached its peak in the 18th century under the Tokugawa *bakufu*.

Today there are schools that practice armored wrestling, in which the participants

close combat) and its popularity has virtually killed the practice of ju-jutsu.

Judo was the first martial art of Japan to gain great popularity in the West. With its concentration on throws and pins, it was ideally suited as self-defence regardless of age, sex and size. Of all the martial arts native to Japan, judo is the only one to have become recognized as an Olympic sport, when it first appeared (not surprisingly) at the Tokyo Olympiad in 1964.

Iaido (the initial "I" is pronounced "e" as in "easy") is often taught alongside kendo in the same dojo, for they are both sword arts. Iaido is called by some "the fast draw," but it more accurately encompasses drawing the

dress up in actual suits of armor and grapple with one another – surely the closest thing to the real thing that there is in the judo/ju-jutsu class of martial arts.

Judo as it is known today was created in 1882 by Kano Jigoro, who – like Ueshiba Morihei would do nearly half a century later for aikido – drew upon his knowledge of several different forms of unarmed combat from his study in many schools of *ju-jutsu*. His combination of physical training techniques and combat techniques (in which little risk of injury existed) advanced judo into the category of sport (ju-jutsu was definitely not a sport but a way of survival in

blade and cutting, in as quick and fluid a motion as humanly possible.

The first school to begin the quick draw technique was (probably) Isasa Chosai's in 1460, when it was called *iaijutsu*. Then, its purpose was to dispatch the enemy – quickly. Modern iaido was begun by Hayashizaki Shigenobu in around 1600. The school he founded was called *batto-jutsu*, which is still practiced by some dedicated "hardliners" today.

In batto-jutsu, cutting techniques are a major portion of the work, and some of the flashier folks one may have seen cutting green bamboo, rolled up matting, or tatami on edge, were likely to have been expert batto-jutsu practitioners.

Kendo may be described as Japanese fencing. While basically accurate, the differences between kendo and fencing are astounding. Western fencing is considered a dignified, quiet and refined sport; those seeing a kendo practice session for the first time often express surprise at the apparent rowdiness as the "fencers" form two opposing sides and come together in what appears to be a grand mêlée of shouting out targets and grunts.

The most famous swordsman in the history of Japan was doubtlessly Miyamoto Musashi (1584–1645). His fame was spread by the phenomenal success of *A Book of Five Rings*, his treatise on sword techniques. For some inexplicable reason, it became an incredible international best-seller in the 1970s, when it was adopted by corporate executive types as a manual of how to succeed in Japanese business.

With advice such as "Do not let the enemy see your spirit," the book became such a hit that rumors have it that a popular American talk show host even tried to book the author of this phenomenal book as a guest, and had to be taken aside and told that the author had died 300 years earlier.

Kyudo is Japanese archery. Like "conventional" Western archery (which also is practiced in Japan and has a separate following and governing organization), the idea is to hit the bull's eye, but kyudo puts considerable emphasis on form, so much so that it may be said that it is of more value to release the arrow with perfect form and miss the target than to make a bull's eye and be sloppy about it.

One of the sports related to kyudo is *yabusame*, in which mounted archers, dressed in Kamakura Era hunting togs, ride a horse at full gallop down a course and release three arrows at three record album jacket-sized targets.

The sport is now invariably tied to Shinto, and is practiced in conjunction with shrine festivals. Actor Mifune Toshiro is said to be a great fan – if not actually a practitioner – of yabusame. There was an early cousin of yabusame in which mounted samurai archers would chase after wild dogs in a large pen and shoot at them, but that was outlawed (mercifully) centuries ago.

Naginata-jutsu is a martial art practiced almost exclusively by women today. The *naginata* is essentially a halberd, and it evolved over the Momoyama years into the weapon used to guard the house. In *jidaigeki*, one often sees a squad of women in kimono, their sleeves tied back, patrolling Edo Castle with halberds at the ready.

Ninpo (literally "the law of stealth and endurance," also called *ninjutsu*) is one of the most romantic of the martial arts of Japan. It has been the star of more movies than any other martial art save China's *kung*

fu. It is also one of the least useful of the martial arts still studied and practiced. Today there are many different ninja organizations, and most are hopelessly romanticized in nature.

Today there are many recognized schools of ninpo, although historically it was the individual clans and their distinctive, but secret, methods of combat that became what we now know as the martial arts action in a Kosugi Sho film.

Ninpo, however, is really a blanket term not unlike budo, as the ninja actually had to master several jutsu to make the grade – to say nothing of the business of staying alive.

Left, exercises at an elementary school. **Above right**, the ancient art of archery.

Of all the many kinds of sports – traditional and "imported" – enjoyed in Japan, baseball is by far the dominant, popular on the high school, college and industrial league levels as well as at the professional rank. High-school baseball fever grips the nation for two weeks in summer as tournaments are held at the Hanshin Tigers Koshien Stadium in March and August, televised nationally. In addition, millions of Japanese play baseball or softball at the sandlot level with friends, neighbors or co-workers, when they are not playing or watching some other sport.

Soccer and tennis are picking up interest as participant sports, especially among youngsters, and the stereotypical Japanese passion for golf does have basis in fact, although expensive green fees and hard-to-get weekend tee-times restrict golfers from playing often.

In professional golf, Japan's top players rank among the best in the world, with Okamoto Ayako a regular on the Ladies Professional Golfers Association tour and Aoki Isao and Ozaki "Jumbo" Masashi frequent competitors in USPGA tournaments.

That's not all. Japanese interest is increasing in American football, basketball, ice hockey, volleyball, bowling, skiing, ice skating, swimming, horse racing, track and field, marathon running, badminton and just about any other sport you can think of.

But all this notwithstanding, baseball remains the winner, so to speak.

Big League Bonanza: When American missionaries began teaching baseball to college students in Tokyo in 1912, they could not have realized how popular it was to become in Japan.

Yakyu, as baseball is called in Japanese, rivals sumo as the national sport. The 12-team, two-league professional baseball system is a money-making industry, drawing more than 15 million spectators to stadiums in all the major Japanese cities each season.

Millions more watch on national television and train commuters devour the pages of Japan's daily national sports newspapers on their way to work each morning from

Left, stepping up to the plate at Seibu Stadium.

April through October for details of the previous night's baseball league action. To put it mildly, Japan is a baseball-crazy country, probably even more so than the United States.

The game enjoyed a good deal of popularity after the first professional team, the Yomiuri Giants, was formed in 1934. Professional play began shortly thereafter and the sport grew until World War II virtually put an end to baseball in the country for two reasons: first, the young men who made up the playing rosters were needed for military service, and second, the language, culture and sports of the enemy – America – were banned by the authorities.

However, as Japan picked up the pieces in the late 1940s, the pro baseball system was also revived. New ballparks were constructed as Japanese cities were rebuilt. In 1950, a two-league alignment was established and the Central and Pacific Leagues in 1989 celebrated 40 years of pro play, progress and profit.

Each league consists of six teams named after the companies which own them. The somewhat more popular Central League includes the Yomiuri Giants and Yakult Swallows of Tokyo, the BayStars of Yokohama, the Chunichi Dragons of Nagoya, the Hanshin Tigers who play near Osaka, and the Hiroshima Toyo Carp, based, of course, in Hiroshima.

The Pacific League is gaining in popularity and its franchises are the Nippon Ham Fighters of Tokyo, the Seibu Lions who are based in the small city of Tokorozawa in Saitama Prefecture just outside the capital, the Lotte Orions of Kawasaki, Osaka's Kintetsu Buffaloes, the Orix Braves who play their games in Nishinomiya between Osaka and Kobe, and the Daiei Hawks team which have made their base in the city of Fukuoka on Kyushu.

Each team plays a 130-game season, as opposed to the 162-game US major league schedule, with opening day the first Saturday in April and the final regular season game played in mid October. The winners of each league pennant meet in the best-of-seven Japan Series, Japan's version of the

World Series, which begins in the third week of October.

Superstars: The reason for the Central League's overwhelming popularity is the presence of the almighty Yomiuri Giants, Japan's answer to the New York Yankees (in better days). The Giants are Japan's first, favorite and most successful team, having won 34 league pennants and 17 Japan Series titles, including an amazing nine straights between 1965 and 1973.

Those were the years during which superstars Nagashima Shigeo and Oh Sadaharu starred for the Giants. Nagashima, a great third baseman, was known as the "Golden Boy" and is considered the most popular

ber) and Akiyama, the centerfielder, had his shirt number changed from 24 to the 1 worn by Oh.

Hired Guns: The Japanese rule allowing *gaijin* players in its pro leagues is one of the most interesting aspects of the system. Each Japanese team can list three foreign players on its 60-man roster, which includes the "major league" team and one farm team. Most teams employ two former US major leaguers and one US minor leaguer or a young player from Taiwan who will be assigned to the farm team for development with the hope that he will become a big star in the future.

There are critics who believe the teams

player ever in Japanese pro baseball. Oh, a first baseman whose father was Chinese and mother Japanese, is known as "Japan's Babe Ruth" because he hit 868 home runs during his illustrious career.

The Pacific League has gained more respectability in recent years, though, with the development of the Seibu Lions as a powerhouse team comparable to the once-invincible Giants. The Lions have won six league championships and five Japan Series since 1982 and are led by young stars Kiyohara Kazuhiro and Akiyama Koji.

Kiyohara, the team's first baseman, wears uniform number 3 (Nagashima's old num-

should be allowed to employ as many foreigners as they wish and the rule should be abolished. Others have said gaijin players are not good for Japanese baseball and should be banned.

Most, feel the situation is fine as is, since the colorful American players make the Japanese game that much more interesting but the limit allows it to keep its identity as Japanese. Since the two-league system was begun in 1950, more than 300 foreign players have appeared in the Japanese leagues – some great, some mediocre, some who simply could not adjust to living in Japan or Japanese baseball.

Most Americans who go to Japan are those who had a chance to play in the majors but for one reason or another could not make the most of the opportunity. Forced with the decision to retire or keep trying while drawing a paltry minor league salary, the lure of Japan can prove to be very attractive.

Those lucky enough to be invited to Japan and who decide to come, do so for the money and the chance to prove they can still be productive ballplayers at a level of play higher than the US minors but lower than the major leagues. Lucrative million dollar contracts are to be had and Japanese baseball is definitely big league in terms of fan following and nationwide media coverage.

in 1983 and enjoyed five great years in Osaka before his son's critical illness forced him to retire in May of 1988.

Bass led the Tigers to the Central League pennant and Japan Series title in 1985 and won batting a triple crown that year and again in 1986. He hit 54 homers in 1985, missing by one Oh Sadaharu's single-season record of 55 home runs, set in 1964.

Americans who've played in Japan have included Yomiuri star Warren Cromartie, a former member of the Montreal Expos, who led the Central League in batting with a 378 average in 1989, as the Giants won the pennant and Japan Series. Cromartie was named most valuable player that season.

You don't play before crowds of 56,000 at the AAA level in the US minors, but that's what the Yomiuri Giants draw to each of their home games at the Tokyo Dome.

Among the better ex-American major leaguers who found success in Japanese baseball are Randy Bass, a journeyman first baseman from Oklahoma, who could not forge a career in his home country despite chances with five big league teams. He joined the Central League's Hanshin Tigers

The Japanese take their baseball seriously, whether at the Little League level (left), or in the lucrative Big League (above).

Others are Olix Braves first baseman Boomer Wells, the 1984 Pacific League triple-crown winner and MVP, Kintetsu Buffaloes slugger Ralph Bryant, who slammed 49 homers to lead the Pacific League in 1989, and Hanshin Tigers pitcher Matt Keough, a 15-game winner in 1989 whose father, Marty, also played in Japan for Nankai Hawks in 1968 after a longstanding US major league career.

Root for the Home Team: The farm system in Japan is simple and differs from the American "bush leagues" in that there is only one minor league team per organization, compared with four or five at various levels in the

Japan's sports world was changed forever in March of 1988 with the opening of the nation's first all-weather stadium, the Tokyo Dome or, as it is affectionately nicknamed, "The Big Egg."

The stadium is a 56,000-seat all-purpose facility located in the center of the city and topped by a soft, air cushion-type cover, much like the Metrodome in Minneapolis and the Hoosier Dome in Indianapolis, and cancels the threat of postponing an athletic, cultural or musical event due to bad weather. Costs were an estimated US$75 million, and it took three years to complete. It is now a landmark and tourist draw.

The Big Egg's name is sort of a semi-acronym cost of ¥350,000–¥500,000, depending of course on the day and time. For information, contact (03) 3811-2111 in Tokyo.

Because sports is so popular in Japan, demand for stadiums is quite high. However, because Japanese cities are also critically short of space, the actual number of seats per capita is remarkably low. Nonetheless, Japan, especially Tokyo, does offer some stadiums of unusual, if not always effective, architectural design. For example, there is the Nippon (or Nihon) Budokan, a covered arena originally built for the 1964 Olympics. It was – before the Big Egg existed – the largest indoor stadium in the country. De-

for "Big *E*ntertainment and *G*olden *G*ames" and there is something happening there every day.

Though it's not ideal for music (what stadium is?) The Big Egg is the site of Japan's largest pop/rock bashes. Popular entertainment figures to appear there are Paul McCartney, Michael Jackson, Madonna and the Rolling Stones, and the building has served as a site for a movie audience, motorcycle races, soccer games, auto shows, conventions and many other events.

The Dome also houses the Japan Pro Baseball Hall of Fame, restaurants and souvenir stands. The charge for a tour is ¥700 per person. To experience what it is like to play a game on the artificial turf under the airdome, bring your team and opponents and rent the field for 2¼ hours at a signed on a shape inspired by the "Hall of Dreams" of Nara's famed temple, Horyuji, this huge octagonal building presents quite a number of drawbacks when used for anything but the judo, kendo and other martial arts competitions for which it was intended. For other activities it has to contend with bad sight lines and horrible acoustics.

Far more successful, both visually and acoustically, is the Track & Field Stadium (a part of the National Yoyogi Sports Center) designed by architect Tange Kenzo, also for the 1964 Olympic Games. Its odd, eye-catching shape is the result of Tange's turning a rectangle "inside out" and twisting it upwards – with results that, though modern, convey a very "Japanese" feeling.

US. The 12 minor league teams in Japan are divided into the Eastern and Western Leagues and the games are played strictly for convenience and player development – not for profit.

The system is very much like the varsity-junior setup operated by American high schools in sports such as baseball, football and basketball.

Going to a Japanese baseball game can be a lot of fun and provide a foreign fan with a sample of Japanese culture. Tickets cost between ¥1,000 for unreserved outfield bleacher space to ¥5,000 for the best box-seats to a Giants home game in the atmospheric Tokyo Dome.

Each team has its own rooting section, complete with trumpets, drums and tambourines, headed by cheerleaders paid by the team. Their job is to keep the crowd interested in the game, no matter what the score, but they often provide a monotonous din that would not be tolerated at a game in the American majors.

The Same Rules – Almost: Of course, the rules of Japanese baseball are generally the same as those of its American counterpart. There are, however, several peculiarities. For example, the ball-strike count is reversed in Japan, making a full count 2-3, rather than 3-2, which causes some confusion to the fan of American baseball observing Japanese baseball for the first time.

In Japan there are tie games, the result of a 12-inning or 4-hour time limit necessiated by the fact that most fans travel to and from the games by public transportation which stops running shortly after midnight. If the games were allowed to continue until decided, as they are in America, the crowds of spectators would have to leave early or risk missing a ride home in case of a 20-inning or 6-hour contest.

Noodles & Neckties: A typical crowd is generally mixed with the "salaryman" business people in jackets and ties, sitting quietly in the more expensive infield seats, sipping their beer and eating *obento* box lunches filled with meat and seafood, rice and pickles on the side. The bleacher fans are mostly the less affluent student types, decked out in clothing of their team's colors, dining on some tea and a styrofoam bowl of steaming *udon* noodles.

Japanese pro baseball continues to improve and American major league teams continually have the opportunity to check the level of Japanese play through visits to the Far East every two or three years. Famous teams such as the Los Angeles Dodgers, St. Louis Cardinals, Baltimore Orioles, New York Mets, Cincinnati Reds and Kansas City Royals have made post-season tours throughout the 1960s, 1970s and 1980s, usually with the results being one-sided in favor of the visitors.

Now the tours are limited to seven-game

series pitting US all-star teams against the All-Japan squad. The scores in previous series have been quite close, a fact that inevitably leads to the question of whether America's World Series will ever live up to its name by inviting Japanese teams (and players from other countries) to take part.

No one so far has come up with the answer, but officials on both sides seem to agree it seems unlikely. However, now that the Japanese are showing more power and speed – if not the sheer physical size – in the game, the chances of them becoming more active on the international baseball scene are good, and getting better every season.

Left, Tokyo Dome, known as "The Big Egg." **Above right**, player for the Daiei Hawks gets some good press coverage.

Japan

240 km / 150 miles

PLACES

Strung like cultured pearls in the Western Pacific off the coast of China, Russia and Korea in the Sea of Japan are the 3,900 islands that make up Japan. They are strung between the remote mountainous lands of the north, which look out across small stretches of water to Russia, to the southwest, off Kyushu, where they stretch for 1,000 km (620 miles) until they come within site of Taiwan. Covering a total of 380,000 sq. kilometers (147,000 sq. miles), Japan is the size of Montana, and a little larger than Italy, but twice as populous with more than 120 million residents. And though the metropolitan areas are dense, it is possible to find corners of quiet and solitude.

The main islands, of Hokkaido, Honshu, Shikoku and Kyushu are mountainous, cut through with narrow valleys. Mt. Fuji, the picture postcard, snow-capped landmark, which can be surmounted in the Julay and August "climbing season", is not an active volcano: some 60 mountains on the island are. In this geologically restless land, earthquakes are a further hazard the Japanese have had to prepare themselves against.

The transportation system of Japan is known throughout the world: its city metros require some shoving to get people on board; and the best train system on earth that will take the traveler anywhere on the four main islands with the punctuality to set chronometers by. Wherever the train stops there will be no disappointment. Indeed, as hoped, there will even be exotic, wondrous and unconventional encounters of the unexpected.

The city's capital is on the main island of Honshu, which has the country's 10 largest cities, including Tokyo which sprawls The 11th, Kitakyushi, is on the southern island of Kyushu.

The Places section of *Insight Guide: Japan* divides the country into four main sections: The Kanto centered on the capital, Tokyo, and Yokohama (*page 189*); The Northlands, which takes in northern Honshu and the island of Hokkaido up to La Perousse Strait, shared with Russia (*page 249*); The Kansai, in southern Honshu, which takes in Kyoto, known as "Everybody's favorite city" and Osaka (*page 271*); and The Southlands, taking in Nagasaki and the island of Kyushu (*page 337*).

Preceding pages: Mt. Fuji and the Shinkansen, two of Japan's major symbols; Chiba's rugged coastline has inspired many artists through the ages; early risers at Asakusa Kannon; women's section at an *onsen*.

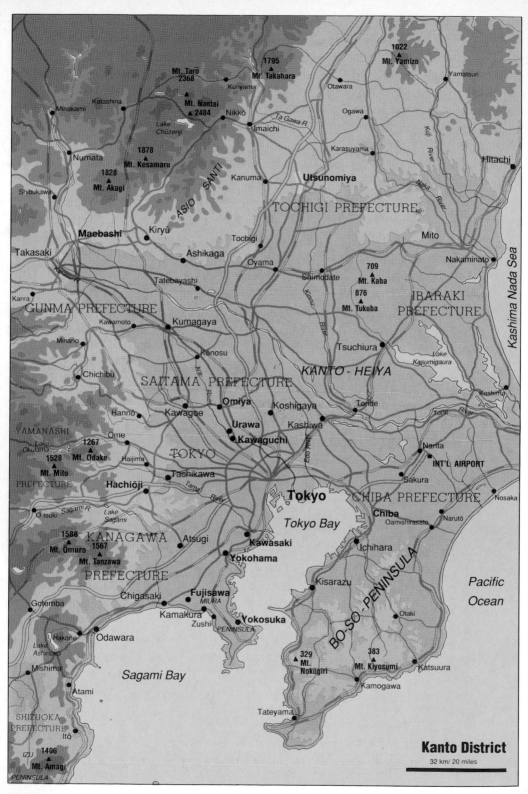

Mt. Yamizo 1022

Yamatsuri

Mt. Taro 2368

1795
Mt. Takahara

Kuriyama

Otawara

Minakami

Katashina

Mt. Nantai 2484

Nikkō

Ta Gawa R.

Ogawa

Hitachi

Lake Chūzenji

Imaichi

Kuji River

1878
Mt. Kesamaru

Numata

Karasuyama

Naka River

Shibukawa

1828
Mt. Akagi

Kanuma

Utsunomiya

TOCHIGI PREFECTURE

ASIO SANTI

Mito

Maebashi

Kiryū

Tochigi

Nakaminato

Takasaki

Ashikaga

Ōyama

Shimodate

709
Mt. Kaba

IBARAKI PREFECTURE

Kanra

Tatebayashi

876
Mt. Tukuba

GUNMA PREFECTURE

Kawamoto

Kumagaya

Kinu River

Minano

Konosu

Tsuchiura

KANTO - HEIYA

Chichibu

SAITAMA PREFECTURE

Lake Kasumigaura

Kashima

Hanno

Omiya

Koshigaya

Toride

Tone River

YAMANASHI

Kawagoe

Urawa

Kashiwa

1267
Ome

Mt. Odake

Haijima

Kawaguchi

Narita

1528
Mt. Mito

TOKYO

Tachikawa

INT'L AIRPORT

PREFECTURE

Hachiōji

Sakura

CHIBA PREFECTURE

Nosaka

O tsuki

Sagami R.

Lake Sagami

Tama River

Tokyo

Chiba

Narutō

1588
Mt. Ōmuro

KANAGAWA

Atsugi

Kawasaki

Tokyo Bay

Oamishirasato

1567
Mt. Tanzawa

Yokohama

Ichihara

BO-SO-PENINSULA

PREFECTURE

Chigasaki

Fujisawa

Kisarazu

Pacific Ocean

Gotemba

MIURA

Kamakura

Zushi

PENINSULA

Yokosuka

Otaki

Hakone

Odawara

329
Mt. Nokogiri

383
Mt. Kiyosumi

Katsuura

Lake Ashinoko

Mishima

Sagami Bay

Kamogawa

Atami

SHIZUOKA PREFECTURE

Itō

Tateyama

IZU

1406
Mt. Amagi

Kanto District

PENINSULA

32 km/ 20 miles

Kashima Nada Sea

188

THE KANTO

Kanto is a large, lumpy circle around the monster metropolis, beginning at Mt. Fuji in the west, through Nikko in the north, down to the southeast through Narita and the Boso Peninsula, across Tokyo Bay to Yokohama and the Miura and Izu Peninsulas on the southwest and back to Fuji. It encompasses six separate, and largish prefectures, and that the total population within that circle is roughly 25 million persons, mean little if you try to ignore the administrative entity called Tokyo-*to* (Metropolitan Tokyo) that sprawls in the center of it all.

The Kanto has a total area of about 1,600 sq. km (600 sq. miles). With Tokyo's population of 12 million or so, Yokohama's nearly 4 million and that of all the adjacent "bedroom prefectures" combined, Kanto's overall population works out to a density of approximately 15,600 persons per square kilometer, three times that of Greater Los Angeles, but not too bad compared to Hong Kong, Bombay, Jakarta or even Mexico City.

Descriptions of the Kanto can be misleading. It is Japan's largest alluvial plain, but it is certainly not an area of wide-open spaces. None of the flat land extends far enough to offer a level, unbroken horizon all the way round the compass. It is also a fact that most of Japan's longest rivers – the Tone, Naka, Ara, Tama, and Sagami – all empty into the Pacific on Tokyo Bay, but Huck Finn would not recognize these concrete-lined trickles, "managed" into almost total obscurity, as rivers at all.

Virtually nothing of interest about the region is recorded until Minamoto no Yoritomo, the first Kamakura Shogun, endowed Tokyo's Asakusa Temple with "90 acres of arable land" around 1180. A village called Edo ("Estuary Gate"), was recorded in 1456, when Edo Castle was built, on the site of the present Imperial Palace, by a man named Ota Dokwan, *Daimyo* of Tamba.

In 1600, the shipwrecked Englishman William Adams became the first foreign "guest" at Edo Palace-nee-Castle, tutoring the soon-to-be shogun. Three years later his pupil, Ieyasu, begun the Tokugawa dynasty. The city suffered history's usual assaults of conflagration, and among its more spectacular disasters was the the last eruption of Mt Fuji in 1707, which covered Edo with 10 centimeters (4 inches) of ash.

Changing Edo's name to Tokyo (Eastern Capital) in 1868 didn't slow the Kanto's steady climb to becoming Japan's richest, most populous and most powerful region. In 1731, Edo's population was more than half a million persons; at the start of the Meiji Restoration, it was nearly two million, second only to London as the world's largest city, but it suffered a calamtous setback in 1923 when the Great Kanto Earthquake claimed 100,000 victims. Although the population of Tokyo proper has stabalized, the population of the region is expected to top 30 million by the 21st century as the urban sprawl spreads.

"Wonder projects" are underway to ease transportation congestion in the region. Among them is the Trans-Tokyo Bay Highway designed to link up the most populous section of the Kanto (the Tokyo-Yokohama strip) with one of its least populous, the Boso Peninsula.

Tokyo

1.0 miles/ 1600 m

ITABASHI-KU

KITA-KU

ARAKAWA-KU

NERIMA-KU

TOSHIMA-KU

Seibu Ikebukuro Line

Tobu Tōjō Line

Hakusan-

Yamanote Line

Komagome Tabata

O-tsuka Dōri Sugamo

Nishi-Nippori

Mejiro

BUNKYO - KU

Kasuga- Dōri Ave.

Takadanobaba

Hibiya- Dōri

Waseda- Dōri

Expressway No. 5

Suidobashi

Higashi-nakano

Chūō Line

Kōenji Nakano

Shin-ōkubo

Iidabashi

Okibanomizu

NAKANO-KU

Ōkubo

Yamate- Dōri

SHINJUKU-KU

Kan

SUGINAMI-KU

Shinjuku

Ichigaya

CHIYODA-KU

Shinjuku-

Dōri Yotsuya

Yoyogi

Ave.

Imperial Palace

Tokyo

Sendagaya

Shinanomachi

Expressway No. 4

Keio Line

Harajuku

MINATO-KU

Shimbashi

Daiichi Keihin Ave.

SHIMOKITAZAWA

SHIBUYA-KU

ROPPONGI

GINZA

CHŪO-KU

Inokashira Line

Aoyama- Dōri

Hamamatsuchō

HARUM

Odakyū Line

Shibuya

SETAGAYA-KU

Expressway No. 3

Yamate- Dōri

Ebisu

Expressway No. 2

Tamachi

Sakurada-Dōri Ave.

Tokyo Bay

Tōyoko Line

MEGURO-KU

Ave.

Meguro

Shinagawa

Expressway No. 1

Keihin Kyūkō Line

Daiichi Keihin

GOTANDA

Mekama Line

O-saki

Hibiya- Expressway No. 2

SHINAGAWA-KU

Jiyūgaoka

✈ Haneda Airport

TOKYO

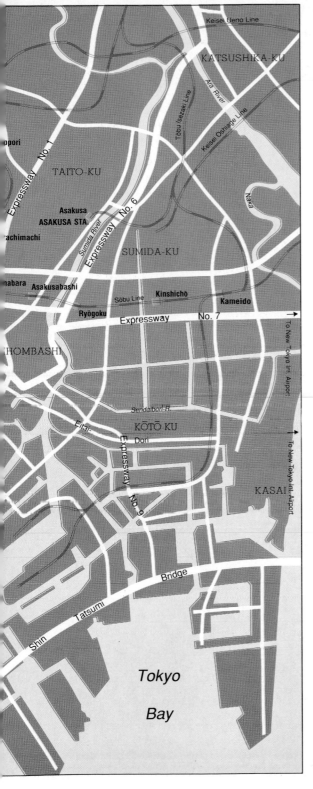

You could explore Tokyo's more "Westernized" parts – such as Akasaka, Shibuya or even Shinjuku – for years and not have a clue that the metropolis still has areas where old Edo is alive and well. Mostly in the north and northeastern regions, these are called, collectively, *shitamachi*. The word literally means "downtown," but then, in the Western sense, "downtown" more properly connotes the Ginza and other, more central locales, so in English we call them "uptown."

If that confuses you, don't fret. The moment you set foot in places like Shibamata, Ueno, Asakusa and even Kanda, you'll know how down-home "uptown" Tokyo can feel.

Shibamata: There is no better place to start a tour of the old Tokyo shitamachi than **Shibamata**. There is little here that can be truly considered tourist; it is essentially a residential neighborhood which has remained for the most part unchanged for decades.

If you are familiar with the Tora-san (*Otokowa Tsuraiyo*) movies – there are more than 40 in the series which started in 1968 – you will recognize the area immediately, for it is here that the hero's family supposedly operates a sweet shop. (Surprisingly, the street really does look like that.)

There is also an old temple, **Taishakuten**. It is Asakusa without the glitzy, tourist-choked feel. Taishakuten was built in 1629, and the ornate carvings ringing its outer walls (covered, unfortunately, by protective netting to keep the birds away) are absolutely gorgeous. Some of the true treats of the neighborhood are the stores lining the street from tiny Shibamata Station to the temple. Recommended Shibamata specialties are *dango* (rice dumplings) and *sembei* (rice crackers), both snacks for which the area is rightfully famous.

Asakusa: It is quintessentially shitamachi (perhaps too much so). This large district's main attractions are, of course, **Asakusa Kannon** or Asakusa Temple (its real name is **Sensoji**). Local legends put the temple as having existed since AD 628, when fishermen from the area pulled an image of the Buddhist Goddess of Mercy – *Kannon* – out of the sea in their nets and enshrined it here. Today, no one seems to know what happened to the image or where it could be, but does it really matter?

The huge, 4-meter-tall, ¾-ton paper lantern at the main gate is called *Kaminarimon* (or Thunder Gate), and was erected in 1960. As Tokyo notably lacks an Arch de Triomphe, a Statue of Liberty or any other structure of note, the lantern serves as one of the city's most popular icons. It honors the God of Thunder, whose statue stands to the right; on the left is the God of the Wind.

Nakamise Dori (Inside-Shop Street) leads from the gate to the temple proper, and its 87 shops offer a variety of goods, from junk to treasures, from replica swords and samurai wigs to Godzilla cigarette lighters. The **Shin** (New) **Nakamise** which intersects it, running perpendicularly, has even more stores; one of the best known is **Sukeroku**, whose miniatures and traditional toys have been fascinating tourists, children and worshipers since the 1800s.

In the myriad of kimono, fabric and clothing shops here, anything from ersatz kimonos and tacky *yukata* to traditional Edo Era formal wear and Japanese cloth by the bolt are sold. The real treasures at Asakusa, however, are *behind* Nakamise and the sidewalks, where, oddly, few people seem to think of going.

There is an endless number of small restaurants in the area serving local meals like *ramen*, *soba* and *yakiniku*. Considering the significant number of tourists, it is perfectly safe to stop in any one of them without giving the proprietors severe culture shock (as might happen in, say, Shibamata). There are some fancier places to eat as well, but one doesn't go to Asakusa for *haute cuisine*.

One of the other interests in the area is **Mokubakan**, a small, old theater of the type that once flourished in Edo. If you speak Japanese, you will love the shows they put on. If you don't speak Japanese, you may be amused at how melodrama and overacting come across in any language. Occasionally there is *rakugo* (humorous monologues), a favorite and a guaranteed house-filler.

There is also a playground, complete with rides, behind the temple – great for those with munchkins. Not as big or self-conscious as Toshimaen or Korakuen, this park is a small affair, just right for the neighborhood in which it is nestled. It seems caught in some time warp, probably locked in the 1960s. You may not be nostalgic over the Japan of 20 years ago, but you can get a chance to see and experience it here.

Asakusa is best experienced during a *matsuri* (festival), when the precincts of Sensoji are covered with stalls selling grilled corn, dango, *kori* (shaved ice), *oden* (stew), *taiyaki* (sweet beanpaste filled pancake-like pastries molded in the shape of fish), *takoyaki* (octopus dumplings – they taste better than they sound), and every variety of munchy and toy imaginable… and *Ramune*.

Ramune is the shitamachi answer to

Sumida River cruise boat passes through Asakusa.

soft drinks. The name is a corruption of lemonade, and indeed it tastes almost like a lemon fizz. It comes in small, thick glass bottles with a glass marble imbedded in the neck to keep the fizz fresh. The trick is to drink it without the marble stopping the flow every three seconds, or getting it up your nose. It is one of the few drinks that tastes better lukewarm than ice-cold, and it is something that is inexplicably and permanently linked to *shitamachi* life.

Asakusa is a wonder and a marvel; there is always something new to discover and experience.

Ueno: The **Tokyo National Museum** complex, which houses some of the best in Japanese art and cultural properties, and Ueno's several other museums, a wonderful park (with less-than-wonderful pigeons – you have been warned) and numerous other attractions make Ueno worth a visit.

You might want to skip the branch of the **Toshogu Shrine** (dedicated to the spirit of Tokugawa Ieyasu, the founder of the Edo *Bakufu*) and the celebrated but depressing **Ueno Zoo,** however.

All of Ueno Park was once within the precincts of the most powerful temple in all Edo. It had close ties to the shogunal family, and during the Meiji Restoration it served as the garrison for troops loyal to the bakufu, hence its destruction. It was burned down and fell into disfavor. Hardly anything remains but a few structures (including a marvelous five-story pagoda) and the memories. The graves of many of the Tokugawa shogun are still there, within an enclosure at the cemetery.

Shinobazu Pond and Park: Near Ueno is a famous lotus pond threatened by developers intending to build an underground parking lot under the pond and replace the latter with an artificial one. So see it while you can. Beside it is the **Tokyo Shitamachi Museum**, where the reconstructed buildings in a well-planned array provide the visitor a reasonably accurate sampling of how life was lived in old Edo – a truly fascinating experience.

Ueno Station is a major juncture

Aerial view of a small part of the city.

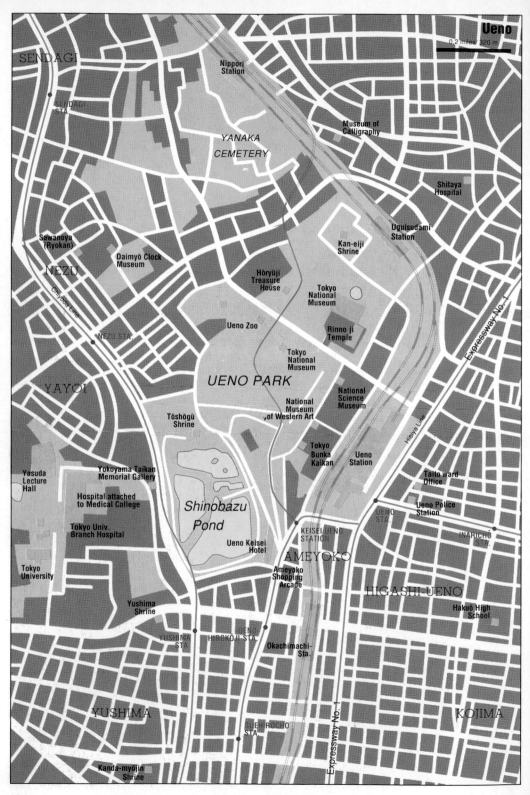

Ueno

0.2 miles/ 320 m

SENDAGI

Nippori
Station

YANAKA
CEMETERY

Museum of
Calligraphy

SENDAGI
STA.

Shitaya
Hospital

Sawanoya
(Ryokan)

Daimyō Clock
Museum

Kan-eiji
Shrine

Uguisudami
Station

NEZU

Hōryūji
Treasure
House

Tokyo
National
Museum

Chiyoda Line

NEZU STA.

Ueno Zoo

Rinno ji
Temple

YAYOI

Tokyo
National
Museum

UENO PARK

National
Science
Museum

Tōshōgū
Shrine

National
Museum
of Western Art

Hibiya Line

Expressway No. 1

Yasuda
Lecture
Hall

Yokoyama Taikan
Memorial Gallery

Tokyo
Bunka
Kaikan

Ueno
Station

Taito ward
Office

Hospital attached
to Medical College

Shinobazu
Pond

UENO
STA.

Ueno Police
Station

Tokyo Univ.
Branch Hospital

KEISEI UENO
STATION

INARICHO
STA.

Tokyo
University

Ueno Keisei
Hotel

AMEYOKO

HIGASHI UENO

Yushima
Shrine

Ameyoko
Shopping
Arcade

Hakuō High
School

YUSHIMA
STA.

UENO
HIROKOJI STA.

Okachimachi-
Sta.

YUSHIMA

SUEHIROCHO
STA.

Expressway No. 1

KOJIMA

Kanda-myōjin
Shrine

("gateway to the north"), so there is plenty of goings-on in the area. One particularly famous gastronomic encounter is **Santomo**, near Marui. Their *fugu* (poisonous blowfish, served – hopefully – without the poison) is to die for… but only figuratively speaking. Another is Japan's oldest operating "Western restaurant," **Ueno Seiyoken**, established in 1872, which overlooks the pond and the **Hongo Woods**.

Tokyo University ("Todai" for short) is a short walk from Ueno Station, and its neighborhood of Hongo 3-chome, too, is considered part of the old Edo. Although there is something antiquarian about the place, it hardly evokes images of, say, old established European universities like Heidelberg or Edinburgh. No student princes here – the aristocracy and Imperial Family sent their children to Gakushuin (once called the Peers' School) in Mejiro.

Most of Japan's big-name politicians and all but a handful of prime ministers have been Todai alumni. Getting accepted almost guarantees success in life. It was founded during the Meiji Restoration, when it was called Tokyo Imperial University. For such a young university, it has a great reputation. Well, in Japan, at least. But if it's so hot, why don't Imperial offsprings go there? It can't be that they couldn't pass the tests…can it?

Jimbocho/Kanda: If there is a book you want but can't find anywhere else, get it here. Dozens of small and large bookstores line the streets in **Jimbocho**. There are stores specializing in art books, secondhand books, comic books – in English, French, German, Russian… anything and everything. Browsing around is a bibliophile's idea of heaven. Some bookstores have books that even those of major universities may have difficulty finding.

Take the advice of many a wise traveler, however: buy your books here, and ship them home.

Jimbocho is only one part of Kanda, however. Adjacent to the book-selling area are numerous stores specializing in equipment for the martial arts – a great place to buy samurai souvenirs – and

practically any other sport you can think of. Many advertise themselves as "discount" shops, and some do offer great bargains on ski gear in the spring, for example. For the most part, however, their prices are about the same as in the department stores.

Ochanomizu: The name of this district literally means "Water for Tea," and is so called, as the story goes, because it is where the water for the Shogun's palace tea ceremonies was drawn. This would not be recommended today, as you can see from the condition of the river – actually part of the palace moat system – that runs past its main train station.

One of Ochanomizu's best known symbols is the great dome of the **Nikolaido**, built in 1884 as the seat of the Russian Orthodox Church in Japan. It is certainly attractive, but overrated as a tourist destination. If you have no intentions to go to Moscow, however, it is likely to be one of your best chances to look at the style of Russian Orthodox (onion top) architecture.

More fun in Ochanomizu is to hang

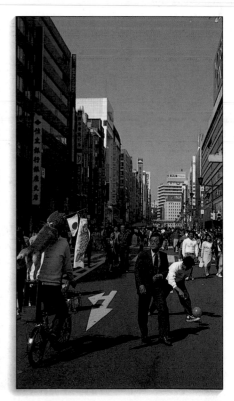

Interesting scene in Ginza on no-car day.

out in the numerous coffee and pastry shops and listen to students from nearby Hosei, Meiji or other universities practice their English or French!

Kanda Jinja: This is one of Tokyo's most important shrines, and just a short walk from Ochanomizu Station. It is dedicated to rebel general Taira no Masakado (d. AD 947) who fought for the rights of the ignored and oppressed Kantoites against Imperial forces. To locals he was a Robin Hood, but to others he was just power hungry (well, he did proclaim himself the "new Emperor"). He was killed in battle and his head sent to Kyoto, from which it is said to have flown – under its own power – back home. There is a *taiko* (drum) troupe attached to Kanda Jinja called **Masakado Daiko.** They are primarily involved in celebrating the life of Masakado, but their main claim to fame is that it is one of the few all-women taiko groups in Japan. They have even cut an album – worth a listen if you like taiko music.

The overall feel of Kanda Jinja, despite being one of the religious centers in Tokyo, is one of the old city. It is hardly a place to see modern Japan.

Across the street is **Yushima Seido**, what is left of the Tokugawa-sponsored Confucian academy. It is a fascinating building, and one of the few Confucian centers in Tokyo, let alone in Japan.

Korakuen: This park, whose name means "Last Paradise," is arguably Ochanomizu's most famous sight. It is a huge themeless theme park with rides and attractions of all kinds. A favorite is a haunted house designed and laid out in line with traditional Edo Era haunted house attractions (yes, they had them even then!) but built with modern technology assistance. Korakuen also has a free-fall parachute ride which combines a bird's eye view of Tokyo with stark raving terror. Next to Korakuen is the **Tokyo Dome**, also called The Big Egg.

Ryogoku: The site of Japan's home sumo arena, called the **Kokugikan** is here, near **Asakusabashi**. Ryogoku is, however, also the home of many of the *sumobeya* (or "stables," as the training

Waiting for friends at the Ginza 4-chome crossing.

196

center/dormitories for the young behemoths are called).

One of the stables, **Takamiya**, is run by the former Hawaiian *rikishi* whose wrestling name was Takamiyama. Restaurants in the area specialize in *chanko-nabe*, a filling and satisfying hodge-podge stew that is the main diet of the rikishi.

Near Ryogoku is the **Fukagawa Edo Shiryokan**, a hall which encompasses a massive reconstruction of a part of shitamachi Edo from the 19th century. It is like walking on to the set of a samurai drama: there is even a lifelike dog relieving himself by the guard tower. Every 20 minutes, the lighting cycles through night and day, and you can wander through the houses and down the alleys to see how dark Edo was before gas lighting. A hall for concerts and public performances is attached to the Shiryokan, so it is advisable to check on current activities held there; sometimes it is a *shakuhachi* recital, or perhaps a *biwa* concert with a recitation of the *Tale of the Heike*.

Akasaka: Once one of the outer defences of Edo castle, this part of Tokyo is primarily known as the downtown nightlife capital – expensive, vibrant and reasonably sophisticated.

Akasaka (which means "Red Slope") is also the home of the State Guest House, on land which during the Edo Period had been the estate of the Kii, one of the three great branches of the Tokugawa family. The eighth and most able shogun, Yoshimune, had spent much of his childhood there. The estate also served as a temporary palace for Emperor Meiji for about 15 years after residences in the Palace proper burned down. Ooka Echizen-no-Kami Tadasuke, one of Yoshimune's capable magistrates, lived here in the early to mid 18th century. His reputation is such that he was the central figure in a samurai drama television series, *Ooka Echize*, for several years running, and a regular character in a series about Yoshimune called *Abarenbo* (Rough–neck) *Shogun*.

Not all of Akasaka was noble, how-

ever; it did have a reputation for bathhouses and "other things" as well. (One may still see – occasionally – a "real" geisha in a "real" stepping from a "real" *jinrikusha* on her way to a meeting in one of the area's swanky teahouses.)

One of the most startling sights is not not far from **Akasaka Mitsuke Station**: the huge, ugly, burned-out hulk of a building – the Hotel New Japan, gutted in a 1982 fire. Like many outmoded or otherwise useless buildings in Tokyo, it stands – an unsightly ghost amid prettier (at least newer) buildings – because there's money in that land, and every year, the value increases.

The big thrill in Akasaka is a sort of gastronomic Russian Roulette: walk down **Sotobori Dori** or **Hitotsugi Dori** and look at all the bars and restaurants (not all restaurants look like restaurants – sometimes you have to open a door and stick your head in) and try to guess if it's one of the cheap ones that just looks expensive, or if it really is one of the expensive ones.

Ginza: Though it once was the epit-ome of the modernized, Westernized Japan, the Ginza (rhymes with "keenza") cannot compete with West Shinjuku for skyscrapers and the like. Its reputation as a great shopping district stands, albeit more among tourists and middle-aged Japanese than the younger crowd and the yuppies who tend to flock to Harajuku for their shopping. Ginza retailers are aware of the problems, and have begun considering steps to lure the youth of Japan back to the area.

Actually, the part of town we are discussing here is more properly called **Nishi (West) Ginza**, comprising the area west of Chuo Dori, east of Marunouchi, north of Shimbashi and south of Kyobashi. That's several dozen square blocks, the center of which is **Ginza 4-Chome** at the intersection of Chuo Dori and Harumi Dori. Stand on this corner around 7.30 in the evening and you will see some of the most beautiful women in the world parade by – "bar hostesses" on their way to work. Don't let their blue-jeans and

Then and now: Shibuya in the 1930s...

cloth coats fool you: on the job they dress (and can afford to!) like pages out of *Vogue*. It is a reminder that prices in most if not all of the thousands of bars, after-hours clubs and posh restaurants in the Ginza can be astronomical. Hidden charges like ¥2,000 per bowl for peanuts, ¥5000 per 30-minute session with a conversational "companion," etc. can add up rapidly. (In this connection, some bars discourage patronage by non-Japanese-speaking foreigners who don't understand "the system." This is not discrimination, merely a safer way to avoid trouble.)

The Ginza has come a long way from when it was a swamp land. The Tokugawa reclaimed it and made it the site of a mint (the name means "silver seat"). After a fire, the area was redesigned by a British architect, and was the first part of Tokyo to have gas lighting installed during the Meiji Era. This added to its overall impression of foreignness, and ...and Shibuya's main crossing, 1990s. the modern appeal made Ginza one of the centers of commerce.

Nihombashi: In older, if not better days, the bridge from which this district takes its name was the spot from which all distances in Japan were measured. Today, however, Nihombashi (also called, confusingly, Nihonbashi and Nipponbashi; they all mean "Japan Bridge") has since become just another place in Tokyo. The bridge (a bridge, anyway) is still there, but obscured under an arching expressway.

One thing hasn't changed: Nihombashi is still an area given to buying and selling. **Kabutocho**, the stock exchange, is not far away, and so is the main office of the Bank of Japan. When the latter was built here in 1896, other government offices followed.

Of historical interest is the fact that in the neighborhood here called **Nihombashi Muromachi**, a man named Miura Anjin lived. His original name, William Adams, was changed to Blackthorne when James Clavell used (some say misused) the Englishman's story as the basis for *Shogun*.

Tsukiji: Until the Great Kanto Earthquake of 1923, the city's fishmarket

was at Nihombashi. Now it is at Tsukiji, a manmade part of Tokyo whose land has been reclaimed from the bay and whose name means "built land."

It was originally designed as a sort of ghetto for foreigners who arrived at the beginning of the Meiji Era. Unlike those of the *dejima* of Yokohama and Nagasaki during Edo, however, the gates of Tsukiji were open, and most foreigners lost no time getting out.

Now, of course, Tsukiji is best known for its boisterous fishmarket. Every morning – well before dawn – trucks arrive with loads of fresh and frozen fish, and chefs from all the best hotels and restaurants come to make their purchases. By noon, it is over and people are sweeping up. If you like fish, or if you just need something to do at four or five o'clock in the morning, a visit to the market is just your cup of tea.

Marunouchi/Otemachi: Most of the Imperial Palace, a huge plot of verdant land smack in the middle of Tokyo, is closed to visitors, of course. You can see some of what the Imperial Family calls their backyard, however, in the **East Garden** (entrance near the Palace-side Building on the north). You can also say you have "been in the Palace" if you visit the offices of the Imperial Household Agency (on the east side, south of the Palace Hotel), where you apply for permission to visit places such as Kyoto's Katsura Detached Palace.

As for **Marunouchi** proper, it is the district that borders the inner palace moat on the east (or Ginza) side, and although there are a few upscale shops here, it is mostly large office buildings (insurance, banks, etc.) with a smattering of foreign airline offices.

Otemachi, too, is mostly down to business, the principal tourist attraction being the statue (in front of the **former City Office**) of **Ota Dokwan** (1432–86), builder and occupant of the first "palace" and the man credited with founding the city.

Kasumigaseki: Yamato Takeru no Mikoto, a legendary warrior of the 4th or 5th century, was fighting back the Ezo (to him a barbarian tribe, to modern

Homeward bound: fighting boredom on the subway.

anthropologists, likely early Ainu) and established a barrier he called Barrier of the Mists (Kasumigaseki). At that time, it overlooked Sagami Bay.

The name stuck.

Now, Kasumigaseki is shorthand for Japanese government. **The Diet Building** is nearby, as are many government ministries including MITI, the all-powerful Ministry of International Trade and Industry. There is in fact nothing interesting about Kasumigaseki from the tourist point of view – even Yamato Takeru's scenery is gone – and it only stands as a monument to government.

Yurakucho: To many, the most famous thing about this part of town was the American who had an office here. Immediately after Japanese surrender in 1945, General Douglas MacArthur established his command headquarters in the **Daiichi Seimi Building**. The office is still there, although it isn't open to the general public.

Oddly enough, Yurakucho was actually named after the man whose estate stood on the spot: Oda Urakusai, tea-master and brother to warlord Oda Nobunaga, friend to Ieyasu and student of master-of-masters, Sen no Rikyu. The "*sai*" (teacher) was dropped from his name, and the suffix "*cho*" (town) was attached. Over time, the pronunciation changed, and the name came to be written in *kanji* as "Happy Town."

Here's another bit of Yurakucho trivia: a skinny wedge of land to the east of the train station was overlooked in MacArthur's rezoning of Tokyo and was – as recently as the 1970s – known as "Sushi Alley" for all the restaurants and bars established there by "squatters" on land "nobody owned." Most were torn down for the construction of the **Kokusai Kanko** office building (home of the Japan National Tourist Organization, JTB, etc.), but perhaps their legacy lingers in the little-known fact that some of the best *yakitori* stalls in the city, if not in the country, are located beneath the Yamanote/Shinkansen train tracks here (and in the neighboring **Sukiyabashi** district immediately to the south). It's probably

Inspecting frozen tuna before the auction at Tsukiji.

Tokyo's best kept dining secret, and you can stuff yourself to near critical mass on beer and yakitori and go home two sizes bigger for less than ¥3,000. Try that elsewhere in Tokyo!

All in all, Yurakucho is rather dingy despite the glitzy department stores on its fringes.

Hibiya: Hibiya Park, Tokyo's pocket-sized version of New York's Central Park, began as a military parade ground for the troops of Emperor Meiji. When plans to build government offices on the site foundered due to the area's weak foundation, it was made into a park – the first Western-style park in Tokyo, which opened in 1903. (Across the street, also on swampy land, is where Frank Lloyd Wright built the original **Imperial Hotel** in the early 1920s; his ingenious "floating pier" foundation helped the structure ride with mushy earth through the Great Kanto Earthquake of 1923, while most other large buildings in the area were reduced to heaps of rubble.)

Hibiya Park is not just known for its

size and scenery: it is famous – rather justifiably, according to records dating back to before 1910 – as a spot for lovers' assignations. It also hosts rock, pop and jazz concerts in its **Outdoor Theater** and classical recitals in its **Small Hall**.

Hibiya has many movie houses and theaters, including the Tokyo home of **Takarazuka**, the famous (if campy) all-women review.

Shinjuku: The image that best serves to represent modern Tokyo is Shinjuku, with its myriad movie theaters, department stores, fashion boutiques, shopping arcades, neon glitz…and confusion. There are parts of Shinjuku that are distinctly seedy; to be fair, there also are "urban residential" parts that are downright comfortable.

In the Edo days, Shinjuku was not even part of the city proper. It was essentially a post town, and its name literally means "new lodgings." Today, **Shinjuku Station** serves over 2 million passengers daily as one of the key western commuter stations in Tokyo. With the opening of two huge skyscrapers to house the new seat of city government, the area has taken on a new dignity – and arrogance: even the street bums now seem to walk with a stut. (Prices have gone up, too, in the surrounding restaurants and shops.)

In a way, Shinjuku may be the part of Tokyo just like New York City, for here are stores and restaurants of every kind, here are skyscrapers, and here are various groupings of theaters, bars, you name it. People come to shop, to visit, to meet, to eat. But unlike New York, there is no unease, no "on your toes" mentality. Perhaps this is Japan.

Kabukicho: This subdistrict of Shinjuku, on the other hand, is a paradox: it is one of the sleaziest parts of Tokyo, yet one of the best places to spend an evening with that Special Someone (or just some friends). Though it offers countless peepshows, "adult toy" shops, soaplands, and other such establishments, it also has some very nice restaurants and several movie theaters. At its heart is **Koma Gekijo**, a conventional theater with offerings ranging

Icons of the rainy season.

from concerts to plays based on samurai drama television series to traditional post-Meiji Japanese theater. The few main streets in Kabukicho can be considered perfectly safe; the only need for concern would be a the side streets, but even there the only likely result would be on encounter with an enthusiastic tout for a less-than-wholesome cabaret or some such.

Kabukicho's chief interest is that it is one of the few places where one can go and observe, from the comfort of the middle of the street or a coffee shop, members of the infamous *yakuza* – or at least persons who appear to be involved in organized crime. They are easy to identify by their punch-permed haircuts, flashy suits (often looking like refugees from a bad movies) and vast quantities of flashy gold jewelry (generally, Japanese men wear little or none). Oh yes: the fingers. One of the more enduring stories about the yakuza is that as apology or by way of atonement (or punishment) for error, they cut off the tip of a finger, usually the pinky.

Ikebukuro: A few stops north of Shinjuku on the Yamanote Line, Ikebukuro strikes one as a smaller, less interesting version of Shinjuku. Its station, too, is a commuter center, and it, too, is home to movie theaters, department stores (including the **Ikebukuro Seibu**, reputedly the world's largest self-contained department store), bars, and a small sleaze center. As a busy commuter station, it is second only to Shinjuku.

One of Asia's tallest buildings, the 60-story **Sunshine 60**, is in Ikebukuro, and stands on the site of Sugamo (previously and later again called Tokyo) Prison, where Tojo Hideki and others were tried, convicted of war crimes and hanged during the Occupation.

Shibuya: Faithful pooch, Hachiko, used to meet his master, a Todai professor, at Shibuya Station every evening. One day the professor suffered a heart attack and never returned, but the dog continued to show up at the station every day for seven years. Hachiko's faithfulness became a local legend. When he, too, died, in 1935, a bronze

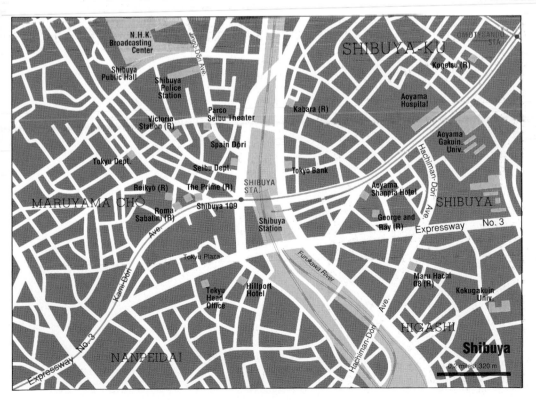

statue of him was erected outside Shibuya Station, soon becoming Tokyo's most famous meeting place. "I'll meet you at Hachiko" is an oft-heard phrase, and the open square in front of the statue is almost always thronged with people – even in the rain.

Although the shopping here is excellent (if you are young, Japanese and very well-heeled), central Shibuya is perhaps best known for entertainment; as there are many theaters, bars, clubs and discos.

Aoyama: It is named after Aoyama Tadanari, one of Ieyasu's advisors, who had his estate in the area. There was even a shrine erected on the spot where his horse fell as he galloped out the boundaries of what was to be his domain: **Komadome** (Colt's Stop) **Hachiman Jingu**. A large number of the shogun's special assistants from Iga, the *ninja*, also lived in the area.

After the end of Edo, Emperor Meiji built his military college here and it was from its huge parade ground, in 1910, that a young Lieutenant Tokugawa made the first airplane flight in Japan. Years later the grounds were requisitioned by the US military to provide housing for Occupation troops, and renamed Washington Heights. For the Tokyo Olympics in 1964, the government reclaimed the land and made the barracks into housing for the athletes, and stadiums were built on the land. Today, much of the land remains as **Yoyogi Park**.

Aoyama Bochi, Tokyo's oldest and largest public cemetery, is the final and permanent address to over 100,000 Tokyoites, many of them foreign; two of the most famous residents are General Nogi, of Russo-Japanese War fame, and Hachiko, of "faithful dog" fame. Today the cemetery is a tranquil spot. With the large number of cherry trees, it is also the unlikely site of annual cherry blossom viewing parties in April. Just lay a blanket down on old Uncle John – he won't mind – and toss a beer back as you glance at the blossoms. Ah, Tokyo.

Harajuku: Known to the tourist and

Funky street art.

resident expat as home to Oriental Bazaar, the best one-stop-shopping in Tokyo for souvenirs, this corner of Shibuya-ku adjacent to Aoyama is the fashion hub in Japan. **Takeshita Dori**, an alley leading into the town from Harajuku Station on the Yamanote line, continues to draw many young shoppers, but most of them are from the countryside (or from the more distant precincts of Tokyo) and are great marks for the pretentious "fashion boutiques" and T-shirt stalls lining the way.

Takeshita Dori is fun to visit, in a twisted sort of way, but even more fun is a Sunday outing to nearby **Harajuku Park**, where there is a parade of fashions gone by. Legions of rock 'n' rollers get caught in what they conceive as the 1950s, meeting for outdoor concerts and dances of the absurd, side by side with ersatz 1960s hippies, pseudo-punk 1970s *poseurs* and numbers of what appear to be persons trying to define the heavy-metal look of the 1990s.

The long, lingering look. The base irony is that it all takes place in front of the entrance to **Meiji Jingu**,

one of the most solemn sites in the metropolis. This is the place to be on New Year's Eve, if you fancy all that noise and the huge crowds.

Roppongi: Long considered the nightlife capital of Tokyo, there are great differences in the night-animal crowds here and the revelers of Akasaka or the Ginza. The latter tend to be well-heeled business executives, bureaucrats, or the generally well-off, and often seem to be mostly in their 40s or 50s; your average Roppongi denizen, on the other hand, is a college student, a young office worker, a member of the *mizushobai* ("water world," or entertainment) profession on a busman's holiday…or a foreigner out for a good time.

In the past few years, Roppongi has been slipping in popularity as people have moved farther and farther out of Tokyo in the search for housing. This is why Shinjuku, Shibuya, and even Kichijoji (an upscale suburb rapidly becoming Yuppie Heaven) have become popular evening spots for many locals; Roppongi is simply not as convenient as it once was.

The party scene has spread from Roppongi proper, so now when one mentions a trip to Roppongi, there is also the possibility of a stop in nearby **Nishi-Azabu** or **Hiroo**, the latter well known as a "gaijin ghetto" where foreign companies subsidize expensive apartments for their executives in Japan.

There is no way of being certain where the name "Roppongi" (meaning "six trees") came from, but the popular theory is that it comes from the names of six great samurai families who owned estates in the area – the Uesugi, Kutsuki, Takagi, Aoki, Katagiri, and Ichiryu – each of which had a kanji or "tree" in their family name.

Others say the name just comes from six big trees that were growing in the neighborhood. Take your pick.

And while you are walking around the area, take in some jazz: Roppongi's **Blue Note**, **Misty's**, **Pit Inn** and several other clubs offer truly first-class jazz of home-grown and imported varieties, and not always at prices that are likely to take the fun out of it.

YOKOHAMA, MAMA!

Yokohama – the very sound of it is exotic. And although the city today is an integral part of the Greater Tokyo Megalopolis and a major urban center in its own right, it has a personality, even a mystique, all its own, much of it stemming from its vital role as one of the greatest international seaports of the Far East.

With a population of 3.1 million, Yokohama is second in size only to Tokyo. Obviously, it would be folly to attempt to savor more than a few of the city's many charms during a brief visit. Happily, however, many of those areas worthy of exploring are concentrated in a relatively small area and can be covered, for the most part by foot, within a single day.

Another thing that makes Yokohama (only a 30-minute train ride from Tokyo) alluring is the fact that its broad, relatively uncrowded streets and laid-back atmosphere provide a perfect antidote for claustrophobia induced by exposure to Tokyo's throngs. But avoid visiting during the weekend. Huge numbers of non-Yokohamans flock here then to check out the latest trends in what is arguably the most cosmopolitan city in Japan.

In short, Yokohama offers just about everything Tokyo can, minus the crowds and the tension. Moreover, the city has ambience that can be quite beguiling, and is enjoyed best not by car but on foot.

Tall Ships & Intelligent Buildings: Start your walking tour of central Yokohama at Sakuragicho Station, which is the terminus for the Toyoko Line originating in Shibuya, Tokyo. Other ways to get here from Tokyo are aboard the JR Yokosuka or Tokaido lines from Tokyo or the Keihin Kyuko Line from Shinagawa. In both cases, you have to transfer onto the Negishi Line at Yokohama Station. Incidentally, Sakuragicho was also the last stop on Japan's first railroad, which began service to Shimbashi in Tokyo in September 1872.

This neighborhood is in a state of great flux at the moment, as work proceeds down near the harbor on the massive **Minato Mirai 21** project, which will totally revamp the port area by the turn of the century. Within its 186 sq. kilometers (73 sq. miles), it includes the 73-story **Landmark Tower**, which at 296 meters (970 ft) is the tallest building in Japan. **The International Zone** will feature a huge convention complex and the **Amenity Zone** will be devoted to landscaped parks next to the port.

You can also visit the *Nippon Maru* "tall ship" and neighboring **Maritime Museum** (both closed Mondays and the Sunday following a holiday), and the **Yokohama Art Museum** with its excellent collection of modernist sculpture (closed Thursdays).

After you cross the pedestrian bridge over the **Ooka River** from Sakuragicho Station, you will find yourself in an area of old government buildings, banks and the like. Push on for four or five blocks to a tree-lined street with red brick sidewalks. Here on **Basha-Michi Dori** (the

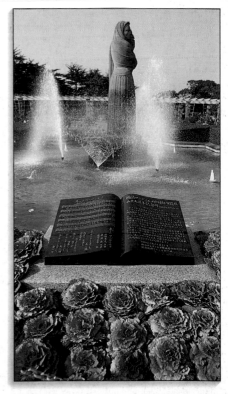

name means "Street of Horse Carriages"), you will find the **Kanagawa Prefectural Museum**. The building, built in 1904, was formerly the head office of the Yokohama Specie Bank, and as one of the best surviving examples of the city's old commercial architecture, it has been designated as an "Important Cultural Property."

Red-Haired Barbarians: When Commodore Perry and his Black Ships arrived in 1853, Yokohama was just a poor fishing village next to a rank swamp. Under the terms of a treaty negotiated in 1858 by the first US envoy to Japan, Townsend Harris, the Port of Kanagawa, smack on the Tokaido, was to be opened to foreign settlement. But the Shogunate reconsidered and built an artificial island on the mudflats of Yokohama (the name means "horizontal beach") instead.

That attempt to segregate the "red-haired barbarians" proved fortuitous for all concerned, since Yokohama's superb natural harbor helped trade to flourish. The wild and woolly early days of the predominantly male community centered around such recreational facilities as "Dirty Village," the incomparable Gankiro Teahouse and the local race track. Periodic attacks by sword-wielding xenophobic samurai added to the lively atmosphere.

However, eventually foreign garrisons were brought in and the merchants could concentrate in a more sedate milieu on their pursuit of lucre. **Honcho Dori**, which is one block further down toward the harbor from the museum, became the center of commercial activities. Turn right when you get there. The wide street is still bracketed with banks and office buildings. There is, for example, the stately **Yokohama Banker's Club** and, on the right, four blocks down, the lovely red brick **Yokohama Port Opening Memorial Hall**, which has miraculously survived the Great Kanto Earthquake of 1923 and the fire bombings of World War II. Also in this area are numerous prefectural offices, and near the waterfront, the **Yokohama Custom House**.

Steamship at dockside in the 1930s.

This district is sometimes called the "Bund," and its oldest buildings have a distinctly European look, something shared with buildings along the Bund in Shanghai, built about the same time.

Incidentally, as legend would have it, in the old days when sailors became so drunk that even they knew it was time to go home, they would ask for "Honcho Dori," knowing that once they were back on the main drag they could get their bearings. The name thus became synonymous with a feeling of security and feeling alright. However, due to the inevitable problems of pronouncing Japanese, it ended up as "hunky-dory."

Well, you can accept that particular story with a grain of old salt.

Freudian Fantasies: By this time, you should be down on the main road alongside the port. The **Yokohama Archives of History**, on the site of the former British Consulate, houses a museum with various exhibits about Yokohama's fascinating history and a library with related audio-visual materials which is closed on Mondays.

Across from it is the **Yokohama Port Opening Square**, where the Japan-US Treaty of Peace and Amity was signed in 1854, and the **Silk Center**, with a delightful museum on the history of that mysterious fabric; at one time, Yokohama owed its prosperity primarily to silk, in which the local Indian community was intimately involved.

A little bit farther down the same road is the **New Grand Hotel**, which although slightly down at the heel is still a civic institution and the best spot for a break over coffee and cake. Next to it is the somewhat garish 106-meter (348-ft) **Marine Tower** and the Yokohama *Ningyo no Ie*, a **Doll Museum,** which closes on Monday.

You will already have noticed **Yamashita Park** across the broad boulevard. It is well worth the hour-long stroll. Among the attractions at the park are "the Girl with the Red Shoes" – a statue dedicated to international friendship among children – and a sculptured water garden that may suggest to some visitors vaguely Freudian fantasies. If seren-

Dancing in the park.

dipity brings you here on a clear summer night, you are likely to hear a rock band wailing away on a temporary stage several hundred feet offshore or sky rockets bursting overhead. But no matter when you visit, you may go aboard the former passenger liner and hospital ship, *Hikawa-Maru*, since she is permanently moored here. Conveniently, there is a beer garden on deck, and boat tours of the harbor leave from next to the ship. Occasionally, distinguished visitors such as the *Queen Elizabeth II* are also to be found in port.

Little China: No visit to Yokohama would be complete without a meal in Chukagai, or **Chinatown**. This dozen or so blocks is the largest Chinatown in Japan, even though Yokohama ranks only fourth in number of Chinese residents, and is nearly as old as the port. The area within its five gates accounts for 90 percent of the former 60-hectare "foreign settlement."

Chinatown also takes pride in the historical role it had in providing staunch support to Sun Yatsen when he was here as an exile trying to drum up support for revolution in his homeland. The Communist Revolution is a different matter, since the community is still bitterly divided between pro-Communist and pro-Nationalist factions.

Some holidays, or days when a baseball game is on at nearby **Yokohama Stadium**, the area is visited by more than 200,000 people, the majority intent on dining at one of the approximately 150 local restaurants. Most also sneak in at least a peak at the exotic shops selling imported Chinese sweets and sundries from Cathay or Southeast and South Asia.

There are also many herbal medicine and tea shops, but you are out of luck if you want a poisonous snake bled into your wine cup for you on the curb; in this and several other ways, Chinatown accommodates itself to Japanese sensibilities. Although in most Chinatowns from San Francisco to London, restaurants basically prepare food for Chinese tastes, in Yokohama everything is adjusted to Japanese tastebuds, with a tad

Kan-Tei-Byo, a temple in Chinatown.

of French influence. Consequently, top chefs recruited from Hong Kong and Taiwan have to be "deprogrammed" to an extent.

Back in the old days, the waterfront Bund where commerce took place was often contrasted with the **Bluff** (Yamate Heights) where the leading foreign merchants lived in palatial homes. **Nanmon Dori** in Chinatown was the central street that ran through the international settlement and connected the two. It became a local tradition known as **Zondag**, from the Dutch word for leisure, that on every Sunday, the flags of the many nations were flown and brass bands strutted down the road. Recently, the Zondag tradition has been revived to an extent, with lion dancing taking place on the same road every first and fourth Sunday.

Epitaths: Virtually every guidebook ever written about Yokohama urges readers to visit the famed **Foreign Cemetery** (*Gaijin Bochi*), where around 4,200 foreigners from 40 countries who somehow found their way to Japanese shores now enjoy their last sleep. Reading tombstones is one of the "thrills" such books usually recommend. The adjacent **Yamate Museum**, with quaint displays on the life of early foreign residents, sits near where Japan's first brewery was located. Both the cemetery and the museum are worth a visit.

And while here, let's also look up some of the city's lesser known attractions. An amble through the hilly **Yamate Residential District** is one that is highly recommended. A cup of coffee in the Edwardian **Yamate Jubankan** should help prepare the visitor in the right mood to descend once again to the turbulent world below, specifically the carnival-like atmosphere of **Motomachi**.

Fickle Fashions: The name of this popular shopping street, just below the Bluff and slightly inland from the portside Yamashita Park, means "Original Town." This is somewhat of a misnomer, because the area was developed long after Yokohama itself was estab-

Below left, main strip in Chinatown. **Right,** Victorian-style building on the Bluff.

lished; still, Motomachi, adjacent as it was to the "foreign district" (now Chinatown), has played an important role in the city's history, as it once was a sort of "Barbary Coast" serving the needs of foreign vessels and their crews visiting the port. Shops offering provisions (and diversions!) were crowded along both sides of its one-kilometer length and, like a town out of some Hollywood western, much of the street was lined with elevated, wooden "sidewalks." (None of this remains, of course, but there are still traces of its "international-ness" – the old German Bakery, for example, a couple of delicatessens and one or two very "European" looking coffee houses.)

In any case, Motomachi's legacy of "foreignness" led to its revival in the 1960s and 1970s as a center of world fashion, with a number of trendy boutiques, a few flashy discotheques, etc. In recent years, however, the focus of fashion in Yokohama has shifted to **Isezakicho**, south of Kannai Station on the Negishi Line, and the big depart-ment stores around Yokohama Station. This means that Motomachi itself is more of a curiosity than a place do to much serious shopping – but it's fun to visit, anyway.

Important Properties: One spot you should not miss while in Yokohama is the **Sankeien Garden** in the hills of Honmoku, past Yamate which is best reached by taxi.

Built at the behest of a 19th-century silk mogul, the 170,000 sq. meters (203,300 sq. yards) of landscaped gardens offer many varieties of trees and flowers, ponds with lotus flowers, water lilies and ducks floating in them. There is also a bamboo "tunnel" and many famous ancient buildings brought from around the country. These include teahouses, a pagoda and the mausoleum Toyotomi Hideyoshi built for his mother. Most have been designated as "Important Cultural Properties" and are well described in the English-language pamphlet available at the entrance to the garden. Sankeien offers refreshment for the soul at any time of the year.

Below left, poolside play. Right, looking out over the yacht harbor at Enoshima.

ENOSHIMA AND THE MIURA PENINSULA

Jutting out like half a seahorse below Kanazawa Hakkei is the **Miura Peninsula** – a lovely place to escape from the mundane. On its right flank is the port of **Yokosuka**, formerly used by the Imperial Navy and now the Northern Pacific base of the US 7th Fleet. The bawdy strip in front of the base – with raunchy dives names like "Bar Atomic" the "Lone Star Bar" – will bring bring back memories to anyone who has served in the military.

But there is much more to Miura: hiking and rock climbing in its verdant, and rolling hills, yachting out of **Aburatsubo**, cormorant viewing on **Jogashima Island** and a visit to the beach town of **Zushi**, home to many artists and writers.

The tip of the peninsula is known as **Kannonzaki** (Cape Kannon). The seas off the point are notoriously treacherous, so it was at this place that one of the first lighthouses in Japan was built. Nearby, to the southwest of the lighthouse, lies **Uraga**, which is still a working fishing port and retains – as much as any in Japan – some of the charm and atmosphere once associated Japan's with fishing villages. A little further on is the beach, **Kurihama**, where Commodore Perry and his fleet of *kurofune* or "black ships" landed in 1853, ending to Japan's two and a half centuries of isolation from its neighbors and the rest of the world.

Then there is **Enoshima**, out on the Shonan Coast. Actually, *Shonan* is a term applied freely to the whole region south of Yokohama. To Japanese, the very name conjures up images of bleached-haired, would-be surfers cruising down the coast highway to the blaring sounds of The Beach Boys.

Enoshima has long fancied itself as the Miami of Japan, and it certainly has the sleaze – if not the danger quotient – to make that claim.

Since it is an island, you have to approach Enoshima over the **Benten-Bashi Causeway**. After navigating your way through a narrow lane filled with souvenir shops and eateries of all kinds, you will reach a red *torii* marking the entrance to a trio of Shinto shrines, linked by an escalator. Automated veneration! At one of the shrines, **Hetsu-nomiya**, you can see the **Hadaka (Naked) Benten** statue, revered by actors and, no doubt, exotic dancers.

Down below the **Nakatsunomiya Shrine** and the **Enoshima Tropical Garden** is a yacht harbor, and by following the narrow path around the back side of the island you can reach the **Chigoga-Fuchi** shore, where in summer you can catch a boat for the short ride back to Benten-Bashi.

On summer weekends, the muddy sands of Shonan beaches from Enoshima westward to **Odawara** are jammed with sun-broiling bodies... and garbage. Snack bars line the length of the shore, especially at the more famous beaches like **Hayama** and **Oiso**, serving everything from cold beer to hot *oden*.

If you suffer from an overdose of the profane at Enoshima, you might consider a more spiritual side trip to the **Taya-no-Dokutsu Caves** near the giant **Kannon Statue**, which stands on a hilltop facing **Ofuna Station** on the JR Tokaido and Yokosuka Lines. Its religious significance aside, the Kannon is more kitsch than culture, but the caves not far away (reached by a bus leaving from the west exit of Ofuna Station) certainly have an unearthly quality to them.

As you wander through the one-kilometer long labyrinth of meditation chambers and stairways, painstakingly hewn out by hand by generations of monks since the early 1500s, you will be awed by sacred waterfalls, Sanskrit inscriptions, and thousands of Buddhist images and carved animals – real and imaginary.

The shift from candlelight to sunlight as you surface from the netherworld might be accepted as a form of enlightenment.

Also in the Enoshima area, about 100 meters (110 yards) northeast of Enoshima Station, is **Ryukoji**, a temple of the Nichiren sect of Buddhism. The founder of the sect, a controversial priest of the 13th century, enraged his elders by challenging their polemics and was beheaded by the Kamakura shogunate in 1271. Somehow, Nichiren caused the executioner's sword to break in half and he managed to escape death. This temple, said to be built on the site of the chopping block, holds an annual **Oeshiki festival** in September to mark the event.

KAMAKURA

Kamakura lies cradled in a spectacular natural amphitheater, surrounded on three sides by wooded mountains and on the fourth by the blue Pacific. For roughly 150 years, from 1192 when Minamoto no Yoritomo made it the headquarters of the first shogunate until 1333 when imperial forces under the command of General Nitta Yoshisada breached its seven "impregnable" passes and annihilated the city's defenders, Kamakura was the *de facto* political and cultural capital of Japan. During those years, the warrior administration based here built numerous impressive temples and commissioned notable works of art, a great deal of it Zen-influenced. Despite the endemic violence of Japan's middle ages, most survived and can be viewed today.

It is a pity that the majority of visitors spend only a day or two in Kamakura, since this "mini-Kyoto" can best be appreciated leisurely, with visits to famous historical sites – there are 65 Buddhist temples and 19 Shinto shrines – interspersed with walks through quiet surrounding hills. Yet, time is the luxury travelers most lack.

The sites discussed in this section are only a sampling. Recommended for those with time on their hands, inclination and good fortune to linger in the town are the rather personal guide *Exploring Kamakura* by Michael Cooper (Weatherhill), which gives a great deal of historical background, and *Enjoying Kanagawa* by Robert Erickson (Kanagawa International Association).

Avoid the Madhouse: Kamakura is only an hour from Tokyo Station and 30 minutes from Yokohama on the JR Yokosuka Line. For that reason much of it resembles an open-air madhouse on weekends. Visitors customarily begin their sightseeing from Kamakura Station or Kita-Kamakura, the station nearest the five great Zen temples. A different approach to the city is recommended, however.

Take the private Odakyu Line from Shinjuku and get off either at Fujisawa or Enoshima. This will give you a chance to ride the delightful **"Eno-den"** (Enoshima Dentetsu) electric trolley line and consequently slip gently into a Kamakura frame of mind. If you start early from Tokyo, you will also be able to avoid some of the chronic congestion in front of the **Great Buddha**.

The Eno-den starts from Fujisawa and ends at Kamakura Station and has 13 stops in between. For about half its 10-kilometer 6-mile) length the cling-clanging, dark-green and cream cars run along ocean and when they are not crowded the conductors even allow surfers to bring their boards aboard.

Older cars (the Eno-den began operation in 1902) are suffused with the smell of wood and oil and you can get the feel of the neighborhoods you pass through, seeing as how private homes and gardens are frequently literally right outside your window and soothing vistas appear after each curve or tunnel.

Your neighbor is likely to be a high school girl, or a housewife out shopping. When the tram stops for a red light along with the motor vehicles, you'll realize that the Shinkansen is not all there is to transportation in Japan.

Majestic Views: Hop off the Eno-den at Hase, the station closest to *Daibutsu*, the Great Buddha. You can either walk up the large road that runs towards the statue or catch a taxi or bus. In the hills to the left on the way are: the **Gongoro Shrine** (next to the Eno-den tracks), which holds a unique festival every September 18 with humorous characters sporting macabre masks; **Hase-dera**, the temple with a 9-meter (30-ft), 11-headed Hase Kannon statue and thousands of small Jiso statues decked out in colorful bibs and bonnets that are dedicated to lost babies (mostly due to abortion); and **Kosokuji**, a temple known for its collection of memorabilia associated with the priest Nichiren.

On a knoll to the right of the approach to the Buddha is the 1,200-year-old **Amanawa-shinmeisha Shrine.** Dedicated to the Sun Goddess, Amaterasu Omikami, the shrine offers a majestic view of the area and the sea beyond.

Daibutsu, the Great Buddha of Kamakura.

Even first-time visitors to Japan have no doubt seen photos of the Great Buddha. But even if you have not, you are in no danger of missing the colossus. At 11.3 meters (38ft) in height – minus the pedestal – and weighing 93 tons, this representation of the compassionate Amida is unlikely to get lost in a crowd. Because the features of the statue were purposely cast out of proportion when it was built in 1252, you should stand 4–5 meters (15ft) in front of the statue to get the full impact of an art work that incorporates influences as foreign from Japanese tradition as those of ancient Greece and really does breathe spirituality. Those without compunctions can even crawl around inside the statue for a fee.

Astonishingly, the Great Buddha has survived almost intact massive typhoons and *tsunami*, like the one that in 1495 ripped away the wooden building which once enclosed it, earthquakes, and even manmade pollution.

Because hilly spines jut out into the basin in which Kamakura is located, the principal sites of interest are scattered in several different compartmentalized areas. This arrangement and the numerous tunnels that pockmark the hills and link the areas make for great atmosphere, but certainly do help the visitor to get about easily.

From the Great Buddha, your best bet is to catch a taxi to Kamakura Station, unless you want to retrace your steps to Hase Station and continue your Enoden odyssey to the end of the line.

Improving with Age: On the east side of the station you will encounter Wakamiya Ave, the broad boulevard that leads under three massive *torii* archways to the **Tsurugaoka Hachiman Shrine**. Paralleling Wakamiya Ave, and lying between it and the Yokosuka Line, is **Kamachi Dori**, Kamakura's modest answer to the Ginza. The area abounds with all kinds of trendy shops and eating places, and many of the Japanese-style restaurants here and elsewhere in the city have incorporated Zen principles of cooking into their cuisine.

Folkcraft shops encourage serious browsing. But Kamakura is most fa-

View of Kamakura Bay over the temple rooftops.

mous for *Kamakura-bori* (lacquer-ware), which originated in the area in the 13th century for the production of utensils used in religious ceremonies. Unlike the traditional Chinese lacquer-ware from which it drew its inspiration, with Kamakura-bori the artist starts by carving the design and only then applies the lacquer. Like fine wine, Kamakura-bori improves with age, taking on richer and subtler hues and luster. You can learn more about this art at the **Kamakura-bori Kaikan** on the right as you start up Wakamiya Ave. towards the Tsurugaoka Hachimangu.

On your approach to the shrine, you will cross a steep, red half-moon bridge that separates the **Gempei Ponds**. The name Gempei refers to the Minamoto (Genji) and Taira (Heike) clans, which of course fought to the end in the samurai power struggle known as the Gempei War. The three islands in the right "Genji" side signify the Chinese character for "birth," that is the victory of Yoritomo and his followers, while the four in the "Heike" pond stand for

Devotees flock to Kamakura's Hachiman Shrine.

the "death" of the rival Taira, Yoritomo's indomitable wife Masako, who ironically was of Taira blood, apparently built the pond to rub in her husband's absolute victory over the ill-fated heirs of Kiyomori.

Art & Archery: Behind the Heike Pond is the **Kanagawa Prefectural Museum of Modern Art** and a little past the Genji Pond is the **Kokuhokan** (National Treasure Hall). The latter each month teasingly changes the limited displays it makes of the 2,000 treasures from the temples of Kamakura which are in its possession. Still, whatever is being shown at any given moment should be stimulating for those interested in Buddhist art. Incidentally, the Kokuhokan building is a copy of the Shosoin repository in Nara.

Continuing up the avenue towards the main shrine, you will cross a 25-meter (82-ft) dirt track along which every September 16 mounted archers gallop and unloosen their arrows at targets in the ancient samurai ritual of *yabusame*. Then you reach an open area

below the steps to the **Hongu** (Shrine Hall.) Here is the red stage upon which Shizuka, Yoritomo's paramour, danced defiantly at the order of his vengeful older half-brother, using the occasion to sing the praises of her lover. The pregnant girl's courage sent Yoritomo into a furious rage, and although he spared her life he later executed her son, whose father was Yoshitsune.

Just past the stage, on the left of the steps, is a huge gingko tree measuring 8 meters (26 ft) around that is reputed to be 1,000 years old. It was beside this track in 1219 that Yoritomo's second son Sanetomo, at 26 already an accomplished poet, was assassinated by his own nephew. Thus came to an end Yoritomo's line and thereafter the shogunate was controlled by Masako's family, the Hojo, through a regency.

The **Hachiman Shrine** might well be considered the physical and spiritual center of Kamakura. Its prominence on the top of Stork Mountain and dedication to Hachiman, the God of War and tutelary deity of the Minamoto, made it the central point of reference for the numerous offices of the "tent government" located below. Actually, the shrine was founded way back in 1063 by one of Yoritomo's ancestors. Yoritomo's very unpretentious tomb is to be found off to the right of the shrine near a hill. It is a grave befitting a samurai, unlike the monstrous art-deco mausoleums for the Tokugawa shoguns at Nikko that look as if were built for *mafioso* dons.

Souls & Scorn: Two isolated temples of great interest and low crowd density are the **Kakuonji**, back in the hills behind Yoritomo's Tomb, and the **Zuisenji** off considerably to the east. The former was founded in 1296. Its **Buddha Hall**, dating to 1354, houses a beautiful **Yakushi Nyorai**, flanked by guardians representing the sun and moon, as well as a shrine to the **Black Jizo**, whose indelible color results from its constantly being scorched by the flames of hell in its efforts to save souls. Access to this temple is strictly controlled. Zuisenji boasts a Zen rock and

Jizo-sama **(Buddhist saints) in a temple collection, Kamakura.**

water garden designed by its founder, the monk Muso Kokushi.

Another spot to visit that is not so far off the beaten track, but nevertheless is largely missed by the tourist hordes is **Harakiri Cave**, a 20-minute walk to the northeast of Kamakura Station, past the shallow, meandering Nameri river. It was here in July 1333, in what was then a temple called Toshoji, the last Kamakura regent, the weak Hojo Takatoki, who had been scorned for his patronage of dog fights, died like a man by his own hand surrounded by over 800 of his cornered followers.

Road to Salvation?: The area due east of Kamakura Station is largely the province of temples of the Nichiren sect. Although most foreigners have heard of Zen, few except those who belong to the right-leaning Soka Gakkai organization know much about Nichiren (1222–82) and his teachings. This was despite the fact that the iconoclast priest founded the only true Japanese Buddhist sect. Nichiren was an imposing personality who in his lifetime was nearly executed, exiled twice and set upon by mobs on more than one occasion and who like Martin Luther and John Calvin continues to generate feelings of both respect and disdain centuries after his death.

Nichiren's importance in political as opposed to religious history lies in his prediction of the Mongol invasion, as divine punishment for the failure of the authorities to accept his argument that faith in the Lotus Sutra was the only valid road to salvation. The irascible Nichiren seems to have been quite put out that the Mongols did not actually conquer the country.

The **Hongakuji, Myohonji, Choshoji**, **Myohoji**, and **Ankokuronji** are all Nichiren temples and are worth a visit. The Myohonji, for example, although only 10 minutes from the station, seems a world apart in its setting at the end of the **Hiki Valley**. It is in this valley that in 1203 the entire Hiki clan was wiped out by the Hojo in a rivalry over shogunal succession.

Double Your Money: To the northwest of Kamakura Station are two "musts." The placid, sublime **Jufukuji** is one of Japan's oldest Zen temples. Among the moss-covered tombs in its cemetery you will find those of the ruthless Masako and unfortunate Sanetomo. Follow the road leading through **Genjiyama Park** until you pass through a stone tunnel and a number of wooden torii. You will arrive at the thriving **Zeniara Benten Shrine** spring; if you wash your money in its waters, Benten, the Shinto Goddess of Fortune, will double its value for you – provided you spend it quickly.

And finally, on the other side of the tracks from the **Engakuji** is **Tokeiji**, a famous "divorce temple." In the old days, women who sought shelter in it or one of the few other *kakekomi-dera* ("run-in temples") in the country, could receive a divorce after they had lived with the nuns for some time. The practice continued at the Tokeiji until 1902. Of course, even if a woman made it here safely and eventually got her divorce, there was no question of alimony. Maybe that's where the Benten spring came in.

Delicate detail at Hachimangu.

FUJI, HAKONE AND IZU

If time does not allow you to go galavanting up and down the archipelago in search of castles, temples, shrines, and quaint farming and fishing villages, the Fuji-Hakone-Izu region, reached in a few hours from Tokyo, is the place to visit. The region, which spans three prefectures and includes such gems as Mt. Fuji, the Fuji Five Lakes, Hakone, Izu Peninsula and the Seven Isles of Izu, has been the inspiration for the works of many of Japan's most celebrated writers, poets and artists. It is also a "continental divide" for Japan, separating the west and south from the cooler north in a strip of volcanic-based topography whose flora and fauna all are both unique and wonderful.

It would be hard to find a mountain more highly praised for its beauty than Fuji, or a lake more often photographed than Hakone's Lake Ashi. Most of the region is designated a "national park," but due to Japan's rather weak laws protecting and restricting commercial exploitation of such assets, some sad and irreversible changes have been wrought upon the area. Still, as evidenced by the millions who return year after year, the magic is still in the air, and if you are able to dodge the crowds, you will find it a rewarding getaway from the big city.

Mt. Fuji: Sweeping up from the Pacific to form a nearly perfect symmetrical cone, 2,776 meters (9,105 ft) above sea level and dwarfing the peaks nearby, the elegant Fuji watches – to employ the anthropomorphic mode many Japanese apply is speaking of her – quietly over her land and people. But she's been known for her temper, too. Fuji's last eruption in 1707 covered Edo, now Tokyo, some 100 kilometers (60 miles) away, with black ash.

Like many natural monuments held to be sacred and imbued with a living spirit, Fuji was off limits to women for many centuries. It was not until 1867, when Englishwoman Lady Parkes boldy scaled the mountain, that there is any record of a woman setting foot on its slopes. Today, about half of the 400,000 Fuji annual hikers are women.

The Climb: Although expeditions are known to set out to challenge the mountain throughout the year, the official climbing season for Mt. Fuji begins on July 1 and ends on August 31. The mountain huts and services found along the trails to Fuji's peak are open only then, and casual hikers are advised to pick this period to make the journey to the top. Expect thick crowds.

The five main trails – Kawaguchiko, Subashiri, Fujinomiya, Fuji-Yoshida, and Gotemba – each is divided into ten stages known as "go." The Kawaguchi trail is the most popular route upward and Subashiri seems to be the preferred way down, but Fujinomiya is more convenient if you are coming from the direction of Kansai, to the southwest. The ascent should take about 9 hours from the first go to the tip of the cone.

For those who wish to see the rising sun from Fuji's peak, considered an important adventure by most, a pleasant

Preceding pages, climbers enjoy the view from the top of Mt. Fuji. Left, the Hakone hills with Fuji in the background. Right, altar at Mt. Fuji Shrine.

way of making the trek is to start in the afternoon, stay overnight at one of the cabins near the top, and make the remaining climb while the sky is still dark. The option is to climb through the night. If any part of the trip is going to be after sunset, remember to bring a reliable flashlight with you. The trails are well-traveled and are hard to miss for the most part, but you will be groping helplessly about at night without a light. The mountain air can be quite cold and rain is not uncommon, so a warm sweater, thick gloves and a waterproof jacket are recommended.

The fifth stations along the Kawaguchi, Subashiri and Fujinomiya – all called *"gogome"* – are accessible by road, and if you feel the 9-hour hike is too long, you may want to take a bus or car to one of those points. Buses to Kawaguchi's *gogome* are available from the bus terminal at Hamamatsucho or Shinjuku JR Stations in Tokyo, and the trip will take about two hours. Those who prefer the train can either catch the JR Chuo Line from Shinjuku Station or the Fuji Kyuko Line via Otsuki to Kawagushi or Gotemba Stations from where buses run to the *gogome* of the respective trails.

To get to the Fujinomiya trail, take the Tokaido Main Line to Fuji, or the Shinkansen "bullet train" to Mishima. Buses should be running regularly during the "official" climbing season.

The Fuji Five Lakes: The Five Lakes district skirts the northern base of Mt. Fuji and provides an ideal year-round resort offering a range of outdoor recreational activities such as camping and water sports during the summer months, and skiing and skating in the winter. From east to west, the lakes are **Yamanaka**, **Kawaguchi**, **Saiko**, **Shoji** and **Motosu**. (A *"ko"* added to the end of these names signifies the respective lake in Japanese.)

Yamanakako, which is the largest in the group, and the picturesque Kawaguchiko are the most frequented of the five, but some of the best spots are hidden near the smaller and more secluded Motosu, Shoji and Saiko. Some

Farming is picturesque in the highlands near Fuji.

recommended visits include the **Narusawa Ice Cave** and **Fugaku Wind Cave**, both formed by the volcanic activities of one of Fuji's early eruptions, the delicate **Shiraito Falls**, and **Koyodai** (Maple Hill), which offers one of the best views of the surrounding area. The primeval forests of **Junkai** and **Aokigahara** nearby are also worth noting.

All five lakes are connected by excellent roads and are also serviced by buses which travel from Gotemba, Fuji-Yoshida and Kawaguchiko.

Hakone: Local history has it that when Toyotomi Hideyoshi, one of Japan's great warriors and the first to unite the country, seized Odawara Castle in 1590, he ordered a rock mineral bath to be built in the neighboring mountains where his men could ease their travel-weary bodies. This area, known as Hakone, is set against the backdrop of Mt. Fuji, and has been a popular place for rest and recreation ever since.

Much of the fun in a visit to Hakone lies in the array of unusual rides in which to get around. The optimal tour starts at Odawara Station, where the **Hakone Tozan Densha** (mountain railway) begins its 8.9-kilometer (5½-mile) zig-zag up to **Gora**. This amazing single-track train, built in 1919, climbs and clangs its 40-minute journey up the steep slope. And it's not just for tourists: in the early morning and late afternoon hours, the small train is packed with local schoolchildren.

Hakone-Yumoto, the first stop on the line and the gateway to Hakone's 16 hot springs, nestles in a shallow ravine where the Hayakawa and Sukumo Rivers flow together. An overnight stay at one of the inns here is recommended; all have natural mineral baths. If you are on a day-trip, the **Tenzan** public bath provides an exquisite hot spring treat for just ¥500. The area is crowded on weekends and holidays, so plan ahead.

Twenty minutes up from Yumoto lies **Miyanoshita**, the oldest and the most thriving of the spa towns. The original *"Taiko no Iwayu"* rock bath attributed to Hideyoshi can be found here, although it is no longer in use. Its name-

One of the most-photographed farmhouses in Japan – for obvious reasons.

sake bath, a block or so away, is open to the public for a small fee.

Miyanoshita is also the home of the famed **Fujiya Hotel** and **Naraya Ryokan**. Fujiya, dating from 1878, is the second oldest existing hotel in Japan. Naraya has a fine reputation and is also used by the Imperial Family on special occasions. For many years, the two establishments competed fiercely for guests to the area. However, in true Japanese fashion, they decided on a compromise: Fujiya would cater to Western tastes and Naraya would remain strictly Japanese style. It was also agreed that Fujiya, which seemed to have the better deal, would pay a fee to cover Naraya's losses.

Outdoor Art: The Tozan Tetsudo also makes a stop at **Chokoku-no-Mori**, an outdoor sculpture garden where the works of Picasso, Rodin, Leger and Takamura Kotaro and many others are on permanent display. If you are blessed with good weather, this will make for a wonderful visit.

At the Gora terminal, change over to the cable car to Sounzan and then transfer to the Hakone Ropeway headed for Togendai. On your journey, you will pass **Owakudani**, the "Valley of the Greater Boiling," in the old crater of Mt. Kami. It is an interesting place but the yellow, sulphurous fumes can be rather overwhelming as there is no breeze.

Togendai lies on the shore of **Ashinoko** (Lake Ashi), a beautiful caldera lake crisscrossed by regular pleasure boats. There are many attractions around this lake and you should rely on the boats and buses here to check out the scene. The **Hakone Shrine**, said to have been founded during the 8th century, is the reason behind the flourishing of the town of **Moto-Hakone**, known as a prominent samurai religious center in its heyday. Of course, the building which stands today was constructed at a much later date, but some interesting relics can be found about.

The **Suginamiki** or Ancient Cedar Avenue makes for a wonderful stroll. This was part of the **Old Tokaido Highway** down which the grand processions

Cruising Lake Ashi.

of the feudal lords and several hundreds of their retainers made their way to the capital at Kyoto. Near here stood the **Hakone Sekisho**, a barrier originally built in 1618 to defend Edo and keep an eye on the comings and goings on the highway. The Hakone Shiryokan Museum nearby offers a glimpse of life as it lived was during the reign of the Tokugawa shogunate.

From **Hakonen**, you can catch the Komagatake Ropeway to reach the summit of **Komagatake**, one of the last of the Hakone volcanos to erupt. The much-talked-about view from the top takes in Lake Ashi and the Amagi Mountains.

Hakone hosts many colorful festivals every year, and if you can bear large crowds, they are bound to be very entertaining. One of the major ones is the **Torii Matsuri** on August 5: a torii gate is burned on Lake Ashi and a thousand lanterns are set adrift. On August 16 is the **Daimonji Yaki**: huge burning torches light up Mt. Myojo and locals and visitors alike enjoy folk dancing and fireworks displays. The **Daimyo Gyoretsu** on November 3 reenacts the processions of the feudal lords down the Old Tokaido, with hundreds of paraders in full costume.

Hakone can be reached via Odawara on the JR Tokaido Line or via the Okakyu Line from Shinjuku to Hakone Yumoto.

Izu: Extending into the Pacific between the Sagami and Sugura bays is the Izu Peninsula, where countless bays, beaches and spas, together with a very inviting climate, give Izu its reputation as a resort for all seasons. It has also managed to leave its imprint on Japanese history together with American Commodore Perry and his "Black Ships" that anchored in Suruga Bay in 1853.

Eastern Izu begins at **Atami**, a hot spring dating back over a thousand years. During the Edo Period, the shogun had its waters brought to the palace so he could enjoy a relaxing bath. Today, Atami is a lively town, albeit somewhat bawdy, offering reasonably sophisticated nightlife and numerous recreational facilities. The MOA Art Museum boasts a fine collection of Japanese

Below left, Shinto shrine on the slopes of Mt. Fuji. **Right**, reclining Buddha at a small temple on Izu.

woodblock prints, ceramics and lacquer works, many have been designated as "National Treasures" and "Important Cultural Properties."

Ito, **Atagawa**, **Inatori** and **Shimoda** are the other major hot-spring towns along this side of the peninsula. Those who have read James Clavell's *Shogun* may recognize Ito as the temporary abode of the shipwrecked Englishman who – so serendepitously, at least in Clavell's version – ingratiated himself into Japanese affairs. The **Ikeda Art Museum** offers some 600 paintings and sculptures by Matisse, Picasso, Chagall, Dali and other masters.

Shimoda is a somewhat sleepy resort town. A fine view of **Cape Iro** to the south can be had from the top of **Mt. Nesugata**, three minutes by ropeway from Shimoda Station. The view includes Oshima, the largest of the "Seven Isles of Izu," but Miyake and Hachijo, considered the best of those islands from the visitor's standpoint, are too distant to be seen. (All seven isles have something to offer tourists, and are growing in popularity. There is limited boat service to some of the islands from the Shimoda area; going by air or overnight ship from Takeshiba Sambashi in Tokyo is preferred, however.)

The Shimoda area also carries many reminders of feudal Japan's first brush with the West. **The Butchered Cow Tree** at the former residence of Townsend Harris, America's first consul to Japan, is an example: the slaughter of a cow here to provide food for the consulate greatly upset the locals, who like nearly all other Japanese at the time did not eat red meat. The fact that it was a *mikan* (orange) tree has led to the battle cry of the citrus and cattle farmers of Japan in their opposition to imports: "Don't tie a cow to an orange tree." Also in Shimoda is **Hofukuji**, a temple exhibiting personal articles of Okichi, Harris' geisha-turned-mistress.

It should also be mentioned that the fresh seafood – particularly the prawns – served in hotels, *ryokan* and restaurants in eastern Izu can be heavenly.

Central Izu is the cultural heart of Izu. **Farming...**

The **Taisha Shrine** in **Mishima** is revered as Izu's first shrine and its treasure hall keeps documents of the first Kamakura shogun as well as swords and other artifacts. The **Egawa Old House** in Nirama is the oldest private dwelling in Japan. **Shuzenji**, along the Katsura River, sprang up around a temple founded by the monk Kobo Daishi; this quiet hot spring town became a favorite hideaway for Japan's great literary talents such as Natsume Soseki, Nobel Prize winner Kawabata Yasunari, and Kido Okamoto.

The west coast is less visited by tourists, for unlike the east, it has no train line. Still, resort towns such as **Toi** and others here are interesting, and some have, reputedly, the best hot springs in the region.

From May 16 through 18, Shimoda celebrates the **Kurofune Matsuri** (Black Ship Festival) in commemoration of Commodore Perry's landing. Various ceremonies, parades and a fireworks display are included. Ito holds its **Tarainori Kyoso** on the first Sunday in

July, with a race of wooden washtubs equipped with sails, followed by fireworks. Then August 8 through 10 sees the **Ito Anji Sai**, dedicated to William Adams (Clavell's model for "Blackthorn"), as Ito townspeople float paper lanterns on the river in his memory. The **Annual Festival of the Mishima Taisha Shrine** at Mishima falls on August 15 through 17, allowing onlookers to get an idea of what the procession of Minamoto no Yoritomo, the first Kamakura shogun, may have looked like. There is also a horseback archery performance on the last day.

The main gateways to Izu are Atami (a stop on the Shinkansen) and Mishima, on the Tokaido Main Line. The JR limited express "Odoriko" also makes direct trips to Ito and Shimoda from Tokyo (the name of the train is the title of Kawabata's famous short story, known in English as "The Izu Dancer"). Travel within the peninsula and along the west coast is not very convenient, as the roads are twisty and narrow, and buses often overcrowded.

…and fishing on Izu.

CHIBA, NARITA AND THE MAGIC KINGDOM

It seems somehow appropriate that William Gibson chose to set the opening of his nightmarish 1984 SF novel *Neuromancer* in Chiba City of the future, a no-man's land where the "sky above the port was the color of television tuned to a dead channel."

Chiba Prefecture, Tokyo's neighbor to the immediate east and northeast, has long suffered from its image as an industrial backwater and home to legions of office workers who commute to jobs in Tokyo from nearly identical box-like apartments, and of *bosozoku* motorcyclists who delight in brazenly violating the stillness of the early morning.

This unflattering image represented at best only a tiny portion of the truth and Chiba is in the midst of phenomenal change anyway.

The Magic Kingdom: What brings most visitors to Chiba today is **Tokyo Disneyland**, located on 874 hectares (2,160 acres) of reclaimed land in **Urayasu City** just across the Edo River from Tokyo. It is only a 15-minute train ride from Tokyo Station on the JR Keiyo Line. Alternatively, one may take the Tozai Subway Line to Urayasu and then catch a shuttle bus.

Over 80 million people have visited the Magic Kingdom since it opened in 1983, nearly 15 million in 1989 alone. In fact, Tokyo Disneyland has already become East Asia's greatest single tourist attraction and 5.5 percent of its visitors come from abroad. Be warned that when school is out, the mammoth crowds can mean 2-hour waits for popular attractions like "Star Tours."

Tokyo Disneyland, where the average visitor spends about ¥8,000, is also big business. Directly and indirectly, the park is responsible for 96,000 jobs and its total economic impact is on par with Japan's entire camera industry.

One area in which the influence of Tokyo Disneyland is readily apparent is the hotel industry. The **Maihama** district of Urayasu, near Tokyo Bay, has sprouted a forest of upscale hotels with out-of-sight prices.

New Conventions: Another symbol of Chiba's coming of age is **Makuhari Messe**, or officially, the Nippon Convention Center, which opened in October 1989. The center is East Asia's largest conventional and exhibition complex, it offers 131,000 sq. meters (1,410,072 sq. ft) of space, as well as state-of-the-art communications and display services. Recently, however, the showcase complex has come under fire from foreign and Japanese critics alike for being an "architectural disaster."

Actually, the Makuhari Messe complex accounts for only 1/20 of a 522-hectare (1,290-acre) futuristic community, which when completed will boast a "Techno-Garden," "World Business Garden" and fashion zone featuring a Hanae Mori Building. It will have a day-time working population of 100,000 and will be home to 26,000 residents. To see the shape of things to come, take the Keiyo Line to Kaihin Makuhari Station.

Also nearby is the **Kazusa Kyuryo**

Left, fun-filled faces on the "Star Jet." Right, the *Mark Twain* sets sail at Tokyo Disneyland.

district, where the 405-hectare (1,000-acre) Kasuza Institute for Life Sciences is being constructed for academic and technical research and development, centering on new materials, biotechnology and raw material distribution.

Technology Tabernacle: Of course, no discussion of Japan's all-out effort to increase its basic research capability would be complete without mention of **Tsukuba Science City**, about 60 kilometers (37 miles) northwest of Tokyo in Ibaraki Prefecture. Despite the fact that many researchers here still prefer the daily 3-hour commute from Tokyo to relocation to the planned city, the population of Tsukuba City reached 220,000 in 1990 and was home to 47 national research institutes or laboratories, Tsukuba University and facilities of over 100 private firms. Among the local residents are 7,000 scientists, engineers and researchers; that this population includes 1,850 foreigners makes Tsukuba perhaps the most internationalized city in Japan, per capita.

Japan's government has been lavish in its support of Tsukuba. Famed architect Isozaki Arata was brought in to design the Tsukuba Center Building, a US$50 million postmodernist tabernacle, as the showpiece of the community. Even so, Tsukuba tends to remind one of the look-alike towns in California, a vaguely threatening environment designed more for the automobile than for people. Appropriately, among the local sights is a completely computerized, totally unmanned "ghost factory" that produces machine parts.

Tsukuba was of course the location of the 1985 International Science and Technology Exposition (Science Expo '85). Its relative failure has served to transfer some of Japan's previous enthusiasm for expos to theme parks: Mitsubishi Corporation is building a ¥300 billion "Space Port" on a 200-hectare (494-acre) site near Tsukuba. Much larger and more expensive to construct than Disneyland, the park will open in late 1992 and is expected to draw 10 million visitors during its first year. Retired astronauts and former

The future beckons at Tsukuba Science City.

NASA personnel are acting as advisors for the project.

Airport Blues: Narita Airport (or, to use the official name, the **New Tokyo International Airport**) is now operating at its limits, handling 18 million passengers a year – half a million during the New Year's week alone – and an average of 360 flights a day are handled by its single 4,000-meter (4,375-yard) runway. Go up to the fifth-floor observation area during the peak hours and you can watch the big birds take off as regularly as trains departing at rush hour.

Things have been, to put it mildly, a mess at Narita from the start. The airport opened in May 1978, seven years late, and before and since it has been plagued by violent protests involving 20,000 anti-airport activists who claim to be supporting the farmers of the area dispossessed by heavy-handed government tactics. (Ironically, "*Narita*" means "Becoming Rice Fields.")

At present, all that is holding up the ¥600-billion second phase of the airport project that would make available new 2,500-meter (2,734-yard) and 3,200-meter (3,500-yard) runways are eight farmers who still adamantly refuse to sell the last 23 hectares (57 acres) out of the 1,065 (2,630 acres) needed.

Prayers of Fire: Most people are in a hurry to leave the Narita area, which is a shame since it has much to offer. First and foremost, there is **Shinshoji**, usually referred to simply as **Narita-san**. A 15-minute walk from JR Narita or Keisei Narita Stations, this temple, said to date back to AD 940, is one of the most important in the entire Kanto region. It draws 12 million visitors a year, worshipers and sightseers alike, including about 3 million during the first three days of the New Year.

There are several reasons for Narita-san's popularity. First of all, there is the image of **Fudo**, the Buddhist "god of fire," which is said to have been carved by Kobo Daishi, the saint who founded the Shingon sect. Prayers in the temple are written on paper or small wooden boards, then burned at the main altar.

Then there is the architectural inter-

Boso Peninsula fishermen prepare their nets for the day ahead.

est provided by the 18.9-meter (63-ft) high Nio entrance gate, the 27-meter (88-ft) high pagoda, the Main Hall and the other buildings of the complex. There are large and quite attractive gardens (and a depressing little zoo) behind the main buildings, but the most interesting sight at Narita-san is at the side of the temple complex, where a "drive-in" chapel welcomes drivers to be blessed – and their vehicles – by a priest and, for a fee, be adorned with amulets to protect them from accidents.

But the most important factor behind Narita-san's popularity is undoubtedly the personality cult of Taira no Masakado, a rebel who tried unsuccessfully to make himself emperor. This Robin Hood-like figure remained a hero to the inhabitants of eastern Japan, who felt slighted and exploited by their cousins in the western heartland. Like the Kanda Myojin Shrine in Tokyo, the temple was built to mollify Masakado's vengeful spirit after he was beheaded in AD 939. The fact that Masakado sought to replace the line of the Sun Goddess has been conveniently forgotten.

Dutch Learning: History buffs should enjoy **Japan Village**, a ¥39 billion pop introduction to Japan's past, located on a 50-hectare (124-acre) site near the airport. When (if ever) completed, it will feature a "Ninja Magic Village" and a replica of the donjon of Edo Castle in miniature. A more credible look at the nation's history can be enjoyed in the former castle town of **Sakura** on the Narita Keisei and JR Sobu Lines. From the 1790s the Sakura fief was known as a center of "Dutch learning," especially Western medical practices. Within the extensively landscaped former castle grounds is the **National Museum of Japanese History** (Kokuritsu Rekishi Minzoku Hakubutsukan), which presents the vast cavalcade of Japanese history from a cultural anthropology, social history viewpoint, with the aid of numerous displays, dioramas and videos. You will not miss the Tokyo museum crowds for a moment.

Up a Lazy River: Other easily accessible places of interest in Chiba are **Kashima Jingu**, the most important shrine in the Kanto district, on the JR Kashima Line from Narita, and the system of canals near **Sawara** and **Itako**, reached by JR limited expresses from Tokyo or Ryogoku Stations. The canals meander through thousands of hectares of marshland where wildlife still abounds; tours using traditional, poled boats take you through portions of the marshes, and usually include a "traditional lunch" and even a spot of fishing.

Around the Horn: If time permits and you have a car, a leisurely drive around the Boso Peninsula is worthwhile. The rather mountainous peninsula, shaped like a pelican's craw separating Tokyo Bay from the Pacific, is ill-served by train lines, but with a car you can enjoy much of what it has to offer.

If you begin on the Tokyo Bay side and head toward the tip, you pass through **Kisarazu**; this small city will be a terminus of the ¥1.5 trillion Trans-Tokyo Bay Highway to be completed in 1995. The bridge-and-tunnel complex will allow cars and trains to cross the bay to Kawasaki in some 15 minutes, shorten-

Waiting for their cue at Chiba Prefecture's *Haniwa* Festival.

ing the total travel time into the heart of Tokyo to about an hour.

Next, near **Sanukimachi**, you will pass the 56-meter (184-ft) **Tokyo Bay Kannon** statue, perched on top of a 120-meter (394-ft) hill. Still further on is **Nokogiriyama** (Saw Mountain), its 329-meter (1,080-ft) summit reached by a ropeway to afford a spectacular view of the bay. While hiking down, try taking in the **Hyakushaku Kannon**, "Hell View," and the **1,500 Disciples of Buddha**, stone *rakan* (statues) which are yawning, crying, laughing, or headless. Finally, you might visit the **Yakushi Nyorai Buddha**, which at 31 meters (102 ft) tall is much bigger than the Great Buddha at Nara. Although dating from the Edo Era, the statue was almost entirely rebuilt in 1969, and looks it.

The **Shirahama-Chikura** area at the tip of Boso is known for its beautiful wild flowers and *ama* diving women, whose shacks can be seen along the shore. You can even watch them at work from glass-bottomed boats.

Then coming up the Pacific side of the peninsula to Amatsu Kominato, you will find **Tanjoji**, a temple dedicated to the area's most famous son, the iconoclastic monk Nichiren.

Next comes **Katusuura**, the farthest point north that coral colonies reach in Japan, and shortly after that, a 17-meter (55-ft) high obelisk marking the site of a 1609 Spanish shipwreck. Before you know it, you will be sailing along **Kujukuri Beach** (the name translates roughly as "99 Miles," though it is much shorter than that); this long sandy beach offers some of the best surfing in the Northern Pacific, and – especially on windy summer days – you can see some of the world's best surfers and sailboarders taking advantage of it.

Further along, the picturesque lighthouse at **Inubosaki** (Dog Howl Point) is worth a visit before you end your drive at **Choshi City** near the mouth of the Tone River; this is the third biggest fishing port in Japan and offers the finest bounty from the sea, thanks to the point where warm from the south meet the frigid currents of the north.

Canal tour through the "Venice of Japan" at Sawara.

NIKKO

After learning that the main attraction at Nikko, the **Toshogu**, comprises 42 structures and that 29 of those are embellished with some sort of carving – 5,147 in all, according to a six-year survey concluded in 1991 by shrine officials – more than a few tourists apply the second meaning of the word "*kekko*" to the phrase "You shouldn't say '*kekko*' until you've seen Nikko." Usually, the phrase is taken to mean that Nikko is "magnificent," but the other meaning of "*kekko*" is "enough."

Still, if only to marvel at the excessive gaudiness of the place (enough gold leaf was used in the decoration to cover 2.4 hectares/36 acres), a visit to the shrine, dedicated to Tokugawa Ieyasu, founder of the Tokugawa shogunate, should in no way be considered a waste of time. In fact, a few hours spent in the precincts, which not incidentally are set amidst one of the richest deciduous forests in

this country, can be a lot of fun – even if the weather (as it probably will be when you visit) is rainy.

The small city of Nikko itself is of little interest, serving merely as a commercial anchor to the splendors (well, some people consider them splendid) that decorate the hillsides and plateau across the river to the west from the Tobu Railway and JR Nikko stations in its heart. It is at the former station that the Tobu train arrives in exactly (and you can set your watch by it) "101 minutes" after departing Tokyo's Ueno Station, something the railway's advertising department has made a catch-phrase of for years.

Somewhat of a Mystery: How this region, once a several-day trek from the shogunate's capital in Edo (now Tokyo), was chosen as the site of Ieyasu's mausolea and all their attendant geegaws is a story in itself. True, Nikko forms a sort of cap or crown at the northern perimeter of the great Kanto Plain of which Edo was the center. However, Ieyasu was a Kansai, not a Kanto man, and established his capital there primarily to distance himself from the Imperial forces in Kyoto to the west, forces he had vanquished to seize power in the first place. The account is still somewhat of a mystery.

Still, Ieyasu's grandson, Iemitsu (1604–51) set in motion the process that turned this once out-of-the-way region into Togugawa turf about 20 years after Ieyasu's death, and who himself, followed by his successor Ietsuna and indeed by shogun and/or Tokugawa princes for the next 250 years or so, made at least three annual pilgrimages to the site to pay tribute to the founder of the dynasty that, among other things, kept Japan and its people isolated and ignorant of the "outside world" for the better part of a quarter of a millennium.

Speaking of mysteries, or perhaps ironies is a better word, there is also the fact that many of those 5,000-odd carvings at Toshogu deal with things foreign. The facade of the main shrine, for example, features carvings of three Chinese men, said to represent important figures of that faraway country who, **Buddhist shrine at Nikko.**

having turned down their chances to be kings or emperors, became folk heros. Perhaps the carvings are meant to convey the fallacy that Ieyasu had come to power only after the Toyotomi emperor had voluntarily abdicated in his favor.

There are also the "foreign" mandarin oranges, prominent among the 1,423 representations of plants and fruits that adorn many of the buildings; they also are Chinese in origin, and were considered delicacies far beyond the reach of ordinary Japanese, especially since Ieyasu had slammed the doors shut on trade with that exotic country.

The "Korean Gate"?: Most ironic of all – and most hypocritical, considering its importance in the annals of "Japanese" art – is the famous, not to say fabulous **Yomeimon**, the gate beyond which only the highest ranking samurai could pass into the inner sanctum of the shrine, and then only after laying aside their swords.

This gate is, indeed, a masterpiece. Technically, it is a 12-column, two-story structure, with hip-gable ends on right and left, and cusped gables on four sides. This description, while accurate, is somewhat misleading, however; the gate, even though its *keyaki*-wood columns are painted white to make it appear larger, is quite small.

Nearly every surface of the gate is adorned ("encrusted" would be a better word) with delicate carvings of every sort – children at play, clouds, tree peonies, pines, bamboo, Japanese apricots, phoenixes, pheasants, cranes, wild ducks and other waterfowl, turtles, elephants, rabbits, a couple of furry tigers, "Chinese" lions, and the traditional symbols of regal power, dragons.

A large white dragon (one of 92 in and around the shrine) is the main feature of the central beam in front of the second story of this fanciful structure, and two drawings of dragons appear on the ceiling of the porticos; in case you're curious, the drawing nearer the entrance is known as *nobori-ryu* or "ascending dragon," the other *kudari-ryu* or "descending dragon."

Yomeimon translates roughly as "Gate of Sunlight," but confusingly, the

Inner courtyard of the mist-shrouded Toshogu Shrine.

structure is also known as the "Twilight Gate," meaning that one wants to stand and examine it till the sun goes down. Well, stand and examine it all you like, but as you do, keep in mind that although it is designated a "National Treasure," and as mentioned, considered an example of the heights of Japanese art, the nameless artisans who created Yomeimon (and many of the other treasures at Nikko) were of Korean, not Japanese, origin.

What lies beyond this gate? Another gate, of course: **Karamon** (Chinese Gate) is also a "National Treasure." It is even smaller than the Yomeimon (about three by two meters overall) and also is laden with carvings – dragons (not only ascending and descending but also just laying around), apricots, bamboo, tree peonies, and more. The ceiling has a carved figure of a fairy playing a harp, while on the ridge of the front gable is a bronze figure of a *tsutsuga* which, like quite a few other carvings and castings in the shrine precincts (e.g., the giraffes and most of the elephants), is not quite a "real" animal, but rather one created from hearsay and myth mixed with a healthy (Korean, perhaps) imagination.

"Sights" Unseen: To help you get your bearings, the Karamon is the last barrier you pass through before reaching the entrance to the **Haiden** (Oratory) and the **Honden** (Main Hall), also "National Treasures," the place everyone remembers because it's where you are requested to take off your shoes.

An official guidebook describes them as the "chief edifices of the shrine." Chief they are, but interesting they are not – at least not to the casual visitor who, not knowing what to look at or for, tends to shuffle along with the crowd and back to the shoe-lockers without a pause. Unfortunately, many of the key elements inside are partially or entirely hidden from the view one gets from the shuffle track, and of course are not identified by signs or labels, museum style. Nevertheless, among the "sights" here are: the Sacred Mirror, believed to represent the holy spirit of the deity; an antechamber formerly reserved for the

One of 42 historic structures at Toshogu.

shogun and the three Tokugawa houses of Owari, Kii and Mito; and an inner sanctum divided into three apartments where a gold *gohei* (wand with paper festoons) is kept, and where, surrounded by "specimens of art of the highest workmanship," is the gold-lacquered shrine called the **Misorandono** (Sacred Palace), wherein are enshrined Ieyasu, with Toyotomi Hideyoshi and Minamoto no Yoritomo as associate deities.

The Sleeping Cat: Confused (and no doubt somewhat bored) after their shuffle through the "chief edifices," most visitors exit, redon their shoes and spend the next 10 minutes or so looking for the famous "**Nemuri-neko**" or "Sleeping Cat" carving. Some never find it at all, and make their way back down the hillside feeling somewhat cheated. To make sure this doesn't happen to you, do *not* follow the logical path back toward the Yomeimon, but turn to your left (your right if you are facing the Haiden/Honden complex) until you are back on the terrace between the Yomeimon and the Karamon. Next, advance straight

ahead (paying the small fee charged at a makeshift entrance to the **Oku-no-In** or Inner Precincts) and into the open-sided, red-lacquered corridor that skirts the foot of the steep hillside atop which is the actual Tokugawa Tomb; the painted relief carving is over the gateway.

This small, gray cat, well-enough executed and rather cute but otherwise unremarkable, is said to symbolize tranquility: the fact that it is asleep is taken to mean that all "harmful mice" have been sent packing and the shrine is, therefore, "safe." The carved sparrows seen behind the dozing cat are not, presumably, a threat.

While here, you might want to climb the 200-odd stone steps to the top of the hill and the Tomb, called the **Hoto**, wherein, it is said, lie the remains of Ieyasu. Some spectacular views of rooftops and the surrounding terrain are had from here.

On the way back down past the Yomeimon to the main entrance and beyond, be sure to stop by the **Yakushido**, one of the few places in

Barrels of sake as shrine offerings at Nikko.

these sacred Shinto surroundings with a Buddhist atmosphere. It's off to the right as you descend (if you can't find it, ask someone). Here, too, you'll have to remove your shoes, but if you're into weird or even pseudo-weird things, it'll be worth it. The attraction of this building (it is not exactly a Buddhist temple, so we'll just call it a building) is the huge **Naku-ryu** drawing on the ceiling. The word means "Crying Dragon," and the really weird thing about it is that it doesn't cry.

Okay, that deserves some explanation. It seems that when people stood under the original – drawn in India ink by Kano Yasunobu (1613–85) – and clapped their hands (as in prayer), the dragon was heard to utter a long, agonized groan. What this was meant to signify is not recorded, and perhaps we will never know, because in 1961, a fire destroyed the building and the drawing along with it.

Today, absurd though it may seem, countless thousands of Nikko visitors line up, after making a small monetary contribution, to clap their hands in prayer under a reproduction of the original "Crying Dragon" and, under the prompting of an enterprising priest, convince themselves into thinking that they, too, have heard the dragon produce its torturous sound.

Among the other sights to take note of as one leaves the shrine are the **Sutra Library**, which boasts nearly 7,000 volumes of the Buddhist Sutras in a large revolving bookcase which was invented by the Chinese.

Its other treasures include numerous stone, bronze and iron lanterns presented by the daimyo paying their respects to the shogunate; a pair of stone **Tobikoe-no-shishi** (Leaping Lions) as the main pillars of the stone balustrade in the middle court and bell presented by a king of Korea. The bronze candelabrum and a bronze lantern and a large revolving lantern were presented by the government of the Netherlands to Japan in 1636. The revolving lantern, in front of the drum tower, is adorned with the three-leaf crests of the Tokugawas, but

Shinkyo, the sacred bridge at Nikko.

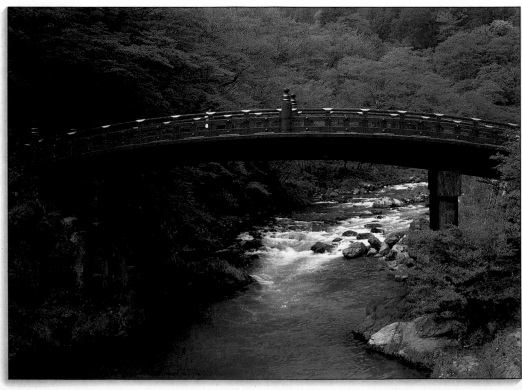

they are placed upside down, "perhaps," as an official Japanese government guidebook to the Sutra Library explains, "by mistake."

Here, also, are the **Sacred Storehouses** on the sides of the middle court – the upper one shows two (imaginary) elephants carved in relief – as well as the **Mikoshigura** (Sacred Palanquin House), the repository for the sacred portable shrines used in the annual festival, and the **Kaguraden** (Sacred Dance Stage). The flower basket in the gilded panel at the right corner probably was inspired by a basket used by early Dutch traders, and is the only carving in the precincts that shows Western-type artistic influences.

First Monkey Trio: Then, as you pass the 40-meter (130-ft) high **Five-Story Pagoda**, its first story decorated with the 12 signs of the Oriental zodiac, and just before you reach the 9-meter (29.5-ft) tall **Omotemon** (Front Gate) with its large images of the two Deva Kings, you will come upon what may be the most famous carvings of all – not just in Nikko but in all the world. There, just under the eaves of the **Royal Stables** building (which happens to be the only unlacquered structure in the shrine precincts, in case you're interested) are, yes, there's no mistake... the "three famous monkeys."

That's right. The **"Hear no Evil, Speak no Evil, See no Evil"** trio is originally, lo and behold, Japanese (or maybe Korean) and right out there in plain sight, no less. Small carvings they are, despite their fame, but like all the other 5,174 here at Toshogu, the stuff from which legends – and travel guides – are made.

Just a short stroll down the broad avenue leading from the "Thousand Steps" (there are only 10) entrance to Toshogu is the **Nikko Treasure House** – a small museum housing various articles (including carvings) from Toshogu and other places around Nikko; during peak tourist seasons there probably will be a number of kiosks set up in the small adjoining park, **Koyoen**, selling beverages and food. After a visit, if you are

Statues of Lords serving the Shogun, Nikko.

still in the mood for more, you could continue along the wide avenue for a few minutes to reach the **Futaarasan Shrine**, on the right hand side and away from Toshogu.

It enshrines the three (main) Shinto dieties: Okuninushi no Mikoto, his consort Tagorihime no Mikoto, and their son Ajisukitakahikone no Mikoto. All three are revered for having helped to create – and then make prosperous – the numerous Japanese Islands.

Within the grounds is a large bronze lantern, called **Bake-Doro** (Goblin Lantern), which is once supposed to have taken on the shape of a goblin so frightening that a samurai attacked it one night; leaving "sword scratches" that are still visible to this day.

Further afield but still within the general area of Toshogu are several other places of interest. One is the **Hongu** (more popularly called Futaarasan-Hongu), one of the oldest shrines in Nikko, established in 767 by Priest Shodo; the present buildings date back only to the end of the 17th century, when the shrine was rebuilt after being destroyed by fire.

Just behind it is **Shihonryuji,** which though also founded in 766 by Shodo, is not a Shinto shrine but a Buddhist temple. It also was destroyed by fire, and the present three-story pagoda was erected in its place at the end of the 17th century. The pagoda, and the image of the **Thousand-Hand Kannon** inside, are the shine's main attractions.

Then there is **Rinnoji**, a temple of the Tendai sect of Buddhism. Its main claim to fame is the fact that General Ulysses S. Grant, the 18th president of the US, stayed here during his eight-day sojourn in Nikko in July 1879.

Actually, the temple has more than that going for it. In its **Spirit Hall** are the tablets of its long line of abbots, all drawn from the Imperial Family, and in another building – built in 1648 and still the largest in Nikko – are three quite amazing Buddhist statues, all measuring 8 meters (26 ft) tall, and worked in gilded wood. The **Bato Kannon**, on the left, has the figure of a horse's head on

Fall in Nikko is a beautiful sight.

its forehead, and is worshiped as the deity for the protection of animals.

The lush forests of Nikko and how pleasant they are, even in the rain, has already been mentioned. Seeing these ancient trees – the majority are *suji*, or Japanese cedar – one would think they have stood here since the beginning of time, or at the very least are part of a primeval "virgin" forest. They don't go back quite that far but they are nevertheless very old – especially those trees in the Toshogu precincts proper and those along the many, many kilometers of avenues and roads within and leading to Nikko. They were all planted as seedlings, one by one, under the direction of a man named Matsudaira Masatsuna (1576–1648).

Matsudaira, so the story goes, was the Daimyo of Kawagoe, and one of the two persons honored by edict of the shogun to supervise the construction of Toshogu. The extent of the man's personal wealth is not recorded, nor how much of it was spent, in addition to the budget he was given by Tokugawa III, for carrying out this worthy task. However, it can be assumed that either he wasn't very well off to begin with, or that he overspent more than he ought to have, because when his turn to present a grand offering to the shrine came – as all the other daimyo were obliged to do – Matsudaira was broke.

What could he do? he wondered. Around 1631, several years before the shrine itself was finished, he began to transplant cedar seedlings – plentiful in the surrounding mountains (which he owned) – into strategic positions around the shrine grounds and along those endless roads. It took him 20 years and an estimated 25,000 seedlings, but it was done and the tale completed.

The benificence continues: the trees – and the banks along the avenues – are now specially protected as "Natural Treasures" and "Places of Historical Importance" under Japanese law.

By the Way: Thanks to the numbers of tourists who flock to Nikko, and to the region's fine scenery, the area abounds with other diversions. If time permits, we can recommend a taxi (not bus) ride up the famed "*I-Ro-Ha*" switchback road to **Lake Chuzenji,** a large and quite picturesque lake whose heavily wooded shores are lined with hotels, inns, camping grounds and the usual sort of outdoor facilities.

If you choose not to stay overnight at the lake, you might try one of the several *onsen* (spas) on the picturesque **Kinu River**, closer to Nikko itself.

Also in the area of the Kinu river is **Nikko Edo-Mura**, a theme park; the not-so-cheap entrance fee entitles you to stroll around the extensive grounds on streets that look like a movie set of the old Edo days. You can see a "real" *ninja* show, confound yourself in a "poetry maze," and other attractions. It's great fun, and a good way to spend a few hours "educating" the family and yourself about the bad old days of pre-Meiji Japan.

You really should "do" Nikko. But when all's done, you'll wonder how President Grant made it through all eight days of his visit. After a day or two, you would think he would have said "*kekko*."

Solitude and serenity at Lake Chuzenji.

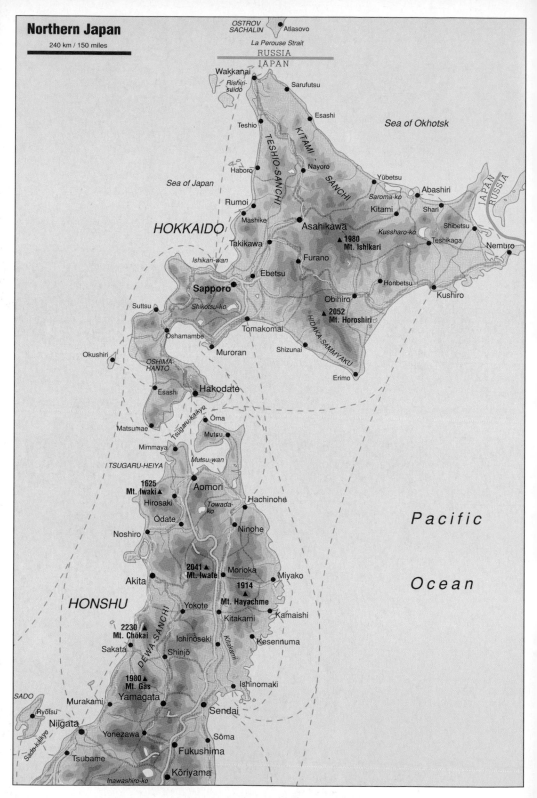

Northern Japan

240 km / 150 miles

OSTROV
SACHALIN · Atlasovo

La Perouse Strait
RUSSIA
JAPAN

Wakkanai

*Rishiri-
suido* · Sarufutsu

Teshio · Esashi

Sea of Okhotsk

TESHIO-SANCHI

KITAMI-SANCHI

· Haboro · Nayoro · Yūbetsu

· Abashiri

Sea of Japan *Saroma-ko*

· Rumoi · Kitami · Shari

HOKKAIDO · Mashike · Asahikawa *Kussharo-ko* · Shibetsu

· Takikawa ▲ 1980
Mt. Ishikari · Teshikaga

Ishikari-wan · Furano · Nemuro

· Ebetsu

Sapporo

· Suttsu *Shikotsu-ko* · Honbetsu · Kushiro

· Oshamambe Obihiro

· Okushiri Tomakomai ▲ 2052
Mt. Horoshiri

*OSHIMA-
HANTŌ* · Muroran · Shizunai

HIDAKA-SAMMYAKU

· Esashi **Hakodate** · Erimo

· Matsumae Ōma

Tsugaru-kaikyo · Mutsu

· Mimmaya *Mutsu-wan*

TSUGARU-HEIYA

1625
Mt. Iwaki ▲ **Aomori**

· Hirosaki *Towada-
ko* · Hachinohe

· Ōdate

· Noshiro · Ninohe

Pacific

2041 ▲
Mt. Iwate · Morioka

· Akita 1914 · Miyako

▲
Mt. Hayachme

HONSHU · Yokote · Kamaishi

Ocean

· Kitakami

2230 ▲
Mt. Chōkai · Ichinōseki · Kesennuma

· Sakata · Shinjō

Kitakami

1980 ▲
Mt. Gas · Ishinomaki

SADO · Murakami **Yamagata**

· Ryōtsu **Sendai**

Niigata · Yonezawa · Sōma

Sado-kaikyo · Tsubame **Fukushima**

Kōriyama

Inawashiro-ko

JAPAN
RUSSIA

DEWA-SANCHI

248

Hinterland, back country; the distant roads; the impenetrable provinces. These are but a few of the terms used over the years by the "sophisticated" people living in Tokyo and points south to describe the north country. The northern prefectures comprise Tohoku (the Northeast) and, since its forced settlement during the Meiji Restoration in the late 19th century, the large northern island of Hokkaido.

This image of inaccessibility is perhaps not so difficult to understand. Travel in the north country is an experience of unconquered nature, high volcanic mountains almost everywhere, severe climate (the western edge of Tohoku gets more snow than any other civilized place on earth), a viable traditional culture, and, in some areas, a language that sounds strangely different from the Japanese spoken in Tokyo. Here in the north you discover strange folklore, legends of evil spirits, creatures that haunt the frozen mountains in winter and, in summer, the exuberant that are festivals unique to this part of Japan.

Even today, the idea of the north as a backwards, somewhat insignificant appendage to the rest of Japan persists. The foreign visitor who openly declares his intention to spend some time traveling in the north can still raise a few eyebrows. He might even find himself the recipient of a torrent of advice by the usually taciturn Japanese; lurid tales of horrendous snowfalls, unacceptable accommodations, the peculiarities of the people, the lack of amenities which we Westerners take for granted. Perhaps the most memorable warning issued in recent years (by a Japanese who, needless to say, had never set foot in the north) was this: "You'll find no toilets with seats in that part of this world."

"I might as well be going to the ends of the earth." That's how Basho, Japan's great 17th-century *haiku* poet put it on the eve of his departure into the north in 1689. It seems a curious notion today, especially when we consider that Sendai, Tohoku's predominant city in Miyagi Prefecture, is only two hours from Tokyo via Shinkansen. Morioka City, deep in the rugged interior of Iwate Prefecture, is only an hour more along the same line. Even Hokkaido, still considered a far-off frontier suitable for only the most adventurous, is now a mere nine hours from Tokyo by train, thanks to the recent completion of the 54-kilometer-long (87-mile) Seikan Tunnel linking Honshu with its northern neighbor. An even more modern alternative, the aeroplane, can get the traveler there in far less time.

Of course, transportation hasn't always been this good. Back in 1689, when Basho decided to prowl the back country, the roads really were narrow, or nonexistent. Yet, despite the rigors of his journey and the beautiful *haiku* he wrote about the north's exotic

Preceding pages: field of greens; fun and games at the Sapporo Snow Festival, held annually.

natural marvels along the way, Basho was never more than 400 kilometers from home.

The north has always been perceived as remote, strange, existing outside the normal sphere of Japanese life. But perhaps this is not so much a matter of distance as of psychology. Even imagining that such a place as Hokkaido exists, for example, is difficult as it is so different from the rest of Japan. Seemingly limitless open space, nature untouched by man, large farms raising cattle and horses, frontier towns, homesteaders. It sounds more like Wyoming or Montana than Japan. There actually are "cowboys" in Hokkaido, something TV producers never seem to tire of "featuring" on daytime shows.

Undoubtedly, the northern mountains have a lot of to do with this sense of remoteness. There are mountains everywhere in Japan, but those in the north tend to be bigger, more imposing and, from late autumn to mid-spring, do not spare a place for the casual tourist. One could begin an imaginary mountain journey in the majestic Japan Alps in Nagano Prefecture. Heading northwest through the central and northern ranges, one would eventually arrive at the industrial seaport city of Niigata in Niigata Prefecture. Here the mountains subside somewhat, leveling off just long enough for the people of Niigata to grow what is considered the best rice in Japan. Then the mountains rise again, forming a huge volcanic spine which literally bisects the entire length of Tohoku, from Yamagata in the south to Aomori in the north. These impressive mountains with their beautiful gorges, waterfalls, volcanic lakes and natural hot springs are as spectacular as they are off the beaten track.

Then too, the people of the north bear some responsibility for the persistence of the area's exotic reputation. Tohoku was originally settled by itinerant warlords and soldiers who constructed castle fortresses to keep out potentially unfriendly neighbors. These castle towns developed into insular communities with their own unique lifestyle, crafts, cottage industries and language. The famous *Toho-kuben* (Northeast dialect), still spoken by many older people here, is actually a series of subdialects with numerous variations. These are a lingering reminder of the area's feudal past, and even today they serve to insulate a part of Tohoku's population from the rest of Japan. At Mt. Osore in Aomori Prefecture there are blind female mediums who reportedly have the ability to contact the spirits of the dead. Unfortunately, the dialect spoken by these women is so rare that only they – and possibly the departed spirits – can understand it. It is not uncommon for Japanese tourists to hire local translators while on a pilgrimage to the sacred mountains.

Traveling in the north country is no longer a matter of going to the ends of the earth. The back roads have opened into highways and train lines. It is perhaps no longer an easy matter to find ourselves – as Basho was able to – alone in some idyllic spot. But for the adventurous at heart, it is still possible, for a little while anyway, to lose oneself in the mysterious backcountry of the north.

Left, the strange and mysterious islands of Matsushima.

TOHOKU: THE UNSPOILED NORTHEAST

The northern quarter of Honshu comprises six prefectures: Aomori, Akita, Iwate, Miyagi, Yamagata and Fukushima. The region is known for its natural beauty, rugged mountains, lovely women, sometimes incomprehensible dialects, innumerable hot springs and – it cannot be denied – its harsh winters.

Here, one still hears the myths that have been told over the centuries, perhaps told as a way of explaining and coping with the difficult realities of weather and topography: clever foxes who turn themselves into beautiful women and lure unsuspecting men to their doom; green-headed river creatures who snatch small children venturing too close to the water; devils and ghosts in great abundance.

By Japanese standards, Tohoku is sparsely populated (10 million people

in a land area of 67,000 sq. km/26 sq. miles). Its climate is comparable to Vermont in the US, with the possible exception of the month of August, when certain parts of southern Tohoku like to pretend they are lying across the equator. (Yamagata City holds the record for the highest temperature ever recorded in Japan, at 40.8°C/ 105°F.)

Long ago the area was known as *Michinoku*, meaning "interior" or "narrow road"; implied in the name is a sense of the uncivilized, the lack of culture. In the old days a barrier wall was constructed at Shirakawa, in southern Fukushima, to separate the civilized world of the south from the barbarians in the north. Although the name eventually changed to the neutral Tohoku, meaning simply "northeast," this image of cultural immaturity lingers.

Escape Modernity: There is a certain irony in this, since it is generally agreed that Tohoku is perhaps the last bastion of traditional Japanese culture, the so-called "real Japan" that one imagines when one conjures up images of this

Although subject to harsh winters, the Tohoku region is very fertile.

land. To a large degree, Tohoku has escaped the rapid "Westernized" modernization which the rest of Japan has undergone since the end of World War II. In the north it is still possible to discover farms growing rice by methods used hundreds of years ago, tiny fishing villages nestled into cliffs overlooking unspoiled sea coasts, isolated hot spring inns, and a people whose open friendliness is unstinting. Here, too, it is still possible to find a remote and empty beach to explore, or to savor the waters of a rustic mountain *onsen* in the company of only the birds and the surrounding forest. No longer unknown, Tohoku is still a place of spectacular beauty, and a must-see for any visitor who desires a taste of the Japan that once was.

Sendai City: This city was originally called Sentaijo, after the Thousand Buddha Statue Temple which once graced the top of **Mt. Aoba**. The name was changed to Sendai, meaning "Thousand Generations," by the Date clan during their reign of the area, possibly in the hope that they would be running things in this port of Tohoku for that long.

Today, Sendai is a cosmopolitan city of approximately 800,000 people, the capital of Miyagi Prefecture, and the pre-eminent city of the entire Tohoku region. It is known as the "Green City" and the "City of Trees," and visitors arriving on the Tohoku Shinkansen from points south will not find it difficult to understand why. From **Sendai Station**, considered one of the most beautiful in Japan, the main boulevards running east to west are all tree-lined.

Those wide, European-style avenues are a pleasure to stroll along. If one is so inclined, the entire downtown area is small enough to cover in an hour or so of leisurely walking. From Sendai's new and tallest **SS-30 Building** (30 floors) one can relax in a variety of top-floor restaurants which afford an excellent view of mountains to the north and west, the Pacific Ocean to the east, and the entire city panorama below.

A 10-minute walk up **Aoba Dori**

Native wildflowers get some tender loving care.

from Sendai Station brings you **Ichibancho,** Sendai's main shopping arcade. Parts of it are covered in rollaway Plexiglass skylights and all of it is of vehicular traffic free.

If nightlife is your interest, walk a little further to **Kokobuncho Dori,** Sendai's main after-hours drag. Here you will find the usual (and seemingly endless) array of Japanese-style bars, nightclubs, discos, *karaoke* boxes and virtually any other kind of nighttime entertainment that can be imagined.

Sendai's atmosphere is casually sophisticated, and the hustle and bustle of Tokyo is conspicuously missing. And, just beneath the surface, the traditional ways of Tohoku remain: the visitor can still watch artisans and craftsmen making knives, tatami flooring and the famed *kayaki tansu* (chests) in the traditional ways in shops tucked into the shadows of much larger and more modern architecture.

Other Sights of Interest: Sendai didn't come into its own until Date Masamune, the great one-eyed warrior lord of the north, moved to his newly constructed castle on Aobayama. Both **Aoba Castle** and the Date family were brought down during the Meiji Era, but the castle walls remain. In addition, a small museum, a souvenir shop, a shrine and a statue of the great Masamune himself now occupy the grounds. Looking northwards and down from the castle grounds, one can see the Hirose River, known locally as the "Miracle of 800,000" because it remains unpolluted even today. Edible trout still swim downstream, so, if you have time, bring your fishing rod.

Zuihoden, the burial site of Date Masamune sits atop **Kyogamine Hill.** There are several cemeteries along the way up, as well as a beautiful Rinzai Zen temple, **Zuihoji.** Above the temple are the steps which lead to the mausoleum at the very top, and nearby are the tombs of samurai who committed ritual suicide when Masamune died. There is also an exhibition room, with pictures taken when the mausoleum was opened during restoration (necessitated by

Wintry night at Haguro Dewa Sanzan Temple.

bomb attacks toward the end of World War II).

Osaki Hachiman Jinja was originally built in 1100 and later moved to its present location by Date Masamune. This shrine is one of Japan's national treasures. Walk up the 100 or so steps to the top (reportedly the count is never the same twice). Follow the stone-paved path lined with enormous cedar trees to the shrine, picturesquely set back in a small forest. It is done in the Momoyama style of gold, black lacquer and bright colors.

On the outskirts of Sendai in Kitayama, a delightful place for a mountain stroll, are two Zen temples, **Rinnoji** and **Shifukuji**, both dating from the 15th century and destroyed and rebuilt many times over the years. They offer beautiful Zen-inspired gardens as well as azaleas and irises in the spring, colored foliage in autumn, and dazzling winter snow scenes.

Then, back in town, there are several more modern attractions worth a look. Sendai has a city museum, the **Hakubutsukan** and a prefectural fine art museum, **Miyagi Bijutsukan**, within its limits. The city museum is interesting architecturally and houses an extensive permanent exhibition of the area's history. There is also a children's room where everything on display can be touched and played with. The prefectural fine art museum has just opened a new sculpture wing with an outdoor sculpture garden.

If you have the time and the energy, you might want to check out the **Tohoku University Botanical Garden**, a great place to cool off on a hot summer afternoon, as well as to observe owls, bats and the flora and fauna within the premises. Sendai observatory is a relatively good place for viewing your favorite constellation, if you don't mind waiting in line. Finally, there's **Kotsu Koen,** a "traffic park" for children, complete with roads, red lights, busy intersections and train tracks. Kids can cruise around in pedal-powered cars and get a taste for what real life is like on Japan's busy and overcrowded roads.

Northward: Sendai is the logical jumping-off point for exploring the rest of Tohoku. A short ride to the northwest will bring you to **Naruko Onsen**, Tohoku's most popular spa. Once a sacred site to honor the gods of the hot springs, Naruko is known for its especially medicinal waters (the treatment of nervous tension is a specialty), and the production of wooden, vaguely phallic *kokeshi* dolls, Tohoku's most famous souvenir.

After your bath, head back to Sendai and then follow the coast north to **Matsushima**, considered one of the three most beautiful spots in all Japan. The bay is filled with strangely beautiful islets of all shapes and sizes, and a fleet of ferry boats is standing by to get you as close to these natural wonders as possible. The poet Basho couldn't get enough of this place, declaring his arrival in Matsushima the happiest moment of his life. These days you can walk the main street along the harbor and rub shoulders with crowds of Japanese tourists. You could try the *sasakamaboko* (molded fish paste) and the

Matsushima offers one of the "Three Beautiful Views" of Japan.

squid-on-a-stick, which are two of the local delicacies.

Continuing north along the coast, you will reach the fishing port of **Ishinomaki**, a great place for seafood of all kinds. Try the *hoya* (sea pineapple) raw in vinegar sauce. Ferries from Ishinomaki take you to **Kinkazan** (Gold Flower Mountain island), a mysterious place of bamboo groves, dense forest and roaming wild deer and monkeys.

At the northeast tip of Miyagi is the city of **Kessennuma**, famous for its variety of shark dishes. Beyond Kessennuma begins Iwate's famed **Sanriku Coast National Park**, 200 kilometers (125 miles) of fantastic coastline, tiny fishing villages and beautiful sandy beaches. **Jodogahama** (Paradise Beach) was named by a visiting priest who assumed that this was as close to heaven-on-earth as he would ever get.

Midway up the Sanriku Coast, you can cut inland, over the mountains to the town of **Tono**, offering a perfectly preserved glimpse into feudal Japan. No modern trappings here. Farming is still done the old fashioned way. Check out the **Magariya**, traditional L-shaped farm houses. The long side is for humans, the short side for animals and ghosts. Do not go too near the rivers here: this is where the legendary green river creature *kappa* lives.

Back to the coast and north lies **Aomori Prefecture** and the **Shimokita Peninsula**. The world's northernmost community of wild monkeys can be found here, as well as the ominous **Mt. Osore** (Mt. Dread). With its bubbling, multicolored mud pits and clinging sulphur clouds, Osore's description of "straight out of hell" seems apt. Here, from July 20–24, the blind Itako women contact the dead.

Japan's Most Beautiful Women: Aomori City, capital of **Aomori Prefecture**, is a logical departure point for Hokkaido, or, if you are heading south again, **Lake Towada** and the **Hachimantai Park** area. **Hirosaki City**, an hour's ride from Aomori, is an old castle town which boasts the most elegant (some say most difficult) regional dia-

Lake Towada: spectacularly beautiful.

lect in Tohoku, as well as reputedly Japan's "most beautiful women."

Still heading south, you will encounter the **Hakkodo** mountain range, which runs down the middle of Aomori Prefecture to the **Oirase River Valley**. Before entering this spectacular valley of steep cliffs, churning rapids and waterfalls, spend a night at **Sukaya Onsen**. The waters here are thought to be curative, and the location is pure rustic-traditional.

The **Towada-Hachimantai National Park** covers a vast area, touching the borders of three prefectures. Excluding Hokkaido, this is Japan's last area of untamed wilderness, with several types of volcanos, bubbling mud pools, steam geysers and scenic splendor. **Mt. Iwate**, the Fuji of the north, is here. **Tamagawa Onsen**, on the Akita side of Hachimantai Plateau, has hot, acidic and slightly radioactive water, considered to be one of the best in the area.

Just to the southeast is **Morioka City**, Iwate's capital and famous for its *wanko soba* eating competitions. Further south is the town of **Hiraizumi**, once called the "Kyoto of the North." Its beautiful **Chusonji** , a temple dating from the 12th century, contains the **Konjiki-do** (Golden Pavilion), Japan's first national treasure.

West from Hachimantai is **Akita Prefecture**, also known for its beautiful women, **Lake Tazawa** (Japan's deepest) and the spectacular **Oga Peninsula**, home of the *Namahage* (the devils of the New Year). These horrible creatures burst into the local homes on January 3 each year, and they are not appeased until fed sufficient quantities of *sake* and rice cakes.

Traveling south through Akita, you enter **Yamagata**, a truly rustic and traditional prefecture. The **Dewa Sanzan** are Yamagata's three holy mountains, where the ascetic Yamabushi mountain men still perform their sacred rituals. Join the other pilgrims and walk the 2,446 steps to the summit of **Mt. Haguro**. Afterwards, you can travel down the **Mogami River** on a flat-bottomed boat, while the boatman sings

to you of the area's legends. To the south is **Tendo**, an *onsen* town famous for its craftsmen who make *shogi* chess pieces, **Yamagata City**, the prefectural capital, and Yamadera, a mountain temple complex established in 860.

More Memories: Finally, your trip to Tohoku wouldn't be complete without at least a brief stop in **Fukushima**, Tohoku's southernmost prefecture. Here you will find **Aizu-Wakamatsu**, an old castle town with much of its historical past preserved for visitors to see. At the center of the city is Aizu clan. Just a short distance across the river is **Hongo**, an ancient pottery town where the craft still flourishes. To the south is **Bandai-Asahi**, yet another vast, verdant national park filled with lakes. Below the park is the southern boundary of Tohoku.

You can leave the area through the ancient **Shirakawa Barrier**, crossing back into the more "civilized" areas of the south. The memories of Tohoku, however, are guaranteed to stay with you long after you leave the place.

Picture-perfect pose in front of a wall of *daikon* (winter radishes).

HOKKAIDO HO!

"Boys, be ambitious!" These were the parting words of Dr. William S. Clark, first President of Hokkaido University, in 1876. This injunction still applies to the traveler venturing to Japan's northern island, where the temples and castles of the south give way to mountains, forests and farms.

Hokkaido has only been part of the Japanese nation since it was settled in Western style late in the 19th century, as an example of the Meiji Restoration development. The real culture and religious history of Hokkaido lies in its aboriginal people, the Ainu, who have been systematically assimilated into the culture (but not the robust economy) of modern Japan. Today, with a population of only 24,000, Ainu are a phantom culture with a forgotten language, whose main occupation is in entertainment at tourist sites.

It's easy in Hokkaido to succumb to the tourist traps. They are numerous, hectic and – it allows you to enjoy the liveliness of crowded resorts – delightful. But add Dr. Clark's dose of ambition, and your Hokkaido experience can be high adventure. This is, after all, the rustic northland. Its climate parallels Quebec and Finland. In winter, icebergs scrape its shores. In summer, hills and fields are riotous with wildflowers and tranquil with dairy cows.

Here too are Japan's own Loch Ness Monster, God's fairies, the Roof of Hokkaido, the End of the Earth and the Gorge of Hell. Volcanoes rumble and spit, threaten the scenery, and fuel a network of scenic *onsen*. Hokkaido is a patchwork of national parks, where Japan's wildest wildlife shares dominion with legions of hikers, climbers, skiers and bikers.

Transportation by bus or train is spotty. A bike is handy in Hokkaido, a car handier. For many young Japanese, the bicycle circuit of the Hokkaido coast (27,000 km/17,000 miles) is an important rite of passage.

The roots of Hokkaido folk are in farming, fishing, hunting and shark trading. The visitor will find the residents here more direct and friendlier than their southern counterparts, but, due to the "Meiji Westernization", culturally sophisticated.

There are seven main areas of exploration in Hokkaido. From "least" to "most challenging" they are as follows.

Sapporo: The capital and largest city (population 1.5 million) of Hokkaido, revolves around Japan's liveliest, most charming boulevard, **Odori Koen (Odori Park)**.

In the first week of February, this broad avenue of parks and fountains contains Sapporo's world-famous **Snow Festival.** In summer, beer gardens spring up on the lawn and people linger outdoors long into the night. After you have visited Sapporo's other tourist "musts," including the **Sapporo Brewery** and its own spectacular beer garden, **Hokkaido University** with its romantic **Poplar Walk**, the **Botanic Garden**, the **Batchelor Museum** of Ainu history, the famous **Clock Tower**

Left, dramatic falls at Tenninkyo, Hokkaido. Right, Onuma National Park.

(**Tokeidai**), and perhaps journeyed to the outskirts to roam **Maruyama Park**, or to **Urigahara Park** for its explosion of lilies, you will return to Odori Koen, the heart of Sapporo.

A tour of Sapporo is easy because it is a new city, laid out in a grid. Just northwest of **Sapporo Station** is Hokkaido University, and the Sapporo Brewery is due east. Otherwise, go south from Sapporo Station, to the Botanic Garden (detour west), the Tokeidai (detour east) and then Odori Koen. Farther south is **Tanuki-Koji Arcade**, a vibrant strip of restaurants and shops. **Nijo Market** serves every dining and household need for locals, and purveys souvenirs in abundance for eager first-time visitors. Finally, **Susukino** is Sapporo's nightlife, strip joint district, where **Ramen Yokocho** is a circus of Sapporo-style "fast food."

Other Sapporo tourist sites include the **Snow Dairy** and **Asahi Brewery**, two restored historical sites – the **Kotani Tondenkei Oku** (Settlers House) and **Hokkaido Settlers Village**
– the **Sapporo Art Forest** and the **Sheep Hill Tower**. But for many, Sapporo is the staging point for trips beyond, including such nearby attractions as the **Jozankei** and **Koganeyu Onsen**, and the **Teineyama**, **Teine Olympia** and **Niseko** ski areas.

Otaru-Shakotan Peninsula: West of Sapporo is **Otaru**, once a fishing and trading center, where the buildings are an eclectic blend of Western and 19th-century Japanese influence.

Otaru is gateway to the **Shakotan Peninsula**, a microcosm of Hokkaido, with its rugged coastlines, abundant campsites, ski areas, boating and fishing in the Sea of Japan, and glorious sunsets from **Capes Shakotan** and **Kamui**. This area's proximity to Sapporo makes sightseeing hectic at times. But along the sideroads and in quiet villages, you can always find an inn.

Hakodate: Wait till dark and take the ropeway up **Mt. Hakodate**. From there, gape at one the world's most beautiful night views. Somewhere there lies **Goryokaku**, a star-shaped bastion

Snow-bound Sapporo.

where loyalists of the Tokugawa shogunate lost the last battle against the Meiji imperial army in 1869.

This is Hokkaido's "historic" city, as Hakodate had Japanese settlers as early as the 13th century, Russian visitors around 1740 and a foreign enclave, at **Motomachi** beneath Mt. Hakodate, in 1854. Visit the mountain, Motomachi and Goryokaku, but don't miss the Fish Market at dawn, when the squid fleet and the crab trappers come in. Sapporo is a night city, Hakodate – at heart – a morning city.

Use the streetcar system to explore. For dinner, have Japan's freshest seafood. *Ika somen,* thinly sliced strips of raw squid, is the city's specialty. Crab and salmon are also abundant and delicious. A unique salmon soup called *sanpei-jiru* – made with *sake* lees – is truly remarkable.

In early August, you can join in the historical pageant that is part of Hakodate's annual **Port Festival**. West of the city are a **Trappistine convent**, famous for its cookies, and **Yunokawa**

Onsen, comfortable and rural. From Hakodate, buses and trains go to **Matsumae**, Hokkaido's only castle town; **Onuma Quasi-National Park**, where views are lovely and the wilderness tame; the picturesque little fishing village of **Esashi**; **Mt. Esan**, a still-active volcano – all very popular with Japanese tourists.

Shikotsu-Toya National Park: Between Sapporo and Hakodate, near Chitose Airport, the **Shikotsu-Toya** area is Hokkaido's most accessible national park. Closest to Sapporo is **Lake Shikotsu**, a huge volcanic caldera. **Shikotsu Kohan**, a fishing village, provides lodgings and tour boats. As in all Hokkaido's national parks, youth hostels are landmarks where anyone – young or old – can get help in renting a bike, locating a trail, getting directions. There are four youth hostels in the area, and seven campsites.

Lake Toya, south of Shikotsu, is round and popular. Tour boats visit its four islands, where the view of **Mt. Yotei** (Hokkaido's Mt. Fuji) is best.

Asahikawa lies near Mt. Asahi, Hokkaido's highest peak.

Climbers can attack Mt. Yotei, **Mt. Eniwa, Mt. Fuppushi** and **Mt. Tarumae**. The latter, a volcano that still steams and fumes, is the best climb. The route to Tarumae from Lake Shikotsu passes through the eerie beauty of **Koke no Domon (Moss Gorge)**.

Lake Toya resort is boisterous in summer, with fireworks during the August festival season. There are many *ryokan*, whose hot spring baths have lake views. The "must" here is **Showa Shinzan**, a small volcano that emerged from the earth in 1944. **Usuzan**, Showa Shinzan's papa, stands nearby. It blew up in 1977, wreaking havoc on the resort. This is preserved on film in a Volcanic Science Museum.

The best route from Lake Toya to the tourist mecca of Noboribetsu is by bus through gorgeous **Orofure Pass**. Noboribetsu's weirdest sight is at the **Dai-Ichi Takimoto-kan hotel**, where 40 baths can soak 1,000 bathers simultaneously. There is nothing else like it. Here, tour the volcanic **Jigokudani (Hell Gorge)** and go up **Mt. Shihorei**.

There are two festivals in August at Noboribetsu – only recommended if you love crowds. For a gourmet treat, in season, ask for *kegani koramushi*, small freshwater crabs.

Akan National Park: Virgin forests, volcanoes, lakes and biological oddities draw thousands every year to **Akan National Park,** whose best staging point is the ferry port of **Kushiro** – where ultramodern architecture contrasts with one of Japan's most congenial dockside scenes.

North is **Lake Akan**, where *marimo*, odd green algae balls – also known as "God's fairies" – will either delight, or bore you. Tour buses dominate this park, which makes a car or a bicycle a plus. **Akan Kohan**, the main town, has ten ryokan. The park has six youth hostels and campsites aplenty. Two volcanoes, **Mt. O-akan** and **Mt. Me-akan**, tempt climbers, with Me-akan the preferred jaunt, partly because **Me-akan Onsen** awaits the weary climber. North of Akan Kohan, **Bokke** features bubbling hot mud. Ainu are abundant in

Easy slider at the Snow Festival.

Akan National Park; they dance and sing on schedule. The best meals here include freshwater fish and venison.

The bus ride between Lake Akan and **Lake Mashu** features wonderful views at **Sogakudai** – overlooking Me-akan and O-akan, and at **Sokodai** – overlooking **Lake Pante** and **Lake Pente**. Lake Mashu is a landmark. Called "Devil's Lake" by Ainu, its 200-meter cliffs, towering over misty waters, have often served as "lovers' leaps."

Also on the Akan circuit, and less touristy, is **Lake Kussharo**, home to *"Kusshi,"* Japan's very own "Nessie." Three congenial spas surround Kussharo: **Kawayu Onsen, Wakoto Onsen,** and **Sunayu** whose hot sands provide a welcome novelty. **Mt. Io**, better known as Mt. Sulphur, steams and reeks impressively, and **Bihoro Pass**, above Kussharo's west shore, is the park's most breathtaking vista.

Daisetsuzan National Park: Wilder and colder than Akan and Shikotsu-Toya, **Daisetsuzan** is the biggest national park in Hokkaido. Known as "The Rooftop of Hokkaido," it is cool here even in summer.

This is a landscape of volcanic peaks and steep highlands, magnificent gorges, carpets of alpine wildflowers and inevitable sightings of the park's rich wildlife – deer and fox and bears, chipmunks and exotic birds. A car, again, is ideal transportation to the interior, **Sounkyo** and **Yokumambetsu Onsen**. A bike is ideal for sightseeing, but there is much climbing.

In the park, there are three good youth hostels (reservations recommended) and a series of campsites. They are useful because, once inside rugged Daisetsuzan, hiking is the preferred recreation. Start at Sounkyo, a busy village near **Sounkyo Gorge (Gorges Reaching to the Clouds)**, chiseled walls of volcanic rock – punctuated with feathery waterfalls – more than 100 meters high. Sounkyo Gorge is 20 kilometers from **Obako** and **Kobako**, at the narrow end, to Sounkyo resort.

From Sounkyo, one of the park's two main ropeways ends near the peak of

Music and dance at an Ainu festival.

Mt. Kuro, jumping off point for hiking territory. The goal is Hokkaido's highest peak, **Mt. Asahi**. Along the way, the hiker comes across vast tracts of creeping pine and virgin forests, timberline barrens, small lakes and side trails, volcanic vents, flower-covered hillsides, patches of year-round snow and the inevitable mosquitos.

There are many hot springs in Daisetsuzan, the most sought-after atop Mt. Asahi, to soothe the hiker. Spas at Sounkyo and **Tenninkyo Onsen** lie at both ends of the Asahidake Trail, while to the south lie **Tomuraushi Onsen** and **Daisetsu Kogen Onsen**. To the north is **Aizankei Onsen**. All these spas can be reached by trail and are much more rustic than their more civilized counterparts in Hokkaido.

Among the best festivals in Hokkaido are Sounkyo's **Kyokoku Himatsuri**, an authentic Ainu fire festival on June 24–25, and Sounkyo's mid-February **Ice Festival** (if you can stand the cold).

Shiretoko National Park: The **Shiretoko Peninsula** is a beautiful, barely civilized finger of volcanic rock jutting into the **Sea of Okhotsk**. It is called the "End of the Earth," and that sensation can be vividly felt in places like **Seseki Onsen**, a south coast hot spring that steams on a rocky shore. There are no hotels in sight, no tourist shops nor places to get something to eat. Like most of Shiretoko's unspoiled south coast, this spot can demand the most of the traveler's ambition.

A car or bike is necessary for exploring most of Shiretoko, and many places require backpacks and sleeping bags for overnight stays.

The north shore, starting from the mundane spa town of **Utoro**, offers more visitors' amenities. From Utoro, there are sightseeing boats and roads east toward **Shiretoko Five Lakes**. Proceed to **Iwaobetsu Onsen**, a lovely, unspoiled place from which you can hike to the top of **Mt. Rausu**, the peninsula's highest mountain.

From here, the hiker can descend southward to another rustic spa, **Rausu Onsen**, or turn eastward along a ridge of

Below, local touch to drying straw. Below left, wilderness at Daisetsuzan National Park.

mountains toward **Mt. Iwo**, a steaming, dramatic volcano. Just north of Mt. Iwo, boasting a waterfall, a hot spring, and a breathtaking view of mountain and ocean, is **Kamuiwakka no Taki**, which for many travelers to Japan is the jewel of Shiretoko.

Starting from the fishing village of **Rausu**, close to Rausu Onsen, a trip along the south coast is rugged and lonely, but adequately relieved by the pleasures of scenic seaside *rotemburo* (outdoor bath).

The best route away from the Shiretoko is north, through the village of **Shari**, toward **Abashiri**, with its interesting but quirky **Prison Museum**, a pleasant walk along **Lake Tofutsuko**, and the **Natural Flower Gardens**. Abashiri, best of all, is at the beginning for Hokkaido's pleasantest, easiest long-distance bicycle trip. This route involves riding north alongside the Sea of Okhotsk, through the attractive **Abashiri Quasi-National Park,** to **Wakkanai** which lies at the northernmost tip of Hokkaido.

Lone kelp collector on the northern coast.

Rishiri-Rebun-Sarobetsu National Park: The small volcanic islands of **Rishiri** and **Rebun** are just west of Wakkanai, but before you take the ferry, a visit slightly south is a trip to **Sarobetsu Alpine Wildflower Refuge**, a rainbow of color as far as the eye can see (especially in July) and breathtaking coastline. This is one of Hokkaido's real wonders, remote, natural, uncrowded and romantic.

Across the water, both Rishiri and Rebun offer delights for the biker, hiker, camper and fisherman. It's possible lodge at a *minshuku* (home-style inn) on either island and get up early in the morning with your host to go fishing in the Sea of Japan.

Hiking is great, with your best bet on Rishiri being a climb of **Mt. Rishiri**, which pokes up from the ocean like Neptune's elbow. On Rebun, hike from **Sukotan Misaki** to **Momiwa**, or bike from **Kabuka** to **Funadomori** to make the most of the rewarding coastline scenery. Joining a youth hostel group is good insurance against getting lost.

Accommodations at this northern outpost are adventurous. There is a hotel, the **Kitaguni Grand**, but staying in a youth hostel (there are three on Rishiri and one on Rebun) or a minshuku is a more appropriate choice.

Coastal Journeys: Besides these seven main regions of interest in Hokkaido, there are a series of coastal journeys that beckon the leisurely traveler. The most challenging of these is the northeast coast from **Wakkanai** to **Rumoi**. On the south coast, the crooked course of **Route 336** from **Tomakomai**, toward **Erimo** and then north to **Kushiro**, is a series of friendly villages, surprising festivals, the green (or snowy) vastness of the **Hidaka Sanmyaku Mountains**, farms, fishing and shipping ports, rocky, isolated, beaches, fascinating food and outdoor recreation.

In the east, the **Nemuro Peninsula** and the marshlands that stretch north toward **Shiretoko** are a recluse's paradise. None of these forays are on the standard tourist itinerary, which means the discoveries you make, the people you meet, will be your very own.

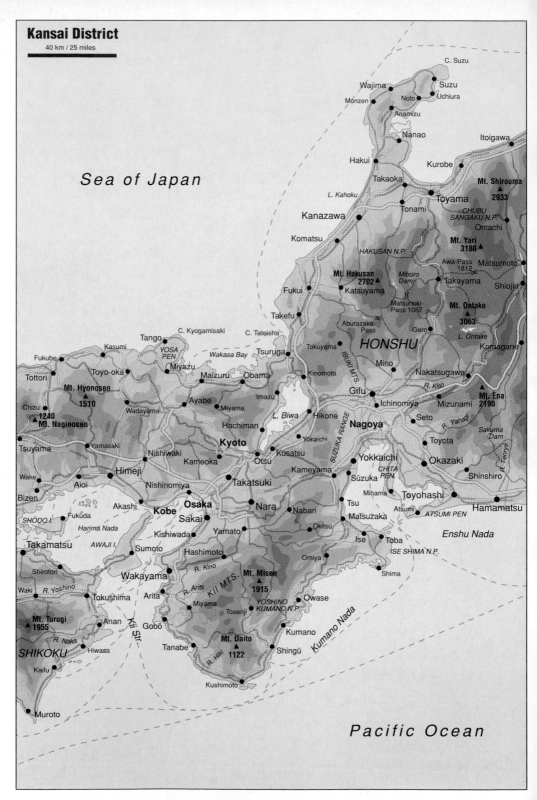

Kansai District

40 km / 25 miles

Sea of Japan

C. Suzu

Wajima · Suzu
Monzen · Noto · Uchiura
Anamizu

Nanao

Itoigawa

Hakui

Kurobe

Takaoka · Mt. Shirouma 2933

L. Kahoku · Toyama · CHUBU SANGAKU N.P.

Kanazawa · Tonami · Omachi

Komatsu · Mt. Yari 3180

HAKUSAN N.P. · Awa-Pass 1812 · Matsumoto

Mt. Hakusan 2702 · Miboro Dam · Takayama

Fukui · Katsuyama · Shiojiri

Takefu · Matsunoki-Pass 1087 · Mt. Ontake 3063

Aburazaka-Pass · Gero

Tango · C. Kyogamisaki · C. Tateisha · Tsuruga · Tokuyama · *HONSHU* · L. Ontake · Komagane

Kasumi · YOSA PEN · Wakasa Bay · Kinomoto · Mino

Fukube · Miyazu · Maizuru · Obama · Nakatsugawa

Tottori · Toyo-oka · Ayabe · Imazu · IBUKI MTS. · Gifu · R. Kiso · Mt. Ena 2190

Mt. Hyonosen 1510 · Miyama · Ichinomiya · Mizunami

Chizu · Wadayama · L. Biwa · Hikone · Seto · R. Yahagi · Sakuma Dam

1240 Mt. Naginosen · Yamasaki · Hachiman · Nagoya · Toyota

Tsuyama · Nishiwaki · Kameoka · Yokaichi · SUZUKA RANGE · Kusatsu

Wake · Kyoto · Otsu · Kusatsu · Yokkaichi · CHITA PEN. · Okazaki

Bizen · Aioi · Himeji · Nishinomiya · Kameyama · Suzuka · Shinshiro

Akashi · Kobe · Takatsuki · Nara · Nabari · Tsu · Mihama · Toyohashi

SHODO I. · Fukuda · Osaka · Yamato · Matsuzaka · Atsumi · ATSUMI PEN · Hamamatsu

Harima Nada · Sakai · Kishiwada · Okitsu · Ise · *Enshu Nada*

Takamatsu · AWAJI I. · Sumoto · Hashimoto · Omiya · Toba

Shirotori · Wakayama · R. Kino · ISE SHIMA N.P.

Waki · R. Yoshino · Tokushima · Arita · R. Arita · KII MTS. · Mt. Misen 1915 · Shima

Mt. Turugi 1955 · Anan · Gobo · Miyama · Tosenji · YOSHINO KUMANO N.P. · Owase

SHIKOKU · R. Naka · Hiwasa · Kii Str · Tanabe · Mt. Daito 1122 · Kumano · *Kumano Nada*

Kaifu · R. Hiki · Shingū

Kushimoto

Muroto

Pacific Ocean

The old Tokaido (Eastern Sea Road) that connected the ancient capital at Kyoto with the seat of the feudal shogunate at Kamakura (and later, after a lapse of several centuries, at Edo, now Tokyo) has all but disappeared. But it was along that much-traveled highway, at a point where it passed through the Hakone hills, that the Kamakura *bakufu* set up a heavily armed security post in the 13th century to stifle any threatening moves by the armies of the western warlords and imperial loyalists. It is from this post at Suzuka on the Tokaido, and another at nearby Fuwazeki on the secondary highway, the Nakasendo, that the regions to the west got their name: Kansai, a word meaning "western barrier."

In the Kamakura days, virtually all lands west and south of those barriers – including the Nagoya-Gifu region – were considered to be in the Kansai. Later, around or just before the beginning of the Edo era, the definition narrowed to include only the Kyoto-Nara-Osaka-Kobe area. Today, the Japan National Tourist Organization and other interested official agencies tend to narrow the definition even further to comprise only the prefectures of Hyogo, Kyoto, Mie, Nara, Osaka, Shiga and Wakayama – an area also known, for better or worse, as the "Kinki."

(Note: we hope that our including chapters on Nagoya and Ise in the Kansai section does not add to the confusion; it was simply more convenient to put them here.)

If Tokyo is where your initial contact with Japan begins, a journey to Kansai some 500 kilometers (310 miles) to the southwest will give you an entirely new perspective on the Japanese experience. Even a few hours seeing the famous sights of Kyoto, while not nearly enough time to do more than just scratch the surface, will no doubt enrich your visit. Seeing the commercial prosperity and mingling with the energetic crowds of Osaka, and a rewarding trip to Kobe with its busy port and international outlook, are things you should not miss.

Naturally, persons native to the Kansai feel an intense rivalry with other parts of the country, particularly Tokyo. Although much of the region is still agricultural, declaring that one is from Kansai doesn't evoke the "country hick" image. This is largely due to the renown and respect of the great commerical-industrial complexes of Osaka-Kobe and the unquestionable urban sophistication of ancient Kyoto, which, after all, was the nation's powerful premier city for well over 1,000 years.

As for the character of the region, well, the words "soft," "sweet" and "smart" come to mind. For example, where in Japan is the language the softest? In the Kansai, with its long vowels, swallowed consonants and gently lilting rhythms. Where is the food the sweetest? In Kansai, where even the *sake* comes with sugar added

Preceding pages: Kiyomizudera, the most popular temple complex in Kyoto; purifying water trough at Shinnyodo.

and, particularly in inland Kyoto, the sweet-tasting *sushi* doesn't even feature fish.

And where are the people the smartest? That depends on what you mean by "smart."

Smartest in the sense of style? No contest: although Tokyo seems now to rank with Paris and New York on the international fashion scene, it is Kyoto – in the heart of the Kansai district of western Japan, and the traditional center of kimono making – where the subdued, astringent elegance of a bygone era (i.e., *shibui*) is still very much in vogue. Likewise, contrary to common believe outside and even within Japan, it is Kobe, not Tokyo, that today dominates the clothing-manufacturing industry of Japan.

If you mean "smart" in the sense of clever or street smart, Osaka may well have a head start over the rest of the country. It is, for example, the center of *yakuza*, or organized crime activity in Japan, if that's any qualification. But it is also the base of Japan's most innovative electronics manufacturer, Matsushita, and is a leader (together with Nagoya) in the development of "clever" or robotic production techniques.

"Smart" in the sense of well-educated doesn't really enter the picture here, for while nearly all of Japan's best universities are in Tokyo, their students come from all over – including the Kansai. But if you consider the practical applications of higher education in advancing the quality of life, the Kansai again is a winner. For example, sensitive city planning in Kobe has turned it into one of Japan's most pleasant urban environments. Also remarkable, considering the population density, is the intelligent management of rail and road transportation arteries in the Kansai that have made it easier and quicker to get around within and among the cities of Kansai than in the Kanto (Tokyo-Yokohama-Chiba) metropolitan mess to the northeast.

The list of examples could go on and on. For instance, smart investments in the preservation and maintenance of tourism resources – temples and shrines in particular – have made the cities of Nara and Kyoto quite wealthy, attracting tens of millions of yen-flush visitors every year. But here we might be running into trouble by continuing the "smart" metaphor, for besides the long-running debate over the new Kansai International Airport recently opened on a manmade island in Osaka Bay, the hottest and most controversial topic of the early 1990s in the Kansai is the "urban renewal" project centered around a new hotel at Kyoto Station; a 120-meter (395-ft) building or other such modern complex in the very heart of that ancient city, argue those against the plan, is hardly a smart way to improve the quality of life *or* perserve the atmosphere for which Kyoto is known.

Smart or not, however, the Kansai does generally manage to show up its major rivals in a number of ways, particularly – as we hope you will discover – in its gracious hospitality: traditionally soft, sweet and unstinting.

Left, all dressed up at festival time.

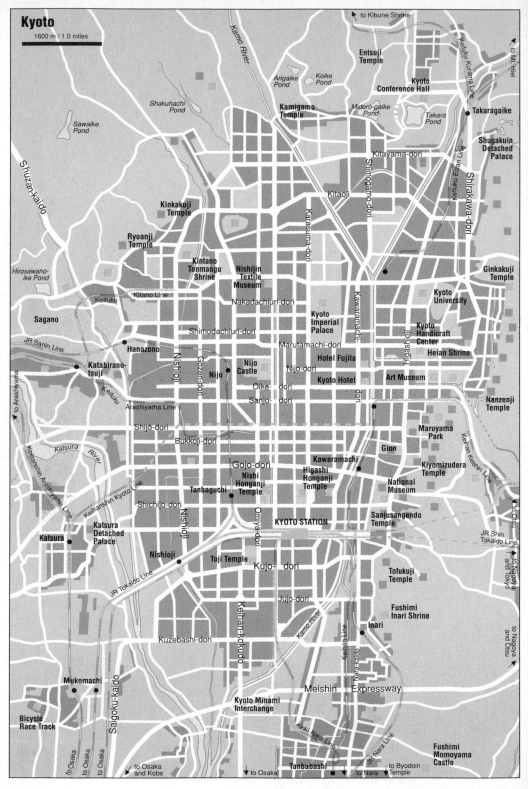

Kyoto

1600 m / 1.0 miles

to Kibune Shrine

Kamo River

Keifuku Kurama Line

to Mt. Hiei

Entsuji
Temple

Kyoto
Conference Hall

Shakuhachi
Pond

Arigaike
Pond

Koike
Pond

Midoro-gaike
Pond

Kamigamo
Temple

Takara
Pond

Takaragaike

Sawaike
Pond

Keihuku Eiden Line

Shugakuin
Detached
Palace

Kitayama-dori

Shimogamo-dori

Shirakawa-dori

Kitaoji

Kinkakuji
Temple

Hirosawano-
ike Pond

Ryoanji
Temple

Karasuma-dori

Ginkakuji
Temple

Kintano
Tenmangu
Shrine

Nishijin
Textile
Museum

Kyoto
University

Kitano Line

Nakadachiuri-dori

Kawaramachi-

Kyoto
Handicraft
Center

Keifuku

Sagano

Shimodachiuri-dori

Kyoto
Imperial
Palace

Higashioji

Heian Shrine

JR Sanin Line

Hanazono

Marutamachi-dori

Nanzenji
Temple

Katabirano-
tsuji

Gozen-dori

Nishioji

Nijo

Nijo
Castle

Nijo-dori

Hotel Fujita

Art Museum

dori

Keifuku

Arashiyama Line

Oike- dori

Sanjo- dori

Kyoto Hotel

to Arashiyama

Shijo-dori

Maruyama
Park

Keihan Keishin Line

Katsura River

Bukkoji-dori

Gion

Keihanshin Kyoto Line

Gojo-dori

Kawaramachi

Kiyomizudera
Temple

to Otsu

Nishi
Honganji
Temple

Higashi
Honganji
Temple

Tanbaguchi

National
Museum

Shichijo-dori

Nishioji

Omiya-dori

KYOTO STATION

Sanjusangendo
Temple

JR Shin
Tokaido Line

Katsura
Detached
Palace

to Nagoya
and Tokyo

Katsura

Nishioji

Toji Temple

Kujo- dori

Tofukuji
Temple

JR Tokaido Line

Keihan-kokudo

Jujo-dori

Fushimi
Inari Shrine

to Nagoya
and Otsu

Kuzebashi-dori

Kamo River

Inari

Keihan Line

Nara-kaido

Mukomachi

Saigoku-kaido

Kinki Nara Line

Meishin   Expressway

Bicycle
Race Track

Kyoto Minami
Interchange

JR Nara Line

Fushimi
Momoyama
Castle

to Osaka

to Osaka

to Osaka

to Osaka
and Kobe

to Osaka

Tanbabashi

to Nara

to Byodoin
Temple

KYOTO

Links to the ancient past, threatened in East Asia by modernization or sometimes by war, are still intact in the city of Kyoto. This may not be apparent on arrival at Kyoto Station by bullet train, the visitor discovering that Kyoto – with its population of 1.5 million sustained by robust electrical, chemical and manufacturing industries – looks much like other modern Japanese cities.

But the maps and guide books have all been studied, and the promises of ancient delights absorbed, and the promises even believed. Soon temple sightseeing becomes an ordeal – if not a hurried marathon – of buses and taxis and sore feet. And then one day, somehow, one of the annual 40 million visitors tastes a drop of the elixir of Kyoto's preserved past. So intoxicating is this old knowledge that the visitor stays on for years and even decades, learning pottery, Zen, calligraphy. Without effort, they have fallen into a lost, almost mystical world that bit by bit has completely overtaken them.

Indeed, behind the modern city, the old arts and old thinking are still very much alive.

From the Beginning: The flat plain where Kyoto sits is enclosed within a horseshoe defined by mountains to the north, east and west. Two small rivers, the Kamo and Katsura, slice down through the city. The Kyoto area is divided into five historically-defined areas. Using Kyoto Station as a focus, to the east is *Rakuto,* usually called *Higashiyama,* and to the west, *Rakusai.* The central district directly to the north of the station is called *Rakuchu,* and beyond, *Rakuhoku.* South of the station is *Rakunan.* These designations are not used so much anymore, but the traveler may run across them.

The first modern inhabitants of the Kyoto region were 7th century naturalized immigrants, *kikajin,* from Korea. About two centuries later, at the beginning of the Heian Period in AD 794, Kyoto was founded as the capital and seat of Japan's imperial court – the name Kyoto means capital, site of the imperial palace. It would remain the imperial capital for over a thousand years until 1868, when the emperor moved his court to Tokyo at the start of the Meiji Period.

At first, the new capital city was called **Heiankyo** and modeled after the Chinese Tang Dynasty capital of Chang'an, now called Xian. The city was initially designed as a rectangle, with the palace to the north and cross streets at right angles, forming exactly 1,200 blocks. The Kamo River's path was shifted to make room, and a series of canals built. Fearing another problem with powerful temple monks, as had happened in Nara, the previous capital, no temples were allowed in the city itself, and it was called by the name Kyoto starting in the late 11th century.

Frequently leveled by fires over the centuries, the buildings of Kyoto have been moved, rebuilt and enlarged, and now represent a mosaic of historical periods. As a result of the fires, few

Maiko on the go.

buildings in Kyoto predate 1600. But despite the ongoing process of rebuilding, the major cultural layers can still be seen today.

Court Life: The golden age was the Heian Period (794–1185), the heyday of the aristocrats. The keynote was elegance and an innocent love of nature, which can be seen in the few remaining Heian buildings and the unlandscaped parks of old estates.

Central to the spiritual life of the times was Esoteric Buddhism. This is the oldest form of Buddhism, and it was called "esoteric" because its symbols were regarded as being so powerful that they had to be kept secret. This influence shows primarily in sculpture, where even the arrangement of divinities have great significance.

Also central Kyoto's traditions is the influence of tea, which has always pervaded the city. Tea masters valued intimate spaces and humble materials such as thatch. The result was an understated architecture, with light timber, and the use of simple natural decoration such as rocks and moss. Tea connoisseurship led to the concentration in Kyoto of traditional craftsmen, and Tea traditions influence many aspects of daily life, and can be seen in restaurants, shop windows, food stores.

A further unmistakable cultural layer can be seen in the city's architecture. Despite modernization, thousands of old traditional town houses still exist. The facades are a never-ending dance of rectilinear patterns: sliding paper doors, window slats in clay walls, lattices, trellises, benches, and hanging blinds made of reeds or bamboo. Most distinctive of these are the *inuyarai,* or dog barriers, which are curved bamboo fences protruding about one foot out from the walls of the houses as a protection against street traffic.

Almost too much: Many visitors have a preconceived idea of Kyoto as a singular, blissful haven of peaceful temples, shrines and other historical or cultural places. Kyoto is, in fact, Japan's seventh largest city and an important industrial center, and these images of Kyoto

Arashiyama lies just west of Kyoto.

are in reality but pockets in an otherwise thoroughly modern city.

There are 2,000 Buddhist temples and Shinto shrines in Kyoto – Buddhist temples are always *temples,* and Shinto shrines are always *shrines.* This book cannot cover every temple and shrine in Kyoto, nor even all the important ones. Nor should the visitor try to visit all the ones below if time is but a day or two. Pick just four or five and savor their elegance, beauty and mystery.

Temples, Shrines and Kyoto: Our description of Kyoto moves counter-clockwise from **Kyoto Station,** touching first the area east of the **Kamo River** near the eastern hills, then following the horseshoe defined by the **Tamba Mountains** around to the north, then down the center of the basin towards the south.

Located in an area called **Higashi-yama,** a few blocks east of Kyoto Station across the Kamo River, **Sanjusan-gendo**'s unusual length – 64 meters (210 ft) by 13 meters (43 ft) – led the shogun to choose the temple in 1649 for the site of an archery contest, which is still performed today: *Yumihiki Hajime,* the first archery, held around mid January on the west side of the temple. Archery was one of the arts favored by Heian courtiers, and later became influenced by the principles of Zen.

Built in 1164 and ravaged by fire in 1249, Sanjusangendo was rebuilt in 1266. The "hall of 33 spaces" separated by evenly spaced pillars or columns is lined with **1,001 images of Kannon,** the god (or goddess) of mercy. They are arranged as a three-dimensional mandala in 10 rows of 50 on either side of a central statue, *Senju Kannon* ("thousand-handed"), a 3.3-meter (11-ft) statue created in 1254 with eyes of crystal. The smaller sculptures are each slightly different, and these symbolize the myriad ways in which Kannon manifests compassion. The back corridor is lined with 30 attendant gods, carved to show the vivid emotion which is characteristic of Kamakura art.

The **Kyoto National Museum,** just north of Sanjusangendo, was opened in 1897 by the Imperial Household Agency

Lighting rope from a sacred fire at Yasaka Shrine.

– guardians to this very day of all things relating to the emperor and his family, including their personal lives – to provide a secure place for the valuable art of the Buddhist temples, Shinto shrines and certain private collections.

Kiyomizudera (Temple of Clear Water) was founded in 798 and is one of the most popular temples in Kyoto. The main hall, dating from 1633, sits high on stilts hanging out over a cliff, and offers a splendid view of Kyoto and beyond. No nails were used in the construction of the woodwork or support girding. Steps lead down to **Otowa Falls** (*Otowa-no-taki*), where visitors sip water from the spring said to have many health benefits, if not sheer divine power for the true believer. A short walk leads up the other side of the valley to a small pagoda with a view encompassing the entire hillside complex.

Rokuharamitsuji is a small temple near Kiyomizu and one of Kyoto's gems. The main hall was built in 1363. At the rear is a museum with two fine Kamakura sculptures: Kiyomori of the Heike clan,

and Kuya, founder of the temple. The eyes of Kiyomori, presaging the tragic destruction of his family, sum up the anguish often seen in Kamakura art. Kuya, who popularized the chanting of the Lotus Sutra, is shown reciting magic syllables, each of which becomes Amida, the Savior. The new year's first cup of tea is served here.

Established next to 17th-century **Yasaka Shrine** as an entertainment district, **Gion** was a sanctioned but elegant red-light district from the early 1700s until as late as the mid 20th century, outshining rival Shimabara on the other side of the Kamo River.

While Gion's prostitution has disappeared, *geisha* and *maiko* (apprentice geisha) may still be seen in kimono – in early evening, around six or so – on their way to expensive and exclusive dinner parties at *ryotei*. The geisha houses are in the style of the old town houses but with added delicate touches, such as the orange-pink plastered walls of **Ichiriki-jaya**, on the south side of Shijo street.

The neighborhood of old wooden

Because of its length, Sanjusangendo was chosen in 1649 as the site of an archery contest...

buildings near the **Gion Shimbashi**, a bridge over the Kamo River, is a national preservation district. **Minamiza Theater**, built in the early 1600s, is the oldest theater in Japan and is still used for kabuki performances.

In summer, downtown restaurants along the Kamo River, between Shijo and Sanjo streets, extend wooden platforms over the river, where diners enjoy the cool evening breeze. The platforms remain until mid September. (The river was once an important line of defense for old Kyoto.) The most enjoyable part of this area is **Pontocho**, a narrow street just to the west of the river lined with bars, restaurants and geisha houses. It matches Gion as one of Kyoto's best-known entertainment areas. **Kawara-machi** is a small but bustling shopping, eating and entertainment neighborhood also located on the Kamo River's west bank. **Shinkyogoku**, or the "Arcade," the main entertainment district established in the 1870s, draws many at night with its lights. **Nishiki-koji** is a stretch of food wholesalers, known among residents for its high-quality fish and produce, essential for Kyoto cuisine.

...which still takes place today.

Antique lovers should not miss **Shinmonzen Street**, a few blocks north of Shijo in the Gion area, lined with dozens of shops selling screens, scrolls, Imari china, lacquer, and bronzes from China, Korea and Japan. Other antique stores are sprinkled nearby: in Higashi-yama north and south of Shijo, along Sanjo street near the Miyako Hotel, and in the neighborhood of Chionin.

Chionin is at the north end of **Maruyama Park** (just east of Gion and popular with the cherry blossom viewing crowd) and is one of Kyoto's largest temples. The original was erected in 1234; the current building was rebuilt in the mid 17th century. Like most of Kyoto's wooden structures and temples, fire frequently ravaged the temple buildings. Those now standing were built in the early 1600s. The two-story, 24-meter (80-ft)-high gate is impressive, as are the temple's extensive collections of art.

Charred by two fires since its estab-

lishment in 1291, **Nanzenji** remains a major Zen temple. The Daihojo Hall (the larger of two abbot living quarters) contains paintings on sliding doors and wall panels by Kano Eitoku (1543–90). In the "Tiger Room" of smaller Shojo Hall, there are 39 murals of tigers, among the greatest paintings in Japan.

Outside, the rock garden is a spread of white sand representing the ocean, rocks and plants portraying the earth, and two rocks depicting a tiger and cub. During the day, it is possible to climb up inside the *Tenka Ryumon,* the Dragon Gate of the World, which affords a good view of Kyoto. Erected in 1628, the gate served as a monument to soldiers who were killed in an early 17th- century siege of Osaka Castle.

A relative newcomer built in 1895 for the 1,100th anniversary of Kyoto, **Heian Shrine** is a five-eighth-scale reconstruction of the Heian Period imperial palace of 794. It has minor historic importance, but the cinnabar beams and elaborate roofs are spectacular. Inside the shrine is a garden built around a lake with a Chinese-style pavilion in the center, a pleasant place to stop and feed the carp. Also in the same area are a number of museums, including the **Kyoto National Museum of Modern Art**.

On the north side of the Heian Shrine and **Okazaki Park**, one of the most convenient places to shop is the **Kyoto Handicraft Center**, featuring seven floors of everything from traditional crafts and foreigner-size kimono to electric appliances for overseas use.

Ginkakuji, the Temple of the Silver Pavilion (1482), is one of the most elusive of all Kyoto buildings, for its main building was never silvered despite plans to do so. The pavilion was built by a shogun as a retreat, a fantasy of peacefulness after civil war had left Kyoto a destroyed city. The sober atmosphere of Ginkakuji is not to be confused with Kinkakuji, the Golden Pavilion (1397), on the other side of town.

The building has two stories: the first floor, the residence, is of the Japanese *shinden* style; the second floor is of Chinese Buddhist style and was used as the altar room. Its mound of white sand

(*Kogetsudai*) in the garden was designed to reflect moonlight down on to the garden. Next door is a smaller building which is said to have the oldest tearoom in Japan.

The two kilometer (1¼-mile)-long **Philosopher's Walk** (*Tetsugaku no Michi*), is a favorite place for viewing cherry trees. The Walk is lined with temples, restaurants and popular specialty stores. Beginning at Ginkakuji and the Silver Pavilion, the Walk backtracks south past Nanzenji to the area of Yasaka Shrine and to 17th-century **Honenin**, which commemorates one of the founders of the popular Buddhist movement of *nembutsu*. The thatched gate is a classic of rustic simplicity, while the garden is formed of unusual mounds of sand with imprints of leaves and flowers.

Beyond Honenin is the **Tomb of Emperor Reizei** (950–1011). Tombs like this abound in Nara and Kyoto, some of them reaching enormous size. The walled-off hill with an altar before it suggests the religious awe in which

A sacred *torii* path at Fushimi Inari Taisha.

the emperors are still held. The Walk is said to have been the favorite walking and meditating path of the philosopher Nishida Kitaro (1870–1945), and this is how it got its name.

Up above Honenin is **Daimonji**, where during Obon, the Chinese character *dai,* or "great," burns across the hillside, sending ancestral spirits back to the other world. Four other bonfire Chinese characters ring Kyoto hills on the same August evening.

To the north: At the foot of the northern hills, the **Shugakuin Detached Palace** (sometimes called the Imperial Villa) was originally built in 1659 as a retreat for a former emperor. It consists of three large and separate gardens with villas. In one of the Middle Villa buildings, *Rakushiken,* is a door of Japanese cedar with carp painted on both sides. It's said that long ago, the carp would leave the picture each night and swim in the villa's pond. Not until an 18th-century artist painted gold nets over the carp images did the fish stay put. From the Upper Villa and garden, the largest and best of the three gardens, is a superb view of Kyoto.

Atop 850-meter (2,780-ft) **Mt. Hiei**, northeast of the Shugakuin Palace, is an historically and religiously important temple, **Enryakuji**, founded to protect the then-new capitol from evil northeast spirits. Apparently this exalted mission gave the temple's monks an inflated sense of importance. Over the decades, they became aggressive friars trained in martial arts who would raid other temples and even Kyoto.

Their not-so-monastic rumbles were quenched by warlord Oda Nobunaga, who destroyed the temple buildings and the monks' power in 1571. Toyotomi Hideyoshi, one of Nobunaga's generals, later revived the temple as a spiritual center, but no doubt to the relief of modern tourism officials, the temple's monks have since then remained tranquil and even-tempered.

Nearby are a science museum, amusement park and an observation point. There were once 3,000 minor temples on Mt. Hiei's slopes but today only

Geishas perform *Miyako Odori* at Kaburenjo Hall, Gion.

three pagodas and just over 100 minor temples remain.

Down below, **Entsuji** is the finest example of a "borrowed scenery" garden, in which hills in the distance are used to complement a garden's design. The garden is composed of three layers: in the foreground is a moss garden with sunken stones, controlled and peaceful; in the middle, less formal, is a hedge and a stand of bamboo; and in the distance, framed by two cedar trees, is Mt. Hiei crowning the scene.

Mostly of the Edo Period, the shrine buildings of **Kamigamo** are a fine example of the Shinto style of architecture, made memorable by the two mounds of white sand used to purify paths before visiting nobility walk on them. On an auspicious day in early May, Kamigamo holds the ceremony of the Purification of the Priestess, a ritual reminiscent of the power of women shamans in ancient Shinto.

The leader of the Aoi Matsuri, dressed in Heian robes, reads a prayer and washes her hands in the sacred shrine waters. In early September a children's sumo tournament is held.

Due north up in the hills, **Kibune Shrine**, dedicated to the god of rain, celebrates the end of the rainy season with a water festival.

Out west: In the gentle hills west and northwest of Kyoto, the area known as Rakusai was a magnet for the Heian aristocracy, who peppered the area with their temples and residences. It is a popular hiking and walking area, and a summer retreat from the asphalt and heat of downtown.

Established as a small monastery in 1315, **Daitokuji**'s present temple buildings were built after 1468, when one of the several fires in its history burned down the temple. It is the holy of holies, where Zen married art. Ikkyu (1394–1481), the greatest Zen calligrapher, the painter Jasoku (15th century), Murata Juko and Sen no Rikyu, founders of the tea ceremony (16th century), all came out of Daitokuji. The great warlord Oda Nobunaga is buried here. Although a brutal warrior, Nobunaga (1534–82) was

Cherry blossom garden at Heian Shrine.

fundamental in the 16th century reunification of Japan after decades of civil war. He was also a leading patron of the arts, and cultivated the aesthetics of Kyoto.

About five out of 20 of Daitokuji's subsidiary temples are open to the public, including **Daisenin**, with perhaps Kyoto's most sophisticated Zen garden. The two-story main gate (1589) was built by Rikyu, a master of the traditional tea ceremony. In the upper story of the gate, Rikyu placed a statue that he himself carved... of himself. Toyotomi Hideyoshi (1537–98), the warlord who finished the unification started by Oda Nobunaga, found this, among other things, reason enough to command Rikyu to commit *seppuku*, the act of ritual suicide, in one of his own tea rooms, in 1591.

Behind Daitokuji is a restaurant where one can eat Zen vegetarian cuisine. Another recommended Zen-type restaurant is **Ikkyuan** (tel: 075-561-1901), near Yasaka Pagoda.

Kinkakuji, the Temple of the Golden Pavilion, was the site of 13th- and 14th-century aristocrats' villas. The pavilion appears to float in a pond like a golden boat – its walls are covered in gold leaf – sailing through the trees. In a small courtyard there is a 500-year-old pine tree that looks like a sailing ship. The current three-story building was erected in 1955, making it one of the youngest old buildings in town. The original was burned down in 1950 by a man who entered the Buddhist priesthood after being seduced by the pavilion's beauty. Thinking that his sense of aesthetics might approach perfection if he burned down the very object that had enchanted him in the first place, he did so. The author Yukio Mishima fictionalized the episode in his 1956 book *Kinkakuji*. In 1987, the gold foil on the outside of the pavilion was renewed.

The Zen temple **Ryoanji**, founded in 1450, has two gardens. Best known is a 300-sq.meter (360-sq.ft) rock garden (ca.1500), the most famous of all Zen rock gardens (known as *karesansui,* or dry landscapes). Much is written about

Amida, the Buddha of Paradise, at Byodoin.

its 15 rocks, one of which is always invisible, but nothing is known for sure about its meaning, its designer, or even when it was built. It simply exists, that's all. The surrounding park used to belong to a Heian estate, with a pond reflecting rounded hills and wild grasses.

In the heart: Established in AD 947, **Kitano Tenmangu Shrine** is a leading shrine of the Tenmangu sect, which has thousands of shrines throughout the country. The shrine commemorates Sugawara Michizane, a 9th-century scholar, statesman and a patron of scholarship. A resident of Kyoto, he died in exile in Kyushu, in AD 903. Lightning, earthquakes and fires hit Kyoto soon afterwards. The shrine was built to pacify Michizane's angered soul.

The present shrine was rebuilt in 1607 after a fire. On *Ema-do* hang small wood votives called *ema,* with a picture of a horse on one side (cheaper than a real horse donation) and a wish or prayer on the other side; most messages today pray for success in school examinations. The shrine also celebrates the first calligraphy of the year; school children offer their writings to the shrine, but all visitors are welcome to try their hand. Michizane loved plum blossoms, known in Japan as the first flowers of spring because they bloom under snow. Geisha from nearby Kamishichigen, an attractive geisha neighborhood, serve tea under the plum trees, in memory of the tea ceremony given here by Toyotomi Hideyoshi in the late 16th century.

Kyoto's textile history extends back to the city's birth. The **Nishijin weaving district**, traditionally famous for silk, received its name – western camp – from the civil wars of the 1400s. The **Nishijin Textile Center** displays Nishijin silk and kimono.

Ura Senke, a leading school of tea ceremony founded in the 17th century, offers special programs for foreigners; Ura Senke has 150 chapters in Japan, and 70 more in other countries. (Call 075-431-3111 for both student information and for demonstration schedules. Beware: this really is a serious venture – no cameras, no levity.)

Decorative ox-cart at Aoi Matsuri.

Originally built as a second palace for the emperor, the **Kyoto Imperial Palace** was used as a primary residence from 1331 to 1868, when Tokyo became the capital. The palace has gone through many restorations over the centuries; the current buildings and structures were built in the mid 1800s, and as such are frowned upon by Kyoto purists. However, the **Shishinden Enthronement Hall**, standing with its sweeping cedar roof before a silent courtyard of white sand, is a truly impressive emblem of imperial rule constructed in the *shinden* style, where all buildings are connected by covered walkways or galleries. The surrounding court town became the present **Kyoto Gyoen**, or the public Kyoto Imperial Park.

For five days in early April, the Imperial Palace opens its doors to the public. At other times it is possible for visitors to take a morning guided tour by applying early in the morning to the Imperial Household Agency.

Nijo Castle contrasts with the delicate characteristics of courtly Kyoto.

Colorful carp flags flutter on Boys' Day.

Construction was begun in 1569 by the warlord Oda Nobunaga and finished by Tokugawa Ieyasu (1543–1616), ally to Oda Nobunaga and Toyotomi Hideyoshi, to demonstrate his military dominance over the city; he in fact assured his dominance over all of Japan by establishing the last of Japan's shogun governments, the Tokugawa Shogunate, from 1603 until 1867.

Rectangular in dimensions, the castle's magnificent stone walls and gorgeous gold-leafed audience halls show where power really lay during the Edo Period. The central main court, encircled by the inner moat, was destroyed by fire in the late 18th century but rebuilt. It was from here that Emperor Meiji declared the centuries of shogunate rule to be over, and abolished. The so-called "nightingale floors" squeak with every step to warn of intruders entering the castle; the sounds actually imitate the call of the Japanese bush warbler. The garden is a grand example of a lord's strolling garden.

Nearby **Nijo Jinya**, just south of the castle, was originally the home of a wealthy merchant, but was used mostly by visiting *daimyo* taking care of business at the Nijo Castle. Containing 20 rooms, the home is famous for its secret trapdoors and other devices – ingenious movable soundproof walls, for example – that protected its occupants and guests. It is a private home now, and permission must be obtained to visit.

The old neighborhood of **Shimabara**, near Kyoto Station and still guarded by a large 17th-century gate, preserves in two old buildings the last of the inns and teahouses dedicated to the *Tayu* courtesans. Tayu used to be the highest rank of geisha, but now only a handful survive. (Pounding of rice cakes for the New Year takes place all over Japan, but only in Shimabara is it overseen by courtesans in full regalia.) In the Edo Period, Shimabara was Kyoto's first quarter for the sensual pleasures, but eventually it lost its popularity to Gion.

As with many other of Kyoto's historical treasures, Toyotomi Hideyoshi was responsible for **Nishi Honganji**, which he established in 1591 when he brought the *Jodo-shinshu* Buddhist sect to the temple's current location. Its Chinese influences are many, and historians sometimes consider it the best example of Buddhist architecture still around. The *Hondo,* or Main Hall, was rebuilt in 1760 after fire destroyed it. Its interior is decorated in no unsubtle fashion. The *Daishido,* or Founder's Hall (1636), contains an effigy of the sect's founder, who carved it himself. Cremated after his death, his ashes were mixed with lacquer and then applied to the effigy. On either side are portraits of the temple's succeeding abbots. The *Shoin,* or Study Hall, contains a number of chambers named after their decorations: Wild Geese Chamber, Sparrow Chamber, Chrysanthemum Chamber. The chambers and their artwork and decorations are exquisite.

Nearby **Higashi Honganji** was established in 1603 when the first Tokugawa shogun, wary of the Jodo-shinshu sect's power at Nishi Honganji Temple, attempted to thwart their influence by establishing an offshoot of the sect. This new sect's headquarters was Higashi Honganji, or East Honganji, in contrast to Nishi Honganji, or West Honganji. Only the Main Hall and Founder's Hall are open to the public. The present buildings were erected in 1895, their predecessors destroyed by fires. When these current structures were being built, female devotees from around Japan cut and donated their long hair, which was woven into 50 ropes used during construction.

Way out west: Off in the hills west of the city, **Arashiyama** was once the playground of Heian aristocrats and is today punctuated with small temples. Young tourists cross over the **Hozu River** on picturesque **Togetsu Bridge** to follow walking courses in the nearby **Sagano** area – a popular locale of Japanese literature – and to promenade by the restaurants and shops along the river. Although a faithful copy of the original bridge crossed by the ancient aristocrats, the present bridge was built in 1934 of steel, unfortunately.

One of the more unusual temples in

Kinkakuji, the Golden Pavilion, reflects the summer sun.

the Sagano area is the **Jikishian Temple**, which over the centuries has become a safe refuge for women escaping messy relationships. Many of the women wrote of their experiences in over 2,000 notebooks called *omoide-gusa,* books of reminiscences.

Over 8,000 old gravestones were collected from the Sagano area and arranged in a temple courtyard at **Adashino Nembutsuji**. For centuries, the bodies of those who died without friends or family were left here. The field of gravestones resembles, some say, the dry riverbed of the Sai River, which in Buddhism divides this world from hell. A festival is held in late August – candles are lit over the stones – to give comfort to the souls without family returning to visit earth during Obon, the traditional time when the living remember the dead.

Ginkakuji, the Silver Pavilion, exudes a more sober atmosphere.

Throughout August, the city rings with the song of cicadas. One way to spend a lazy summer afternoon is to view the lotuses floating on the pond of **Tenryuji**. The 13th-century pond lies within one of the oldest Zen gardens in Kyoto, predating the use of raked sand. The rocks jut upwards in Chinese style, and the shoreline is in the shape of the character meaning "heart."

One of the most famous strolling gardens is at **Katsura Detached Palace** (early 17th century) on the Katsura River, south of Arashiyama and due west of Kyoto Station. Its garden has a large central pond with several tea houses overlooking it. The design of the garden ensures that regardless of where one is standing, one always has a frontal view... the back of something, or of a view, is never seen.

Katsura, with its severe refinement, has exercised more influence on contemporary architecture than perhaps any other building in the world. (Shugakuin Detached Palace, with its lake floating in the sky, and its three levels separated by "farms" to give the emperor the illusion of living in the country, is pure fantasy. Katsura appeals to the perfectionists; Shugakuin appeals to romantics. Visitors to both require permission

from the Imperial Household Agency.

South of Kyoto station: On the other side of the shinkansen – or bullet train – tracks, south of Kyoto Station, the temple at **Toji** boasts one of the nation's enduring postcard images: the **Five-Story Pagoda**, or Goju-no-to, rebuilt in 1644 and **Japan's** tallest pagoda (55 meters/180 ft). The temple itself was established in 796, around the same time as Kyoto. Built next to the old city's main gate, the temple became the main Buddhist temple in Japan, the site of all important ceremonies dedicated to Japan's peace and safety. The temple's main hall, or *Kondo,* reflects the Buddhist traditions from India, China, and Japan. The hall dates from 1603 and contains sculptures of the 8th and 9th centuries. The appropriately named Treasure House is the home of many priceless treasures.

Tofukuji Temple, founded in 1236, is one of the best places for autumn foliage. It contains Japan's oldest, and perhaps most important, Zen-style gate (ca. 1428). Yet it is rarely visited and the grounds are usually quiet among the 25 subsidiary temples. Three major fires since 1319 have led to major reconstructions over the centuries. The main building was started in 1236, taking 19 years to finish. Be sure to walk through the *Hojo* (abbot's quarters) to the little platform over the ravine looking down on the Tsuten bridge, one of the most delightful views of all of Kyoto.

In the last week of November, **Shokaku-an**, a subsidiary temple of Tofukuji, holds a service in honor of brushes and pens which have outlived their usefulness. Writers and painters bring their old pens and cast them into a sacred fire.

Fushimi Inari Shrine, the "fox shrine" south of Kyoto Station, was founded in the 9th century, although the main shrine dates from 1499. For centuries, if not millennia, Japanese farmers believed the fox to be the god of harvest's messenger. The fox deity, with over 30,000 shrines across Japan, has since become associated with financial success, and the hillside behind Fushimi

Shrine maiden in *juni-hitoe*, a 12-layered kimono from the Heian Period.

Inari Shrine is lined with tens of thousands of cinnabar *torii* gates donated by local businesses.

To truly experience Fushimi, walk the full four-kilometer (2½-mile) course (approximately one or two hours) up along the paths behind the main shrine. As you pass under 10,000 or so red torii, the scene develops a dreamlike quality, especially when you reach the *tsuka* "mounds," where altars to natural spirits stand protected by images of foxes, horses, and even crocodiles. Traditional Japanese candles are for sale, and these burn everywhere with spooky, flickering flames. Amongst the altars, mystics and faith healers pray, and the scene amounts to a close encounter with the animistic roots of ancient Shinto.

Over the hills to the southeast of central Kyoto, on the other side of the Meishin Expressway, **Daigoji** is well worth a visit. Built on a hillside, there are two parts: *Kamidaigo* on the summit, and *Shimodaigo* at the base. Altogether the shrine has 70 buildings. The five-story pagoda (38 meters/125 ft) is the oldest building in the temple, built in 952. The other structures were rebuilt at the order of Hideyoshi after he came to view the cherries in 1598 and found the temple in a state of disrepair. The garden of **Sampoin**, designed by Hideyoshi, was one of the first stroll gardens, and its riot of rocks illustrates the exuberance of the Momoyama Period. On the second Sunday of April, the temple holds a parade reliving Hideyoshi's cherry viewing party.

Further south along the banks of the Uji River is **Byodoin**, the Phoenix Pavilion, a Buddhist architectural embodiment of the Western Paradise. At the end of the Heian Period, many thought that the Buddhist judgment day was near. The Byodoin reflects that belief. The main hall, or *Hoo-do,* (1053) enshrines Amida, Lord of the Western Paradise, surrounded by angelic musicians. The wings of the building are purely decorative, giving it the vague look of an alighting phoenix, a *ho-o*. From across the lake one can see the face of the Buddha framed in a window,

through which he sends out beams of saving light. The main hall's image is on the Japanese ten yen coin. (There is also a termite-resistant concrete replica of Byodoin in Hawaii.)

Manpukuji, near Uji, is one of the most unusual temples in Japan. Founded by a Chinese Zen monk in the early 17th century, it retains a strong Ming Dynasty flavor. Its main hall is of teakwood from Thailand.

The 12 Months of Kyoto: Tradition in Kyoto infuses the year with a natural rhythm. In 1994, Kyoto celebrated its 1,200th anniversary... 1,200 cycles of the four seasons that the Japanese, especially in Kyoto, define with festivals, rituals and ceremonies. Lucky indeed is the resident of Kyoto who can spend the whole year indulging in both seasons and festivals.

January: Beginning at midnight on the first day of the year, people dress in their best kimono and flock to shrines and temples for the first worship of the year. The peak period is January 1–3, but visits continue for the first ten days of January.

February: The last day of winter, *Setsubun* (or, separation between winter and spring), falls in the first week of February, depending on the old lunar calendar. The Japanese celebrate the end of winter with ceremonies symbolizing the driving out of demons. People throw beans into every corner of the house, crying "Oni wa soto, fuku wa uchi!" ("Out with the devils, in with good fortune!") There are many setsubun festivals in Kyoto, including at Yasaka Shrine in Gion, where geisha perform dances and then throw beans into the crowd in the afternoon.

March: In March the camellias fall, as complete flowers, not petal by petal. This disturbed the samurai, who were reminded of falling heads. But the flower is a favorite of tea masters, for whom one camellia bud symbolizes the coming of spring. One place to see falling camellias is Enrian, near Seiryoji.

April: Spring arrives with a vengeance, celebrated by cherry blossom parties, geisha dances and flower arrangements. Of all flowers, cherries are the most loved for the spirit of evanescence felt in their brief flowering and snow-like falling. Kyoto has numerous cherry blossom viewing spots, the most famous being at Daigoji. Don't expect private moments amidst the cherry trees; blossom viewing is a vigorous social affair, the partying perhaps more important than admiring the blossoms.

May: If April feels like spring, May really is. Azaleas, peaches and rhododendrons bloom, while temples air their treasures in the fresh spring breeze. Jingoji displays its art collection, normally hidden from the public, in the annual *mushibarai* "insect drying."

For a city steeped in the tea ceremony, the arrival of the new year's tea was, and still is for many, a major event. At 1pm, Kenninji recreates the parade that delivered the first tea of the season to its citizens in the Edo Period.

Early May is the time when Kamigamo waits for an auspicious day on which to hold the ceremony of the Purification of the Priestess. The ritual involves the leader of the Aoi Matsuri,

Weird and wonderful bargains can be found at Toji flea market.

dressed in Heian robes, reading a prayer and washing her hands in the sacred shrine waters.

June: From about June 10 through July 10, Kyoto enters the *tsuyu,* the rainy season that Japanese claim to dislike but love to talk about ad infinitum, as if no where else on the planet had a rainy season. Rain falls constantly in a light drizzle, the perfect filter for viewing Kyoto's sights. Kibune Shrine, dedicated to the god of water, celebrates the end of the rainy season with a vibrant water festival.

July: With the end of tsuyu comes the heat of summer, and *Tanabata.* According to legend, two stars, who are actually lovers, cross the milky way to meet each other only once a year on this day. Everywhere you will see bamboo stalks hung with colored papers in their honor. Kyoto's biggest Tanabata festival is at Kitano Tenmangu.

The Gion Festival, dating from the 10th century, is the premier festival of Kyoto. On July 17, about 30 floats, decorated with brocades from China and old dutch tapestries, parade downtown. The night before, several thousand people clad in light summer kimono throng the streets along Shijo between Karasuma and Kawaramachi, fanning themselves and listening to the hypnotic rhythm of the chimes struck by children in the floats. Many homes and shops open their doors to the public with displays of family treasures.

August: This is the month of *Obon,* when the spirits of the dead revisit their families, to be entertained for a few days before returning to the other shore. Lamps and fires are lit to guide them on their way.

From August 7–10, visitors ring the bell at Chinkoji, whose sound reaches to the depths of hell to announce that the spirits are now free to come to earth. The eastern slopes near Kiyomizu were once the site of an immense burial ground. The largest remaining cemetery is Higashi Otani Honmyo, where thousands of paper lanterns are strung by the gravestones in mid August. The grounds are open all night for visitors to pay their

The *Jidai Matsuri* features some lovely period dress.

respects and wander amongst the gently swinging lanterns.

On August 16, at Gosan Okuribi, the spirits' send-off to the other world is spectacular, with the evening lighting of bonfires hundreds of meters long on five hills surrounding the city. The most famous is to the east, in the shape of the word "Great." The other four are: "Wonderful Law," the "Boat," another "Great" to the west, and the "Torii."

While Obon is celebrated throughout Japan, only Kyoto actively preserves one for children, called Jizo-bon (in honor of Jizo, protector of children).

September: September is a neutral month, a good season for Zen. Mid September is the time for moon viewing, with numerous events across town. Osawa Pond behind Daikakuji has been known since Heian times as one of Japan's three great moon-viewing sites.

October: October is a month of dress-up and strange happenings. The Bull Festival at Koryuji is known as one of the "Three Weird Festivals" of Kyoto. It features demon caricatures, a god riding a bull, and a long slow announcement (punctuated by cries from the audience of "Speed up!"). The ceremony is both humorous and bizarre.

Yuki Shrine, in Kurama far north of town, holds another of the "Three Weird Festivals," a Fire Festival in the third week of October. In a sea of flame and sparks, youths bearing 250 huge pine brands gather before the shrine. At the moment of greatest tension, a portable shrine bursts out from the main building and makes a circuit of the village.

Jidai Matsuri (Festival of the Ages) is the third of the orthodox "Three Weird Festivals" of Kyoto, and the climax to October's round of fancy dress. About 2,000 participants lead a colorful parade representing all the famous people in Japanese history, dressed in the styles of their times.

November: In November people travel out of the city to see the changing leaves. North of Kyoto by bus is the little town of Ohara with several small temples. Sanzenin has a wondrous garden of moss and maple trees.

December: Kaomise, at Minamiza,

means "face showing," and it is Kyoto's annual gala kabuki performance, so called because the greatest actors show their faces for the occasion. Typically kabuki programs run two per day, about five hours each. On the exterior of the theater hang wooden placards with actors' names in old kabuki script.

Radish boiling at Senbon Shakado celebrates the day of Buddha's enlightenment; the radishes are inscribed with magic Sanskrit letters.

In December, temples and shrines literally begin dusting in preparation for the coming of the new year. The dusting at Higashi Honganji is surely one of the world's great cleaning experiences. From early morning, hundreds of volunteers pound the tatami, wipe the pillars and steps, and brush away the dust of the year.

On the last day of December, the old year departs at midnight with 108 strikings of temple bells across the country - *Joya no Kane,* the New Year's Bell. In Kyoto, at Chionin, it takes 17 monks to ring Japan's largest bell, cast in 1636.

Below, well-manicured gardens at Taizoin. **Right**, lad in his festival finery.

292

NARA

Nara belongs to an era before Zen gardens and tea ceremony, before Japan became Japan. Founded in AD 710, the city flourished during the golden age of Tang China. Buddhist thought from India and arts from as far as Greece and Turkey flowed east along the Silk Road, and Nara was the last stop. Preserved here, long after extinction in their home countries, are the finest examples of Tang architecture, early Korean religious sculpture, and treasures from Central China and Iran. To explore Nara is to look beyond Japan, into the greater Asian past.

Japan had its capital at Nara from AD 710 to 784, after which the government moved to Kyoto and the area lost political importance. This was Nara's great blessing. As a result, it avoided the wars which destroyed all the other ancient capitals of China, Korea and Japan.

"Nara" stands for something much larger than its brief span as the capital. It climaxed centuries of development in the surrounding Yamato Plain, birthplace of Japanese culture, and this history can be felt today in the remains of earlier capitals, imperial tombs, and Japan's oldest shrines.

The joy of Nara comes from exploring outside the modern city. You may find it in the quiet of the hill temples, bypassed by tour buses and the millions of school children. Or you may stand beside a tomb mound and listen to the sound of cicadas in the trees. Outside of Nara Park, there are no perfectly raked sand gardens. Everything is dark, worn, even shabby, and what a relief!

Exploring the Yamato Plain and its surrounding hills is complicated without the use of a car. If you use trains and buses, the best way is to plan each day in advance using maps, and in approaching Japanese-speaking friends, and the concierge at your hotel for assistance. But at some point it may be necessary to rent a car or taxi, which is

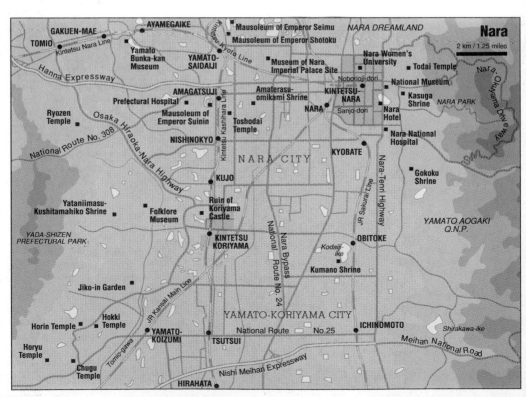

expensive, but not too burdensome if you go in a group of three or four people. The way to enjoy Nara is to take picnic excursions with friends.

Cultural Background: Japanese see in their early, pre-Chinese culture an "Age of the Gods," when men were pure and close to nature. This can be felt in the tomb mounds of the kings and nobles, built under Korean influence from the 3rd to the 7th century AD The typical tumulus consists of a stone chamber covered in a mound of earth in a "key-hole" shape, and surrounded by a pond. The earthen covering can be as tall as a small hill, making these mounds among the largest mausoleums in the world. The tombs of emperors are wholly controlled by the Imperial Household Agency and are closed to the public. Heavily wooded, these forbidden precincts harken back to mysterious origins, the "Age of the Gods."

While the early Japanese layer still exists, the Buddhist and Chinese layer is much stronger in Nara. In fact, fear of the power of the Buddhist temples led the Imperial court to move the capital away from the Yamato Plain.

Nara Buddhism represents an early exuberant form of Buddhist thought, rich in symbolism. Everywhere in Nara you will see mandalas, diagrams or arrangements representing cosmic truth. At the center is the essence of the main god being illustrated. Expanding outward in circles or squares are other gods exerting their powers to help the center. Mandalas can be elaborate, from the arrangement of statues on an altar to the layout of temple buildings.

Every placement and gesture has meaning. For example, you will see two guardian figures flanking the gates to large temples. One has his mouth open, the other closed. These symbolize the sounds "A(lpha)" and "Om," the first and last letters of the Sanskrit alphabet. Being first and last, they encompass all, and hence have magical power to protect against evil.

Hand gestures, clothing and implements are significant. Most ornate are the *mandorla*, or halos, in which can be seen the intercultural impact of the Silk Road. The halos originated in Indian Buddhism, and traveled east to Japan, and west to Europe, where they were adopted by Christianity. The flames in the halos signify divine light.

Statues with great power were hidden from the public, and these became the so-called "Secret Buddhas," shown only on rare occasions. For instance, the Kuze Kannon of Horyuji was hidden from the public for a thousand years before seeing the light of day in the late 19th century. Many statues are still only shown in the spring or fall, or on religious holidays.

The principal Buddhist images one may see in Nara are:

Shaka (Sakyamuni), the historical Buddha; and

Nyorai, Buddhas who have achieved the final stage of perfection.

The important Nyorai are:

Vairocana, the Cosmic Buddha;

Yakushi, the Healer of Souls, who holds a medicine bottle; and

Bosatsu (or Bodhisattva), Buddhas devoted to saving all living beings.

Preceding pages, the stone lanterns at Kasuga Taisha. **Below**, Nara street scene.

The important Bosatsu are:

Kannon, the Buddha of Compassion;
Miroku, the Buddha of the Future;
Monju, the Buddha of Wisdom;
Amida, the Buddha of Paradise, who sends out beams of light to save and lead souls to the Western Paradise;
Jizo, the Guide After Death, who holds a pilgrim's staff and a light in his palm to guide souls (especially children) after death;
Nikko, the Light of the Sun; and
Gakko, the Light of the Moon. Nikko and Gakko frequently stand as attendants to the central image.

Guardians: The role of the Guardians is to protect the truth. Wrathful in countenance, the Guardians brandish weapons and are wrapped in flames. Guardians include deities (such as the **Ashura**) who were once evil and now have a benign appearance.

Disciples: The disciples of Buddha were a favorite theme of Nara art. These statues have great character, with eyes and faces showing the effects of the disciples' religious lives.

Many Nara masterpieces owe their beauty to the technique of dry lacquer, in which the contours of the figure are molded out of a paste of lacquer applied over a central core. The use of a soft plastic material rather than carving allows for great subtlety of expression.

Nara Park: Old Nara, much larger than the city today, followed the model of Chinese imperial cities: a sacred square, with streets radiating from the central palace. During the centuries of neglect after 784 the palaces disappeared, but the temples and shrines on the northeastern edge of the city survived. This corner of the city is now a public park. Tame deer, sacred to Kasuga Taisha shrine, are its symbol.

The best place to begin exploring the park is **Kofukuji**, a temple located near the Kintetsu Railway station, and with one of the convenient parking lots in the area. The patrons of Kofukuji were the Fujiwara clan, who gained power in the mid-7th century and succeeded in dominating the government for the next 500 years. Even after the capital moved to Kyoto, the Fujiwara continued to support Kofukuji as the family temple. Kofukuji is known for its two pagodas. The five-story pagoda, built in 1426, is a copy of an original dating from 730; the three-story pagoda dates from 1114.

The attached **Kokuhokan Museum**, although a dreary, concrete building, offers the best introduction to Japanese sculpture available. Most famous is the set of guardians (734) with sweet childlike faces molded out of dry lacquer. Of these, the six-armed **Ashura** is one of the best loved statues in Japan. In addition, the museum displays a cast bronze head of **Yakushi Nyorai** (685) practically Egyptian in its abstract simplicity, and massive heads of temple guardians, from statues which must have been 15 to 20 meters (50 to 65 ft) high. Nara developed in an age before Japan became the land of the miniature. The buildings and statues aimed to exceed even the grandeur of Imperial China.

From Kofukuji walk across the street to the **National Museum** if you are inclined to see more sculpture. The most interesting part of the National

Quaint tea shop entrance.

Museum is the **East Gallery** (reachable via an underground walkway) which houses temporary shows. Once a year the Annex displays objects from the Shosoin Treasury.

The museum borders on Nara Park's central avenue. Walk north to the **Nandaimon** gate, dating from 1199. This gate, with its 18 pillars and elaborate roof construction, is one of the outstanding monuments of the Kamakura Period. Inside the gate stand great wooden statues, called Nio, who guard the entrance to Todaiji. They were carved by the sculptors Unkei and Kaikei (circa 1200).

Straight ahead is **Todaiji**, the temple also known as the Hall of the Great Buddha. Founded in 743, it is the most important temple in Nara. Enshrining a monumental bronze image of Vairocana, the Cosmic Buddha, the hall was meant to proclaim the power of the Imperial state. It was destroyed numerous times by fire. The present building dates from 1706. The Buddha has been greatly altered in later restorations, but the petals of the lotus on which the Buddha sits retain original engravings in fine lines showing Shaka (the historical Buddha) as one of 110 billion avatars of the Cosmic Buddha.

Although only two thirds of its original size, Todaiji is said to be the largest wooden structure in the world. The present building is not entirely a first-rate piece of architecture (note the pillars made of bound timbers rather than single beams such as those of the Nandaimon gate). Still, the interior retains a sense of the dark medieval grandeur that was old Nara.

The bronze statue, by the way, is 16 meters (55 ft) tall and weighs 500 tons. Like the statuary found in the **Sangatsu Hall** and the **Kaidan Monastery**, it shows off Tempyo Period (729–764) art and craftsmanship.

Behind Todaiji is a quiet part of the park where you can rest from the milling crowds. In late October and early November, you will be able to catch a glimpse of the exterior of the **Shosoin Treasury**. Built in 756 to house a col-

Tame deer roam Nara Park.

lection donated to Todaiji by Emperor Shomu, the Shosoin is constructed in log-cabin style, raised high on stilts. It was the world's first humidity controlled museum. This style, called Azekura, is found in the storehouses of many Nara temples. The Shosoin is a time capsule, having preserved through the centuries hundreds of objects from across Asia, some of which are the world's only surviving examples.

The road behind Todaiji, lined with picturesque clay walls, leads up the hill to the Nigatsudo and Sangatsudo temples. **Sangatsudo**, built in 746, contains a large central statue of Fukukenjaku Kannon (God of Compassion), radiating light beams, and surrounded by a mandala arrangement of attendants and guardian beings.

Next door is **Nigatsudo**, the perfect place for a final view of the park. Raised high over the city, this pyramidal building was frequently burned and rebuilt, most recently in 1669. Every March 13 since its founding in 752, the Emperor sends an emissary at midnight with water symbolizing the coming of spring. The arrival of the water is the occasion for a fire festival, where monks with burning pine brands run around the verandah spinning sparks into the night.

Hardy souls will enjoy the walk south from Nigatsudo along the foot of **Mt. Wakakusa**. This is also the site of a fire festival on January 15, when priests fire the dry grass, setting the whole mountain ablaze. At the end of the walk lies **Kasuga Taisha**, the shrine of the Fujiwara family, known for its sacred deer and for its collection of hundreds of stone lanterns.

The city of Nara contains numerous other temples of historical importance. The most interesting temple outside Nara Park is **Shinyakushiji**, built in 747. This, along with Sangatsudo, is one of the few original Nara buildings. The central figure of Yakushi Nyorai (the Healer) grants aid to those suffering from ailments of the eyes and ears. Most unusual is the set of 12 clay guardian images still standing intact. Shin-

Watching the Procession of Buddhas in Nara.

yakushiji, tucked away among crowded streets in a forgotten part of town, is a favorite of Nara lovers.

Nara Environs – Northwest: The premier site outside downtown Nara is Horyuji to the southwest. If you have time to explore the lesser known temples of the northwest suburbs, the best place to begin is **Hannyaji**, the Temple of Wisdom. Surrounded by a garden of wild flowers, it has great charm. In the garden is a Kamakura gate with elegant upturned gables, and a 13-story Heian stone pagoda. The temple houses a Kamakura statue of Monju, the God of Wisdom. Monju rides on his sacred lion, carrying in his hand the sword to cut through ignorance.

From Hannyaji, the road turns west. Here, about 2 kilometers (1½ miles) from Nara Park, was the center of the ancient city. Of the **Heijokyo Palace** nothing survives but a large field, with circular clipped hedges showing where the pillars used to stand. Near the palace field is **Hokkeji**, a nunnery known for its 8th century statue of Kannon. The statue is of unpainted wood, with features said to be copied from the face of Empress Komyo, and surrounded by a halo of sprouting lotus leaves. Beware: the statue is one of the "Secret Buddhas," only on view from March 30 to April 7, June 6 to 8, and October 25 to November 8.

Near Hokkeji is the tiny temple of **Kairyuoji**, "the Temple to the Dragon King of the Sea." It houses a 4-meter (13-ft) high model of a pagoda. Washed up on the shores of time, this pagoda is on record as being the oldest architectural model in the world.

North of Hokkeji are imperial tomb mounds surrounded by moats, and beyond them is **Akishinodera**, patron temple of the arts. The original temple was founded in 775, but the present hall dates from the Kamakura Period. Inside is **Gigeiten**, God of the Arts, a favorite of Nara cognoscenti. The head is original Nara with the delicacy of expression typical of dry lacquer. The body, a re-creation from the Kamakura Period, has taken on the S-curve of Chinese sculp-

Below left, Todaiji, Hall of the Great Buddha. Right, the Buddha himself.

ture, creating a graceful swaying motion.

Nara Environs – Southwest: The southwestern temples are a major tourist destination, easily reached by train or bus from Nara City. Going south, the first temple is **Toshodaiji**, founded by a Chinese monk called Ganjin in 751. As you approach, the roof of the **Kondo** (Main Hall) spreads out before you, the finest surviving example of Tang Dynasty architecture. Note the inward curving fish tails on the roof, unique to Nara, and also found on the Hall of the Great Buddha.

Inside the Main Hall is a triad of images centered on **Vairocana**, the Cosmic Buddha. Chinese influence can be seen in the sway of the torso, and the magnificent *mandorla* in which the Cosmic Buddha manifests himself in space and time through an infinity of other Buddhas. To the left is the **Thousand-Hand Kannon**, who manifests mercy through the devices held in his hands: the rosary, the bottle of tears, the axe, the wheel of the law, the lotus, etc. On Vairocana's right is **Yakushi**, the Healer, whose mandorla takes the shape of a medicine bottle.

Behind the Main Hall is the **Kodo**, or Lecture Hall. Although altered in later times, this building is the only extant example of Nara courtly architecture, since it was originally part of the Heijokyo Palace. Enshrined within is **Miroku**, the God of the Future, positioned in a mandala arrangement directly behind the Cosmic Buddha. Toward the right of the Main Hall are two storehouses built in the Azekura (log cabin) style.

Yakushiji is a 10-minute walk from Toshodaiji. All of the original buildings have been destroyed by fires except the **Eastern Pagoda** (698, rebuilt 718). This is constructed of a harmonious arrangement of three roofs with smaller roofs underneath creating the illusion of six stories. Unfortunately, the complex as a whole lacks the Nara charm, due to modern reconstructions of the Western Pagoda (1981) and the Main Hall (1976). The Main Hall houses an original triad (considerably restored) of Yakushi flanked by Nikko, Light of the Sun, and Gakko, Light of the Moon.

The goal of most travelers in this area is **Horyuji**, which boasts the oldest wooden buildings in the world. Horyuji was founded in 607 by Prince Shotoku, the pivotal figure who established Chinese religion and culture in Japan. It is another time capsule, like the Shosoin Treasury, preserving hundreds of art works from the 7th and 8th centuries.

Horyuji is divided into two wings. Most visitors start from the **Western Cloister**. The main gate, dating from 1438, leads to an avenue lined by earthen walls characteristic of Horyuji. Note the wood grain patterns created by pressing the earth with boards, thought to make the walls earthquake resistant. At the end of the avenue is the **Chumon** (Middle Gate). The pillars of the gate (607, rebuilt circa 670) are famous for their entasis (outward curvature), a feature of Greek architecture which traveled to Japan via the Silk Road.

Inside the Western Cloister are the **Pagoda** and **Kondo** (Main Hall) circa 670. The Kondo houses a rare group of

Lighting a fire at Kasuga.

bronzes (circa 620) in Wei (pre-Tang) style. They are distinguished by elongated faces, the "archaic smile," and the abstract, almost art deco lines of the falling drapery and the flames of the mandorla. In the center is the Shaka Triad (Sakyamuni, the historical Buddha, with attendants). To the right is Yakushi and to the left is **Amida**, the Buddha of Paradise. The wooden guardians, standing on demons, are Japan's oldest "Four Heavenly Kings."

On entering the **Daikodo** (Lecture Hall) to the rear of the complex, you come to the sophisticated world of Heian. The Daikodo, transferred here from Kyoto in 990, houses a triad of Heian statues of Yakushi, flanked by Nikko and Gakko.

One of the pleasures of Horyuji is the walk out through the cloister, an old example of a Chinese form which influenced temples and palaces across East Asia. Outside the cloister, walk east to the two concrete buildings of the **Daihozoden** (Museum). These buildings are even uglier than the Museum of

Kofukuji, but the treasures are so important you simply cannot resist going inside. Among the displays in the museum are: the **Kudara Kannon** from Korea, and the **Portable Shrine of Lady Tachibana** (both circa 650), and the **Hyakumanto Pagodas**, the "Million Pagodas," containing strips of paper printed with short prayers. Published in 764 in an edition of one million, they are the world's oldest printed material.

From the Museum, there is a walk bordered by temples and earthen walls to the **Eastern Cloister**. In the center of the cloister is an octagonal building of Chinese inspiration surmounted by a flaming jewel, known as the **Yumedono**, Hall of Dreams. Built circa 740, it commemorates a dream of Prince Shotoku in which an angel appeared to him while he was copying the sutras. The Yumedono contains a "Secret Buddha," the Kuze Kannon, only on view in the spring and fall.

Behind the Eastern Cloister is **Chuguji**, a nunnery housing a wooden

Rooftops of the Taimadera complex.

statue of Miroku, God of the Future, the supreme statue of Nara. Possibly of Korean workmanship, it dates from the early 7th century. With one leg hanging down in the posture known as "princely ease," Miroku sits with his head tilted slightly and a hand raised to his cheek in a thinking gesture. Although Miroku is enshrined in a drab concrete building, this is an ideal place to stop, rest, and meditate for a while. The attendant will turn off the recorded announcement if requested to do so.

Slightly removed from the Horyuji complex are the two temples of **Hokkiji** and **Horinji**. Hokkiji contains a three-story pagoda built in 706. Horinji, was rebuilt only in 1975, but is enjoyable to visit, being situated in picturesque surroundings just one kilometer (½ mile) north of Chuguji.

South Yamato and Asuka: From Horyuji, you proceed to the south Yamato Plain. To the west are **Taimadera** and **Shakkoji**, famed for their thousands of varieties of peonies. Taimadera contains two Nara Period pagodas, and a

"secret" mandala painting (an Edo Period copy is on view). On May 14 parishioners don masks of the Buddhas and parade through the grounds, in a unique display of walking sculpture.

East of Taimadera is the city of Yagi, with its old town area preserved, known as **Imai-cho**. This is a veritable museum of Edo Period town life, with over 600 old houses including six designated as Important Cultural Properties.

A short drive south are the ruins of **Asuka**, the capital before Nara. Asuka (552–645) was the great beginning. It was the first city to have avenues on the Chinese pattern and large Buddhist temples. It was here that Prince Shotoku introduced Chinese law and religion. And it was here that the poems of the *Manyoshu*, Japan's first poetry anthology, were written. Today, there is only a village of farmhouses and rice paddies, but the ruins conjure up a "scent" of the past, as reflected in the village's name Asuka-ko, "Asuka Incense."

In Asuka, two burial mounds are open to the public. **Takamatsuzuka**, ca. 700, contains Japan's only known tomb murals. Excavated in 1972, they are displayed in a modern building often crowded with visitors. More evocative is the **Ishi-no-Butai Kofun**, the Stone Stage. This was the inner chamber of a 7th century tumulus. The earthen covering has disappeared, leaving the 75-ton boulders exposed like a stage for titans.

Tachibanadera stands at the site of Prince Shotoku's birthplace. Most of the temple's buildings date from the Edo Period, but the pleasant country surroundings exude something of the Asuka "scent." Most important of the area's temples is **Asukadera**, enshrining the **Great Buddha of Asuka**, a bronze image of Shaka which is Japan's oldest large-scale Buddhist statue. Although frequently burned and restored, the essential quality of the original still remains.

The year 643 was a pivotal point in Japanese history. The powerful Soga clan plotted against the emperor, and was defeated with the help of Nakatomi Kamatari, founder of the Fujiwara House. This led to the Taika Reforma-

Bicycle gets bamboo protection.

tion of 645, establishing the victory of continental civilization. Pillar bases of the **Asuka Itabuki no miya**, the palace where these events took place, are visible in a field near Tachibanadera.

The Asuka area is ideal for day excursions, and it is possible to rent bicycles in front of Kintetsu Asuka Station. Other sites of interest include: **Okadera**, with a 4.5-meter (15-ft) high plaster statue of Kannon, **Amagashi-no-oka**, the hill beloved of *Manyoshu* poets for its view of the valley, and **Tanzan Shrine** situated in the western hills. Tanzan, meaning "Talk in the Mountains," is where Kamatari met in secret to plan his attack against the Soga clan. The shrine contains an elegant Kamakura Period 13-story pagoda with cedar roofs.

The Northern Hills: The Yamato Plain suffers from typical Japanese modern development, and it is only a matter of time before it disappears under a layer of electric wires and pachinko parlors. As this happens, lovers of Nara turn more and more to the mountains. The northern and eastern hills are convenient for relaxing afternoon drives out of Nara, notably the **Nara Okuyama Driveway** starting from behind Todaiji. The hill roads wind through beautiful valleys, past temples, stone carvings, and waterfalls.

The jewel of the northern hills is **Joruriji**, one of the few surviving Heian temples. Joruriji (1179) is a miniature Pure Land, the Buddhist paradise. In the center is a pond, symbolizing the lake of heaven. To the right is the Western Paradise, the temple of **Nine Amida**, each representing a step on the ladder of spiritual progress. During the year the rays of the sun sweep across the temple, lighting each Buddha image in turn. In a direct line across the pond is a pagoda with a statue of Yakushi, lord of the Eastern Paradise. Joruriji contains other great sculptures, including **Kisshoten**, a "secret" image of an Indian goddess, only visible on January 1 to 15, March 21 to May 20, October 1 to November 30.

About one kilometer's walk into the hills are the **Tono-o Sekibutsu**, stone carvings dating from the Kamakura Period. These are Magaibutsu "Buddhas on Hillsides," cut into the rock. Carved in an abstract, even crude style, and covered with lichens, the **Magaibutsu** have a magical aura about them. The hills of Nara contain hundreds of such carvings, worth a study in themselves. One kilometer further you arrive at **Gansenji**, boasting another group of stone carvings and a fine view from the hilltop behind the temple.

Yamanobe-no-Michi: The foothills bordering the Yamato Plain to the east have become a popular hiking course. The **Yamanobe-no-Michi** (Path on the Edge of the Mountains) has existed since the Yamato Plain was still a swamp. With its tumuli and ancient shrines, this is the area closest to the "Age of the Gods." The 16-kilometer (10-mile) walk, with detours to see sites, and time to reflect before ancient tombs, takes a full day to complete.

Begin from **Isonokami Jingu** in the town of Tenri. It houses the sword with which the legendary first emperor

Temple buildings on the outskirts of Nara.

Jimmu conquered the world. After about 1½ hour's walk past the small shrines and the remains of old temples, you finally arrive at **Chorakuji**, well known for its **Amida Triad**, the first Kamakura statues to have crystal eyes. The neighborhood has many Buddhist stone carvings.

Some 15 minutes' walk from Chorakuji are two great tumuli: **Sujin Tennoryo** (Tomb of Emperor Sujin), and neighboring **Kushiyama Kofun**. These are the most beautiful tombs in the Nara area. Ten minutes walk further on is **Keiko Tennoryo** (Tomb of Emperor Keiko).

Another 1½ hour's walk brings you to **Miwa Shrine**. The present building dates from early Edo, but the shrine is one of Japan's oldest. There has never been a "Main Shrine" to house a sacred object, since the mountain behind the shrine is seen as divine in its own right. Miwa Shrine is the classic example of Shinto nature worship. Miwa is also known for its *somen* noodles, which are a refreshing meal for the hungry hiker.

Ten minutes south of Miwa are the **Kanaya Sekibutsu**, images of Shaka and Miroku carved on coffer stones taken from old burial mounds. These carvings give a good illustration of the cultural overlay of Shintoism and Buddhism and make a fitting end to the Path at the Edge of the Mountains.

The Eastern Mountains: For nature lovers, the Eastern Mountains are most enjoyable. Soon after leaving Sakurai, at the southeastern end of the Yamato Plain, the road begins to climb into verdant hills. The first stop is **Hasedera**, the "Flower Temple," known for its peony festival held in the last week of April. A covered stairway of 399 steps hung with lanterns leads up to the Main Hall, which enshrines Japan's largest wooden statue, an **Eleven-Headed Kannon** carved in 1538. From the temple platform there is a good view of the picturesque town of Hasedera and the surrounding hills.

A half hour's drive to the east brings you to the village of Ono, where you turn south on the winding road along the

Below and facing page, spring arrives in the hills around Nara.

Muro River. Across the river you see the **Miroku Magaibutsu** cut into the cliff face. This is the largest hillside carving in Japan, dating from 1207.

Two miles further up the river is **Muroji**, the temple which epitomizes the appeal of Nara: cultural treasures, a mixture of mystery and charm, in a numinous natural setting. Muroji, founded in the 8th century, became one of the few Esoteric Buddhist sites to be open to women, earning it the name Nyonin Koya, the "woman's Koya," in distinction to the all-male Mt. Koya monasteries to the south. Enter the enclave over the arched bridge spanning the river. After about 90 meters (300 ft) you come to the foot of a roughhewn staircase, capped by the rustic roof of the **Kondo** (9th century). The appearance of a helmet surmounting a ribbed suit of armor gave this staircase the name **Yoroizaka** (Armor Slope). Inside the Kondo, five Heian statues of Kannon, Monju, Shaka, Yakushi and Jizo stand placidly behind the twisting forms of 12 guardians, blown by a gale

of Kamakura energy.

Behind the Kondo is the Kamakura-Period **Kanjodo**, containing a 9th century statue of **Nyoirin Kannon**, whose mark is the wish-fulfilling wheel. On the walls are paintings of the Two Spiritual Worlds: the Diamond Mandala, and the Womb Mandala.

Nearby is a small five-story **Pagoda**, with an almost doll-like quality. From here, the path leads to the **Oku-no-In**, the Inner Sanctuary. A small sanctuary removed from the main complex is a feature of hillside temples borrowed from early Shinto. It derives from the belief in the power of mountains typified by Miwa Shrine. The path stumbles upwards with huge stone steps made for giants rather than human beings, past the snaking roots of towering cryptomeria pines. Eventually you reach the little Kamakura **Mieido** at the top, where you can receive the seal of the temple, as proof of having sought and found the heart of Nara.

Beyond Nara: Muroji is the gateway to deeper mountains. To the east is natural scenery, including the **48 Waterfalls of Akame**, one of Nara's best picnic sites; the gorges of **Koochidani** and **Oku-Koochidani**; the temple of **Enjoji** with a Heian garden designed for boating parties; and the village of **Yagyu**, birthplace of a school of martial arts.

To the south are numerous temples and shrines leading up to **Mt. Yoshino**, hideaway of Imperial loyalists in the 14th century, and famous for its cherry blossoms in spring. There are many good inns in this area. **Zaodo**, at Mt. Yoshino, is a leading temple of the mystical cult, with tapered columns made of natural tree trunks.

Farthest south is **Mt. Koya**, sacred center of Esoteric Buddhism, founded by Kobo Daishi in AD 816. On the hilltop are temples with collections of Buddhist art. Around the tomb of Kobo Daishi is a graveyard with monuments to old families and historical figures. Pilgrims visit Mt. Koya all year and you can spend the night in one of the temples. The circuit of the mandala of Nara and its hinterland is now completed.

THE GRAND SHRINES OF ISE

If it makes you feel more comfortable, you might think of it as a pilgrimage to the heart of what is simple, good and lasting in the Japanese aesthetic, instead of one to the seat of a faith which to some radical freethinkers in Japan is anachronistic, right wing and ultra-nationalistic. However you think of it, though, do try to visit these magnificent shrines, just a short detour from the "bullet train" stop at Nagoya, for here you will see – and no doubt feel – a corner of Japan as "pure" as it comes.

No one can say exactly how long the two main shrines of what are collectively called the **Grand Shrines of Ise** have existed; historical evidence shows that the Naiku, or **Inner Shrine**, has been in place since around the 4th century, and the Geku or **Outer Shrine** since the late 5th century, but it's likely that some sort of shrine or another has been here much, much longer. The re-

ally impressive aspect of their antiquity, however, is not their age, *per se*, for there are many religious and other structures in the world far, far more ancient, albeit most lie in ruins. At Ise, however, the venerable cypress-wood buildings stand today in perfect condition – almost brand-new – mocking the ravages of time.

The Gods Move House: The secret of the "mint condition" of these most sacred of all Shinto shrines is in a practice called *sengu*, or "shrine removal," observed every 20 years, with few exceptions, over the last 13 centuries.

(For trivia buffs: the exceptions were during the century of internal warfare during the 15th and 16th centuries; in the "modern period" since the Meiji Restoration, sengu have been held in the years 1869, 1889, 1909, 1929, 1953 [delayed due to war], and 1973.)

The 61st such sengu took place in October 1993, with the razing of the two main buildings (the **Toyouke-Daijungu** of the Outer Shrine and the **Kotaijingu** of the Inner Shrine), along with 14 smaller auxiliary structures (*betsugu*) on the grounds of both shrines, and associated fences, gates and so on.

Actually, before the existing structures were destroyed, new shrine buildings of identical scale and materials as the old ones were erected in adjacent plots set aside for that purpose. When all was ready, Japan's largest and most important festival, **Jingu Shikinen Sengu**, began and the deities of the respective shrines were invited to pass from the old into the new structures.

Interestingly, not only the buildings are "reborn" but also a long list of "divine apparel and treasures" – clothing, decorations and accoutrements for the gods – and various ritual tools used during the rites accompanying the sengu. Included are such things as thread-spinning tools, swords and other weapons, equestrian accessories, musical instruments and writing implements and, of course, saws, hammers, etc.

The making of these items – all done by hand, from the basic raw materials – began early, as did the "prefabrication" of the new buildings from *hinoki* (Japa-

Offerings of rice at Ise.

nese cypress) timber harvested from a special state forest far to the north in the Kiso Mountains of Nagano Prefecture and blessed in a ceremony held there in May 1985.

Removal Equals Rebirth: Why all this "extra work?" Shrine officials offer three good or at least plausible answers.

First, the 20-year period can be viewed as forming a kind of border. For example, in human life, the period "forms a substantial line of demarcation in generations." Thus, the sengu perpetuates an appreciation and an awareness of the cultural and religious significance of the shrines from age to age.

Next, two decades is also "perhaps the most logical period in terms of passing on, from generation to generation, the technological expertise needed for the [re]construction."

The third answer, or hypothesis, is a bit more shaky. It was long thought that when Emperor Tenmu ordained the practice of shrine removal at Ise, which was first implemented in AD 690, during the reign of the next empress, Jito, it was to

avoid the deterioration that wooden buildings such as these normally suffer. However, Horyuji, the Nara temple – now the world's oldest standing wooden structure – had already been around a good while, so it's more likely the good Emperor Tenmu was motivated by the first explanation. Or, maybe he had the fate of his nation's carpenters and craftsmen in mind. Or both.

The Outer Shrine: The "proper practice" when visiting the Grand Shrines is to stop at the Geku first. This shrine, located a few blocks from Ise Station in a magnificent grove of age-old Japanese cedars, is dedicated to **Toyouke no Omikami**, the Goddess of Farms, Crops and Food. She has been worshiped in the Ise region for some 2,000 years; during that period, prayers have been offered at Ise for the continuity and safety of the imperial house, the security of the nation, and the peaceful lives of the people.

The tradition is that this deity, accompanying Prince Ninigi no Mikoto on his trip to Earth, was originally enshrined at

Priest enters a building in the Outer Shrine.

Manai in Tamba Province (Kyoto Prefecture). But in accordance with a revelation of the Sun Goddess Amaterasu Omikami imparted to Emperor Yuryaku, the shrine was moved to its present location in AD 478. This shrine has always been regarded with almost the same reverence as the Inner Shrine, and the same head priest *or priestess* serves in both.

The grounds of the Outer Shrine cover about 89 hectares (225 acres) (23 hectares larger than the Inner Shrine). After crossing the bridge in front of the first *torii*, the **Kiyomori-no-Kusu** is on your right. A tale is attached to this large camphor tree, about 6 meters in circumference but otherwise unremarkable: it seems that when the famous general Taira no Kiyomori (1118–81) visited the shrine as an imperial messenger, his ornamental coronet got caught in a branch of the tree. He became so angry that he ordered the branch cut off. Is that scar on the trunk proof of the tale? One can only wonder.

Ultimately, the object of your stroll is the **Shoden** (Main Hall) – or at least the thatched gateway standing at the outermost of the three formidable fences, which is as far as anyone, except imperial personages, envoys and shrine officials ever get to that sacred building.

Physically, the Shoden is 6.1 meters (20 ft) high, with a base of 10.2 by 5.8 meters (33 by 19 ft), is made of unpainted *hinoki*, and has a thatched roof. However, this description hardly does it justice – neither do the official photographs (ordinary visitors are prevented from taking pictures here by *very* alert guards) – and it has to be seen in person to be appreciated. The clean, simple lines of the building are the very essence of uniquely Japanese architecture, showing nary a trace of the often garish Chinese and Korean influences that dominate such shrines as the Toshogu at Nikko and most others in Japan. The barest minimum of metal ornamentation on its roof and uprights, and the pristine, raked-gravel grounds surrounding it, add to the impression of "purity" to which we referred earlier.

By the way, courtesy calls for removing headgear and overcoats in front of fences here and in the Inner Shrine. If that seems strict, remember that you are lucky to be able to stand here at all: before the Meiji Restoration (1868) no non-believer, particularly any Buddhist priest or nun, was permitted to enter either of these sacred Shinto precincts.

Also by the way, if your visit falls in early or mid spring, you might want to stop at the **Magatama Ike**, a pond surrounded by lush iris plantings.

The Inner Shrine: You'll need a taxi or bus (or very strong legs) to get to the precincts of the Naiku, a few kilometers from the one we've just described. From the taxi/bus plaza and cluster of souvenir shops and restaurants at the **Ujibashi Watarihajime Shiki** entrance, you cross the **Isuzu River** via the **Ujibashi**, a long, arched footbridge entirely rebuilt (as part of the Removal) in 1989. Proper form requires walking on the left side (although even many Japanese don't seem to know this). Propriety also asks that one proceed a few hundred meters upstream (through a torii just past the only public restroom – and the only place smoking is allowed – in the precincts) to a stone-faced "beach" on the shore to bathe (hands at least) and rinse one's mouth for purification. (Note: It's said that all watershed lands feeding this 19.2-km (12-mile) long river are kept free of pesticides, etc., in order to keep the waters clean. One taste of the murky stuff, however, reveals this to be a crock.)

In any case, you will then return to the "main street" lined with huge cedars, and walk past the **Shrine Office** and **Kagura Hall** (both on your right) onwards to the **Kotaijingu** (Main Hall).

Here, as in the Outer Shrine, the object of your attention is enclosed in a series of fences, and can be viewed only from the front of a thatched-roof gate in the outermost fence. Here, too, the view is limited (and the anti-photo patrol is, if anything, even more alert) but worthwhile: the Kotaijingu, while a little larger than the Main Hall of the Outer Shrine, seems even more pristine – the same clean, simple shape, the same natural glow of the unpainted wood, the same sharp lines of the massive thatched roof, but more so.

The Kotaijingu is said to contain the **Yata no Kagami** (mirror), which along with a sword and a comma-shaped jewel, constitute the Three Sacred Treasures which are the regalia of the Japanese imperial throne.

Japanese mythology says that the mirror was handed by Amaterasu Omikami to Ninigi no Mikoto, her grandson, when the latter came down from the Great Plain of Heaven to reign on earth. She gave him the gift of rice agriculture, together with a blessing to the effect the land and people of Japan should continue to prosper forever.

According to the Sun Goddess' instructions, the mirror was to be kept at the palace of Emperor Sujin (AD 92). Then about the 3rd century, for fear that too close contact might possibly desecrate it, the mirror was moved to Kasanui in Yamato Province (near Nara), where it was placed in a shrine. Some 88 years later it was moved to its present site of rest.

Sidetrips: The shrines are part of the 52,036-hectare (130,000-acre) **Ise-Shima National Park** in the southern extremity of Mie Prefecture, on that lumpy peninsula that juts southward from Nara. The coastline, particularly at Matoba, Ago and Gokasho bays, is marked by many narrow inlets, dotted with pine-clad islands.

Besides offering the famed *Ise-Ebi* (a small lobster) and other seafood goodies, this is pearl-culture country: the touristy **Toba** or "Pearl Island" is just south of Ise City, although it was further south, in Ago Bay, where a man named Mikimoto first succeeded with his oyster-torture experiments. A "paddle-wheel boat" cruise around Ago Bay, complete with barbecue lunch, passes the very spot.

Also, the Yamaha Music Foundation has a "music camp" near here, with resort hotel open to the public; this is also a part of Japan where a seafood dinner and relaxing overnight stay in a *ryokan* (inn), while no cheaper than elsewhere, is a darn good investment.

Pearl cultivation at Ago Bay.

OSAKA

Osaka is positively peripatetic. It bustles and bursts. You can see it in the restless crowds disembarking at Osaka airport or getting off the Shinkansen at **Shin Osaka Station**. No respectable Osakan, whether he is driving or walking, would think of waiting for the light to turn green to move. This is the city of business where lost time means lost opportunities and lost profits. It thrives as it has for centuries on the manipulation of the abacus, which many here claim has a language all its own that only Osakans understand.

Foreigners may look at Japan as unique, but many Japanese look at Osaka as if it belonged to another, somewhat unrelated part of the world. Everything is different in Osaka from the famous greeting ("Are you making money?") to the rollicking Osaka-style humor. Even the language and intonation has a distinct, earthy flavor, raising eyebrows of disdain in sophisticated metropolis of Tokyo.

Tax Rebates: It goes by all sorts of nicknames; the **City of Water** for one because of its numerous rivers and canals (many of which in recent years have been converted to streets). But perhaps more appropriate is **City of Merchants**, because what makes the city tick is its continuing love affair with doing business.

The business connection is documented as far back as the 4th century when Emperor Nintoku, who had made Osaka his capital, astutely decided to rebate all taxes to local businessmen for a period of three years after he was informed of an impending recession. His ploy worked and the Osaka business ethic was born.

The city's fine port played an important role in its economic and cultural development as well. Merchants from around the country and from China and Korea poured into the city. Osaka continued to grow in strength and economic power, culminating with the reign of the legendary Toyotomi Hideyoshi, who chose Osaka for his seat of government, built Osaka Castle, and turned the city into Japan's foremost commercial and industrial city. For the next 270 years Osaka became the "kitchen" of the country, with raw materials pouring in and high-quality finished products flowing out.

There were notable cultural developments here through the centuries as well, such as the poet Basho and the country's foremost playwright, Chikamatsu Monzaemon. *Bunraku* puppetry was another Osaka cultural contribution, and one that still thrives today.

Although the Osaka of today now sits firmly in the back seat of Tokyo's ever more powerful car, it still is an industrial and business dynamo, and its people still outshine their Tokyo cousins when it comes to creativity, ingenuity, enthusiasm and friendliness.

Two Faces of the City: It is relatively easy to get around using the extensive and user-friendly subway, train, and bus system. First, note that there are basically two faces to Osaka, and visi-

Preceding pages, Osaka castles, ancient and modern. **Left,** Tsutenkaku, "Tower to Heaven." **Right,** suburban Osaka.

tors would be wise to see both. One centers on **Kita** (North) **Osaka**, around **Osaka Station**, the other on **Minami** (South) **Osaka**, around **Namba Station**. They are only 10 minutes apart by subway (and 15 minutes by taxi on a good day) but they are worlds apart in mindset and manner.

Kita, which also goes by the name **Umeda**, is Osaka's newer face, where most of the new skyscrapers, office blocks, hotels and shopping centers are found. Minami, also known as **Namba**, is where you will find the "real" Osaka, the unpretentious side of the city. This is where anything that hints of Tokyo is looked at askance, where the friendly, funny Osaka dialect is spoken with pride, and where Osakans feel most at home. Most Osakans will tell you that Kita is where you might work, but Minami is where the good times are.

Going Underground: Most visitors to Osaka don't usually plan on spending much time exploring the city. The best way, then, to see the city and enjoy both its faces is to do it on foot, starting from Kita and ending up in Minami (or vice-versa). A straight walk would take only about 45 minutes, but there is so much to see that it is better plan on at least a day ahead.

Since most trains (except the Shinkansen) arrive at one of the three stations in Kita (Osaka Station, Hanshin Umeda, or Hankyu Umeda), it is from here that a walking tour of the city should start. Before even getting out of the station area, you should head underground to explore the vast subterranean shopping network, one of the largest in Japan. Corridors stretch in every direction and for the uninitiated it can be quite confusing.

The finest example of underground architecture and planning is found at **San Ban Gai**, located on two levels directly under the Hankyu Umeda Station. The creative use of water and lights make this a state-of-the-art facility. The main underground shopping area, the massive (and oddly named) Whitey Osaka covers an area equal to 1.7 hectares (4¼ acres) of land.

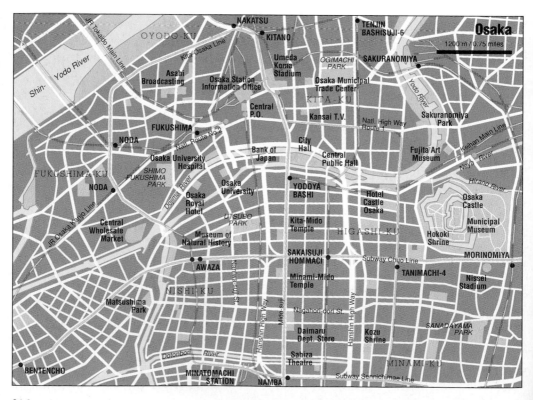

Prime Real Estate: Back on the street again, find north-south **Midosuji Boulevard** and head south until you come to the river. When you cross the bridge you will be on **Nakanoshima**, one of the most important pieces of real estate in the city. This narrow island is the center of the city government and the home to many major Osaka companies as well. Straight ahead on the west side of the street is the lovely old **Bank of Japan** building.

Also nearby are **Osaka City Hall**, **Nakanoshima Library**, the venerable **Central Public Hall** and half a block to the east, the **Museum of Oriental Ceramics**, housing the famous **Ataka Collection**, of about 1,000 Chinese and Korean masterpieces, of which 150 are normally on display. The museum is located within the attractive **Nakano-shima Park**, which continues on for several blocks alongside the river. **The Rose Garden** within the park is a good place to sit and relax and watch Osaka whizz by above and beyond you.

Tiger Bones: Getting back to Mido-

Neat rooftop restaurant.

suji, cross the river again and you are on solid ground at **Yodoyabashi** and walking south under the gingko trees. Japan's thriving pharmaceutical industry started in Osaka just east of Hommachi, and many of the largest drug companies today still have their headquarters in the **Doshomachi**, just a few blocks away. Tucked away in a corner there is the **Sukuna-Hikona Shrine**, the "drug shrine." It's a tiny little place that blossoms in importance all out of proportion to its size once a year on November 22–23, when a huge festival is held to memorialize when Osaka drug companies discovered that a medicine that included ground tiger bones was effective in combating malaria.

Continuing south you will come to the district known as Hommachi, which is actually where Midosuji and Hommachi boulevards cross. Just south of the crossing is **Semba**, the traditional home of the textile industry. Most big mills have outgrown their Semba homes, but 800 smaller retailers are still found in the **Semba Center Building**, a

two-story structure entirely under a 930-meter (½-mile) expanse of elevated highway. Many of Osaka's business greats got their training in Semba years past; most Japanese will tell you there is no one quite as astute in business as a Semba-trained businessman who can manipulate a *soroban* (abacus) faster than a calculator.

Walk south once again along Midosuji until you come to the next major crossing, **Nagahori**. The first landmark to look for is the **Sony Tower** at the opening of Osaka's premier covered shopping street, **Shinsaibashi**, which extends toward **Takashimaya Department Store** and **Namba Station**. Here you have ancient little shops sitting in apparent ignorance of the outrageously fancy boutique plazas that stand on either side. The **Shinsaibashi Daimaru**, flagship of the prestigious chain of department stores, is worth a few minutes of your time if for nothing else than to admire its lovely art deco interior (be sure to seek out the elevators).

Villages: At the southeast corner of Daimaru turn left and walk east a couple of blocks. This area is **Europa Machi** (European Village) and it is full of chic boutique shops and restaurants catering to the wealthy young workers of the city. Architecturally elegant buildings line the cobbled streets and the whole district has a distinctly Continental feeling to it.

Back at Daimaru again, this time go west, cross Shinsaibashi and Midosuji and continue in the maze of streets there for a block or two and you will come to the raucous, colorful **America Mura** (American Village), where the streets are lined with everything from surfer shops to nonstop flea markets. A triangular park in the middle of the main street here is generally humming with all sorts of activities and ongoing entertainment. A favorite picture here is of smirking visitors standing under the giant painting of Marilyn Monroe pursing her lips. This is seventh heaven and a good place to mingle with the crowds, sit in coffee shops, or find discos.

Both of these *mura* areas were estab-

Osaka boasts some of the best shopping complexes in the country.

lished in the late 1980s, as Osaka celebrated the 400th anniversary of the founding of the castle, and used it as a theme for its "21st-Century Plan," an urban-renewal-cum-chamber of commerce pitch for expansion.

Flash Gordon: South on Shinsaibashi is one of the most fascinating stretches of road in the city. At the **Dotombori Canal**, Shinsaibashi ends and **Ebisu-suji** begins, and this is where your journey to the heart of Osaka begins in earnest. At this point the *son-et-lumiere* **Kirin Building**, architecturally akin to something out of Flash Gordon comic books, stands on your left just at the foot of the Ebisu bridge. It's a good idea not to venture any further than about halfway across the bridge.

Squeeze in along the wall and sit tight, for you are about to see one of the best nonstop parades in the country – Osakans from every walk of life out for a good time, a bit of shopping, or just a cheap meal. Osakans pass through Dotombori frequently enough to reaffirm their affiliation with the city. Even those whose financial success has allowed them to move out to the hoity-toity suburb of Ashiya periodically come back to Dotonbori to renew ties with their roots.

Great Stories: There is more to Dotombori than just the passing crowds, however. For many years in times past, this place resembled the theatrical heart of the country. At one point there were six kabuki theaters, five bunraku puppet theaters, and myriad others where the great storytellers and comics of Osaka performed. Today most of the old theaters have been replaced by movie houses, among which the elegant old **Shochikuza** is an architectural link to the time when movies were movies and young Japanese thrilled like their American counterparts to Fred Astaire flicks. The venerable **Nakaza** with its kabuki and geisha dances, and the vaudevillian **Kadoza**, are still active, but they are the last of the legitimate theaters left on Dotombori. Several years ago the Bunraku Puppet Theater moved from the old Asahiza to

Youngsters being "bad" in Dotomburi.

the **National Theater,** a few blocks to the east.

One of the alleyways just south of the Nakaza is called **Hozenji Yokocho**. Along this narrow way are located dozens and dozens of eating and drinking establishments. (Be sure to confirm prices in these before entering.) Continue down the alleyway to **Mizukake Fudosan,** one of the most visited and venerated temples in Osaka. Local businessmen come to pray for good luck, young couples come to ask for happy futures and older people pray for good health. A very serviceable temple, indeed, with something for everyone. Do like everyone else: make your wish, ladle water over the moss-covered statue, throw in a donation, and pray for the best.

From here walk south for a few minutes till you come to the wide boulevard called **Sennichimae Dori**. Cross the street and walk east a block and you will arrive at **Printemps Department Store**. From here turn right and enter the Sennichimae shopping arcade, a typical blue-collar area full of pachinko parlors, old movie theaters and cheap restaurants. As you continue down the arcade the street narrows and you enter one of Osaka's most famous wholesale areas, **Doguyasuji**, an entire market devoted to kitchen and restaurant furnishings and accessories: plastic food, colorful lanterns, uniforms, imitation flowers, chopsticks. (There are several other wholesale markets around the city including **Machamachisuji**, the toy and doll center of the country; **Nipponbashi**, where you will find great bargains in the latest electronic goods; **Tachibana Dori** for good furniture at attractive prices; and **Hakimono tonya-gai**, where the specialty is Japanese slippers, clogs, and umbrellas.)

From Doguyasuji it is two blocks to Namba Station and **Takashimaya Department Store**. There is nothing too remarkable here save the vast underground shopping arcade of **Namba City** and **Rainbow Town**. Several subways have stations here; Namba is also the terminus for both the Kintetsu and

Three "bums" in a row: two yakuza show off their tattoos...

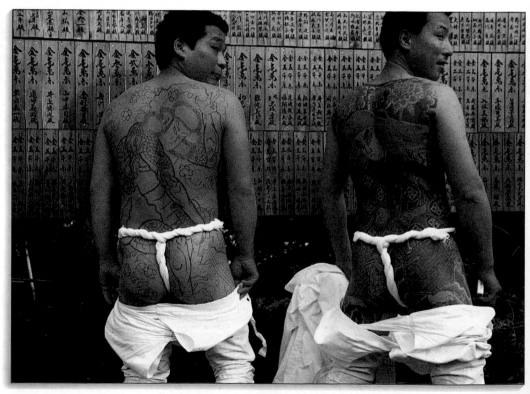

Nankai Railways. Namba is the jumping-off point for Nara and points south of Osaka. From downtown Osaka, Namba is the best way to get to the new **Kansai International Airport**, opened in 1994 built on a manmade island in Osaka Bay.

To the Castle: Though the walking tour is over, there is at least one place that no visitor to Osaka could possibly *not* go and still say she had seen the city. **Osaka Castle** is one of the most visited site in the country. It is an ode to everything that was great in the past and a symbol of the possibilities of Osaka in the future. The main *donjon*, which towers over the vast expanse of gardens and stone walls, is a replica of the original building which legendary leader Hideyoshi built in the late 16th century, at Osaka's peak. He commanded that all the feudal lords of the nation participate in the construction. Within three years, thanks to the labor of tens of thousands, the castle was completed and became the largest fortress Asia had ever seen. Much of the original grounds, moats

...while pink "gorilla" parades its posterior.

and giant walls still stand. In late winter and spring the gardens come alive with plum blossoms and cherry blossoms; in fall the beautiful Japanese maples add to the grandeur of the castle.

Adjacent to the castle is the **Osaka Business Park**, worth a visit to see what the future of Osaka may be like. Planners aim to make this the center of Osaka someday, but even now it sports a slew of state-of-the-art skyscrapers, theaters, shopping centers and hotels. It is a pleasant place to spend time – lots of flowers and greenery and seats.

Get Out of Town: Purveyors of kitsch and assumed glamor might want to make the trek (about 30 minutes by Hankyu Railway from Umeda) out to **Takarazuka**. Every month, year after year, troops of highly trained women have been putting on musical extravaganzas that boggle the mind and the senses. Back in 1910, Takarazuka was a small town at the end of the newly opened Hankyu train line. In order to attract passengers the train company built a hot spring and put together an all-female operetta company. Today it is a booming business and a popular form of entertainment in the country. There are 400 performers divided into four groups, two of which perform simultaneously in the home theater and the Takarazuka Theater in Tokyo while the other two troupes rehearse for the next production. Their specialties are Japanese-style spectacles and Las Vegas-type high stepping. One of their perennial favorites is the musicalization of *Gone With The Wind*. To this day a man has not appeared on the stage as a performer, though. Instead, the more masculine-looking stars sport fake moustaches and sideburns.

A nice side trip in Takarazuka is a visit to **Kiyoshi Kojin Temple** (at the Hankyu station of the same name). This is a very charming temple located at the end of up a winding, climbing path. Along the way are myriad shops selling antiques, bamboo goods, and local medicines. Festival days (the 27th and 28th of every month) are especially fun, and the temple precincts themselves are very picture-worthy.

KOBE

Although the characters bearing its name translate as "God's Door," **Kobe**, 30 kilometers (19 miles) down the east coast of Honshu from Osaka, is more like a door sill – a long narrow ledge squeezed in between the Rokko Mountain range and the Inland Sea. Known for the port (which Commodore Perry forced open in 1868), its pearl and fashion industries, and its local beef, Kobe boasts no world-class tourist objectives and is consequently bypassed by most foreign travelers.

However, thanks to a rich history of trade and foreign contacts, plus a Hong Kong-like topography that ensures one is never more than a few minutes' walk from either harbor cruising or mountain climbing, Kobe represents a rarity for Japan: a dynamic yet pleasant city (population 1.4 million) with topnotch hotels, strollable neighborhoods and superb international food.

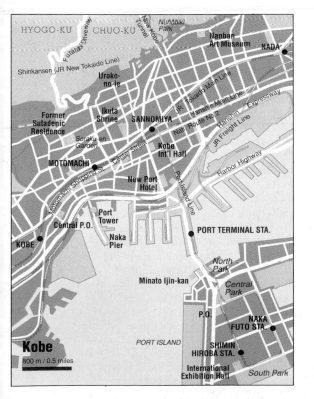

Left, shopping street in Kobe.

The cardinal point on the Kobe compass is **Sannomiya,** a popular shopping and entertainment district served by three inter-city train lines (*not* the Shinkansen though). Due north of the Hankyu Station, (site of the **International Tourist Office**, 392-0020, in the mezzanine alongside JR's West Exit), look for Kitanozaka Street. Leading uphill past the India Social Club to **Kitanocho.** Here, on this high, airy ground, rich foreign traders staked out impressive residences at the turn of the 20th century, their growing influence freeing them from the ghetto originally prescribed near the wharfs.

Presenting a fanciful potpourri of European and American architectural styles, more than a dozen of these *ijinkan* – now sharing the hill with trendy boutiques and restaurants – are open to the public. Westerners tend to find the interiors unexceptional (and full of cheap souvenirs for domestic tourists) but standouts include the impeccably-restored **Kazamidori** (an "Important Cultural Property"), the **Choueke House**, which offers an intimate glimpse into the lifestyle of one longtime resident family, and **Persia House,** outfitted with museum-quality Persian folkcraft and pottery.

Also agreeable, especially in summer after hiking the steep Kitano slopes, is an ijinkan offering a garden view of Osaka Bay. Finally, you might try the game of locating the mosque, the synagogue and the Jain temple, plus the Catholic, Baptist and Russian Orthodox churches, all within a few blocks' radius. It is a unique assemblage for a city this size in Asia and attests not only to Kobe's melting pot role – look for Indians in the pearl business, Germans in bakeries and Russians in the confectionery trade – but also to the thousands of new style corporate transferees who have consistently chosen cosmopolitan Kobe over Osaka.

Black Market Memories: Extending due west from Sannomiya's Flower Road, parallel shopping arcades extend to **Motomachi** and beyond. The one directly under the tracks – the remnants of a huge black market that surfaced amid the post-war rubble – is a mecca for sailors and bargain-hunters seeking secondhand, salvage and imitation goods. These tiny, low-overhead shops end at **Motomachi Station**, although still cheaper and more unusual items await inside the nondescript alley-entrance in the south wall of the station.

One block south of the tracks runs a far fancier series of pedestrian malls beloved by Kansai shoppers for their all-inclusiveness. The Sannomiya half tends to cater to the clothing and consumerist needs of younger Kobeites, while Motomachi specializes in atmospheric emporia dealing in traditional items like kimono, tea, antiques and beanpaste buns.

South of Motomachi Station and just west of elegant **Daimaru Department Store**, look for the dragon gate announcing Kobe's two-block-long **Chinatown**. This small but vibrant enclave, like Kitanocho, surpasses in its aura of foreignness anything that can be seen in the equally historic ports of Yokohama and Nagasaki, thus cementing Kobe's reputation as the most "non-Japanese" corner of the country.

From Chinatown it is another 10 minutes south to **Meriken Park**. Named after the American consulate that stood nearby in the early days, this redeveloped wharf frontage is now the site of the strikingly-designed **Maritime Museum** which tells the story of the seafaring town. It is an informative, user-friendly resource with audio explanations in English. A visit here should include a ride to the top of adjacent **Port Tower** and the 45-minute **Harbor Cruise**, to buoy up one's understanding of the world of international shipping and the significance of Kobe Port then and now.

Recycled Mountains: As for tomorrow, in a feat investing in science fiction technology with a biblical dimension, Kobe has been able to "recycle" several of its surplus mountains and build up from the sea floor the world's two largest manmade islands. This massive increase in berths and storage area promises to preserve the city's status as Japan's foremost international trading port – it already has sea links with 150 countries – and its position as a world leader in efficient handling of containerized cargo.

For an intriguing look at the cultural side of foreign trade, drop in at the nearby **Kobe City Museum**, housed in a former doric-columned bank next to the Oriental Hotel. This small, admirable museum focuses on Japan's early encounters with the West and features a rare collection of Namban ("southern barbarian") Art, works inspired by contacts with the first Portuguese and Spanish traders who arrived here in the 16th and 17th centuries.

Bird's-Eye View: Returning to Flower Road and Sannomiya – perhaps pausing to enjoy a bird's-eye view of the above itinerary from the top floor of the **City Hall** – one completes the circuit of central Kobe.

For those who do not relish tramping about, the **City Loop** bus shuttle for tourists retraces a similar route and offers a day pass that permits getting on and off at will. Taxis, alas, are not recommended. Partly due to the short-distance trips (and possibly because many of them are seasonal workers in the famed local *sake* distilleries), Kobe cabbies are probably the surliest in the nation. Even for destinations further away from the center, public transportation is best as systems are modern and easily graspable.

The **Portliner** monorail from Sannomiya, for instance, provides a convenient elevated loop ride around **Port Island**. Here – and on neighboring **Rokko Island**, also reachable by a monorail from JR Sumiyoshi Station – visitors can get a firsthand look at the future of container vessels, the center of the island has been zoned to accommodate Kobe's burgeoning fashion industry, hotel, sports and convention facilities, plus an amusement park and spacious sea-view apartments for 20,000 residents. Port Island's size had nearly doubled by 1994 when the **Kansai International Airport** was opened. Also situated on a manmade island in the ever-shrinking Inland Sea, it is an extraordinary engineeryng achievement.

Port Island, incidentally, offers a good vantage point from which to gaze back nostalgically at the "old" Kobe, especially at night when it becomes a flickering tiara augmented by two eliminated insignia on the mountainside. One symbol is an anchor and the other a pair of interlocking fans that represent the marriage of Hyogo and Kobe ports. It was due to the fan-shaped perfection of the harbors of these neighboring villages that, prior to AD 700, a trading port came into existence and Kobe's destiny was set.

Nude Bathing?: Moving away from the sea, a bus or subway from Sannomiya can transport you to the tucked-in-the-mountain **Shin-Kobe** "bullet train" station, behind which you can hike the ravine to the **Nunobiki Falls**, or, if the idea appeals, further to a reputed nude bathing pool.

More water – this time from scalding hot springs – awaits the weary traveler deep in the backside of Rokko Mountain in the *onsen* town of **Arima**. Reached by bus, cable car and ropeway from Hankyu Rokko station, this oldest spa in Japan boasts all the usual onsen amenities, plus a nationally-recognized basket maker named Shochikusai. One bargain in town is **Arima Onsen Kaikan**, the public bath where, for a few hundred yen, one can bathe in the same curative waters as at inns costing 100 times more.

Arima's two sources, by the way, are said to be capable of soothing all human ailments except love – itself an irony since, over the centuries, the town has done much to increase that particular affliction. Enquiries may be directed to Arima Tourist Office, tel: 904-0708, preferably in Japanese.

Finally, back to the sea, 15 minutes on JR down the coast from Sannomiya takes you to the only significant beach in western Japan.

A more interesting reason to visit **Suma**, however, is its **Aqualife Park,** which has a state-of-the-art aquarium and a mini-amusement park replete with a walk-through piranha tank and a dolphin show.

Busy Kobe Port.

NAGOYA AND GIFU

Nagoya may be the biggest small town you will ever visit. Although it ranks as the third largest city in Japan, and the capital of the crab-shaped Aichi Prefecture, it has a feel more like a *furusato* (home town) that has gotten way too big for its britches.

Known for its flat white *kishimen* noodles, its pickles known as *moriguchi-zuke* and its confection, *uiro*, Nagoya is better recognized as a center of industry, producing construction materials and automobiles. (Nagoya is sometimes called the "Detroit of Japan.")

Another of Nagoya's claims to fame is the pinball game, *pachinko*, invented (actually adapted from a Western game) here just after World War II. Most of Japan's millions of pachinko machines are made in this region.

But **Meieki**, as Nagoya Station is known, is the only part of town some folks see, as Nagoya is located almost precisely in the center of Japan, along the Tokaido Route, and is a major connecting point for transportation to and from other cities, including Tokyo and Osaka. Behind the station lies, **Eska**, a sparkling clean underground shopping mall, and **Apita**, a pricey department store, stand out among a number of business hotels, ancient love hotels and tiny art cinemas.

The Shinkansen tracks are near the back of the station, but if you cross to the front you will find an entirely different scene. There are three major department stores in the immediate vicinity, along with numerous cinema complexes, and a wedge of a building called **Lejac**, in which much of Nagoya's affluent youth seems to experience its nightlife. Nearby is the venerable **Dai Nagoya Building** with the odd orange globe on its roof. That globe is one of the original commercial symbols of modern Japan and it belongs to Morinaga, a caramel company in the late 1800s that has since become one of Japan's food giants. Morinaga maintains one of its restau-

Pachinko parlors like this one sprang up after the game was invented in Nagoya.

rants in the building, which at night is illuminated by a violet light that lends the entire area an eerie glow.

Clocks, Castles & Carp: A statue of **Serve**, Nagoya's celebrated seeing-eye dog, guards one of the entrances to two subway lines, the Meitetsu and Kintetsu train stations and a network of underground shopping malls less extensive than Osaka's but no less diverse. **Unimall** runs nearly to the next subway stop, near the glass-walled **Kokusai Center** housing an information center, two lending libraries, comfortable reading rooms and a slew of businesses.

You can spend the day at Meieki without leaving the station but you would be missing a lot. For one thing, if you walk above ground from Meieki to the Kokusai Center, you will pass one of Nagoya's many *karakuri* dolls, automated wooden puppets, devised during the Edo period, that emerge from clocktowers to announce the time. For another, Nagoya was originally planned to be a castle (not a mall) town by Shogun Tokugawa Ieyasu; he built

Nagoya Castle in 1612 for his ninth son, Yoshinao. But the town didn't quite develop that way and, at any rate had to be redesigned and reconstructed after suffering extensive air raids in 1945. The castle, rebuilt in 1959 and now functioning as a cultural/historical museum, is considered Nagoya's primary attraction. The golden dolphins on the roof of its restored *donjon* are *the* symbols of Nagoya.

Nagoya Castle is a short taxi or subway trip from the Kokusai Center and **Hisaya-Odori Park** at the center of **Sakae**. The 180-meter TV tower in the park affords one of the two best views of Nagoya. Below the tower and extending every which way is yet another underground arcade, a portion of which is known as **Central Park**. Sakae is the center of Nagoya's legal nightlife and a shopping paradise for non-bargain-hunters. Its two main east-west streets, which begin at Meieki and parallel the Higashiyama subway line, are Hirokoji Dori, about which more later, and Nishiki Dori, where you can discover a showroomful of chinaware made by the Nagoya-based firm, Noritake, On the second weekend of every October, these avenues are thronged with Nagoyans celebrating the **Nagoya Festival**, which features a parade of men in armor and a streetside theatrical display arranged by **Atsuta Shrine**.

A Blessing on Your Car: Both Hisaya-Odori and the Meijo subway line run straight down from Nagoya Castle through Sakae to **Yabacho**. From there you can walk west to **Shirakawa Park**, whose science museum offers a "**Theater of the Stars**." On the way you may pass **Wakamiya-Odori Park**, or, you may choose to continue down the Meijo line for one more stop (or walk down Hisaya Odori, which later becomes Maezu Dori below Yabacho) to **Kamimaezu**, where tiny, overstuffed secondhand bookstores mark nearly every corner. From Kamimaezu you can venture east until you reach calm **Tsuruma Park**, a 24-hectare (60-acre) collection of gardens in Eastern and Western styles.

Or you can walk northwest and enter

another shopping arcade, this one above-ground but roofed. The bargains are here: **Ameyoko** is an electronics haven, and the **Komeihyo** area is a combination of pawnshops and five-and-dime stalls. In between these are shops of every description; you can purchase used kimono, old coins and traditional Japanese dolls, all at reasonable prices. The arcade ends at the bright orange **Osu Kannon Temple**, perched high atop its white stairway and specializing in blessings for automobiles. (Aichi Prefecture is infamous as the home of Japan's worst drivers.) On the 18th and 28th of every month, antique dealers spread their wares over the temple ground for a flea market of grand proportions, and every weekend, Komeihyo has a giant used-kimono sale. During the last week of July/first week of August each year, the arcade whirls with the **Osu Merchants' Street Performances Festival**.

You may also take the subway to the **Port of Nagoya**, where the **Nagoya City Exhibition Hall** and the **Nagoya Port Building** are located. The latter houses an observatory, a restaurant and the **Nagoya Maritime Museum**, whose principal attraction is the retired Antarctic icebreaker, *Fuji Maru*. It is in this area where the **Port Festival**, in July, attracts thousands with fireworks, a brass-band parade and a mini-*matsuri* complete with *omikoshi*.

Another subway line will take you to Jingu-mae, site of the **Atsuta Shrine**, second only to the Ise Shrine in Mie Prefecture in its importance to the Imperial Family. One of the family's three "sacred treasures," the **Kusanagi** (Grass-Mowing Sword) is kept here, and hundreds of ancient trees thrive amid equally ancient artifacts, including the 600-year-old **Nijugocho Bridge**, made of 25 blocks of stone. The shrine's festival is in June.

Culture, Culture Everywhere: There are museums all over Nagoya, ranging from the treasure-laden **Tokugawa Art Museum**, including heirlooms of the Owari-Tokugawa family, to the **Aichi Bijutsukan** (Fine Arts Museum), near the TV Tower, which often displays the

Strategically-sited Nagoya Castle.

works of Japan's up-and-coming artists. (You may participate in a quiet tea ceremony at the former, which can be reached by bus from Sakae.)

Nagoya is also jam-packed with universities and junior colleges. Its two most prestigious, **Nagoya University** (Meidai) and **Nanzan University** are set within shouting distance of each other along Yotsuya Dori, a high-tech, high-fashion boulevard that forms a major intersection with a little backstreet and the same Hirokoji Dori you may have shopped on back in Sakae. From here, **Yotsuya Dori** snakes uphill, wanders past the two schools and mysteriously becomes Yamate Dori by the time it culminates in Yagoto, on the Tsurumai line.

These two fascinating streets take their names from quite famous sections of Tokyo, and the **Meidai/Nanzan** area is in such a hurry to develop itself on par with these namesakes that even its newer buildings, less than a decade old, are often torn down to make way for edifices a touch more state-of-the-art.

A trek between subway lines will take you from cafe to boutique, from below street level to well above it. An airy, post-modern, experimental architecture now characterizes the district. Glass and bent-chrome columns are illuminated in ice-cream colors, atria and loft-like cafes look out upon the hill. It's the closest you will ever come to True Glitz in Nagoya, so enjoy it! Further up the Higashiyama line is the **Higashiyama Zoo**, with 3,200 captive animals, and the **Botanical Gardens**. The zoo's **Sky Tower** provides the other splendid view of Nagoya.

Beyond the Limits: What is the best way to get out of Nagoya? If you are planning to fly, you should take the bus instead. That's right: the Nagoya Airport is in neighboring Komaki, which is a rather tedious bus ride from the center of town. (Actually, the best way into and out of Nagoya is the Shinkansen, as mentioned earlier.)

But don't leave yet, as the Nagoya environs hold much to be explored. There is, for example, nearby **Kasugai**, with its peach orchards and paper factories; a town called **Toyota**, whose main industry has become a household name around the world; **Suzuka**, locale of a racing circuit used to test vehicles built by a hometown boy named Honda; **Gamagori**, with its motorboat-racing; **Tokoname**, also with a motorboat race course in addition to a number of kilns whose output has notable style; **Arimatsu**, the home of Japanese tie-dying and known for the unique methods of fireproofing its houses; and **Ama-gun**, famous for its cloisonne.

Smashing Times: Then there is **Seto**, a kiln town whose name has found its way into the generic term for all pottery in Japan: *setomono*. Every September, the potters of this sleepy hamlet bring their wares out to be sold at discount rates in stalls along both sides of the Seto River. This **Setomono Ichi** (market) lasts only three days.

Meieki is also the best starting point for most other out-of-city ventures. The Meitetsu Inuyama line will carry you to **Inuyama Castle** within 10 minutes, perched on a cliff above the Kiso River.

Outdoor artist inspects her work.

It claims to be Japan's oldest tower and is a lovers' lane for some. Also in the Inuyama area are **Little World**, an outdoor ethnic museum of dwellings from all over the world; **Japan Monkey Park**, where you can mingle with some of the approximately 1,000 simian residents; and **Meiji-Mura**, where Meiji-Era trains chug through a "village" full of Meiji (and post-Meiji) buildings (including a section of Frank Lloyd Wright's original Imperial Hotel) collected from all over Japan. Other attractions include a riverboat ride and cormorant fishing on the **Kiso River**, also known as "The Japan Rhine."

The Big One: Every March, one of Japan's strangest festivals occurs not far from Inuyama at a little shrine dedicated to phalluses. A huge one is carried through the streets and crowds of men and (especially) women try to touch it, hoping to enhance their fertility. Sake flows freely and amiable mass confusion reigns.

The **Tagata Shrine** is open all year round to visitors and its gift shop is stocked with appropriately shaped sweets, toys and reminders.

Gifu City: This quiet town has a modern apparel industry, attracting international buyers (especially from underdeveloped nations), but is probably better known for its 200-year history of cormorant fishing on its three rivers, the Kiso, the **Ibi** and the one that bisects the city, the **Nagara**. In the 16th century, Oda Nobunaga legitimized the profession of *uaki*, as fishing with cormorants for the river "trout" called *ayu* is known; later, Shogun Tokugawa Ieyasu, who liked *sashimi* cut from ayu and often presented this delicacy at court, popularized the dish in Edo.

Today, uaki is a lucrative tourist attraction, with the collared birds doing their thing at night to the light of small fires suspended in iron baskets from the front of the boats.

Gifu Castle commands an impressive view from the top of Kinkazan (Golden Flower Mountain) in the city; it was built about seven centuries ago, suffered numerous razings, and was re-

An *onsen* visit is just the ticket in winter.

built in 1956. A 3½-minute gondola ride to the foot of the mountain brings you to **Gifu Park** and its **Museum of History** and **Museum of Insects**. The latter contains various bugs, butterflies and spiders (some of which are gigantic!) from around the world.

Spas and Battlefields: Mountainous Gifu Prefecture has much to offer in the way of natural beauty. There are the resort towns of **Gero** and **Takayama**, with their onsen spas and ubiquitous hikers, tennis buffs and other vacationers. The buses to Gero from Gifu are often crowded with aged citizens, making their way to the baths (or the **Gero Onsen Hospital**) where the natural hot springs are said to ease the effects of numerous ailments.

The JR trains bound for Takayama (from Nagoya's Meieki Station via Gifu City) on the other hand are more often crammed with more youthful travelers, especially in mid-April when the town's Hachiman shrine holds its annual festival which has at its center two dozen colorfully decorated floats.

Takayama is sometimes called "**Little Kyoto**," and is packed with museums and other points of interest; the quiet beauty of the town, its *shunkeinuri* lacquerware and its famous *sake* make it a good off-the-beaten-track place to visit.

Finally, no summary of the sights in the Nagoya region would be complete without mention of **Seki**, a blade-forging village and the site of the Battle of **Sekigahara**, waged in the early 17th century between the forces of Tokugawa Ieyasu and Toyotomi Hideyoshi. Though Tokugawa was outnumbered nearly two to one, his warriors slaughtered more than a third of his enemy's troops to put their leader in the shogun's seat which he and his descendants held for the next 250-odd years.

It is considered by some to be sad that today, only an unassuming stone marks the spot of Tokugawa's heroic triumph, and in lieu of a memorial to him or an appropriate museum, Sekigahara offers only an amusement park and an ice-skating rink.

Typically rugged Gifu landscape.

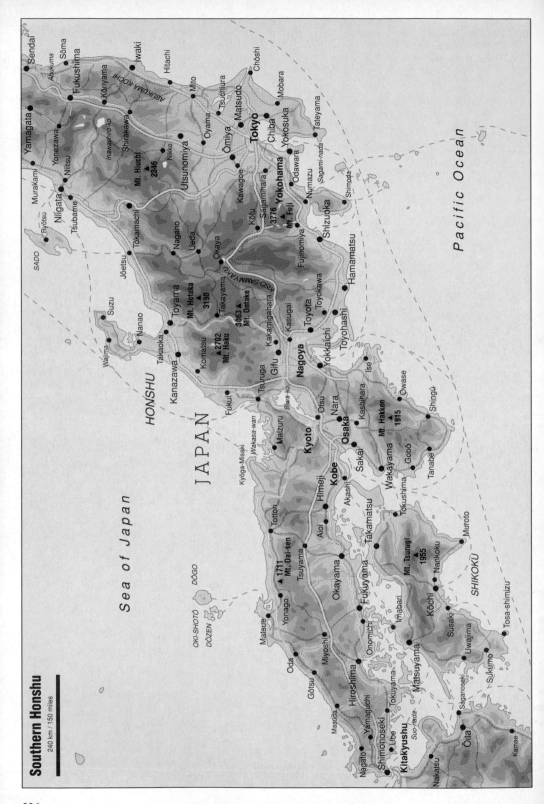

Southern Honshu

240 km / 150 miles

Pacific Ocean

Sea of Japan

JAPAN

HONSHU

SHIKOKU

SADO

OKI-SHOTŌ
DŌGO
DŌZEN

Abukuma
Inawashiro-ko
ABUKUMA KŌCHI
KISO-SAMMYAKU
Biwa-ko
Sagami-nada
Wakasa-wan
Suō-nada

Sendai
Sōma
Iwaki
Hitachi
Chōshi
Fukushima
Kōriyama
Katsuyama
Mito
Tsuchiura
Mobara
Yamagata
Yonezawa
Murakami
Niitsu
Shirakawa
Nikko
Utsunomiya
Oyama
Ōmiya
Matsudo
Tokyo
Chiba
Yokosuka
Tateyama
Mt. Hiuchi
2346
Niigata
Byōtsu
Tsubame
Tokamachi
Nagano
Ueda
Okaya
Kōfu
Sagamihara
Yokohama
3776
Mt. Fuji
Odawara
Numazu
Shimoda
Shizuoka
Suzu
Nanao
Joetsu
Toyama
Mt. Hotaka
3190
Takayama
3063
Mt. Ontake
Kakamigahara
Kasugai
Fujinomiya
Toyokawa
Hamamatsu
Wajima
Takaoka
Kanazawa
Komatsu
2702
Mt. Haku
Tsuruga
Gifu
Nagoya
Toyota
Yokkaichi
Toyohashi
Ise
Owase
Fukui
Maizuru
Otsu
Nara
Kashihara
Mt. Hakken
1915
Shingū
Kyōga-Misaki
Kyoto
Osaka
Sakai
Wakayama
Gobō
Tanabe
Kobe
Akashi
Himeji
Tottori
Tsuyama
Takamatsu
Tokushima
Muroto
Matsue
Oda
Yonago
1711
Mt. Dai-sen
Okayama
Fukuyama
Mt. Tsurugi
1955
Nankoku
Miyoshi
Kōchi
Susaki
Gōtsu
Hiroshima
Onomichi
Imabari
Matsuyama
Uwajima
Tosa-shimizu
Masuda
Yamaguchi
Tokuyama
Sukumo
Ube
Nagato
Shimonoseki
Saganoseki
Ōita
Kitakyushu
Nakatsu
Kamae

336

As in most other conventions, Japan does not quite suit itself to the usual geographical shorthand of North, South, East and West. That's because the four main islands do not lie on a direct north-south axis. But take a jog toward the left of the map below Tokyo, at the midpoint of the largest one, Honshu. It's not quite correct to put the remainder of Honshu, all of Shikoku, the Inland Sea and Kyushu in a box labelled "Southlands." More properly, these regions should be called "Western," or "Southwestern" at the very least. "Western Japan," however, is the term generally used to refer to the Kansai (Kyoto/Osaka/Kobe). The word *Kansai* itself means "Western Barrier." So why fight it? In the name of bibliographical convenience, then, if not cartographical precision, we'll stick with "Southlands" and define it, loosely, to signify those regions south (and west) of the Kansai – throwing in Okinawa for good measure.

Here we should add that beyond geography and the fact they are all Japanese, these regions bear little or no resemblances to each other. That section of Honshu from, say, Okayama down the coast of the Inland Sea to Hiroshima is markedly different from the Japan Sea coast side, from the section beginning at Tsuruga and the Bay of Wakasa, for example, passing through Tottori, Matsue and on to the tip at Shimonoseki. Likewise, Shikoku, though the smallest of Japan's four main islands, could as well be on a different planet from the one occupied by the islands in the Ryukyuan group (i.e. Okinawa). As for Kyushu – well, there are those who believe that this large island, particularly the southern part, is a nation unto itself, and who cite the long tradition of fierce independence stemming from the Satsuma Clans as proof.

Life here is considerably less frenetic than in the industrial belt extending from Tokyo to Osaka. Even in the most populous and industrial cities of Kyushu, or even large and well-developed cities like Honshu's Okayama and Hiroshima, the pace may strike you as laid-back, if not downright placid compared with Tokyo and Osaka. In the smaller cities and towns, you could shut your eyes and imagine yourself back in Japan of the 19th or an even early century. Well, almost.

Another generalization would be that the climate is kinder and gentler in these regions of Japan than elsewhere: very little snowfall (none, of course, in semitropical Okinawa and the Ogasawaras), hardly any seasonal differentials (wet and less wet are the seasons, period) and, except in the mountains, temperatures high enough to make sweaters and overcoats mere fashion accessories.

But as with all generalizations about life and the weather, there are two annoying and not-so-little exceptions worth mentioning.

One, most of the Southlands lie in the path of seasonal typhoons, and thus are regularly given good soakings by torrential rains riding

Preceding pages: within the walls of Himeji Castle; pigeons at Hiroshima's Peace Park.

The Southlands 337

up the Black Current. Typhoons also frequently hit central Honshu and elsewhere from late summer through November or so, but years may pass between major landings; in Okinawa and southern Kyushu, the average is about four per year.

Two, there are more active volcanoes on Kyushu than on any other Japanese island. Among the most notable are Mt. Sakurajima, near Kagoshima; Mt. Aso (the world's largest), east of Kumamoto; and Mt. Unzen (in the news since mid-1991 for its pyroclastic activities) that forms that thumb of land between Nagasaki and Kumamoto.

Speaking of typhoons and volcanic eruptions, both happen to be associated with major historical aspects of the Southlands, especially Kyushu, that were to have significant impact on the rest of Japan. Volcanoes first. Thanks to them, the amount and variety of ceramic-quality clays (and chemicals for glazes) in Japan are virtually without limit. Historians and sociologists link this to Japan's early development of technologies (chemistry, the control of heat, etc.) as well as to the nation's abilities to exploit, if not actually assimilate, the talents of Korean potters who immigrated to Japan, at first voluntarily and later by force, bringing with them new technologies as well as new artistic and architectural ideas. When the kilns around Imari in Kyushu got into full gear in the 17th century, Japan had itself an export item that made a lot of Japanese (and Dutch) very rich.

Secondly, it was a "Divine Wind" (*Kamikaze*) that defeated a 13th-century invasion of Japan by the Mongols. This particular ill wind did the nation a lot of good, for it lent credence to the government's claim that a Japan united in faith (under the watchful eye of the Kamakura *bakufu*, of course) could withstand any outsider's blow.

Wind and fire of another, more frightening, sort also played major parts in the history of the Southlands and, indeed, of the whole world. So major, in fact, that no one on earth can, or should be able to, even utter the names of two of the region's major cities without being reminded of them: Hiroshima and Nagasaki.

In selected parts of the Japan Sea coast of Honshu, there are sights worth seeing. Sadogashima (Sado Island) and the Noto Peninsula, for example, while not part of the Southlands, are treasurehouses of culture and folklore, along with offering some quite rustic scenery. Likewise, there are quite a few well-known temples in the Fukui and Tsuruga areas, including the beautiful and important Eiheiji, where the mysteries of life have been pondered by Zen novitiates – including many foreigners – since the 13th century. And let us not ignore, further down (westward) the coast, Amanohashi-Date ("Heavenly Bridge"), one of Japan's "Scenic Trio," nor the sand dunes of Tottori, where *Woman of the Dunes* was filmed. And last, at least, we mustn't fail to mention the still-sleepy town of Matsue, where a lonely Lafcadio Hearn taught English and waxed poetic a century ago, and the nearby Grand Shrine of Izumo (Izumo Taisha), the oldest Shinto shrine in Japan and second in importance only to those of Ise.

<u>Left</u>, in Japan, even the rice terraces have aesthetic value.

THE OTHER END OF HONSHU

The rapidly growing city of **Okayama** has once again asserted itself as the region's most dynamic and, for this reason, finds itself often playing host to visiting foreigners. But they are here on business, not for sightseeing.

If you should find yourself here, however, you will enjoy Okayama's most notable attraction, the **Korakuen Garden**. Originally laid out in 1686 for Lord Ikeda, it is generally regarded as one of the three most beautiful gardens in Japan, along with Kairakeun Garden (Mito) and Kenrokuen Garden (Kanazawa). It is situated on an island in the Ashi River, across from the black (and thus called "Crow") **Okayama Castle**, a reconstruction. Korakuen is unusual for its large grassy areas and cultivation of edible crops, including rice and wheat. Tea is also grown and harvested and there are teahouses scattered throughout the garden.

Other sights in Okayama's "culture zone" include the **Orient Museum**, with exhibits tracing the impact of Near Eastern civilization on Japan, the **Okayama Prefectural Museum of Art** and the **Yumeji Art Museum**, with works by Yumeji Takehisa.

Bizen, about 45 minutes by train from Okayama, is famous for its unglazed, coarse pottery that is frequently enhanced by kiln "accidents," such as a stray leaf or bit of straw sticking to the side of a pot, leaving an interesting pattern after firing. There are more than 100 kilns in **Imbe**, the 700-year-old pottery making section of Bizen, and several museums, including the **Bizen Togei Bijutsukan** (Ceramics Museum) and **Fujiwara Kei Kinenkan** gallery.

Kurashiki: This small and rather shabby textile-producing city boasts the pearl of Japanese tourist attractions. Its arts district brings world-class Japanese and international art and traditional crafts together in an exquisite setting. Thirteen and a half hectares of 300-year-old rice warehouses, Meiji factories, and the homes of samurai and wealthy merchant families have been elegantly preserved and converted into museums, craft shops and art galleries.

The streets and alleys bordering on Kurashiki's central canal look much as they did at the town's cultural and economic zenith, around the 18th century. During the Edo Period, Kurashiki was a central collection and storage site for taxes and tribute, paid in rice, from communities throughout western Honshu, the Inland Sea and Shikoku. The numerous stone rice warehouses, called *kura*, clustered around willow-lined canals, gave the town its name. Their unique, striking designs employ dark black tiles deeply set in bright white mortar, capped by black tile roofs. Stone bridges, arched so that barges piled high with sacks of rice from the hinterland could pass below them, span the waterways.

Streetscapes like these first captured the imagination of Europeans when Japanese porcelain depicting similar places was widely exported in the 1800s. Today, Kurashiki is about the only such city to escape the ravages of wrecking balls, Allied bombing, and urban development. It attracts millions of visitors annually, so it is best to avoid weekends and holidays when tourist crowds are likely to be thickest. Most of its many fine museums are closed all day on Mondays.

Kurashiki is for walkers, with most of the attractions within a block or two of the canal. Automobiles are not allowed to disturb the elegant ambience of its preserved quarter. The centrally located Tourist Center provides maps, information, and a free and cheerful place to rest weary feet.

Kurashiki's preservation was largely the work of the Ohara Magosaburo, the wealthy scion of Kurashiki's leading family. The Ohara family's textile mills were the principal source of employment in Kurashiki during the Meiji period, by which time rice levies had been replaced by cash taxes, making the city's huge rice warehouses redundant.

Museum Hopping: Ohara Magosaburo built the nation's first museum of West-

The much-photographed "Floating Torii" at Miyajima hasn't suffered from overexposure.

ern art in 1930, the **Ohara Museum**, and stocked it with works by El Greco, Monet, Matisse, Renoir, Gauguin and Picasso. The neoclassical building remains the centerpiece although new galleries have proliferated around it over the years. The restored kura next to the main gallery are likely to be of more interest to visitors already familiar with European art: they contain Japanese folk art and a fine collection of ancient Chinese art. Semi-separate rooms are devoted to the works of each of the great *mingei* (Japanese folk art) potters such as Hamada Shoji, Bernard Leach, Kawai Kanjiro and Tomimoto Kenkichi, who gained famed in the 1920s and 1930s.

Many of Kurashiki's warehouses-turned-art-houses are devoted to preserving and revitalizing mingei. Among the most interesting is the **Japanese Rural Toy Museum**. The first floor is packed with traditional Japanese toys, dolls and kites, while a collection of toys from around the world can be seen on the second floor. The adjacent toy store is as interesting as the museum. The **Kurashiki Museum of Folk Craft** displays about 4,000 simple, handmade objects that are, or were, used in everyday life. The building that houses this museum, parenthetically, is itself of historical interest: it is remodeled from four two-story wooden rice granaries.

Visitors can learn a little about the daily life of one of Kurashiki's leading families at the **Ohashi House**. It was constructed in 1796 for a merchant family that was granted samurai status and is much larger than typical merchant houses of that time (note the unusual roof tiles). The curious can delve into the region's ancient history at the **Kurashiki Archaeological Museum** and the **Kurashiki City Museum of Natural History**. **Ivy Square**, an arts complex created out of the red brick textile factories which brought about the Ohara family fortune, houses the **Kurabo Memorial Hall** with displays on the textile industry, as well as shops and restaurants.

Leaving the canal area, weary tra-velers might want to stop for a drink at the **Kurashiki Kokusai Hotel**, designed by Kurashiki native Shizutaro Urabe, before heading for the city's more distant attractions. These include the **Seto Ohashi Memorial Museum of Bridges** (the building is shaped like an arched *taiko* bridge) and Washuzan Hill, which offers tremendous views of the great bridge as well as the Inland Sea. There is also Kurashiki's former city hall, designed by Japan's most famous architect, Tange Kenzo, which was transformed in 1983 into the **Kurashiki City Art Museum**.

Onomichi: This city at the center of the Inland Sea was an important commercial port 800 years ago. Wealthy merchants flocked to the city during the Edo Period, building 81 temples on the steep slopes overlooking the sea to celebrate their prosperity. With the coming of the railroad in the late 19th century, however, commerce literally passed the city by. Because of its relative lack of importance, American bombers also passed by Onomichi, and when the shinkansen

Kurashiki was the tax-collecting center of Southern Honshu.

route was mapped Onomichi was passed over again, a station being placed in the up-and-coming Fukuyama instead. As a result of its slide into relative obscurity the city has unselfconsciously retained much of its pre-Meiji heritage. Some 25 of the temples remain, the most interesting being **Senkoji**, which is best reached via the ropeway tram.

Hiroshima: One moment – 8.15am, August 6, 1945 – irrevocably changed world history. The atomic flash, signalling Hiroshima's instant destruction and the ultimate loss of over 200,000 lives, has been reflected in the subsequent lives of people everywhere, shaping their political, military and technological milieu. The immediate and lasting impact on Hiroshima gives concrete reality to the abstract horrors of nuclear war, just as the city's renewal demonstrates in steel and concrete the incredible path of reconstruction the entire nation undertook in a few short years following the war.

Amazingly, Hiroshima's people

Streets along Kurashiki's canals have changed little over the years.

quickly rebuilt a vibrant city from the radioactive ashes which was larger and more prosperous than the old one, leaving only a few carefully chosen scars to remind them and the millions of visitors of its abiding atomic legacy. Forever associated with the atomic bomb, the city's ebullient renaissance also shows something of the resilience of the human spirit.

Unlike Nagasaki, which seems to turn its collective back on its bombing, there are reminders around virtually every corner in Hiroshima. But the remembrances do not tend toward the morbid or sorrowful; they point to the pride with which the city's residents have recovered, and to fervent hopes that the example of Hiroshima will be sufficient to prevent repetition of such horrors again.

The best way to see Hiroshima is through the window of a street car. As most other Japanese cities tore up their streetcar tracks, their cars were added to Hiroshima's collection. The city has acquired an eclectic collection of cars,

many dating back to the 1940s and maintain them as a sort of moving transport museum.

A Castle Town: Hiroshima's military significance predates World War II by several hundred years. Troops were staged here in preparation for the invasion of Korea in 1582. A castle incorporating the latest construction and defensive techniques was built on the spot seven years later by the Mori clan. It rests on pilings driven into reclaimed swampland. The outer moats were built above the level of the surrounding land so that their walls could be breached, flooding the plain where siege troops would likely mass. The castle was an important bastion of the Tokugawa Shogun's forces, a western outpost facing the often hostile Choshu and Satsuma clans. In the 19th century, **Hiroshima Castle** was occupied by the emperor during the occupation of Manchuria. It also served as an important Japanese Army headquarters during World War II and was completely destroyed by the atomic bomb. Reconstructed in 1958, the castle contains an excellent museum, which is appropriately devoted to castles.

A few blocks east of the castle, **Shukkeien Garden** was built on the banks of the Kyobashi River in 1620 in emulation of a famous Chinese lake. Early spring brings cherry blossoms, azaleas bloom a little later, and multicolored carp inhabit the central pond throughout the year.

Half an hour away and northwest of central Hiroshima, **Mitaki Temple** is set in a lush forest with three waterfalls. Buddhas adorn the hillsides and a fierce, life-size baby-killing devil statue of wood hangs out on the temple's porch. A friendly dog often welcomes visitors to the teahouse, which is decorated with a colorful collection of masks and kites. The walk from the train station to the temple grounds passes a grouping of graves of unknown victims of the bomb called "Little Boy."

Peace Park: The **Heiwa Kinen Koen** (Peace Memorial Park) is adjacent to the infamous **Genbaku Domu** (Atomic

The Atomic Dome, a grim reminder of the horrors of nuclear war.

Dome), marking ground zero of Hiroshima's atomic explosion. At its maximum intensity, the temperature approached that on the sun's surface, and almost everything within sight was vaporized instantly. The building with the (now carefully maintained) skeletal Dome once housed the Industrial Promotion Hall, and was one of the few surviving vertical structures.

Tange Kenzo designed the heart of the park complex, which comprises the **Peace Memorial Museum**, **Peace Memorial Hall**, **Cenotaph** and **Peace Flame**. The museum contains graphic portrayals of the bombing and its consequences for persons and places within its reach. Although the museum is filled with powerful images of terrible suffering, it certainly is not a "hall of horrors" as one may expect. It is something every visitor here should see, and feel, to comprehend the realities of nuclear war, remembering that today's weapons are far more powerful than the Hiroshima and Nagasaki bombs.

A visit to the museum is an emotional experience for most, even though the exhibit has been justly accused of failing to place the bombing in historical perspective: "It is as though the bomb fell on Hiroshima, figuratively as well as literally, out of the blue. Nowhere is there any suggestion that it might have been triggered by past actions. Nowhere is there the least sign that any other nation or race might have suffered comparable wartime tragedies," charges writer Alan Booth.

The **Cenotaph**'s inverted U-shape reflects the design of the thatched roof houses of Japanese antiquity. It contains a stone chest with the names of the victims of the nuclear bombing, and bears the inscription: "Sleep in peace: the error will not be repeated." **The Peace Flame** and **Atomic Dome** can be seen through it.

The **Statue of the A-Bomb Children** is dedicated to a child who died of leukemia caused by atomic radiation. She believed that if she could fold 1,000 origami cranes the act would prevent her death. She died just after the 954th

Below Left, pagoda on Miyajima; **Right**, paper cranes at Peace Park.

crane. School children come from around the country to place wreaths of folded cranes around the statue's neck.

Many visitors ring the Peace Bell before crossing the Motoyasu River to the Dome. Colorful row boats can be rented by the hour near the **Heiwa Ohashi** (Peace Bridge) for a more cheerful perspective on Hiroshima, and regular cruises depart from the pier in front of the Dome.

Miyajima: Though it is formally called Itsukushima (Strict Island), this major Hiroshima-area tourist attraction is more often, and more appropriately, called **Miyajima** (Island of Shrines). Literally littered with tourists, tame deer, and their respective droppings, much of the spirit and splendor of this, one of the country's holiest sites, manages to shine through. The great crimson *torii* (shrine gate) rising out of the sea in front of the **Itsukushima Shrine** is probably the most familiar Japanese cultural icon. The familiar sight, plastered on nearly every travel poster and guidebook sold abroad, hasn't suffered from the exposure. It is especially breathtaking at sunset – even when the tide is out.

The current gate was built in 1874, but a similar torii has awed visitors for seven centuries. The island's spiritual roots are much older, however. The first shrine, honoring Amaterasu's three daughters, goddesses of the sea, was built in the 6th century. To maintain the island's "purity," births and deaths have been prohibited on Miyajima from the earliest times – and perhaps this explains the "strict" part.

The entire island of Miyajima was dedicated as a sanctuary by Taira no Kiyomori, who ordered the Itsukushima Shrine completely rebuilt in 1168. Kiyomori and his clan prospered, eventually attaining a brief rule over Japan, which ended tumultuously in 1185. The shrine rests on stilts and seems to float like a giant ship when the tide comes in. Costumes and masks used in the *bugaku* dance festival (first week of January) and the *noh* plays which are performed in mid April are on display in the **Asazaya** (morning prayer room), which is reached via a vermillion-colored bridge.

Next to the Itsukushima Shrine, the oldest noh theater in Japan, built in 1568, also seems to float a few inches above the sea.

The nearby **Treasure House** contains hundreds of "National Treasures" and "Important Cultural Objects", including illuminated sutras made by members of the Taira clan in the 1160s.

A five-story **Pagoda**, built in 1407, and **Senjokaku** (A Thousand Mats) **Hall** are at the top of a hill behind the shrine. Senjokaku, built in 1587, is Toyotomi Hideyoshi's contribution to the island of Miyajima.

Most of the island is covered with uninhabited virgin forest. A good way to see it is from the 1.6-kilometer (5,250-ft) long ropeway (cable car) that runs over **Momijidani Koen** (a park) to the top of **Mt. Misen**.

Shimonoseki: The western limit of Honshu, Shimonoseki is the gateway to Kyushu and to Korea as well, with shinkansen service to Hakata and daily ferries to Pusan, South Korea. There isn't much reason to linger here, but the largest aquarium in Asia, the **Shimonoseki Suizokukan**, and **Akamon Shrine** may be of interest to those waiting for a boat. History and literature buffs will recall that the final scenes of *Tale of the Heike* took place here, as the exiled Empress Dowager hurled herself and the infant emperor into the swirling tides; several spots in the area claim to be the actual spot, but in fact, any would do, as the cliffs are high and the waters do, indeed, swirl frighteningly as the waters of the Japan Sea meet those of the Inland Sea.

Himeji: A 15-minute stroll from the shinkansen station, along a road lined with modern sculptures brings visitors to the main attraction in the city, **Himeji Castle**. It is called the White Egret Castle as it quite resembles a nesting crane, majestically resting on the banks of the Senba river. It is the largest, and most elegant, of the dozen existing Japanese medieval castles. Although the city was extensively bombed during World War II, the castle itself emerged unscathed and has been maintained in pristine condition.

The site occupied by Himeji Castle has been fortified since 1333. A castle was built here in 1580 by Toyotomi Hideyoshi. In 1681, Ikeda Terumasa, Tokugawa Ieyasu's son-in-law, rebuilt and expanded the castle to its present form. Castles in this period served both as military strongholds and as administrative centers. Terumasa's design achieved with funds from the Shogunate, elegantly merged martial necessity and artistic form on a scale previously unknown in Japan.

The castle's construction was a Herculean task, requiring 387 tons of wood, 75,000 tiles weighing 3,048 tons, and a huge number of large stones. These stones weren't easy to come by, and tales of their procurement live on in the ramparts. Ancient stone coffins, mined from nearby tombs, can be seen in one part of the precincts. The contribution of a millstone, from a woman living in the town below the castle, is still remembered today.

The castle's seemingly impregnable defences were never tested in battle. They started with three concentric moats, surrounding high, curved stone ramparts punctuated with several gates and watchtowers. The walls and watchtowers feature small holes, from which arrows and bullets could be fired at attackers. Roads within the castle grounds twist and turn, the better to confuse hostile forces in the event the outer defences were to be breached .

Himeji Castle is a "hillock" (as distinct from a mountain or flatland) castle, atop a 46-meter (150-ft) hill. There are spectacular views from the main *donjon*, which rises 31 meters (102 ft) from the castle grounds. *Shachihoko*, huge ornamental fish, which were strategically placed on the roof as charms to ward off fire, can be seen close up from the top floor.

The **Hyogo-Kenritsu Rekishi Hakubutsukan** (History Museum) nearby contains displays about Japanese castles, including the most magnificent of all, the "White Heron."

Hall and pagoda overlooking Itsukushima Shrine, Miyajima.

SHIKOKU

The least developed and least frequently visited of Japan's four main islands, **Shikoku**'s attractions (and drawbacks) are attendant on its relative isolation. The island can provide a more "Japanese" experience than Honshu or Kyushu: its people are less familiar with foreigners and its places have been less influenced by the homogenizing aspects of modern culture. It is also more diffused; places likely to be of interest to international travelers are relatively far apart and more difficult to get to than in more widely traveled pathways.

Shikoku's separate identity may not be long-lived. The smallest of the main Japanese islands, it was the last to be linked by bridge with Honshu. Its physical separation ended in 1988 with the completion of the **Seto Ohashi**, a bridge which carries automobiles and trains from Kojima on Honshu to Sakaide on Shikoku. There is considerable debate on Shikoku as to whether this will stimulate the island's economic development or speed the departure of its young people to the brighter lights of Osaka and Tokyo.

The Seto Ohashi is actually a series of 11 bridges which use four small islands as stepping-stones. At 12.3 km (7.6 miles), it is the longest double-deck bridge in the world, carrying four lanes of automobiles above dual train tracks. First suggested by a prefectural assemblyman in 1889, officials were finally persuaded of its logic in the late 1960s. Construction was set to begin in 1973 but was postponed in the aftermath of the first "oil shock" until October 1978. After 9½ years of work and expenditures exceeding ¥1.1 trillion, the first cars and trains finally rolled across in April 1988.

The most numerous and distinctive visitors to Shikoku today, arriving by plane as often as not, are *ohenrosan*, devote Buddhist pilgrims making the rounds of the 88 holy temples and shrines established by the priest Kobo

Shoreline near Takamatsu, gateway to eastern Shikoku.

Daishi 1,200 years ago. In the feudal period it was common for white-robed pilgrims carrying staffs to complete the circuit on foot, a feat requiring more than two months. Today's similarly-adorned pilgrims usually make the rounds in two weeks or less, via air-conditioned buses.

Shikoku is split into northern and southern sections by steep, rugged mountains. The relatively dry northern part, facing the Inland Sea, is more industrialized. The south is wilder, warmer, and wetter. The weather is most favorable in early spring and at the beginning of the fall.

Takamatsu: This city, the capital of Kagawa Prefecture, is the main railway terminal and port in eastern Shikoku. **Ritsurin Park** contains one of the finest traditional gardens in Japan, comprising 54 hectares (133 acres) of ponds, hills, pine forests and a botanical garden. One of the garden's best rewards is a cup of tea at the beautiful **Kikugetsutei** teahouse. The **Sanuki Mingeikan** (Folk Art Museum), near the entrance, displays comprehensive collections of crafts from Shikoku and throughout Japan. The local wood crafts – trays, etc. – are particularly valued. However, the region's most popular craft (not on display here) are the distinctive *sanuki-udon* noodles, presented daily at thousands of *udon* restaurants throughout Kagawa.

About 20 minutes by train from the center of Takamatsu is **Yashima.** The architectural embodiments of Shikoku's past – an open-air kabuki theater, a vine suspension bridge, thatch-roofed farmhouses, and a variety of other traditional buildings – have been collected and preserved in **Shikoku Mura** (village). The **Yashima Plateau** was once an island; now a narrow strip connects it to the mainland. It juts out into the Inland Sea, providing extensive views, particularly from **Yashima Temple.**

Kotohira: One of the most famous and popular shrines in Japan is here – **Kotohiragu**, also called Kotohira-san. It is dedicated to Okuninushi no Mikoto, the Guardian of Seafarers. Sail-

Heading back after a refreshing visit to the onsen.

ors and fishermen have come here seeking propitious sailing since the shrine's inception in the 11th century. In recent years their numbers have been swelled by the 4 million Japanese and foreign tourists arriving each year. The main shrine is at the end of a long, steep path lined with stone lanterns. A trip to the top of the 785 stairs and back takes at least an hour.

The **Kanamaruza**, restored to its original (1835) condition is the oldest existing kabuki theater in Japan. Its stage, resonating with the echoes of thousands of performances, is exciting to visit even when empty. In the third week of April the nation's best kabuki actors bring it alive. The revolving section is turned by strong men pushing the 150-year-old mechanism under the stage and the audience is seated on cushions on tatami.

Tokushima: This area is famous for the Awa-Odori, summer "crazy dance" festival held from August 12 to 15. It is the most humorous Japanese festival, with residents and tourists joining in proces-

THE IYA VALLEY

For 1,000 years, Iya was the most secret place in Japan. Defended by Japan's deepest gorges, Iya Valley became Japan's Shangri-La, the place of last refuge. In the 12th century, Heike courtiers fled here, and their descendants held the outside world at bay until 1920, when the first road was built. Iya retains a mystical atmosphere, a realm of peaks enveloped in clouds and mist, and so strong is the feeling of having gone up and away from the world, that even now the villagers refer to outsiders as "people from below."

As in a Sung landscape, the mountains rise jaggedly, and the houses do not cluster in the lowlands, but are scattered far over the hills. Sometimes, high on a cliff, you see a single cottage with a thatched roof, like the dwelling place of a sage.

For a "person from below," the quest for Iya starts from the town of **Ikeda**, almost the geographical center of Shikoku. From Ikeda, you may travel by car or bus via the old Iya Kaido (road). After 40 minutes, the bus stops at **Iya Onsen**, a hot springs built at the most spectacular point in the gorges. In another 20 minutes, the ride terminates at **Kazurabashi**, the vine bridge. Although surrounded by tourist developments, the vine bridge gives a sense of the almost "pre-historic" quality of life in old Iya.

Few travelers proceed beyond Kazurabashi. From here on you will need your own car. One winding road takes you to the hamlet of Tsurui, with two historic houses: the **Kimura House** (designated an "Important Cultural Property") and **Chiiori** (this writer's house, recently rethatched). Another takes you to Kyojo, where there are several small inns. In nearby **Asa**, the lineal descendants of the original Heike lord reside under a splendid thatched roof. Past Asa, the road winds upwards for tens of kilometers (about one hour's drive) before ending at sacred **Mt. Tsurugi**.

From Mt. Tsurugi, you descend to Sadamitsu (about 40 minutes), or you drive slowly down through the mountains to Tokushima (about 2 hours). Soon you are back "below," and Iya recedes into the high hills and the world of secrets.

Rice planting season on Shikoku.

sional dances and contests for "the biggest fool of all." Another home-grown entertainment, puppet shows, featuring giant puppets accompanied by *samisen*, are performed here by farmers between seasons. **Otaki Hill** is topped by the **Peace Memorial Pagoda**, built in 1958 and which can be reached by a ride in a cable car. Over a quarter of the 88 Kobo Daishi temples are in the immediate vicinity of Tokushima.

Nearby **Naruto** faces the **Naruto Straits**, a narrow channel where rushing waters, propelled by the tides, form whirlpools. The swirling vortices can be observed at close range from sightseeing boats or from more distant terrestrial perches.

Kochi: The capital of Kochi prefecture, **Kochi City** is best known for the role its leading families played in forging the alliance between the Satsuma and Choshu clans and the ensuing imperial restoration. Its most renowned citizen from this period is Sakamoto Ryoma, who was assassinated in 1867, a year before the restoration. He is remembered in the museum at **Kochijo**, an elegant castle that was built in the 17th century and rebuilt in the 18th. Ryoma's statue graces **Katsurahama**, a beach which is more famous as one of the few locations in Japan where dog fighting is legal.

The steep cliffs of the **Ashizuri** and **Muroto Capes**, continuously battered by fierce seas offer some of the most beautiful scenery on Shikoku. The **Ashizuri-Uwaki National Park** is popular for swimming and diving.

Matsuyama: Near this city is the **Matsuyamajo**, one of the most spectacular castles in Japan, built in 1603 (rebuilt to the same specifications following a fire in 1854) atop a mountain. The industrial city's other principal attraction is the **Dogo Onsen Honkan**, as famous for its waters as its literary associations. Some of Japan's most famous literary figures have frequented the spa since its construction in 1894, including Natsume Soseki, who used it as the setting for his novel *Botchan*. Dogo Onsen retains the flavor of an old fashioned bath house.

Uwajima: Bovine sumo, in which bulls, fattened and feted like their human counterparts, collide in an effort to push each other out of the **Togyujo** (bullfight ring), can be seen here. The **Taga Jinja**'s extensive sex museum is equally exotic, and probably more stimulating. Less exciting sights include the **Date Hakubutsukan** museum and the **temple quarters.**

Ozu: Another of Shikoku's animal oddities, cormorant fishing, can be observed in the summer at Ozu. Ozu has a number of renovated Edo- and Meiji-period houses and stores. The **Garyusano** villa features beautiful gardens overlooking a river.

Uchiko: A few minutes to the east of Ozu, Uchiko's **Yokaichi** street is lined with the homes and shops used in the late 19th century by vegetable-wax merchants. The **Kami Hagatei**, with displays of the tools of the wax-making trade as well as a gallery and tea shop, is particularly interesting. So is the beautifully restored Meiji-Era **Uchikoza** kabuki theater.

Offerings at Shikoku's Kompira Shrine are dedicated to seafarers.

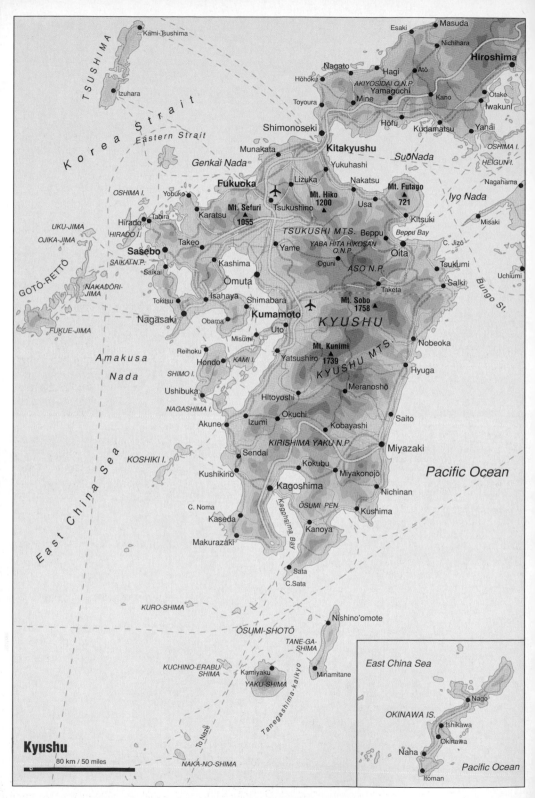

Kyushu

80 km / 50 miles

KYUSHU

Sometimes called "city in search of a soul," **Kita Kyushu** (North Kyushu) is an amalgamation of five cities (Moji, Kokura, Yawata, Tobata and Wakamatsu) with a combined population of just over a million. The civic marriage was arranged by Tokyo bureaucrats in 1963 and is yet to be consummated by a blending of culture or politics. Kita Kyushu is linked to Shimonoseki by the **Kanmon Bridge**. Monster steel mills (now an endangered species) and factories were built here to take advantage of the region's rich coal deposits, but they hold little interest for tourists, except, perhaps, the one converted into a "space camp" theme park.

Fukuoka/Hakata: During the Nara and Heian Periods, the Fukuoka area was the principal Japanese port for trade with China and Korea. In 1274, a scouting party of some 30,000 Mongols landed near Fukuoka, having decimated garrisons on Tsushima and Iki Islands. The invaders were similarly successful on Kyushu, but the death of their commander and serious storms which threatened their ships encouraged a hasty departure. Seven years later, in 1281, Kublai Khan sent a force of 150,000 soldiers, the largest amphibious assault in history prior to World War II. After 53 days of fighting, during which the Mongols overwhelmed fanatical Japanese resistance, a terrific typhoon, the famous *kamikaze* (divine wind) sent most of the invading fleet to the bottom of the sea.

In 1601, **Fukuoka Castle** was built on the west side of the Naka River, and the town that grew up around the castle was also called Fukuoka. A town for merchants, named **Hakata**, was built on the other side of the river. Hakata has been a mere ward within Fukuoka City since 1889, but the name has stuck and **Hakata Station**, the southern terminus of the Shinkansen, **Hakata clay dolls,** Japan's most sophisticated and highly valued, and the popular **Hakata Yamagasa** festival, are all named after the merchant city.

Fukuoka City is the capital of Fukuoka Prefecture and, with a population of 1.1 million, competes with Kita Kyushu for designation as the largest city on Kyushu. It is the main port of entry to Kyushu and is famous for its *fugu* (blowfish) meals, particularly in winter.

Relics of Fukuoka's most famous visitors are preserved at the **Genko Kinekan** (Mongol Invasion Memorial Hall), along with a statue of Nichiren, who was among the mystics who took credit for the fortuitous kamikaze storm mentioned above.

In its role as the crossroads between Japan and China, Fukuoka was the place that Zen Buddhism first touched the nation. **Shofukuji**, founded in 1195 by Eisai on his return from years of study in China, is the oldest Zen temple in Japan. Eisai is also credited with bringing the first tea seeds into the country and shrubs here are said to be their descendents.

The **Sumiyoshi Jinja**, the oldest extant Shinto shrine on Kyushu, was built

in 1623. It sits atop a hill that provides an excellent city overview.

Other points of interest in Fukuoka are: **Fukuoka-shi Bijutsukan**, an art museum housing a collection of Japanese art; **Ohori Koen**, a park containing the remains of Fukuoka Castle and reconstructions of its turret and gates; and the **Shiritsu Rekishu Shiryokan** (near Tenjin station), a museum dedicated to Fukuoka's history.

Sections of defensive walls built after the first Mongol invasion can still be seen on the road to **Dazaifu**. Forty minutes from Fukouka, Dazaifu is home to the **Dazaifu Temmangu Shrine**, built in 1591 to commemorate the scholar Sugawara Michizane. Students clamber over its orange bridges to pray for success in examinations.

Karatsu, Imari & Arita: Karatsu, Imari, and Arita, west of Fukuoka, are pottery towns whose fame dates to the 16th century, when captive Korean artisans were brought to the area. Anyone with an interest in Japanese ceramics could easily spend a day, or week, investigating these villages.

Karatsu is famous for its stoneware. Several galleries and workshops, including the **Nakazato Taroemon** and the **Ryuta** kilns, are open to visitors. The **Hikiyama Tenijo** museum exhibits 19th-century **Karatsu Kun-chi Festival** floats. A famous pine grove, **Niji-no-Matsubara**, stretches 5 kilometers (3 miles) along Matsuuragate Beach.

Imari porcelain, which is actually produced in nearby **Okawachiyama** and **Arita**, is famous around the world. The first kilns in this region were created in the early 1600s by Ri Sanpei, a Korean prisoner of the Nabeshima daimyo. Sanpei and his countrymen were not allowed to leave the small villages that were established around their kilns. Some of their graves are in Okawachiyama's **Nabeshima Honyo Koen** along with a replica of one of the original kilns.

Kyushu Toji Bunkakan (Kyushu Ceramic Museum) in Arita is the best place to view the full range of Kyushu pottery. **Imaizumi Imaemon** and **Sakaida Kakiemon** are famous work-

shops with galleries and shops open to the public.

Hirado: Continuing west, the focus shifts to Japan's early Christians. The first foreign settlement in Japan was established on Hirado Island in 1550, where the Dutch began trading activities. The **Francis Xavier Memorial Chapel** consecrates the saint's visit to Hirado. European activity was terminated when the Dutch were forced to move to Dejima in Nagasaki harbor in 1641, but crypto-Christians maintained a version of the faith here for centuries. This bit of historical lore has provided the basis for a thriving domestic tourist industry here, with "real" icons for sale.

Nagasaki: A city of nearly half a million, Nagasaki clings to steep hills wrapped around a very active deep-water harbor, competing with Kobe for designation as Japan's San Francisco. Like San Francisco, it has a lively **Chinatown** (Shinchimachi) and a spirit of receptiveness to novel ideas. One of the most interesting cities in Japan, travelers on a restricted time budget should

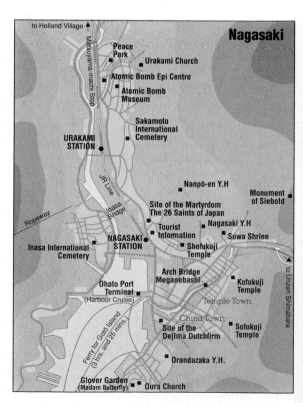

allow for at least two days in Nagasaki.

Nagasaki's harbor has played a prominent role in Japan's relations with the outside world. Dutch traders organized the first sustained European presence on an island in Nagasaki Harbor. Most of the early Christian missionaries came through this harbor. Its Mitsubishi Shipyards, the first modern shipbuilding facility in Japan, was the target of the second atomic bomb.

The port at Nagasaki was established in 1571 to serve Portuguese traders. A decade later, Omura Sumitada, a local *daimyo* who had grown rich on trade with the foreign barbarians, turned over partial administration of the port to the Jesuit missionaries who came in the merchants' wake. A generation later, fearing that the Christians and their converts would subvert his authority, Hideyoshi banned Christianity. He had six Spanish priests and 20 Japanese Christians rounded up in Kyoto and Osaka and brought to Nagasaki, where they were crucified in 1597 as a warning to the largest Christian community in

Painted stone Buddha in Oita.

Japan. A memorial, constructed in 1962, stands in **Nishizaka Park** on the spot of the crucifixions.

Christianity was completely and brutally suppressed following the Christian-led Shimbara Rebellion of 40,000 peasants south of Nagasaki in 1637–38. Japan's sole officially sanctioned contact with Europeans for the succeeding two centuries was through a settlement on **Dejima**, in Nagasaki Harbor. The artificial island was built for Portuguese traders, but was occupied by Dutchmen after the Portuguese were banished in 1638. Its occupants were confined to this small, walled area and contact with Japanese was limited to a small circle of officials, traders, prostitutes, and, in the later years, scholars. As no other Europeans were permitted in Japan until 1854, whatever news of European technology and culture that filtered into Japan came through this settlement. The **Dejima Museum** near the site preserves relics of the settlement.

Like the Dutch, Nagasaki's Chinese, mostly from Fukien, were officially

confined to a walled ghetto, but restrictions on their movements were not as strictly enforced. They left the only pure Chinese architecture, and one of the two Chinatowns (the other is in Yokohama) remaining in Japan. Shin-chimachi's narrow winding streets are filled with Chinese restaurants which cater to tourists, there being very few Chinese left in Nagasaki.

Two popular "Chinese" dishes in Japan, *saraudon* and *champpon*, were invented in Shi-nimachi. Like most of the Chinese food served in Japan, they bear only a passing resemblance to the original, but they are at the same time quite delicious.

The Chinese community was granted permission to build its own temples. **Teramachi** (Temple Town) contains two of the oldest Chinese temples in Japan, as well as numerous Japanese Buddhist temples and graveyards. **Kokufuji**, founded in 1620, was built on the edge of the original Chinatown, which was burned down in 1698, the current Shinimachi occupying land designated for Chinese merchants following the fire.

Sofukuji is a bright, elaborate, Ming-style temple. It is in better condition than most Ming Era temples in China. A Zen priest from Fukien built Sofukuji in 1629. Shaka and 18 disciples inhabit the main hall. The **Masodo** (Hall of the Bodhisattva) contains an image of the Goddess of the Seas, flanked by fierce guardians reputed to have thousand-mile vision.

Spectacles Bridge, so named because of the resemblance of it and its reflection to a pair of eye glasses, is the oldest stone arch bridge in Japan, built in 1634 by the priest from Kofukuji.

Cho-Cho San: True to its traditional receptiveness to new ideas and peoples, Nagasaki embarked on an aggressive modernization campaign in the later part of the 19th century. Thomas Glover, a Scotsman, was one of the first and most important of the European traders who arrived soon after Commodore Perry's Black Ships reopened the country. Glover helped Nagasaki

Temple detail at Sofuku.

achieve many Japanese firsts: the first railroad, the first mint, and the first printing press with movable type were all built in Nagasaki as a result of his efforts. He was also very active in supporting the rebels who defeated the Shogun's forces, "restoring" the emperor's rule. There is considerable controversy over whether Glover's marriage to a geisha did, as many guidebooks assert, inspire Puccini's opera *Madame Butterfly*.

Glover also built the first western-style mansion in Japan. Glover Gardens contains this house, built in 1863, and several other early Meiji Era houses which present elegant mixtures of Japanese and European architectural styles. The grounds provide excellent views of the harbor and the city. If you are not fortunate enough to visit during the annual **Okunchi Festival** in October, a trip to the **Kunchi Shiryokan** museum on the edge of the gardens shows what you are missing: Chinese dragon dances, floats and energetic revelry.

The Second Bomb: If construction of Glover's mansion marked the beginning of an era of infatuation with European technology, political and social institutions in Nagasaki and in the country as a whole, the detonation of a plutonium bomb over Nagasaki 82 years later marked its tragic, cataclysmic end.

A simple stone obelisk stands at the epicenter (usually called "hypocenter" here) of the atomic blast which devastated Nagasaki on the morning of August 9, 1945. The plutonium bomb, which was three times more powerful than the uranium bomb dropped two days before over Hiroshima, landed about 3 kilometers (2 miles) off target over Urakami, a Christian village.

Urakami Church, the largest Christian church in Japan, stood a few hundred meters from the epicenter; it was rebuilt in 1958. Headless statues of saints, scorched in the blast, remain as silent witnesses.

The **International Culture Hall** (housing the **Atomic Bomb Museum**) contains photos, relics, and poignant details of the blast and its 150,000 vic-

Glover House, the first Western-style dwelling in Japan.

tims. Simple objects – a melted bottle, the charred remains of a kimono, etc. – as well as photos of victims provide stark evidence of the bomb's horror and destructiveness. Many visitors say they wish that everyone in the world, particularly national leaders, could see this museum and more fully appreciate the horrors of nuclear war.

As important as its displays are, the museum, like the more elaborate one in Hiroshima, fails to provide any historical context or background to the bombing. Nothing is said about the reasons for the war, and there is no comparison with other mass killings of civilians, such as those committed by Japan in China. Additional explanation might lead visitors to conclude that, while there can be some debate about the logic, however terrible the calculation, for the initial atomic bombing of Hiroshima, it is far more difficult to come up with any humane rationale for this second, and more lethal, bomb.

The **Peace Park** is dominated by the **Peace Statue**, depicting a man with right hand pointing to the sky (signalling the threat from the atomic bomb) and left hand extended (symbolizing world peace). The **Peace Fountain**, on the south side of the park, was built in remembrance of the A-bomb victims who died crying for water.

Other Nagasaki sights: The ropeway cable car to the top of **Mt. Inasa** provides fantastic vistas of the harbor and surrounding hills, especially at night; **Oura Cathedral**, the oldest gothic structure in Japan; **Nagasaki Museum of History and Folklore**; and **Holland Village**, just outside the city, which is presumably of more interest to Japanese than to foreign visitors, the chief attraction being numerous Dutchmen and women and replicas of windmills and other foreign exotica.

Shimbara Peninsula and Amakusa Islands: The most scenic route between Nagasaki and Kumamoto takes travelers through the Shimbara Peninsula and the Amakusa Islands, on a combination of buses and ferries.

Down the peninsula, roughly midway between Nagasaki and Kumamoto, is **Unzen**, whose *jigoku* ("hell") pits of boiling mud and colored mineral waters are less dramatic, and less commercialized, than Beppu's. Christians who refused to renounce their faith were thrown into these jigoku in the 17th century. Unzen was a popular resort among colonial officials based in Shanghai in the days of the British Empire. The town is named after the **Unzen Volcano**, which is in the center of the peninsula and is surrounded by **Unzen-Amakusa National Park**.

Unzen erupted in 1991, causing considerable death and damage. The castle at **Shimabara**, which was destroyed along with virtually all of the Christian rebels in the 1637 rebellion, was reconstructed in 1964. It houses a museum displaying the *fumi-e* Christian images which suspected believers were forced to walk on to demonstrate that they were no longer Christians.

The **Amakusa Islands**, about 70 in all, lie between Unzen and Kumamoto. The **Kirishitankan** in Hondo is a museum which contains relics of the

Nagasaki's emotive Peace Statue.

Amakusa Christians. Hondo is also home to the **Amakusa Ocean Floor Natural Aquarium**.

Kumamoto: Although it isn't a popular tourist destination, **Kumamoto City** is an interesting, dynamic provincial capital. The city of half a million people is best known for its 17th-century castle, 350-year-old **Suizenji Park**, and, believe it or not, its horse-meat *sashimi*. Eager to retain its vitality into the 21st century, Kumamoto also boasts the most successful **Technopolis** research park (adjacent to the airport) in Japan. Kumamoto province has a sister state relationship with Montana, which is due more to the power and influence of the former ambassador to Japan, a Montanan, than to any similarity between the two places. The Texas swing music on one of the newer street cars is explained by Kumamoto's sister-city relationship with San Antonio, Texas.

Kumamoto Castle was built in 1607 by Kato Kiyomasa. Unfortunately, its 49 towers were made of wood and most were incinerated in a siege in 1877. The restored donjon, housing a museum, as well as original turrets, moats and stone palisades evoke the grandeur of what was one of Japan's most impressive castles. **Honmyoji**, a Nichiren temple which houses Kato's tomb, can be seen from the castle's towers.

You can enjoy a cup of tea in the basement of the **Kumamoto Traditional Crafts Center** across the street from the castle. The first floor features a colorful collection of toys, tools, jewelry and ceramics produced by Kumamoto craftsmen. The museum is part of the prefecture's efforts to sustain traditional crafts, which were largely abandoned after World War II. Most of the items are on sale in the museum's shop.

Suizenji Park, designed in 1632, contains landscaped models of Mt. Fuji and the 53 stops of the Tokaido.

Mt. Aso National Park, an hour's drive from Kumamoto, contains the world's largest volcanic crater, an active volcano, and a **volcano museum**. Mt. Aso (1,592 meters/5,220 ft) erupts every two or three years. The drive

Kumamoto kindergarten kids.

away from Kumamoto takes you past **ASPECTA**, the largest outdoor theater in the world.

The recently restored Edo-style **Yachiyoza** in Yanaga, 50 minutes by bus from Kumamoto, is one of 10 kabuki theaters in Japan, and well worth a visit. Built in 1910, it is a mixture of traditional Japanese construction and imported innovations such as a revolving stage and concealed trap doors. Patrons sat on tatami, warming themselves with a *hibachi* in winter. Around the corner, the **Lantern Museum** displays hundreds of handmade lantern headdresses worn by young women in the local annual festival.

Minamata Bay, in the southern part of Kumamoto Prefecture, is a monument to the excesses of industry, the results of laissez-faire government controls, and to sheer ignorance, greed and disregard for ethical conduct in general. The reason: a severely debilitating and often fatal ailment known as "Minamata Disease" (nicknamed "*Itai-Itai Byoki*" or "Hurt-Hurt Disease") was traced to shellfish and other products taken from its waters, waters into which local industries had been discharging mercury and other heavy-metal wastes for decades. Legislation hurriedly passed by the Diet soon after the discovery in the 1970s now constitutes the basis of Japan's pollution control law, for what it is worth, and Minamata Bay itself is being reclaimed and turned into an ecological park.

Elsewhere in the region, the **Yamanami Highway** runs across Kyushu from Kumamoto to Beppu, through some of the most attractive scenery in the country.

Beppu: If you want to "go to hell" and enjoy the trip, head for Beppu on the northeastern coast of Kyushu. The resort town is famous for its jigoku, variously colored ponds of water and mud that steam and boil, as well as its spas. A popular destination for Japanese tourists, Beppu is gaudy and commercial, a far cry from the serene elegance of Japanese travel posters. A popular tour encompasses half a dozen hellish attrac-

The main crater at Mt. Aso National Park.

tions, including: **Blood Pond Hell** (a vermillion colored boiling pond); **Sea Hell**, a boiling mud pond 120 meters (395 ft) deep; **Mountain Hell** (a mud pond in the hills, complete with statues of gorillas); **Oniyama Hell** (mock-ups of crocodiles); **White Pond Hell**, **Golden Dragon Hell**, and others. All these are far too hot for bathing, but out on the beach and in the many *onsen* inns, comfortable hot-sand and hot-mud baths are available.

Beppu is also well-known for its fugu (blowfish). **Takasakiya Hill**, 15 minutes from Beppu, is covered with wild monkeys. Nearby is **Yufuin**, a rustic *onsen* resort providing a tranquil counterpoint to Beppu.

Takachiho: The **Takachiho Shrine** is where the *Iwato Kagura*, a sacred dance, is performed for tourists every night. The **Takachiho Gorge**, featuring 80-meter (130 ft) cliffs, is the mythical cradle of Japanese civilization, where the Sun Goddess Amaterasu emerged from her cave to create the islands and people of the country. A cave near the

Kushifuru Shrine at Iwato is said to be the very one.

Usuki: The **Usuki Sekibutsu**, a collection of more than 60 stone Buddhas, is all that remains of the Mangetsuji, once an important temple. They are the most exquisite and mysterious Buddhist images in Japan. Archaeologists have dated their carving to slightly over 1,000 years ago, but have not determined who created them or why.

Miyazaki: This small city is considered the hometown of Jimmu, the mythological progenitor of the Japanese imperial family. Jimmu is enshrined in **Miyazaki Jingu**, which also features an interesting museum containing relics from local ancient tombs.

Heiwadaikoen (Peace Park), built in 1940, has a 40-meter-high (130-ft) tower; if you clap your hands at the correct place the tower resonates with a strange groaning sound. Reproductions of *haniwa*, clay figurines found in ancient burial mounds near the Miyazaki, are scattered throughout the park.

Saitobaru, north of Miyazaki, is one of the richest archaeological sites in Japan. About 300 burial mounds of 5th–6th century have been excavated here and two of the larger ones can be visited. Artifacts, including original haniwa, are on display at the **Saitobaru Shiryokan** (museum).

Kagoshima: This prefecture, in the far south of Kyushu, consists of two peninsulas, Satsuma and Osumi, and a chain of islands stretching off in the direction of Okinawa. A distinct, rapid-fire dialect is spoken here. The speech of older people, lacking the homogenizing influences of national television and radio announcers, is almost incomprehensible to other Japanese.

Kagoshima City, the southernmost metropolis in Kyushu, is situated on a large bay, and is famous – perhaps infamous is the better word – for being Japan's most polluted: the pollution (some people say it's harmful to health, others ignore the fear) comes from **Sakurajima** and its very active volcano. The mountain has erupted over 5,000 times since 1955. More than half a million people live within 10 kilometers (6 miles) of Sakurajima's crater. No other major city is as precariously positioned; Naples, Kagoshima's sister city, is twice as far from the volcanic Vesuvius.

Volcanic ash frequently rains on the city's residents, dirtying their laundry and bringing out the umbrellas, literally.

Sakurajima (Cherry Island) itself can be reached via a short ferry ride from Kagoshima. As the name indicates, it was once an island, but an eruption in 1914 spilled some 3 billion tons of lava out of the cone to join the island to the Satsuma Peninsula. The peninsula actually contains three volcanoes: the Minadake, Nakadake, and Kitadake. There are dramatic views from the **Yogan Tenbodai** on the southeast side of Sakurajima. Extra large *daikon* (radishes) grow in the rich volcanic soil, along with kumquats, summer oranges, and other fruits.

Aside from the gritty ash and often polluted air of Kagoshima, the city itself is delightful, and retains much of the spirit of the once-powerful Satsuma clans from whom the area takes its name. The Satsumas were ruled by the Shimazu daimyo, who were among the most dynamic of the Japanese hereditary rulers, for seven centuries. The Shimazu's distance from Edo bred a fierce independence.

The Shimazu were open to new ideas from abroad. They welcomed Francis Xavier to Kagoshima, the first Japanese city he visited, in 1549. Returning from Japan's ill-fated invasion of the Korean peninsula in the early 17th century, the Shimazu brought captive Korean potters to Kagoshima, the originators of "satsumaware."

The Satsuma clans opposed the Edo Shogunate's capitulation to European demands that Japan open its ports to trade. Demonstrating its resistance to the shogun's edicts, Shimazu retainers killed an Englishman near Edo in 1862. The British retaliated the following year, sending a squadron of ships to bombard Kagoshima. To the British sailors' surprise, the lords of Satsuma reacted favorably to this demonstration

Blood Pond Hell, volcanic springs at Beppu.

364

of modern naval power. They welcomed her majesty's officers to the still smoking city and purchased some of their ships, which later were incorporated into the Japanese navy. Satsuma clansmen dominated the Japanese navy until the Pacific War, and close relations between the Japanese and British navies lasted until the 1920s.

In 1866 the Satsumas joined with the rival Choshu clan in a successful military coup against the shogun which "restored" Emperor Meiji's sovereignty. Ironically, a decade later, the Satsumas led a bloody, and unsuccessful, rebellion against the new order which they had empowered.

Satsumaware and the more rustic Kuro-Satsuma pottery can be viewed and purchased in **Naeshirogawa**, a village that was settled by Korean potters in the 1600s. In addition to pottery, Kagoshima is known for *kiriko* cut glass. Local artisans were compelled to cease kiriko production under the terms of peace imposed on the region in 1877. They resumed kiriko production in 1985, following a hiatus of 180 years.

Iso Park, containing a garden which was laid out in 1661, provides excellent views of Sakurajima. Just outside the park, the **Shokoshuseikan** housed the first Western-style factory in Japan. It contains exhibits on the factory and the Shimazu family. The **Shimazu Yashiki** (mansion) has been preserved.

Nanshu Cemetery holds the remains of Takamori Saigo (1827–77) who led the forces which defeated the shogun's forces and later perished after leading the 1877 rebellion against the regime he had created. Saigo made his last stand on **Shiroyama Hill.** When defeat was inevitable, he had a loyal follower decapitate him. Saigo is worshiped at **Nanshu Shrine**; he was buried at **Jyokomyoji.**

Ibusuki is a spa town with hot sand baths, near **Mt. Kaimon,** a volcano noted for its resemblance to Mt. Fuji.

Japan's ambitious space program, if small by American and Soviet standards, operates a launch pad at **Uchinoura** on the Osumi Peninsula.

A hot sand bath at Ibusuki cures many ills.

OKINAWA

The 100-odd *Nansei* (Southwestern) islands in the Ryukyu chain stretch like an immense bow for 1,000 kilometers (6,250 miles) from just off Kyushu to within sight of Taiwan.

Most visitors arrive on the main island of Okinawa by plane, although the ferries from Kagoshima, Osaka and Tokyo are still packed during summer. Try to book far in advance if you plan to visit in September. More enjoyable are the visits in the fall – if you manage to avoid the typhoons that blow up with incredible force – and spring. During these times you can savor Okinawan hospitality to its fullest.

Is Okinawa a "tropical paradise"? Well, it has the highest unemployment rate of any prefecture in Japan and an average annual income that at ¥1.7 million is less than half Tokyo's ¥3.45 million. Despite this, the ever-ready smiles of its gentle, friendly people give no hint of the incredible suffering Okinawa has known through times of war–and even during times of peace.

Soundwaves Old & New: The center of tourist activity in the main city of Naha is **Kokusai Dori** (International Road), which is the city's equivalent of Waikiki (but without the beach). But only a short distance away are typically Okinawan neighborhoods. The quickest way to get a feel for the differences between Okinawa and the rest of Japan is to visit a local pub.

Here you can enjoy a break from the disco or *karaoke* music that are *de rigueur* at big city clubs in Japan, and relax to the frequently plaintive sounds of the *sanshin*, the three-stringed snake-skin-covered Okinawan banjo known elsewhere as the *jabisen*.

Traditional Okinawan dance and theater, which differ considerably from their Japanese counterparts, are performed frequently at various locations in Naha or can be caught on television. Many people in Okinawa speak good English, so arrangements are easy.

Okinawan crafts are also a delight.

Don't miss the **Tsuboya** pottery-making district off Himeyuri Dori in Naha. Active since 1682, it houses two dozen kilns, which make everything from the *kara-kara* flasks country gentlemen used to carry with lion "roofs" on top. A central **Pottery Center** sells items from all the kilns.

Bembo (Matsuyama 2-21-8; tel. 68-1867) is a store-cum-workshop that offers red and black *Ryukyu-shikki* lacquerware with gold decoration resembling relief. The **Fukuya Mingeiten**, on Kokusai Dori, offers crafts from throughout the Ryukyus.

Undoubtedly, Okinawans are very proud of their exquisite textiles, which are typically handwoven from ramic fiber and pongee silk, and feature beautiful designs created from with dyes. The designs and details of craftsmanship traditionally differed by production area. The *bingata* stencil-dyed fabric, originally made exclusively for aristocrats, is the most highly prized. It uses exotic "tropical" patterns.

Naha is also the perfect spot to make

Okinawa's azure waters are invitingly warm.

your initial experiments with Okinawan "soul food." Having gotten used to raw fish, *unagi*, *fugu* and other exotic delicacies in central Japan, you should now be ready to plunge into *mimiga* (sliced pig ears with vinegar), *ashite-bichi* (stewed pigs' legs) or with *rafutei* (pork simmered in *miso*, sugar, rice wine and soy sauce), *goya champuru* (stir-fried meat and bitter melon) or one of the many kinds of local noodles. *Awamori*, the local distilled rice brew, packs a wallop that puts *sake* to shame.

If you get tired of the glitter around Kokusai Dori, try the fascinating back alley markets off Heiwa Dori near Mitsukoshi. **The Naminoue Shrine**, a small Confucian temple and the **Gokokuji**, a temple which was once considered a national religious center, are down by the ocean, just north of an old pleasure quarter that even today retains its fair share of bars, cabarets and steak houses.

A Part, but Apart: In pre-modern times, most of these far-flung islands shared the same distinct Ryukyuan culture.

Today, of course, Okinawa and the other islands here are all part of Japan, yet it does sometimes seems like another world. Most "experts" agree that even racially, Okinawans are Japanese. But even their body language tells you that they are somehow different from their fellow countrymen.

For centuries the Okinawans minded their own business and accommodated themselves to outsiders. But during the age of imperialism in the late 19th century, their independence fell prey to the ambitions of powerful neighbors.

A Mighty Palace: The first castle on **Shuri**, the magnificent mountain overlooking the vast countryside and the oceans beyond, was established in 1237. Under the second Sho Dynasty, which was established in 1469 by King Sho En, it became a mighty palace and temple complex. Shuri remained the political and cultural center of the Ryukyus until 1879, when the last Okinawan king, Sho Tai, was forced to abdicate by the Meiji Government. The definitive history of Okinawa in English, *Okinawa:*

Golf is one of Okinawa's many pleasant diversions.

The History of an Island People by George H. Korr, recounts in magnificent fashion the fascinating story of the Ryukyuan kingdoms.

During the Battle of Okinawa in 1945, Shuri became the headquarters of the imperial forces. It was destroyed during the fighting and Ryukyu University now stands on the former site. Pre-war accounts describe a marvel, on a par in architectural and artistic interest with Kyoto, Nara, and Nikko. Much of the castle's stonework has been rebuilt.

On the way to Shuri by bus from Kokusai Dori, get off at **Ike no Hata** bus stop. First stop is the **Okinawa Prefectural Museum**, which provides a handy crash course on Okinawan history and culture. Several gates and bridges have been built since the war. The **Tama-udon Mausoleum**, five minutes from the famed gate called **Shuri no Mon**, contains the bodies of King Sho En and other members of his family.

Reminders of the bloodiest battle of the Pacific War, which cost the lives of 13,000 Americans, 110,000 Japanese and 140,000 Okinawan civilians (one-eighth of the population) are few at Shuri but hard to pass by in the southern part of the island, where major Japanese units made their last stand.

Tug-of-War: On the way stop at **Itoman**, the home of some of the most fearless sailors in the world. The **Hakugindo** cavern shrine is dedicated to the guardian deity of the town. Itoman's mid-August tug-of-war with intertwined "male" and "female" ropes draws crowds from afar.

Spots not to miss in the far south are the tunnel labyrinth at **Romogusuku** near Naha Airport, which was the last headquarters of the Imperial Navy and in which over 4,000 men committed suicide, the **Himeyuri no To** (Lily of the Valley Tower) where a group of high school girls and their teachers committed suicide after singing their school song, and **Mabuni Hill**, a promontory overlooking the ocean where the last resistance took place.

Coming up the east coast of the island along Highway 331, you will reach **Gyokusendo Caves**. Only about one-fifth of Asia's largest cavern is open to the public. Next door is the **Habu Koen**, where you can witness fights between mongooses and *habu* snakes, whose venom is strong enough to fell a horse or water buffalo.

Further Adventures: The central portions of Okinawa Island are largely occupied by military bases (Okinawa has about half the total number of military bases in Japan), most important of which is the US airbase at Kadina. Okinawa City (Koza) outside Kadina is sleazy and garish, but there are good beaches in the area, notably **Manza Beach** and **Moon Beach**, offering all kinds of marine sports, and many chances to enjoy A&W root beer or Foremost ice cream. The **Nakamura Home** at Nagasuku lets you see how an 18th-century gentry family lived and the ruins of **Nagasuku Castle**, built in the mid-15th century, are the largest in Okinawa.

The **Motobu Peninsula** was the site of the 1975 World Ocean Exposition. Several exhibitions concerning Okinawan culture or the ocean are open

Okinawa's colorful costumes offer tropical appeal.

every day except on Thursday. The ruins of **Nakijin Castle** are a 20-minute drive away and a tiny sombrero-shaped isle offshore is where the famous US war correspondent, Ernie Pile, "bought the farm."

Unique Religion: A 5-kilometer (3-mile) ferry ride from the Chinen Peninsula on Okinawa Island's southeast coast brings you to small, flat **Kudakajima**, the "Island of the Gods." This is where the Great Ancestress of the Ryukyuan people, Amamikiyo, supposedly descended from heaven and bestowed on them the five grains. Normally sugar cane and *fukugi* tree-covered Kudakajima, which has a resident population of only about 270, is somnolent. But it attracts great interest in mid November every 12th year when the five-day-long **Izaiho** festival is held, in which local women between the ages of 30 and 41 temporarily serve collectively as *noro*, or priestesses, to perform rites and communicate with the gods.

Directly across from Kudaka on the Chinen Peninsula is the **Seifa Utaki Shrine**, at which the Ryukyu monarchs personally worshiped and which was sacred to the common people as well as the aristocracy.

Another sacred island is **Iheya** to the northeast of Okinawa Island. According to Okinawan legend, Emperor Jimmu Tenno began his conquest of Japan from here and a huge cave on the island, referred to as the "Hiding Place," is said to be the very cave where the Sun Goddess Amaterasu hid herself until the other gods and goddesses could coax her out, thereby restoring light to the world. Priestesses governed that island until the 19th century.

The Far North: A visit to the far north of Okinawa Island, or *yanbaru*, will reward you with vistas of rugged hills, pristine beaches and secluded fishing villages, while bringing you into contact with some of the friendliest people anywhere. In the village of **Kijoka** you can observe the various steps required to produce the plantain-fiber textile, *bashofu*. The view at **Cape Hedo** at the northern tip of the island is stunning.

Local rooftops sport Shisa (roof gods) to ward off evil.

But don't go wandering off in the bush in *yanbaru*, since this is *habu* country.

The Outer Islands: Your best bet for experiencing the Ryukyuan way of life as it used to be is to visit the outer islands or *Sakishima*, which are reached by ferry or air from Naha.

Kerama, only 35 kilometers (20 miles) west of Naha, with numerous sea snakes among its gorgeous coral reefs, is an excellent SCUBA-diving haunt. **Kumejima**, 3½ hours by ferry from Naha's **Tomari Port**, has preserved several fine traditional homes in **Nakazato** and elsewhere. Don't forget to purchase some Kumejima-Tsumugi, silk pongee.

Further afield is the **Miyako group** of eight islands. **Miyakojima**, the main one, is an hour by air or 10½ hours by boat from Naha. At its port of **Hiraya** you will see the *nintozeiseki* (head tax stone), a 1.45-meter (5-ft)-high stone. After the samurai of Satsuma (now Kagoshima) invaded the Ryukyu Kingdom in 1609, it became in everything but name a tributary to that fief's lord, even though the country continued to pay tribute to the Ming Empire in China.

All the children on Miyakojima were paraded once a year before the nintozeiseki. Those taller than it had to pay the tax or were shipped off to work as forced labor.

So burdensome were the taxes that on some remote islands in the **Yaeyama group**, that the islanders had to resort to killing the weak and old because there was not enough food to go round. The *nintozei* system was not finally abolished until 1918.

Miyakojima earned a place in Japanese school books when five local fishermen spotted the Czarist fleet steaming towards Japan during the Russo-Japanese War (1904–05). The timely warning allowed the Imperial Navy under Admiral Togo Shigenori to surprise and annihilate the Russians in the Battle of Tsushima Straits. Nearby **Irabu Island**, which can be reached by boat from **Hiraya**, offers attractive scenery and fine diving.

The Yaeyama group, best reached by air (the ferry from Naha only docks

Fast ferry to the tourist isle of Taketomi.

about once a week), was long relatively isolated from the rest of the Ryukyus. It will appeal to those interested in folk-lore or the outdoor life.

The main island of **Ishigakijima** is presently embroiled in a controversy regarding whether an offshore airport should be built near **Shiraho**, one of the largest and most beautiful coral reefs in this part of the Pacific.

The **Municipal Yaeyama Museum** near the harbor has a collection of local artifacts and folkcrafts. **Kabira Bay** is an idyllic lagoon-like area with small islands and sandy beaches.

Spectacular Jungle: A short ferry or hovercraft ride from Ishigaki harbor will take you to **Taketomi**, a flat island famed throughout Japan for the star-shaped sand at **Cape Kondoi**. The island is beautiful and peaceful, but locals warn tourists to beware not only the habu but also the undercurrents in the surf. A ferry or jetfoil will also whisk you to the large island called **Iriomote**, a touch of New Guinea in Japan.

Except for the two towns of **Ohara** on the southeast and **Funaura** on the north, the island is primarily tropical rain for-est designated as a national park. Thank-fully, development on the island has been limited, with only one resort. *Minshuku* abound and you can even camp on the beach at **Hosisuna no Hama**, which provides free showers. A river boat will take you up the Urauchi River to Mariudo and Kampira falls amidst the spectacular jungle. You can even take a dip in the pools below the falls. If you are adventurous, you may like the challenge of the cross-island trail. But here, too, is habu territory, so take care.

If SCUBA-diving is your thing, you may have heard of "**Manta Way**" be-tween **Iriomote** and **Kohama** Island. Awesome giant manta rays can be seen here. Make sure you find a good local diver to take you down, since many of the divers offering their services to tour-ists have little or no training. The deep-sea fishing in the area and off Yonaguni is also interesting, but the price of going on a trip is high.

Nothing but beautiful blue on the horizon.

INSIGHT GUIDES
Travel Tips

OYSTER *GLX*

🌀 **Samsonite**[*]

Our Strengths Are Legendary[*]

TRAVEL TIPS

GETTING THERE

The most practical way of entering Japan is by air and through one of its several international airports. **New Tokyo International Airport (Narita Airport)**, 60 km (37 miles) from Tokyo city center, is the busiest and one of the two main aerial gateways to Japan. Flights on China Airlines are served by **Haneda Airport**, Tokyo's domestic airport located between Tokyo and Yokohama. Osaka's 24-hour, offshore **Kansai International Airport**, the other main gateway, serves routes plying the Americas, Europe and Asia. **Nagoya Airport** connects flights to and from various points in the Pacific and the Americas. Three airports on Kyushu – **Fukuoka**, **Kumamoto** and **Kagoshima** – serve those from cities in Europe, Korea and mainland Asia. Three major domestic airlines maintain air routes throughout Japan: Japan Air Lines (JAL), All Nippon Airways (ANA) and Japan Air Systems (JAS).

There is a ¥2,000 airport tax for all passengers departing on international flights.

TRAVEL ESSENTIALS

VISAS & PASSPORTS

A proper visa is necessary for foreigners living in Japan and engaged in business or study. Passengers with confirmed departure reservations can obtain a stopover pass for up to 72 hours.

Visitors from the following countries are not required to obtain a visa prior to arrival in Japan, provided they do not intend to stay for more than 90 days nor receive remuneration in Japan: Argentina, Bahamas, Bangladesh, Barbados, Belgium, Canada, Chile, Colombia, Costa Rica, Cyprus, Denmark, Dominican Republic, El Salvador, Finland, Greece, Guatemala, Holland, Honduras, Iceland, Israel, Italy, Lesotho, Luxembourg, Malaysia, Malta, Mauritius, Norway, Pakistan, Peru, Portugal, San Marino, Singapore, Spain, Surinam, Sweden, Tunisia, Turkey, Uruguay, USA.

Visitors from the following countries may reside in Japan for up to 6 months providing they are not earning an income: Austria, Germany, Ireland, Liechtenstein, Mexico, Switzerland and the United Kingdom. New Zealanders may visit Japan for 30 days without a visa.

MONEY MATTERS

The unit of currency is the yen (indicated as ¥), and the coins are ¥1, ¥5, ¥10, ¥50, ¥100 and ¥500. Bills are ¥1,000, ¥5,000 and ¥10,000. Foreign currencies are accepted at few hotels, restaurants and souvenir shops. You can buy yen at foreign exchange banks and other authorized moneychangers on presentation of your passport. At Narita Airport, the bank is open 24 hours.

Major credit cards, such as American Express, Diner's Club, MasterCard and Visa, are accepted at many establishments in the large cities and there is no surcharge for their use.

Using credit cards can be confounding sometimes, as they are a rather new item in Japan compared to North America and Europe. Outside the urban areas, not so many places accept them. Even places displaying acceptance of Visa or MasterCard, for example, may not – or cannot – accept your particular card, as it wasn't issued by a Japanese bank. Acceptance, or approval, can be erratic and without logic, but generally you won't know until you try. If your card is rejected, don't get upset. There's *nothing* you can do except pay cash or go elsewhere.

No tipping remains the rule in Japan, except for unusual or exceptional services. Porters at large stations and airports charge around ¥300 per piece of luggage.

BANKS

Despite the wide use of computers and on-line systems, Japanese banks are often slow and inefficient in many fields. Especially when transferring money in or out of the country, you can expect the process to take a long time and to be costly. Also, small neighborhood branches are often not able to process any international transactions. In order to send money out of the country, or cash foreign checks, you will find it much easier to go to a major branch, where someone will be able to speak English and usually understand what you want. The bank charges for remitting money out of the country are ¥2,500 to ¥8,000 depending on how fast you want the money to be sent. Banks are open Monday to Friday between 9am and 3pm for normal banking. Cash dispensers are open from 9am to 6pm on weekdays, and 9am to 2pm on Saturdays.

Swatch.
The others just watch.

seahorse/fall winter 94-95

shockproof
splashproof
priceproof
boreproof
swiss made

swatch ✚
SCUBA 200

Pack your trunks for a holiday that's smooth as silk.

Few countries can provide such a choice of exotic holiday experiences as Thailand.

Elephants still roam wild in Thai forests and have played an important cultural and working role since the early days of the Kingdom.

Today, you can enjoy the unforgettable thrill of a trek atop your own private elephant, on trails that lead through lush northern forests.

If riding a two-ton elephant isn't the holiday you had in mind, how about sailing aboard a traditional seventeen metre junk in the Andaman Sea?

Or relaxing in a luxury hotel and swimming in crystal blue waters at one of Thailand's famous beach resorts?

ROYAL ORCHID

Holidays

Then there's the shopping - but that's another story.

The first thing you need is our Royal Orchid Holidays brochure. In it you'll find every holiday imaginable in this exotic and mystical land.

Pick up a free copy from your travel agent or nearest Thai office and discover the treasures of the Kingdom.

And, of course, the best way to fly to Thailand is on Thai International, where you'll enjoy our world renowned Royal Orchid Service while you fly there smooth as silk.

INSIGHT GUIDES

COLORSET NUMBERS

HEALTH

In general, levels of hygiene are very high, and it is very unlikely that you will become ill as a result of eating or drinking something. The tap water, though heavily chlorinated, is potable. Most food is of a high standard, however, because the Japanese place so much emphasis on presentation and how food looks, there is wide use of chemical fertilizers in Japan, and therefore it is not recommended to eat the peels of fruits and some vegetables.

Toilets: Apart from major hotels and some train stations, most toilets in Japan are of the Asian squatting type, which takes some getting used to, but are supposed to be the most hygienic (no part of your body actually touches them) and physiologically best. In Tokyo and other major cities, they are slowly being replaced with Western-style toilets in many establishments. By law, every coffee shop and restaurant etc. must have its own toilet, or access to one in the same building.

CUSTOMS

Japan strictly bans the import and use of narcotic drugs, firearms and ammunition. If caught in possession of any of these, the offender will not face the death penalty, but can expect no leniency. Many a foreigner is still sitting in a Japanese prison, long forgotten by everyone but himself. Pornographic magazines and videos showing any pubic hair are technically forbidden in Japan.

This issue of films and magazines displaying pubic hair is a curious one. Photographs in *Playboy* magazine, for example, are literally sanded to obliterate pubic hair, but maybe only every other photo. Yet at convenience stores like Seven-Eleven, teenage boys can buy magazines with very, very explicit photographs or *manga* illustrations. Likewise, films sometimes will have fuzzy flesh-colored spots or electronic mosaics floating over offending parts. Other films are shown untouched.

You can bring in any currency, personal ornaments and other valuables into Japan, but there is an official limit of ¥5 million that can be taken out.

You are also allowed to bring with you into Japan, free of tax, three 760 ml (25 fl oz) bottles of spirits, 400 cigarettes and 100 cigars or a total of 500 g of tobacco, and 2 fl oz (50 g) of perfume.

EXTENSION OF STAY

Foreigners wishing to extend their stay in Japan must report, in person, to the Immigration Bureau within two weeks before their visa expiration. Present your passport, a statement with the reasons why you want an extension of stay, and documents certifying the reasons. The fee is ¥4,000.

Foreigners living in Japan must obtain a re-entry permit from the Immigration Bureau if they leave Japan and plan to return. Present, in person, your passport and certificate of alien registration (held by foreign residents in Japan) along with the appropriate re-entry form to the Immigration Office. The fee for a single re-entry is ¥3,000 and for a multiple re-entry ¥6,000.

Those wishing to transfer visas to new passports must report to the Immigration Bureau in Tokyo. Present both old and new passports and certificate of alien registration.

The main and branch office addresses are:

Tokyo Regional Immigration Bureau, 1st Otemachi Common Government Office 2nd Floor, 1-3-1 Otemachi, Chiyoda-ku, Tokyo, tel: (03) 3213-8111. Hours: 9am to 12pm, 1pm to 5pm, until noon on 2nd and 4th Saturdays; closed on Sundays.

Hakozaki Immigration Branch Office, Tokyo City Air Terminal, 42-1 Nihombashihakozaki, Chuo-ku, tel: (03) 3664-3046. Hours: 9am to 12pm, 1pm to 5pm, until noon on 2nd and 4th Saturdays; closed on Sundays.

ALIEN REGISTRATION

Foreigners planning to stay in Japan for more than three months are required to register at the ward office in their residing area. The application must be made in person within 90 days. The applicant must have his/her passport containing the proper visa and two photographs (3 cm x 4 cm).

If the alien registration card is lost or defaced, report to the ward office within 14 days. Take your passport and two new photographs and you will be issued a new one.

For visitors under 16 years of age, applications may be made by a parent or legal guardian by producing the applicant's passport. No photograph is necessary.

Ward office hours are from 8.45am to 5pm, Monday through Friday, and 8.45am to 12.30pm on Saturdays. Contact:

Minato Ward Office, 1-5-25 Shibakoen, Minato-ku, Tokyo, tel: (03) 3578-2111. English service is available on Monday, Wednesday, and Friday from 9am to 4pm at its public affairs department.

Tokyo Metropolitan Government, Tokyo Daisan Chosha, 3-5-1 Marunouchi, Chiyoda-ku, Tokyo, tel: (03) 3211-4433. English service is available on Monday and Thursday from 1pm to 4pm.

Information regarding alien status and visas presented above is general and subject to change. For further information contact your appropriate embassy, consulate or the Japan Immigration Bureau.

375

GETTING ACQUAINTED

GEOGRAPHY & POPULATION

Japan is made up of four main islands, Honshu, Hokkaido, Kyoshu and Shikoku, and several hundred smaller ones that stretch nearly 3,000 km (1,865 miles) in the temperate and sub-tropical zones, between 20° and 45° latitude. The total land area is 377,435 sq. km (145,728 sq. miles), 85 percent of which is mountainous. The country is divided into four different climatic and cultural zones by mountain ranges: the Japan Sea and Pacific Ocean on the northeast half, and the Japan Sea and Inland Sea on the southwest half. The famed Mount Fuji, seen on clear days from many places in and around Tokyo, is the country's highest mountain at 3,776 meters (2.3 miles). The population of Japan is about 123 million.

CLIMATE

"Japan has four seasons" is a phrase you will hear often, though it is still not clear why the Japanese feel that it is a feature unique to their country. The climate in Tokyo can be a bit of everything, and in recent years, the manifestation of the "four seasons" has not been all that clear, but generally in spring it is pleasant until May. In June begins the rainy season which should last about a month, but often longer. The summers are hot and sticky through to September. The typhoons usually come through in August and September. Fall begins in late September and lasts through mid-November and is cool and pleasant. The winter lasts from mid-November to the end of February or beginning of March.

CULTURE & CUSTOMS

At work and in most formal situations, the Japanese may seem a very reticent and reserved people, lacking in spontaneity or personality. There are books and theories explaining this behavior, but it only provides one side of the picture. Japanese (especially men) can become extremely raucous when drinking, and often let out their real opinions and feelings after a few drinks.

On the crowded trains you will find yourself being pushed and bumped around. You do not need to be polite here; just push along with everyone else. It is often said that "the Japanese are only polite with their shoes off," which means that they are polite and courteous with people they know well and would be indoors with (where shoes are almost always removed).

The Japanese distinguish between inside and outside the home. Inside the entrance to all homes (and some restaurants) is an area for removing shoes. You then step up into the living area, wearing slippers or in your stockinged feet. (Slippers are never worn on *tatami* mats, however.) Taking shoes off keeps the house clean, besides being more relaxing, and it also increases the amount of usable space, since you can sit on the floor without worrying about getting dirty. The toilet, however, is one area of the house that is considered "dirty," so separate slippers are provided there.

The custom of bowing has, in many cases, become somewhat a conditioned reflex. Foreigners, in general, are not expected to bow, and this is especially evident if a Japanese person first reaches out to shake hands.

As to punctuality and keeping appointments, the Japanese have a reputation for not being very punctual. At several of the famous "meeting places" you can observe people waiting, often for an hour or more, for someone. After several apologies and explanations, everything is usually forgotten and forgiven.

The way the Japanese usually speak and express themselves gives a very good picture of their culture. Direct statements of fact are most often avoided as this implies that the speaker has a superior knowledge, and this is considered impolite. Therefore, much "beating around the bush" is done which often leads to misunderstandings and seems like a waste of time to foreigners, but this must be taken into consideration when dealing with the Japanese.

When eating with Japanese, if you don't know what to do, the best policy is to just watch what the people around you are doing and do as they do. Below are a few helpful tips:
• Do not rest your chopsticks vertically in your rice as this is associated with death.
• Do not pass food from chopstick to chopstick as this is only done with the cremated bones of the dead at funeral services.
• When drinking beer or sake, one person will pour for the other, who will hold up his glass while it is being filled. Each person takes turns at pouring until enough is drunk and people will often begin to pour their own.

In any case, whatever happens, foreigners are usually forgiven for any breach of etiquette, so there's no need to spend time worrying about what is right and wrong. Japanese behavior in general is situational, and the Japanese themselves often do not know the right thing to do in any given situation. "It all depends on the situation," remarks the smart alec, but it's often fun for everyone involved when one of "us" makes a slip. Sometimes it actually does help to break the ice and put everyone in a more relaxed mood.

REMY XO BECAUSE LIFE IS WHAT YOU MAKE IT

INSIGHT *Pocket* GUIDES

United States: Houghton Mifflin Company, Boston MA 02108
Tel: (800) 2253362 Fax: (800) 4589501

Canada: Thomas Allen & Son, 390 Steelcase Road East
Markham, Ontario L3R 1G2
Tel: (416) 4759126 Fax: (416) 4756747

Great Britain: GeoCenter UK, Hampshire RG22 4BJ
Tel: (256) 817987 Fax: (256) 817988

Worldwide: Höfer Communications Singapore 2262
Tel: (65) 8612755 Fax: (65) 8616438

" I was first drawn to the Insight Guides by the excellent "Nepal" volume.
I can think of no book which so effectively captures the essence of a
country. Out of these pages leaped the Nepal I know – the captivating
charm of a people and their culture. I've since discovered and enjoyed
the entire Insight Guide Series. Each volume deals with
a country or city in the same sensitive depth, which is
nowhere more evident than in the superb photography. **"**

Sir Edmund Hillary

PEOPLE

Population: 123,231,000 (Japanese 99.4 percent; Korean 0.5 percent; other 0.1 percent)
Population density: 326 persons per square kilometer
Urban population: nearly 80 percent
Age distribution (1986): Infancy–14: 20 percent; 15–59: 64 percent; 60+: 16 percent
Life expectancy at birth: 75.6 male; 81.4 female

Life expectancy has been steadily rising for the last three decades, and the "greying" of Japan is becoming a major social concern. In 1985, only 10.3 percent of the population was 65 or older; in the year 2000 it is expected to reach 16.2 percent.

Retirement age for salaried employees, stable at 55 during most of the port-war era, is now gradually being raised to 60 by many major companies. Private and national pension plans are provided, covering 99 percent of the country's working population.

GOVERNMENT

Form: Parliamentary Democracy
Head of State: Emperor Akihito (born December 23, 1933, took office January 7, 1989)

While it is generally felt that the emperor's actual power is less than that of, say, the Queen of England, his social, cultural and political influence is much stronger than intended by the Allied Powers who, during the Occupation of Japan following World War II, "guided" the drafting of Japan's present constitution.

Although Article 1 of that document states the the "Emperor shall be the symbol of the State," and that he derives his position from the will of the people, the exact powers of the emperor are not specifically defined.

Prime Minister: (President of majority party in Lower House, currently – and since 1955 – the LDP)
Age of Suffrage: 20
Election Turnout (average): Rural 60 percent; Urban 50 percent
House of Representatives: 512 members (130 districts); 4-year term
House of Councillors: 252 members (1–4 from each of 47 prefectures); 6-year term

EDUCATION

Japan's public education system is tax-funded (although many private schools exists). Compulsory for all children are 6 years junior high school (enrolment 100 percent); high school (3 years) is elective (enrolment over 90 percent nationwide, nearly 100 percent in urban areas); Higher education at college/university (4 years) or trade schools is also elective (over 30 percent of all high school graduates go on to higher educational studies).

The school year begins in April; vacations include about 40 days in summer and around 100 days each for spring and New Years.

The three-year high school program is compressed to two in many of the best high schools to allow students to prepare for college entrance exams.

There are about 95 national, 34 public and 31 private 4-year universities/colleges in Japan. The quasi-national radio/TV network NHK runs the University of the Air (patterned after Britain's Open University) that combines radio and TV and correspondence.

Lietracy: 99 percent
Juku: These "after-school schools" are estimated to number about 200,000, earn ¥490 billion annually, and attract as many as 1.5 million elementary and 2 million high school students. In the main, they focus on preparing students for entrance exams.

CRIME

About 13 million crimes are reported a year, about one-eighth the number reported in the United States in the same year. Murders and violent assaults each average about 1.5 per 100,000 population. Although the crime rate has risen by 20 percent in Japan over the past decade, its growth is far lower, and the arrest/conviction rate remarkably higher, than in other industrialized nations.

ELECTRICITY

The power supply is 100 volts AC. Eastern cities in Japan, including Tokyo, run on 50 cycles while those in the west such as Kyoto, Osaka and Nagoya, use 60 cycles. Most hotels have adaptors for shavers and hair dryers.

BUSINESS HOURS

Officially, business is done on a 9am to 5pm basis, but this is in theory only. The Japanese will often do overtime till 8pm or 9pm. In general government offices are open from 8.30am or 9am to 4pm or 5pm Monday to Friday, and from 9am to noon on the 1st and 3rd Saturdays of the month. Main post offices are open 9am to 7pm Monday to Friday, 9am to 5pm on Saturday, and 9am to noon on Sunday and holidays. Branch post offices are open 9am to 5pm Monday to Friday. Major companies and offices are open from 9am to 5pm Monday to Friday. Some are also open on Saturday mornings.

In cities, department stores are open daily from 10am to 7pm, except for one day during the week. Restaurants are open for lunch from 11.30am to 2pm and for dinner from 5pm to 9 or 10pm. Most shops open between 9am and 11am and close between 6pm and 8pm.

The main national holidays are:

January 1: *Shogatsu* (New Year's Day). The Japanese visit Buddhist temples and Shinto shrines to make wishes for the new year. They also call on relatives and friends.

January 15: *Seijin no Hi* (Adults' Day). A holiday on which young boys and girls who have reached the age of 20 put on *kimono* and visit the shrine for a special ceremony.

February 11: *Kenkoku Kinen no Hi* (National Foundation Day)

March 21: *Shumbun no Hi* (Vernal Equinox Day)

April 29: Birthday of the late Showa Emperor's. Now named as *Hana to Midori no Hi* (Flower and Greenery Day). The Golden Week holiday period also begins on this day.

May 3: *Kempo Kinembi* (Constitution Memorial Day).

May 5: *Kodomo no Hi* (Children's Day). Though the emphasis is on little boys, in theory it is for all children. Carp banners (*koinobori*) are flown from homes where boys live. The carp is a symbol of strength and manhood, and parents hope their sons will grow up big and strong like the carp. Samurai dolls are also displayed inside the home.

September 15: *Keiro no Hi* (Respect for the Aged Day).

September 23: *Shubun no Hi* (Autumnal Equinox Day).

October 10: *Taiiku no Hi* (Health and Sports Day).

November 3: *Bunka no Hi* (Culture Day). Various events organized to encourage the people to promote and preserve the nation's heritage and culture.

November 23: *Kinro Kansha no Hi* (Labor Thanksgiving Day).

Note: When a national day falls on Sunday, the following Monday becomes a holiday.

COMMUNICATIONS

TELEPHONE & POSTAL SERVICE

To use the public telephones, which are colored either green, red, pink, blue or yellow, just insert a ¥10 coin and dial the number desired. ¥10 for three minutes.

Yellow and green phones accept ¥100 coins, which make them more convenient for long-distance calls (for more information, call 0051), but no change is returned for unused portions thereof. Green phones accept telephone cards (in denominations of ¥500 and ¥1,000) which can be obtained at any Nippon Telegraph and Telephone (NTT) office, KDD office, tobacco shops, or through special vending machines.

Postal supplies and services are available at all post offices. Post your letter in the red or blue (for overseas destinations) mail boxes. Approach your hotel guest relations officer for assistance.

EMERGENCIES

MEDICAL SERVICES

Try to remember that you are in Japan, and that you must be prepared to adapt to the Japanese system. Although some doctors may speak English, the receptionist and nursing staff may not, so it is advisable to bring along a Japanese friend or someone who can speak both languages. Protestant and Catholic mission hospitals in major cities are accustomed to treating visitors.

Most hospitals and clinics do not have the appointment system, so you have to be prepared to wait your turn, however frustrating that may be. Hospitals and clinics in Japan have different hours and systems, so be sure to phone before going.

The ambulance and fire services can be reached at telephone number, 119; and the police at 110.

GETTING AROUND

FROM THE AIRPORT

From Narita Airport: A taxi to downtown Tokyo from Narita costs between ¥20,000 and ¥30,000, depending on destination and traffic. Most people prefer either the bus or train, a tenth of the price of a taxi. Either way, it's 2–3 hours by road.

Bus. A regular limousine bus service runs between Narita and TCAT (Tokyo City Air Terminal) in downtown Tokyo, to Tokyo and Shinjuku stations, and to most major hotels in Tokyo. Tickets (just under ¥3,000) are bought at the airport after clearing immigration and customs. There are several routes depending on destination. Buses arc boarded outside the terminal at the curb, and will accept any amount of luggage at no extra charge. The buses leave every 20 minutes or so, taking two to three hours to arrive at the hotel. There are also buses to Yokohama and Haneda, the domestic airport.

Trains. There are two train alternatives into Tokyo: the Keisei Skyliner and the JR Narita Express. Both are twice as fast as by taxi or bus, but not as convenient.

In terms of connections, the Narita Express is more convenient, stopping at JR stations in Chiba, Tokyo (Station), Shinjuku, Ikebukuro, Yokohama and Ofuna. The Skyliner stops just at Ueno Station and nearby Nippori. Both take about the same time to reach Tokyo, an hour, and both have no restrictions on luggage. (Be warned, however, that carrying luggage through train and subway stations in Japan, especially in Tokyo, is a feat of considerable effort with long hikes and Fuji-like climbs. If carrying more than one piece of luggage, and if not taking the limousine bus directly to a hotel, consider a baggage delivery service. *See below.*)

The Narita Express costs about ¥3,000 for regular class, and tickets must be bought in advance. The Skyliner costs ¥1,740 and tickets can be bought in advance or at the Ueno Keisei Station for the next available train.

The Skyliner is far more comfortable than the Narita Express (unless traveling in first class, which is a delight). Narita Express's regular seats are small with almost no leg room: usually you sit facing another seat, knee to knee, in groups of four. When traveling with families, the Japanese prefer this style. But for the arriving traveler trying to shake jet lag, or exhausted from last-minute sightseeing before leaving Japan, this arrangement leaves a lot to be desired, especially for the price and especially when the train is overcrowded. (JR permits standing passengers when trains are full, making them even fuller.)

The Keisei Skyliner, on the other hand, is never overbooked or crowded, and the seats are quite comfortable with lots of leg room. Considering the difference in price, the Skyliner is far and away the better deal, both in price and in comfort. If one isn't carrying a lot of luggage, a connection can be made at Ueno Station to JR trains or the subway.

Note: If making a domestic airline connection, you must take the taxi, bus or train into Tokyo and make the connection at Haneda Airport. No domestic flights are made out of Narita. The limousine bus will take you directly from Narita to Haneda, as will a very expensive taxi.

Baggage delivery. Most residents of Japan take advantage of Japan's fast and reliable delivery network. After clearing immigration and customs, take your luggage to the ABC counter in the main terminal (there are several). Often a line indicates the counter. For about ¥1,500 per bag, ABC will deliver the bag by the following day wherever you are. If carrying more than a couple of bags, *seriously consider this alternative.*

From Haneda Airport: If you are coming into Haneda Airport, then a taxi to the town center will cost about ¥5,000 to ¥6,000 and takes about 30–40 minutes. Provided your luggage is light, you can take the Monorail to Hama-matsucho Station on the JR Yamanote Line. The trip takes about 17 minutes.

Osaka: In autumn of 1994, the new Kansai International Airport opened, replacing the old Osaka Airport near downtown. The new airport, constructed on a manmade island in Osaka Bay, is perhaps the world's most expensive airport for users, airlines and passengers alike. It is architecturally impressive, however.

Unlike Tokyo, where there is a two-hour bus ride between the international and domestic airports (no doubt the world's worst connection), domestic and international connections at the Kansai airport are made at the same terminal in a matter of minutes.

Despite being on an island, getting to and from the airport is relatively easy: two railways, two expressways, 10 limousine bus services, and high-speed ferries connect the island with the mainland.

To/From Osaka:

Trains. The JR Haruka Express runs between the airport and both Shin Osaka (a Shinkansen stop) and Tennoji stations, taking 45 minutes from Shin Osaka. Fare, about ¥3,000. From Osaka itself, take a local express for about ¥1,200.

A private line, Nankai Electric Railway's limited express called "Rapi:t" (sic), travels nonstop from Namba Station in downtown Osaka to the airport in only half an hour. Fare is about ¥1,300.

Buses. There are a number of deluxe buses, which take about an hour and a half from downtown Osaka.

Ferries. The airport is connected by ferry to Osaka's Tenpozan port (40 minutes), Kobe's Port Island (30 minutes), and Awaji Island (40 minutes).

To/From Kyoto:

Trains. The JR Haruka Express goes nonstop from Kyoto Station, costing about ¥3,500.

Buses. A bus leaves from Uji, south of Kyoto, and stops at Uji Station on the Keihan Line, the JR Uji Station, and Okubo Station on the Kintetsu Line. From downtown Kyoto, the bus takes almost three hours; from Uji, about two hours.

From Nagoya Airport: Nagoya's international airport at Kamaki is 30 minutes by bus to Nagoya Station. It is 45 minutes from Tokyo by air and 2 hours by rail on the Shinkansen.

From Fukuoka Airport: Kyushu's major airport at Itazuke is 20 minutes away from metropolis Hakata and is linked to it by regular bus services.

Domestic flights connect the airport with Tokyo (one hour 40 minutes) and Osaka (one hour).

RAIL TRANSPORT

Japan has one of the most efficient and extensive rail networks in the world.

Rail service is provided by **Japan Railways (JR)** and several regional private lines. The trains on important routes run every few minutes. Trains, such as JR's **Shinkansen** (the "Bullet Train") which travels at speeds of up to 136 mph (220 kph), offer alternatives to air and long distance bus travel.

Japanese trains are well-known for being crowded, especially during rush hours. Trains and subways are sometimes packed to three times their specified capacity.

All subway stations post a timetable. Regular services are operated Monday through Saturday. The Sunday and holiday schedule has fewer runs. Trains run until after midnight, so be sure to check the time of the last train.

All subway and train stations have a route map with fares for each stop near the ticket machines. The fares are regulated on a station-to-station basis, so if you cannot determine the fare required, just purchase the cheapest ticket available. You can pay the difference upon arrival at your destination.

The ticket machine will dispense the ticket and give the correct change. A child's ticket is half fare; a plastic shield is in front of the red buttons for children's tickets. Several types of prepaid train cards are also available.

Transportation cost savings can be made by buying a *teiki* (train pass), valid for one, three or six months. Major subway and train stations issue passes. Fill out the appropriate form with the names of the two destination points and where transfers will be made. Another way to save on train fares is to buy a *kaisuken*, a series of 11 tickets between two destinations for the price of 10. One-day tickets good on either subway lines or JR trains are available.

Station arrivals are announced in Japanese inside the trains. The names of the stations are usually written in both Japanese and English.

Timetables and subway maps in Japanese can be obtained at most stations. Subway maps in English are available in various English-language publications and at some major train and subway stations.

BUSES

Buses are plentiful in the cities, and during the commuting hours are, like the trains, often packed beyond capacity. They are not as easy to use as the trains, as their routes and destinations are written in Chinese characters (*kanji*) only. So until you are familiar with where a particular bus goes, it is best to ride in one with someone who knows the system.

TAXIS

Taxis are the most convenient way of getting around, but unfortunately, also the most expensive. In Tokyo, for example, the basic fare starts at around ¥600 for the first 2 kilometers (1½ miles), and ¥80 for each 370 meters (400 yards) thereafter. Once again, no tipping is expected or required.

Taxis are readily available on almost every street corner, and can certainly be found at every major hotel and railway station. There is a red light on in the front window if the taxi is free and available. The doors on taxis are opened and closed by the driver, who has a lever in the front, so when you've hailed a taxi and it stops, just wait for the door to open, and after arriving at your destination and paying, the door will open again by itself. You can get out and just walk away without trying to close the door, because you can't! Most taxi drivers speak only Japanese, so it can be helpful to have your destination written in Japanese.

PRIVATE TRANSPORT

You will need an international driving license or a Japanese one. However, be warned that driving in Japan can be a headache and tedious. The major cities seem to be in a perpetual stage of renovation; there is always construction work going on somewhere, and road divisions are often not easy to see. The streets are narrow, crowded and often confusing. Most street signs are in Japanese.

Remember that in Japan, driving is on the left-hand side of the road. Renting a car will cost from about ¥6,000 for 6 hours, or from ¥10,000 for 24 hours.

You can obtain the *Driver's Map of Japan* issued by the JAF Publishing Co. 9-3, Shiba Sakaecho, Minato-ku, Tokyo. Tel. (03) 3433-8731.

LEFT LUGGAGE

If possible, carry as little luggage as possible when traveling in Japan. Trains and stations, especially, are not designed for travelers with more than a small overnight bag. If you think you can make all your Tokyo train and subway connections while hauling several large bags, forget it. The train/subway map looks neat and tidy. The train/subway station connections are serious hikes with no carts or porters available, and lots of steep stairs.

Hotels, of course, will usually store luggage for guests heading off on adventures.

Narita Airport. For security reasons, bombs in particular, the international airport at Narita has no coin lockers. There are checkrooms, however, at the airport:

ABC Skypartners: between the South Wing and the Central Building. ¥400 or ¥800/day per bag, with no time limit for storage. 7am–10pm.

GPA (Green Port Agency): South Wing, 1F and

4F. ¥400/day per bag, 30 day limit. 7am–10pm.

Train and subway stations. Most train and subway stations have coin lockers of varying sizes for ¥200 to ¥500 per day, depending on station and size of the locker. Time limit is 3 days. After that, contents are removed.

Checkrooms for large bags are located at several main JR stations. Luggage can be stored for up to two weeks, ¥400/day per bag for the first five days, ¥800/day per bag for each additional day.

Tokyo Station, outside Yaesu south exit, 8.30am–6pm.

Ueno Station, in front of central exit, 8am–8pm.

Shin Osaka Station, outside the central exit, 5am–10pm.

Kyoto Station, Karasuma central exit and Hachijo central exit, 8am–8pm.

LOST PROPERTY

Fortunately, the Japanese are quite honest about turning in found items. If you've lost a wallet packed with cash or a camera, or simply an overnight bag with dirty socks, chances are you will recover it.

JR trains: Items left on trains will usually be kept for a couple of days at the nearest station. After that, they are taken to one of the major stations to be stored for five more days. Inquiries can be made in Japanese to lost-and-found centers at Tokyo Station (03) 3231-1880, or Ueno Station (03) 3841-8069. In English, inquiries can be made with the JR East Infoline (03) 3423-0111 from 10am–6pm weekdays.

Subways: Things left on Eidan trains are stored for three or four days at the station nearest to where the item was found, then taken to a lost-and-found center. In Japanese, call the center at (03) 3834-5577, 9.30am–7pm weekdays, 9.30am–4pm Saturday. On the Toei trains, or on Tokyo city-operated buses inquire about lost property at terminals the same day, or call the lost-and-found center, in Japanese, at (03) 3815-7229, from 9am–6pm weekdays.

Taxis: All taxi companies in Tokyo report unclaimed items to a single center, the Tokyo Taxi Kindaika Center. Call (03) 3648-0300, in Japanese.

Police: At last resort, contact the police. The Tokyo Metropolitan Police Department maintains an immense – a *very* immense – lost-and-found center in Iidabashi, with everything from forgotten umbrellas (zillions of them) to bags full of cash. Call (03) 3814-4151, 8.30am–5.15pm weekdays. English sometimes, Japanese mostly.

IMPERIAL PALACE VISITS

All Imperial palaces and villas – in Tokyo, Kyoto and elsewhere – come under the jurisdiction of the Imperial Household Agency, which controls every little aspect of the Imperial family, both ancestral and present. As only the palaces and villas in Kyoto can be visited, the following information is applica-

ble only for the **Kyoto Imperial Palace**, the **Shugakuin Detached Palace** (sometimes called Shugakuin Imperial Villa), and the **Katsura Detached Palace** (sometimes called Katsura Imperial Villa). Tours are in Japanese, with English pamphlets, and take 1–2 hours.

Visitors wishing to visit the palaces or villas in Kyoto must obtain permission in advance. The exact procedure seems to change occasionally. Most recently, one must apply in person, not by mail.

Kyoto Imperial Palace. Children must be accompanied an adult of 20 years or older. Group size is limited. Two tours daily. A passport or alien registration is required.

Katsura Detached Palace and **Shugakuin Detached Palace.** Adults only permitted on tours. Groups must be smaller than four people. Katsura has four tours daily, Shugakuin five tours daily. No tours on Sunday or national holidays.

Apply early, up to three months in advance. Current procedure is to apply in person at the Kyoto office of the Imperial Household Agency, in Kamigyo-ku in Kyoto, near the Imadegawa subway station. Open Monday-Friday, 8.45am–4pm. The Tokyo office (tel: 3213-1111) of the agency accepts applications for Kyoto, but approves only a limited number. (Apparently Japanese can apply by mail.)

Information required on the application: desired tour date and time, full name, age, sex, occupation, passport number and nationality. Be sure to indicate all people who will be in your group. Last-minute additions are not allowed.

Imperial Household Agency, Kyoto Office
3 Kyoto-Gyoen, Kamigyo-ku, Kyoto 602 Japan
tel: (075) 211-1215

Yes, it's a lot of work, but these places are simply exquisite and worth the effort.

WHERE TO STAY

Western-style hotels offer rooms whose rates may vary from ¥8,000 to ¥30,000. There are hotels which also provide Japanese-style guest rooms and landscaped gardens. Others have restaurants serving Continental food as well as local *sukiyaki*, *sushi*, *tempura*.

Ryokan (Japanese-style inns) exude an atmosphere of traditional Japanese living. They charge an average of ¥9,000 per person, depending on the type of bath facilities offered.

There are about 80,000 ryokan in Japan, of which 2,000 are members of the Japan Ryokan Association (JRA), who ensure that a high standard of service is maintained. Guests sleep in rooms covered with *tatami* (straw) mats, on *futon*. The baths are communal, though there are usually separate baths for men and women. Morning and evening meals are served in the guest's room and the futon laid out at night.

Minshuku are bed-and-breakfast lodgings without the frills (toiletries and *yukata* gowns etc). Rates are from ¥5,000 up. The Japan National Tourist Organization (JNTO) lists some 230 minshuku for overseas visitors.

The following is a brief list of accommodations in Japan, categorized by region: Kanto, The Northlands, Kansai and The Southlands – in that order.

KANTO

IN AND AROUND TOKYO

In Tokyo there are hotels everywhere and most of them are up to international standards. Those that are reflect it in their prices. However, convenience is a very dear commodity here, so often you are paying for the location more than the service or luxury. In most hotels and all ryokan, you are provided with a yukata robe, toothbrush, razor, shower cap etc.

ASAKUSA

Asakusa View Hotel, tel: (03) 3842-2111. Ideal for sightseeing and shopping.
Mikawaya Bekkan, tel: (03) 3843-2345. Ryokan near Asakusa Station on the Ginza line. Japanese-style rooms only, communal bath and showers. Meals not included.

UENO

Hotel Park Side, tel: (03) 3836-5711. Overlooking Ueno Park; delightful atmosphere; easy access to public transport.
Tourist Hotel, tel: (03) 3831-0237. Minutes away from Ueno Station.

KANDA

Diamond Hotel, tel: (03) 3263-2211. Near Hanzomon Station; nice quiet area.
Grand Central Hotel, tel: (03) 3256-3211. Central location and convenient to Kanda and Tokyo Station.
Hilltop (Yamanoue) Hotel, tel: (03) 3293-2311. Near Ochanomizu Station; pleasant hotel and old favorite of writers and artists; excellent food and service.
Hotel New Kanda, tel: (03) 3258-3911. Quiet; near to busy Akihabara electronic quarter.

AKASAKA

Akasaka Prince Hotel, tel: (03) 3234-1111. Modern, efficient; rooms with great views.
Akasaka Tokyu Hotel, tel: (03) 3580-2311. Conveniently located.
ANA Hotel Tokyo, tel: (03) 3505-1111. Convenient for business and fun.
Capitol Tokyu Hotel, tel: (03) 581-4511. Comfortable and relaxing setting, blending Japanese and Western design.
Hotel New Otani, tel: (03) 3265-1111. Largest hotel in Asia; with 400-year-old Japanese garden, and in good location.

GINZA

Hotel Atamiso, tel: (03) 3541-3621. Convenient to the Kabukiza (Kabuki Theater) and to all Ginza shopping. Near Higashi Ginza on the Hibiya line.
Ginza Dai-Ichi Hotel, tel: (03) 3542-5311. Conveniently located, minutes from Shimbashi Station.
Ginza Nikko Hotel, tel: (03) 3571-4911. Near Shimbashi Station.
Ginza Tokyu Hotel, tel: (03) 3541-2411. Close to the Kabukiza Theater in Ginza.
Mitsui Urban Hotel, tel: (03) 3572-4131. Great location.

NIHOMBASHI

Imperial Hotel, tel: (03) 3504-1111. Built in 1890, with new tower completed in 1983; near government offices and Ginza shopping.
Palace Hotel, tel: (03) 3211-5211. Old but quiet and peaceful surroundings overlooking the Imperial Palace moats and gardens.
Royal Park Hotel, tel: (03) 3667-1111. Next to the City Terminal. Indoor pool, fitness club, Japanese garden and executive floors.
Tokyo Marunouchi Hotel, tel: (03) 3215-2151. Short walk to Tokyo Station and the Imperial Palace grounds.

SHINJUKU

Century Hyatt Tokyo, tel: (03) 3349-0111. Japanese-style Hyatt service and accommodation, with health facilities and disco.
Inabaso, tel: (03) 3341-9581. Near Shinjuku Sanchome Station. Ryokan with Japanese- or Western-style rooms, each with a bath attached. Meals not included.
Keio Plaza Hotel, tel: (03) 3344-0111. A 45-story skyscraper with health facilities and executive salon.
Okubo House, tel: (03) 3361-2348. Youth hostel at economy rates.
Shinjuku Prince Hotel, tel: (03) 3205-1111. In the heart of exciting Shinjuku.
Star Hotel, tel: (03) 3361-1111. Popular hotel; convenient location.

Taisho Central Hotel, tel: (03) 3232-0101. Budget-class; next to Takadanobaba Station on the JR Yamanote Line.
Tokyo Hilton International, tel: (03) 3344-5111. Completed in 1984; health facilities and executive salon.
Tokyo International Youth Hostel, tel: (03) 3235-1107.
Washington Hotel, tel: (03) 3343-3111. Very modern, reasonable and convenient, though rooms are rather small.
Yashima Ryokan, tel: (03) 3364-2534. Near Okubo Station. Both Western- and Japanese-style rooms, communal bath and showers. Meals not included.

SHIMBASHI & SHIBA

Hotel Okura, tel: (03) 3582-0111. Rated the second best hotel in the world; with health facilities and excellent restaurants.
Shimbashi Dai-Ichi Hotel, tel: (03) 3501-4411. Central location, suitable for business, shopping and sightseeing.
Tokyo Prince Hotel, tel: (03) 3432-1111. Next to Zojoji temple; garden restaurant.
Takanawa Prince Hotel, tel: (03) 3447-1111. Convenient to Shinagawa and southwest Tokyo; traditional Japanese garden.

SHIBUYA

Hillport Hotel, tel: (03) 3462-5171. Short walk to Shibuya Station. Near restaurants, department stores and theaters.
Shibuya Tobu Hotel, tel: (03) 3476-4891. Good location.
Shibuya Tokyu Inn, tel: (03) 3498-0109. Good location.
Hotel Sunroute Tokyo, tel: (03) 3375-3211. Old standard; near Shinjuku Station.

AOYAMA

Aoyama Shampia Hotel, tel: (03) 3407-2111. Conveniently located.
The President Hotel, tel: (03) 3497-0111. Located near the Crown Prince's residence and the Roppongi and Aoyama areas.

ROPPONGI

Hotel Ibis, tel: (03) 3403-4411. Located where a lot of the action can be found.
Roppongi Prince Hotel, tel: (03) 3587-1111. Near Roppongi Station. Outdoor pool.

OUTSIDE TOKYO (AREA CODE)

YOKOHAMA (045)

Bund Hotel, tel: 621-1101.
Hotel Aster, tel: 651-0141.
Hotel Empire, tel: 851-1431.
Hotel New Grand, tel: 681-1841.
Satelite Hotel Yokohama, tel: 641-0202.
Shin Yokohama Hotel, tel: 471-6011.
The Hotel Yokohama, tel: 662-1321.
Yokohama Prince Hotel, tel: 751-1111.
Yokohama Tokyu Hotel, tel: 311-5114.

KAMAKURA (0467)

Hotel Tsurugaoka Kaikan, tel: 24-1111.

ENOSHIMA (0466)

Iwamotorou Bekkan Enoshima Grand Hotel, tel: 26-4111.

NARITA (0476)

ANA Hotel Narita, tel: 33-1311.
Holiday Inn Tobu Narita, tel: 32-1234.
Hotel Let's Narita, tel: 23-0222.
Hotel Nikko Narita, tel: 32-0032.
Narita Tokyu Inn, tel: 33-0139.
Narita View Hotel, tel: 32-1111.

CHIBA & FUNABASHI (043)

Chiba Grand Hotel, tel: 41-2111.

DISNEYLAND (0473)

Daiichi Hotel Tokyo Bay, tel: 55-333.
Sheraton Grand Tokyo Bay Hotel & Towers, tel: 55-5555.
Tokyo Bay Hilton, tel: 55-5000.

HAKONE (0460)

Fujiya Hotel, tel: 2-2211.
Goura Kadan, tel: 2-3331.
Hakone Kanko Hotel, tel: 4-8501.
Hakone Kowakien, tel: 2-4111.
Hakone Prince Hotel, tel: 3-7111.
Hotel Momijien, tel: 2-3185.
Hyouseki Kaku, tel: 4-8531.
Matsuzakaya Honten, tel: 3-6511.
Mikawaya Ryokan, tel: 2-2231.
Naraya Ryokan, tel: 2-2411.
Taiseikan, tel: 2-2281.
Yumoto Fujiya Hotel, tel: 5-6111.

IZU (0558)

Fuyoso, tel: 48-0464.
Hotel Amagi, tel: 48-5041.
Matsushirokan, tel: 48-0072.

NIKKO (0288)

Chuzenji Hotel, tel: 55-0333.
Hotel Harumoto, tel: 54-1133.
Kamaya Bekkan, tel: 62-2141.
Konishi Ryokan Bekkan, tel: 54-1105.
Nikko Grand Hotel, tel: 62-2411.
Nikko Green Hotel, tel: 54-1756.
Nikko Lakeside Hotel, tel: 55-0321.
Nikko Prince Hotel, tel: 55-0661.

THE NORTHLANDS

WITHIN TOHOKU

SENDAI (022)

Chatelet in Sendai, tel: 221-4191.
Miyako Hotel, tel: 222-4647.
Sendai Hotel, tel: 225-5171.
Sendai Royal Hotel, tel: 227-6131.

MATSUSHIMA (022)

Hotel New Komatsu, tel: 354-5065.
Hotel Taikansou, tel: 354-5214.
Matsushima Century Hotel, tel: 354-4111.

AKITA (0188)

Akita Castle Hotel, tel: 34-1141.
Akita New Grand Hotel, tel: 34-5211.
Ryokan Shibata, tel: 62-3274.

AOMORI (0177)

Aomori Grand Hotel, tel: 23-1011.
Aomori Green Hotel, tel: 23-2001.
Hotel Aomori, tel: 75-4141.

LAKE TOWADA (0176)

Kohanso, tel: 75-2021.
Towada Kanko Hotel, tel: 75-2111.
Towadako Grand Hotel, tel: 75-2121.

YAMAGATA (0236)

Green Hotel, tel: 22-2636.
Hotel Castle, tel: 31-3311.
Yamagata Grand Hotel, tel: 41-2611.

MORIOKA (0196)

Hotel Royal Morioka, tel: 53-1331.
Kobayashi Ryokan, tel: 22-4181.
Morioka City Hotel, tel: 51-3030.
Morioka Grand Hotel, tel: 25-2111.

HIROSAKI (0172)

Hirosaki Prince Hotel, tel: 33-5000.
Hotel New Castle, tel: 36-1211.
Ishiba Ryokan, tel: 32-9118.

IZAKA SPA (0245)

Hotel New Tachibana, tel: 42-2164.
Iseya, tel: 42-3131.
Matsushimaya Ryokan, tel: 42-3155.

BANDAI KOGEN (0242)

Hotel Kogenso, tel: 32-2531.
Urabandai Kogen Hotel, tel: 32-2211.

ON HOKKAIDO

SAPPORO (011)

ANA Hotel Sapporo, tel: 221-4411.
Century Royal Hotel, tel: 221-2121.
Fujiya Santus Hotel, tel: 271-3344.
Hotel Alpha Sapporo, tel: 221-2333.
Hotel New Otani Sapporo, tel: 222-1111.

HAKODATE (0138)

Hakodate Harbor View Hotel, tel: 22-0111.
Hakodate Kokusai Hotel, tel: 23-8751.
Hanabishi Hotel, tel: 57-0131.
Hotel Hakodate Royal, tel: 26-8181.
Meigetsu Pacific Hotel, tel: 57-0181.

SHIKOTSU-TOYA NATIONAL PARK (0123)

Hotel Manseikaku, tel: 5-2171.
Ito Onsen Hotel, tel: 25-2620.
Shikotsuko Kanko Hotel, tel: 25-2211.
Toya Kanko Hotel, tel: 5-2111.

NOBORIBETSU (0143)

Daiichi Takimotokan (Ryokan), tel: 84-2111.
Hotel Iwai, tel: 84-2281.
Noboribetsu Grand Hotel, tel: 84-2101.

KUSHIRO CITY (0154)

Kushiro Pacific Hotel, tel: 24-8811.
Kushiro Park Hotel, tel: 22-1919.
Ryokan Kawatani, tel: 23-8221.

WAKKANAI (0162)

Kanno Ryokan, tel: 23-3587.
Kitanoyado, tel: 28-1137.
Wakkanai Station Hotel, tel: 23-2111.
Wakkanai Sun Hotel, tel: 22-5311.

KANSAI

NAGOYA (052)

Hotel Nagoya Castle, tel: 521-2121.
Nagoya Crown Hotel, tel: 211-6633.
Nagoya Daiichi Washington Hotel, tel: 951-2111.
Nagoya Hilton Int'l, tel: 212-1111.
Nagoya Terminal Hotel, tel: 561-3751.
Nagoya Tokyu Hotel, tel: 251-2411.

ISE (596)

Asakichi Ryokan, tel: 22-4101.
Business Hotel Ise, tel: 25-5959.
Ise City Hotel, tel: 28-2111.
Ise Kokusai Hotel, tel: 23-0101.
Okunoya, tel: 22-2589.
Town Hotel Ise, tel: 23-4621.
Yamadakan, tel: 28-2532.

NARA (0742)

Hotel Fujita Nara, tel: 23-8111.
Hotel Pacific Nara, tel: 27-5808.
Kasuga Hotel, tel: 22-4031.
Kikusuiro (Ryokan), tel: 23-2001.
Nara Hotel, tel: 26-3300.
Shikitei (Ryokan), tel: 22-5531.
Wakakusa Hotel, tel: 22-2577.

KYOTO (075)

ANA Hotel Kyoto, tel: 231-1155.
Arashiyama Ladies Hotel, tel: 882-0955.
Kyoto Central Inn, tel: 211-8494.
Kyoto City Hotel, tel: 431-7161.
Kyoto Palaceside Hotel, tel: 431-8171.
Kyoto Prince Hotel, tel: 781-4141.
Kyoto Shin Hankyu Hotel, tel: 343-5300.
Kyoto Tokyu Hotel, tel: 341-2411.
Miyako Hotel, tel: 771-7111.

OSAKA (06)

ANA Sheraton Hotel Osaka, tel: 347-1112.
Hotel New Otani Osaka, tel: 941-1111.
Hotel Nikko Osaka, tel: 244-1111.
Hotel Plaza, tel: 453-1111.
Onoya Geihinkan (Ryokan), tel: 252-2000.
Osaka Hilton, tel: 347-7111.
Osaka Terminal Hotel, tel: 344-1235.
Osaka Tokyu Hotel, tel: 373-2411.
Plaza Osaka, tel: 303-1000.

KOBE (078)

Grand Hotel Rokko Sky Villa, tel: 891-0140.
Hotel Kobe, tel: 221-5431.
Kobe Portopia Hotel, tel: 302-1111.
Ohmori Ryokan, tel: 341-0591.
Oriental Hotel, tel: 331-8111.
Rokko Oriental Hotel, tel: 891-0333.

THE SOUTHLANDS

IN SOUTHERN HONSHU

OKAYAMA (086)

Hotel New Okayama, tel: 23-8211.
Ishiyamakadan, tel: 25-4801.
Okayama Kokusai Hotel, tel: 73-7311.
Okayama Plaza Hotel, tel: 72-1201.

HIMEJI (0792)

Hotel Himéji Plaza, tel: 81-9000.
Hotel Okuuchi, tel: 22-8000.

BIZEN (0869)

Daikokuya Ryokan, tel: 2-0203.
Ikedaya Ryokan, tel: 2-0530.
New Kibiji, tel: 3-5454.

KURASHIKI (086)

Kurashiki Ishiyama Kadan (Ryokan), tel: 22-2222.
Kurashiki Kokusai Hotel, tel: 22-5141.
Mizushima Kokusai Hotel, tel: 44-4321.

HIROSHIMA (082)

ANA Hotel Hiroshima, tel: 241-1111.
Hiroshima City Hotel, tel: 263-5111.
Hiroshima Kokusai Hotel, tel: 248-2323.
Hiroshima Riverside Hotel, tel: 227-1111.
Hiroshima Station Hotel, tel: 262-3201.
Mitakiso (Ryokan), tel: 237-1402.

MIYAJIMA (0829)

Kamefuku (Ryokan), tel: 44-2111.

TOTTORI (0857)

Hotel New Otani Tottori, tel: 23-1111.
Hotel Taihei, tel: 29-1111.
Kozeniya (Ryokan), tel: 23-3311.

MATSUE (0852)

Horaiso (Ryokan), tel: 21-4337.
Hotel Ichibata, tel: 22-0188.
Matsue Tokyu Inn, tel: 27-0109.

HAGI (0838)

Hagi Grand Hotel, tel: 5-1211.
Hagi Kokusai Kanko Hotel Rakutenchi,
tel: 5-0121.
Senshunraku (Ryokan), tel: 2-0326.

SHIMONOSEKI (0832)

Sanyo Hotel, tel: 32-8666.
Shimonoseki Grand Hotel, tel: 31-5000.
Shimonoseki Marine Hotel, tel: 46-3111.

ON SHIKOKU

TAKAMATSU (0878)

Hotel Rich Takamatsu, tel: 22-3555.
Keio Plaza Hotel Takamatsu, tel: 34-5511.
Takamatsu Grand Hotel, tel: 51-5757.
Tokiwa Honkan, tel: 61-5577.

MATSUYAMA (0899)

ANA Hotel Matsuyama, tel: 33-5511.
Hotel Oku-Dogo, tel: 77-1111.
International Hotel Matsuyama, tel: 32-5111.

TOKUSHIMA (0886)

Hotel Astoria, tel: 53-6151.
Hotel Isaku, tel: 22-1392.
Kanko Hotel Bizan, tel: 22-7781.
Tokushima Grand Hotel Kairakuen , tel: 23-3333.
Tokushima Park Hotel, tel: 25-3311.

KOCHI (0888)

Hotel New Hankyu Kochi, tel: 73-1111.
Joseikan, tel: 75-0111.
Keishokaku, tel: 42-2225.
Kochi Dao-ichi Hotel, tel: 83-1441.
Sansuien Hotel, tel: 22-0131.

ON KYUSHU

KITA-KYUSHU (093)

Hotel New Tagawa, tel: 521-3831.
Kokura Hotel, tel: 531-1151.
Kokura Station Hotel, tel: 521-5031.

FOKUOKA (092)

ANA Hotel Hakata, tel: 471-7111.
Hakata Miyako Hotel, tel: 441-3111.
Hakata Shiroyama Hotel, tel: 281-2211.
Hakata Tokyu Hotel, tel: 781-7111.
Hotel New Otani Hakata, tel: 714-1111.
Hotel Nikko Fukuoka, tel: 482-1111.
Hotel Station Plaza, tel: 431-1211.
Nishitetsu Grand Hotel, tel: 771-7171.

IMARI (0955)

Hotel Iwataya, tel: 23-3133.
Imari Grand Hotel, tel: 22-2811.

ARITA (0737)

Takeo Century Hotel, tel: 22-.2200
Ureshino Kanko Hotel Taishoya, tel: 42-1170.

NAGASAKI (0958)

Hotel New Nagasaki, tel: 26-8000.
Nagasaki Grand Hotel, tel: 23-1234.
Nagasaki Tokyu Hotel, tel: 25-1501.
Yataro (Ryokan), tel: 22-8166.

UNZEN-AMAKUSA NATIONAL PARK

Fukiya Ryokan, tel: 73-3211.
Hotel Toyokan, tel: 73-3243.
Unzen Kanko Hotel, tel: 73-3263.

KUMAMOTO (096)

Kumamoto Hotel Castle, tel: 326-3311.
Kumamoto Kotsu Center Hotel, tel: 354-1111.
New Sky Hotel, tel: 354-2111.

ASO NATIONAL PARK

Aso Kanko Hotel, tel: 7-.0311

BEPPU SPA (0977)

Beppu Fujikan Hotel, tel: 23-6111.
Kamenoi Hotel, tel: 22-3301.
Nippaku Hotel, tel: 23-2291.
Suginoi Hotel, tel: 24-1141.

MIYAZAKI (0985)

Hotel Phoenix, tel: 23-6111.
Hotel Plaza Miyazaki, tel: 27-1111.
Miyazaki Kanko Hotel, tel: 27-1212.
Seaside Hotel Phoenix, tel: 39-1111.

KAGOSHMIMA (0992)

Kagoshima Dai-ichi Hotel, tel: 55-0256.
Kagoshima Hayashida Hotel, tel: 24-4111.
Kagoshima Sun Royal Hotel, tel: 53-2020.
Shiroyama Kanko Hotel, tel: 24-2211.

ON OKINAWA

NAHA (098)

Hotel Ekka, tel: 868-3135.
Naha Tokyu Hotel, tel: 868-2151.
Okinawa Fuji Hotel, tel: 868-1118.
Okinawa Grand Castle, tel: 886-5454.
Okinawa Harbor View Hotel, tel: 853-2111.
Pacific Hotel Okinawa, tel: 868-5162.

OKINAWA CITY (098)

Hotel City Plaza, tel: 933-5599.
Hotel Star Hill Okinawa, tel: 935-4321.
Koza Kanko Hotel, tel: 933-1173.

MIYAKO (09807)

Hotel New Marukatsu, tel: 2-9936.
Miyako Grand Hotel, tel: 2-3351.
Miyakojima Tokyu Resort, tel: 6-2109.

ISHIGAKI (09808)

Hotel Miyahara, tel: 2-6111.
Hotel Nikko Yaeyama, tel: 3-3311.
Ishigaki Grand Hotel, tel: 2-6161.
Ishigaki Hotel Sun Coast, tel: 2-6171.
Villa Fusaki Resort, tel: 3-3040.

TAKETOMI (09808)

Izumiya (Minshuku), tel: 5-2250.

IRIOMOTE (09808)

Takemori Ryokan, tel: 5-5357.
Uehara, tel: 5-6516.

FOOD DIGEST

Food in restaurants and cafes is generally "safe." Many outlets specializing in foreign (Chinese, French, etc) dishes might communicate or have menus only in that language or in English. The very hungry tourist can always point to the plastic dish models displayed on the glass showcase at the eatery.

Listings, as with the previous section on hotels, are categorized by region, starting with Kanto, The Northlands, Kansai and ending with The Southlands. Effort has been made to identify places offering local specialties. Telephone numbers are excluded from the listings as most of the staff (including receptionists) at these outlets speak and understand only Japanese. Seek assistance from the hotel's front office if necessary.

KANTO

IN AND AROUND KYOTO

Most restaurants in Tokyo, regardless of their dinner prices, have special lunch menus with prices from ¥800. Budget-conscious tourists might want to opt for **Tengu**, a famous chain of cheap food and good drinking spots. Just look for the black and red picture of the long nosed goblin, or just ask for the nearest Tengu.

GINZA

Araliya, 11am to 8.20 pm; Sri Lankan meals from ¥950. Closed 3rd Wednesday.
Buono Buono, Italian food from ¥5,000.
Darie, lunch and dinner; Romanian food from ¥3,000. Closed Sundays.
Ginza Suehiro, well-known Japanese steakhouse serving steak, *shabu-shabu* and *sukiyaki*.
Gomi-Hatchin, 4pm to 10pm; *kushi-age* meals from ¥5,000. Closed Sundays.
Ketel Restaurant, lunch and dinner daily from ¥1,600.
Kiyota, *sushi* from ¥10,000; reservations required. Closed Sundays and holidays.
Kushino-bo, *kushi-age* meals; lunch and dinner from ¥5,000. Closed Sundays and holidays.
L'ecrin, French cuisine; lunch and dinner from ¥15,000. Closed Sundays.
Maxim's de Paris, French cuisine; lunch and dinner from ¥20,000. Closed Sundays.

Miracle, 5pm to 4am daily. Korean barbecue (*yakiniku*) from ¥2,500.

Shabusen, inexpensive *shabu-shabu* restaurants in town; from ¥2,300.

Sharaku, 6pm to 2am *Sushi* set from ¥1,500.

Sushi Sei, *sushi* lunch and dinner from ¥3,000. Closed Sundays.

Ten-Ichi, famous *tempura* restaurant in Tokyo; lunch from ¥4,500 and dinner from ¥5,500. Closed Sundays and holidays.

Tenkuni, *tendon* meals from ¥1,400, and others from ¥2,500. Closed 1st and 3rd Wednesday.

Tokyo Hanten, Chinese cuisine; lunch and dinner from ¥6,000. Closed Sundays.

Tonki, 5pm to 9.30pm for dinner; *tonkatsu* meals from ¥1,500. Closed Sundays.

NIHOMBASHI

Sunaba, lunch and dinner; *soba* and *udon* meals from ¥500 to ¥2,000. Closed Sundays and holidays.

Ten-mo, lunch and dinner; *tempura* meals from ¥4,500. Closed Sundays and holidays.

Yamamura, Japanese meals from ¥6,000. Closed Sundays and holidays.

SHINJUKU

Aoba, lunch and dinner daily; Chinese dishes from ¥400.

El Flamenco, lunch and dinner; Spanish cuisine; from ¥5,500. Closed Wednesdays.

Hofbrauhaus München, German cuisine; evening meals from ¥4,000.

Indonesia Raya, Indonesian cuisine; lunch and dinner; from ¥2,500. Closed Sundays and holidays.

Iseto, *sushi* dinners from ¥2,000. Closed Sundays and holidays.

Keika, *ramen* noodles for lunch and dinner; from ¥520 to ¥780.

Keitel, lunch and dinner; German cuisine; from ¥4,000. Closed Mondays.

Pas-A-Pas, French cuisine; dinner only; from ¥2,500. Closed Sundays.

Shinjuku, lunch and dinner daily; favorite with tourists; *shabu-shabu* course from ¥8,000 and *sukiyaki* from ¥7,500.

Shirakawago, Japanese meals from ¥4,000.

Suzume No Yado, daily evening Japanese meals from ¥2,000; country-style dishes.

Tonton-Tei, *tonkatsu* meals between ¥600 and ¥1,600. Closed 1st and 3rd Thursdays.

Zuien, morning and evening; Chinese dishes from ¥650.

SHIBUYA

Ankor Wat, Cambodian dishes for lunch and dinner; from ¥2,500. Sundays and holidays closed at lunch.

Antonio (Daikanyama), Italian cuisine; lunch and dinner; from ¥6,000.

Basta-Pasta, lunch and dinner daily; Italian cuisine; from ¥5,000.

Chaco, 11.30am to 10.30pm daily. and 4pm to 9pm on Sundays and holidays; great steak dinners from ¥1,700.

Chez Lui, lunch and dinner; French cuisine ¥1,700 to ¥6,000. Closed Tuesdays.

Daiichi Jingu, Korean barbecue for dinner; ¥7,000.

Dolphin Club, lunch and dinner; French courses from ¥3,500. Closed Sundays.

El Castellano, dinner only; Spanish cuisine. Closed Sundays and holidays.

El Pollo Loco, Mexican meals from ¥590.

España, Spanish cuisine; lunch and dinner from ¥3,000. Closed Sundays. On holidays open for dinner only.

George & Ray, steak lunch and dinner; from ¥4,000. Closed Sundays

Hidano Takayama, lunch and dinner daily; Japanese meals from ¥3,000.

Hope-Ken, open 24 hours daily; *ramen* noodle dishes from ¥500.

Ichikan, *sushi* lunch and dinner from ¥5,000.

Kabara, 6pm to 11.30 p.m; courses from ¥4,000. Closed Sundays.

Kogetsu (kyo), dinners from ¥13,000; Japanese zeals. Closed Sundays.

La Vita, buffet-style lunch ¥1,500 and dinner; French cuisine; from ¥2,500 to ¥6,000.

Los Reyes Magos, Spanish cuisine; dinner daily from ¥3,500.

08 (Maru Hachi), 5pm to 12.30am from ¥5,000. Closed Sundays and holidays.

The Prime, 11am to 11pm daily; wide variety in open cafeteria-style; about 16 different counters serve *sushi*, pasta, bagels, salads, stews, tacos, Oriental and continental dishes. **La Meme Paris** serves Vietnamese food; **Performance Restaurant–Shiryo Hiroba**, serves lunch and dinner buffet daily; popular eating spot; from ¥2,000.

Madame Toki's, French courses; lunch and dinner; from ¥15,000. Closed Mondays.

Maisen, day and night meals from ¥650.

Phnom Penh, Cambodian specialties; dinner from ¥2,500; 5pm to 11pm. Closed 1st and 3rd Sunday.

Reikyo, lunch, dinner, supper; Chinese cuisine; from ¥2,000. Closed Thursdays.

Roma Sabatini, lunch and dinner; Italian cuisine; from ¥6,000. Closed 1st and 3rd Monday.

Sasan, 7-course Chinese dinner for ¥5,500; 5pm to midnight. Closed Sundays.

Sergeant Pepper's, *yakiniku* lunch and dinner daily; from ¥4,500.

Victoria Station Shibuya, 11am to 2am daily. Meals from ¥3,000.

Xing Fu, lunch and dinner; *kanpo ryori* (Chinese herbal cooking) from ¥5,000. Closed Sundays and holidays.

Zapata, Mexican lunch and dinner; from ¥1,500; drinks till 1am.

AOYAMA

Antonio (Aoyama), lunch and dinner; Italian food from ¥5,000. Closed Mondays.

Daini's Table, 5 pm onwards; Chinese dinners from ¥7,000.

Kay, 6.30pm onwards; Thai food. Closed Sundays.

La Mex, lunch and dinner; Mexican menu from ¥5,000. Closed Sundays.

L'orangerie de Paris, lunch and dinner daily; French menu from ¥8,000. Closed Sunday evenings.

Selan, 8am to 9.30pm daily. French menu from ¥8,000.

Tony Roma's, lunch and dinner daily. Steaks and ribs from ¥4,000.

ROPPONGI

Bengawan Solo, lunch and dinner daily; Indonesian meals from ¥4,500.

Brasserie Bernard, lunch and dinner; French cuisine from ¥3,000. Closed Sundays.

Chisen, 5.30pm to 11pm daily; *kushi-age* from ¥4,000.

Fukuzushi, 5.30pm to 11pm; *sushi* dinners from ¥8,000. Closed Sundays.

Hamato, lunch and dinner; *sushi* from ¥10,000. Specializes in *fugu* (blowfish).

Hard Rock Café, from 11.30am onwards till 2am; till 11.30pm Sundays and holidays; succulent steaks.

Moti, lunch and dinner; Indian meals from ¥2,000. Closed Saturdays.

Naruse, 5pm to 10.30pm daily; all the *shabu-shabu* or *sukiyaki* you can eat for ¥3,900 per person.

Ryorijaya Hashimoto, 5.30pm to 10pm; Japanese dinners from ¥4,000. Closed Sundays and holidays.

Serina Roppongi, 5pm to 10.30pm daily; steakhouse.

Toricho 5pm to 10pm; *yakitori* meals from ¥3,500.

Torigin , lunch and dinner, daily; *yakitori* from ¥900.

Victoria Station Roppongi, lunch and dinner daily from ¥3,000.

Vidrio, Spanish lunch and dinner meals from ¥2,500. Closed 3rd Sundays.

Yagurajaya, Japanese cuisine from ¥3,000. Ample space for groups.

YOKOHAMA

YAMASHITA-CHO & CHINATOWN

Chonkin Hanten Bekkan, Sichuan Chinese.
Kanton Hanten, Guanchou Chinese.
Kaseirou Shinkan, Beijing Chinese.
Pekin Hanten, Beijing Chinese.

KANNAI

Casa de Fujimori, Spanish dishes.
Hungry Tiger Kannai, Western dishes.
Pino Blanc, French dishes.

Restaurant Kawori, French dishes.
Serina Isebura Kan, *shabu-shabu*.
Suehiro, Western dishes.
Victoria Station, Steak.

YOKOHAMA STATION VICINITY

Hamazen Honten, Japanese dishes.
Ranten, Shanghai Chinese.
Sagano, *shabu-shabu*.
Shabusen, *shabu-shabu*.
Yokohama Seiyouken, French dishes.

OUTSIDE TOKYO & YOKOHAMA

KAMAKURA

Hachinomoto, near Kenchiuji; *Shojin-ryori*.
Kittei, near Kamakura Station; *kaiseki-ryori*.
Rai Tei, Kamakurayama; *kaiseki-ryori*, *soba*.

ENOSHIMA

Mikasa-kaikan Restaurant, near Kugenuma-kaigan; French dishes.

NARITA

Kikuya, Nakamachi; Japanese dishes.

CHIBA/FUNABASHI

Toutenkou, Chiba City; Chinese dishes.
Funatamazushi, Funabashi City; *sushi*.
Inariya, Funabashi City; Japanese dishes.
Victoria Station, Funabashi City; steak.

HAKONE

Hagehachi, *sushi*.
Hatsuhana, *soba*.
Shikachaya, *soba*.

FUJI

Jinbei-chaya, Houtounabe pot dishes.
Katsuyama Minshuku Village, lamb.

ATAMI

Chirindoron, Spanish dishes.
Italian, pasta.
Scott, French dishes.

ITO

Amanokoya, near Kawana Pier; *miso* soup.
World, near City Hall; French dishes.

NIKKO

Asahiya-shokudo, Kawaji Spa; local dishes.
Ikari, Kawaji Spa; *ramen*.
Shousendo, Shiobara Spa; Chinese food and dumplings.
Tsuruya, Kawaji Spa; *soba*.
Western Village, Kinugaea Spa; barbecue.

THE NORTHLANDS

WITHIN TOHOKU

SENDAI

Numerous restaurants are located in the **Ichiban-cho** area, near the Mitsukoshi Department Store.
Kakitoku, oysters.
Kaiseian, eel.

MATSUSHIMA

Market in Shiogama Suisan Nakaoroshi Ichiban offers seafood in the morning.

AKITA

Hamanoya, Kawabata Dori; local dishes.

AOMORI

Daruma, Aoyagi Dori; seafood.
Kyosai, in Shosai Kaikan BF; seafood.

LAKE TOWADA

Yasumiya, Towadako-cho; local dishes.

YAMAGATA

Agetsuma, Midorimachi; seafood.
Chitosekan, Nanokamachi; local dishes.
Shabukin, Kasumimachi; *shabu-shabu*.
Shougetsu, Toukamachi; Japanese food.
Toriya, Nanokamachi; local chicken dishes.

MT. ZAO

Green House, near Zao Spa; coffee shop.
Shokudou Juhyou, near Zao Spa; local dishes.

MORIOKA

Morning Market, at Kyabatake and near Minami Ohashi on the Kitagami River, daily from 5am.
Night Market, at Zaimoku-cho, Saturdays, 3pm to 9pm from April to November.
Tawaraya, Honmachi Dori 1-chome, Wanko *soba*.

HIROSAKI

Osakaya, in Honcho; local confections.
Yamauta, near Station; pub with Tsugaru-jyamisen music.

BANDAI KOGEN

Goshikijaya, entrance of Goshikinuma; coffee shop.
Ura Bandai Royal Plaza; various dishes.

ON HOKKAIDO

SAPPORO

Ramen Yokokyo, famous street with 16 *ramen* shops; open until 4am.
Aji-no-Sanpei, Minami-ichi-jyo Nishi 3-chome Daimaru Fuji Central Bldg, 3F; *miso-ramen*.
Ganso Ryuho, near Tokei-dai; *ramen*.
Kanikko, Minami-5-jyo Nishi 4-chome Nanko Bldg; crabs.
Sapporo Biru-en, Kita-6-jo Higashi 9-chome; draft beer and Jingisukan pot dishes.
Satohoro, Sapporo ANA Hotel; local dishes.
Tonden-no-yakata, Tanuki Koji; local dishes.

HAKODATE

Chiaki-an, in Horai-cho; handmade Japanese confections.
Mikasa, in Suehiro-cho; Ika-*somen*.
Renga-tei, in Shinonome-cho; local dishes.

SHIKOTSU-TOYA NATIONAL PARK

Shikotsu Lake, famous for *himemasu*, a trout, *sashimi*, etc.

KUSHIRO CITY

Market, near Station; seafood & fresh vegetables.
Kani Doraku, near old Kushiro River; crabs.
Sakae Zushi, in Sakae-cho; sushi.

WAKKANAI

Ezo no Sato, Chuo 2-chome; local fish dishes.
Hitoshi no Ie, near Wakkanai Station; local dishes.
Wakkanai Shinai Kanko Center, near Wakkanai Station; local dishes.

KANSAI

NAGOYA

Yamamotoya, in Matsuzakaya Department Store in front of Station; *miso-Nikomi-Udon*
Torikyu, Minami 1-chome; local chicken dishes.
Kadoya, Iwai Dori; *yakitori*.
Kishimen Tei, in Nishiki 3-chome; *kishimen*.

Nagao, in Sakae Walk Gai; local dishes.
Yabu, in South-Main Matsuzakaya Department Store; *soba*.

ISE

Akafuku Honten, near Ise Naiguu; Japanese confections.
Nojima, near Ise-shi Station; coffee shop.
Taiki, near Yamada Station; *tempura*.
Tsutaya, near Kita-Shinbashi; *udon, soba*.

NARA

Chiyonoya Honten Takimura; Japanese confections.
Hiraso, Kakinoha; local *sushi*.

NARA CITY

Bekkan Kikusuiro; *kaiseki* and *bento*.
Isuien Sansyutei; local dishes.
Okyadokoro Tokiwa; local seasonal dishes.

KYOTO

KAWARAMACHI

Seigoin Yatsuhashi, at Sanjyo Kawaramachi; Japanese confections.
Tankuma Kitamise, Kawaramachi Dori; local dishes.

KIYAMACHI

Matsuzushi, near Sanjyo Dori; Kyoto-style *sushi*.

PONTOCHO

Matsutomo, reasonable Ryotei *bento*.
Takara, Ryotei; local dishes.
Uzuki, Ryotei; local dishes.

TERAMACHI

Mishimatei, *sukiyaki*.

GION

Gion Suehiro, beef.
Ippei Chaya, beside Kamo River; local seasonal dishes.
Matsuba, near Minami za; Nishi *soba*.

ARASHIYAMA

Nishiki, at Nakanoshima Park; Ryotei *bento*.
Seizansodo, in Tenryu-ji grounds; *yudofu*.

SAGANO

Hirokawa, near Nonomiya Jinjya; eel.
Ohkochi Sanso, Japanese tea and confections in beautiful garden setting.
Tsutaya, Ayu trout dishes.

OSAKA

STATION VICINITY

Ippo, in Hankyu Department Store; *tempura*.
Kikkyo, Acty Osaka 14F; *tenshin*.
Torihei, at Shin Umeda Shokudo Gai; *yakitori*.

SONEZAKI

Hyotei, Sonezaki 2; *soba*.
Rogetsu Honten, Sonezaki Shinchi 1; pot dishes.
Suehiro Honten, Sonezaki Shinchi 1; *shabu-shabu*.

NAKANOSHIMA

Alaska, Asahi Shinbun Bldg,13F; Western dishes.
Mimiu, Hirano-cho 4; *udonsuki*.
Shibatoh, Nakanoshima 2; eel.
Yotaro Honten, Koraibashi 2; Tai fish with rice.

SHINSAIBASHI

Honfukuzushi, Shinsaibashisuji 1; Osaka-style *sushi*.
Kagairo, in Holiday Inn Nankai Osaka 3F; *kaiseki*.
Kitamura, Higashi Shinsaibashi 1-16-27; *sukiyaki*.
Matsubaya, Minami Senba 3; Kitsune *udon*.

DOTONBURI

Daikoku, Dotonbori 2-2-7; Kayaku rice dishes.
Maruman, Dotonbori 1-9-3; Matsumae *sushi*.

KOBE

SANNOMIYA

Jyujiya, Edo machi, 96; Western dishes.
Restaurant Burge, in Boeki Center Bldg 24F; French dishes.
Sky Restaurant, in Oriental Hotel; Western dishes.

SANNOMIYA CENTER GAI

Morozoff, Sannomiya-cho 1-8-1-160; café.
Totenko, Center Plaza 19F; Chinese dishes.

MOTOMACHI

Fook, Higashiten, Sakae-cho Dori 2-9-11; steak, wine.
Hon Takasagoya, Motomachi Dori 3-2-11; Japanese confections.
Rohshoki, Motomachi Dori 2-1-14; Chinese pork dumplings.

IKUTA

Aragawa, Naka Yamate Dori 2; Tajima beefsteak.
Nishimura Coffee, Naka Yamate Dori 1; café.
Shinsenkaku, Shimo Yamate Dori 2; Beijing Chinese food.

THE SOUTHLANDS

IN SOUTHERN HONSHU

BIZEN

Horikeya, near Kibitsu-jinja; coffee shop.
Kinki, in Houfuku-ji; vegetarian dishes.
Momotarou, near Kibitsu-jinja; coffee shop.

TOTTORI

Hananoren, near Tottori Mingei Museum; local dishes.
Takumi Kappo, near Tottori Mingei Museum; crabs.
Watanabe Ryokan, Karo-cho; crabs.

MATSUE

Kaneyasu, near Station; seafood.
Matsumoto, at Teramachi; Izumo *soba*.
Minami, at Shinji Lake; Tai fish in rice.

HAGI

Fujitaya, in Kumagaya-cho; *soba*, *udon*.
Hyakumangoku, in Shimo Goken-cho; seafood.
Ochadokoro, near Kikuya Yokocho; Japanese tea and confections.

SHIMONOSEKI

Nakao, in Akama-cho; *fugu*.
Torafuku, near Station; *fugu*.

ON SHIKOKU

TAKAMATSU

Kawafuku, Sanuki *udon*.
Nicho; *kaiseki*.
Tenyasu; *tempura*.

MATSUYAMA

Hyakumi, seafood.
Menbo Goshiki, *somen*.
Yamabiko, *fugu*.

TOKUSHIMA

Banya, Sakaecho Pulaza Maruyama 1F; *robatayaki*.
Ebiten, near Tensaku; shrimps.

Fujiya; Japanese confections.
Fuwomi, near Tokushima Station; coffee shop.
Tensaku, near TokushimaStation; *sushi*.

KOCHI

Erupii, coffee shop.
Lump, Obiya arcade; coffee shop.
Momoya, *yakitori*.
New Monda, *shabu-shabu*.
Nishikawaya, Japanese confections.
Soho, bar.
The Square, near Kouchi Castle; coffee shop.
Tosahan, Harimayabashi; local dishes.

ON KYUSHU

KITA-KYUSHU

Itakura, Kokurakita-ku; *kaiseki ryori*.
Kaneyasu, Wakamatsu-ku; seafood.
Sekisui, Yahatahigashi-ku; *kaiseki ryori*.
Shigeru, Moji-ku; *fugu*.

FUKUOKA

Fukuya, Nakasu Market; Karashi mentaiko.
Miyake Udon, in Kami Gofukucho; *udon*.
Suigetsu, in Shoko Kaigisho Bldg in front of Station; Mizutaki chicken stew.

IMARI

Bordeaux, Nirimachi; French dishes.
Kurokame, Nirimachi; eel.

ARITA

Ryusuitei, Nishi-Arita; river fish.

NAGASAKI

China Town, in Shinchi; Champon *sara-udon*.
Ikesu, Shippoku local dishes.

UNZEN-AMAKUSA NATIONAL PARK

Ginsui, local confections.
Himematsuya, in Joshin-cho; local dishes.
Unzen Jigoku, volcano boiled eggs.

MATSUE

Danjyuro, in Ginza Dori Urban 21 Bldg, 1F; seafood.
Komurasaki, Kumamoto *ramen*.
Moriyama, *soba*.

ASO NATIONAL PARK

Asoji, in front of Ichinokawa Station; Takana rice dishes.
Dengaku-no-sato, local dishes.

BEPPU SPA

Tsukinoya, Shiroshita kare, local flatfish.

MIYAZAKI

Lamp Tei, Nishi Tachibana Dori; Japanese steak house.
Shiruan, Nishi Tachibana Dori; local seasonal dishes.

KAGOSHIMA

Aoyagi, Nigiwai Dori; Japanese confections.
Kuroiwa, Nigiwai Dori; Kagoshima *ramen*.
Satsumaji, at Tenmonkan Dori; local dishes.

ON OKINAWA

NAHA

Yotsutake, Kokusai Dori; Ryukyuan dishes.

OKINAWA CITY

Chuo Park Avenue, more than 100 restaurants and shops.

MIYAKO

Koja, Miyako *soba*.
Restaurant Nomura, shrimp.
Taiyou, eel.

ISHIGAKI

Iso, local dishes.
Steak House Ishigakijima, steak.
Yakko, seafood.

TAKETOMI

Gurukun, coffee shop.
Yarabo, cafe & restaurant.

IRIOMOTE

Iriomote
Marine Lodge & Restaurant Atori, local dishes; reservations required.
Robinson Cottage, coffee shop.

CULTURE PLUS

The following lists museums, galleries and theaters in Tokyo.

MUSEUMS

Asakura Sculpture Museum, 7-18-10 Yanaka, Taito-ku, tel: (03) 3821-4549.
Bridgestone Museum, 1-10-1 Kyobashi, Chuo-ku, tel: (03) 3563-0241.
Hara Museum, 4-7-25 Kita Shinagawa, Shinagawa-ku, tel: (03) 3445-0651.
Matsuoka Art Museum, 5-22-10 Shimbashi, Minato-ku, tel: (03) 3437-2787.
National Museum of Western Art, 7-7 Ueno Park, Taito-ku, tel: (03) 3823-6921.
National Science Museum, 7-20 Ueno Park, Taito-ku, tel: (03) 3833-4191.
Nezu Art Museum, 6-5-36 Minami Aoyama, Minato-ku, tel: (03) 3400-2536.
Seibu Art Museum, 1-28-1 Minami Ikebukuro, Toshima-ku, tel: (03) 3981-0111.
Suntory Art Museum, Tokyo Suntory Bldg, 1-2-3 Moto Akasaka, Minato-ku, tel: (03) 3470-2536.
Sumo Museum, 1-3-28 Yokoami, Sumida-ku, tel: (03) 3622-0366.
Tokyo Central Museum, Ginza Boeki Bldg, 5th Fl, 2-7-18 Ginza, Chuo-ku, tel: (03) 3564-0711.
Tokyo Metropolitan Museum, 8-36 Ueno Park, Taito-ku, tel: (03) 3823-6921.
Tokyo National Museum, 13-9 Ueno Park, Taito-ku, tel: (03) 3822-1111.
Tokyo National Museum of Modern Art, 3 Kitanomaru-koen, Chiyoda-ku, tel: (03) 3214-2561.
Ueno No Mori Museum, 1-2 Ueno Park, Taito-ku, tel: (03) 3823-0111.

GALLERIES

There are art galleries all over the Ginza area and other parts of Tokyo, but below are four well-known ones that almost always hold interesting shows.

Kaneko Art Gallery, Mitsunari Bldg, 3-7-13 Kyobashi, Chuo-ku, tel: (03) 3564-0455. 11am to 6.30pm. Closed Sundays and public holidays.
Maruzen Gallery, 2-3-10 Nihombashi, Chuo-ku, tel: (03) 3272-7211. 10am to 6.30pm. Closed Sundays.
NichidoGallery, 7-4-12 Ginza, Chuo-ku, tel: (03)

3571-2553. 10am to 7.30pm daily.

Parco Gallery, Parco Part 1, Udagawacho, Shibuya-ku, tel: (03) 3477-5781. 10am to 8.30pm daily.

THEATERS & CONCERTS

ABC Kaikan Hall, 2-6-3 Shibakoen, Minato-ku, tel: (03) 3436-0430.

Akasaka La Foret (avant garde), Akasaka Twin Tower Bldg, 2-17-22 Akasaka, Minato-ku, tel: (03) 3582-9255.

Aoyama Enkei Gekijo (avant garde), 5-53-1 Jingumae, Shibuya-ku, tel: (03) 3797-5678.

Ginza Nogakudo (*noh*), Ginza Noga-kudo Bldg, 9th Fl., 6-5-15 Ginza, Chuo-ku, tel: (03) 3571-0197.

Hakuhinkan Gekijo, 8-8-11 Ginza, Chuo-ku, tel: (03) 3571-1003.

Hayuza Gekijio (actor's theater), 4-9-2 Roppongi, Minato-ku, tel: (03) 3470-2880.

Hibiya Kokaido (public hall), 1-3 Hibiyakoen, Chiyoda-ku, tel: (03) 3591-6388.

Hitomi Memorial Hall, 1-5-57 Taishido, Setagaya-ku, tel: (03) 3422-5131.

Honda Gekijo (contemporary), High Town, 2-10-15 Kitazawa, Setagaya-ku, tel: (03) 3460-0005.

Jean Jean (recitals/intimate), Yamate Church, B1, 19-5 Udagawacho, Shibuya-ku, tel: (03) 3462-0641.

Kabukiza (*kabuki*), 4-12-15 Ginza, Chuo-ku, tel: (03) 3541-3131.

Kanze Nogakudo (noh), 1-16-4 Shoto, Shibuya-ku, tel: (03) 3469-4843.

Kinokuniya Hall (Japanese drama), 3-17-7 Shinjuku, Shinjuku-ku, tel: (03) 3354-0141.

Kokuritsu Gekijo (contemporary Japanese drama), 4-1 Hayatocho, Chiyoda-ku, tel: (03) 3265-7411.

Kosei Nenkin Hall, 5-3-1 Shinjuku, Shinjuku-ku, tel: (03) 3356-1111.

Meijiza (historical Japanese drama), 2-31-1 Hamacho Nihombashi, Chuo-ku, tel: (03) 3660-3939.

Nakano Sun Plaza, 4-1-1 Nakano, Nakano-ku, tel: (03) 3388-1151.

National Theater Nogakudo (*noh*), 4-18-1 Sendagaya, Shibuya-ku, tel: (03) 3423-1331.

NHK Hall (classical events). 2-1 Jinan, Shibuya-ku, tel: (03) 3465-1111.

Nihon Budokan, 2-3 Kitanomaru Koen, Chiyoda-ku, tel: (03) 3216-0781.

Nissei Gekijo, 1-1-1 Yurakucho, Chiyoda-ku, tel: (03) 3503-3111.

Shibuya Kokaido, 1-1 Udagawacho, Shibuya-ku, tel: (03) 3463-5001.

Shinjuku Koma Gekijo (musicals), 1-19-1 Kabukicho, Shinjuku-ku, tel: (03) 3202-0131.

Studio 200 (avant garde), Ikebukuro Seibu Department Store, 1-28-1 Minami-Ikebukuro, Toshima-ku, tel: (03) 3981-0111.

Suehirotei (*rakugo*), 3-6-12 Shinjuku, Shinjuku-ku, tel: (03) 3351-2974.

Sunshine Gekijo (Japanese versions of Western box office hits), Sunshine City Bunka Kaikan, 3-1-4 Higashi-Ikebukuro, Toshima-ku, tel: (03) 3987-5281.

Suntory Hall (mostly classical events), 1-13-1 Akasaka, Minato-ku, tel: (03) 3505-1001.

Teikoku Gekijo (Imperial Theater), 3-1-1 Marunouchi, Chiyoda-ku, tel: (03) 3213-7221.

Theater Apple (modern drama), 1-19-1 Kabukicho, Shinjuku-ku, tel: (03) 3209-0222.

The Tokyo Globe (Shakespeare/Opera/Visiting troupes), 3-1-2 Hyakunincho, Shinjuku-ku, tel: (03) 3360-1151.

Tokyo Bunka Kaikan (two halls, Classical/Opera), 5-45 Ueno Park, Taito-ku, tel: (03) 3828-2111.

Tokyo Dome (Big Egg), 1-3 Koraku, Bunkyo-ku, tel: (03) 3811-2111.

Tokyo Takarazuka Gekijo (all-female revue), 1-1-3 Yurakucho, Chiyoda-ku, tel: (03) 3591-1711.

Yubinchokin Hall, 2-5-20 Shibakoen, Minato-ku, tel: (03) 3433-7211.

SHOPPING

SHOPPING AREAS

Japan is a very expensive place to shop, but there are still bargains to be had if you look them up. The quality of Japanese products is well known, and there are some items which can only be bought in Japan. Certain areas promote only certain kinds of merchandise, which means that some domestic travel is involved for the serious shopper.

Following is a guide to the main shopping attractions in the cities and other areas throughout Japan.

IN AND AROUND TOKYO

Akihabara: The electronic jungle of the world featuring hundreds of discount stores.

Aoyama: High-class fashion boutiques.

Asakusa: Traditional Japanese toys, souvenirs, workmen's clothes, etc.

Ginza: The most expensive shopping center. Several major department stores are located here, such as **Hankyu**, **Matsuya**, **Matsuzakaya**, **Mitsukoshi**, **Printemps**, **Seibu** and **Wako**, and exclusive boutiques. Also some traditional Japanese goods stores.

Harajuku: Another fashion area, though mostly geared to the young, which makes shopping relatively cheap. Several antique shops, and **Kiddyland** for the kids.

Hibiya: Mostly antique shops, jewelry shops, and art galleries.

Kanda and **Jimbocho:** Many second-hand bookstores.

Nihombashi: A good place to pick up traditional craft work. Two of Japan's oldest department stores, **Mitsukoshi** and **Takashi-maya** are located here.

Roppongi: Several antique shops in the area, the **Axis** design building which features interior design as its main theme, and Seibu's **Wave** building which specializes in audio-visual equipment.

Shibuya: A good place to start with, Shibuya has a little bit of everything. **Tokyu Hands** is a must to visit; probably the most complete do-it-yourself department store in the world. Also here are the **Seibu, Tokyu** and **Marui** departments stores, the **Parco** "fashion buildings" besides the hundreds of small boutiques geared to young shoppers.

Shinjuku: Several big camera and electronic discount stores such as **Yodobashi** and **Sakuraya.** Also, **Isetan** and **Marui** department stores.

Ueno: Ameyoko is good for cheap food, cosmetics, clothing and toys. One of the few open markets in Tokyo. The shops in the back streets sell traditional Japanese goods.

ANTIQUES

In most of the shops listed here, the staff speak English and are helpful. Watch out for badly restored pieces that have been given a quick coat of glossy lacquer and sold like new at steep prices.

Antique Gallery Kikori, Hanae Mori Bldg, B1, 3-6-1 Kita Aoyama, Minato-ku, tel: (03) 3407-9363. Small but interesting selection of *tansu* and other items.

Antique Gallery Meguro, Stork Bldg, 2nd Fl, 2-24-18 Kamiosaki, Shinagawa-ku, tel: (03) 3493-1971. Antique market of sorts covering 740 sq. meters (885 sq. yards) that houses several small antique shops.

Edo Antiques, 2-21-12 Akasaka, Minato-ku, tel: (03) 3584-5280. Large selection of *tansu* and *hibachi*.

Hasabe-ya Antiques, 1-5-24 Azabu Juban, Minato-ku, tel: (03) 3401-9998

Harumi Antiques, 9-6-14 Akasaka, Minato-ku, tel: (03) 3403-1043. Mostly *tansu* that have been restored, but some unrestored pieces can be purchased.

Japan Old Folkcraft and Antique Center (Tokyo Komingu Kotto-kan), 3-9-5 Minami Ikebukuro, Toshima-ku, tel: (03) 3980-8228. 35 dealers covering 600 sq. meters (718 sq. yards) and displaying various antique items.

Oriental Bazaar, 5-9-13 Jingæmae, Shibuya-ku, tel: (03) 3400-3933. Apart from antiques, it is also a nice place to browse and pick up traditional Japanese toys, paper (*washi*), *kimono*, etc.

CERAMICS

Besides workshops, department stores are the best places for Japanese ceramics offered at reasonable prices. On back streets, small shops also sell ceramics but prices are higher.

Iseryu Shoten, 3-8-2 Ningyocho, Nihombashi, Chuo-ku, tel: (03) 3661-4820. Closed Sundays and holidays.

Saga Toen, 2-13-13 Nishi Azabu, Minato-ku, tel: (03) 3400-3682.

Tachikichi & Co. Ltd, 6-13 Ginza, Chuo-ku, tel: (03) 3571-2924.

DEPARTMENT STORES

Daimaru, 1-9-1 Marunouchi, Chiyoda-ku, tel: (03) 3212-8011. Closed Thursdays.

Isetan, 3-14-1 Shinjuku, Shinjuku-ku, tel: (03) 3352-1111. Closed Wednesdays.

Marui, 3-30-16 Shinjuku, Shinjuku-ku, tel: (03) 3354-0101. 10.30am to 7.30pm. Closed 2nd or 3rd Wednesday.

Matsuya, 1-4-1 Hanakawado, Taito-ku, tel: (03) 3842-1111. Closed Thursdays.

Matsuzakaya, 3-29-5 Ueno, Taito-ku, tel: (03) 3832-1111.

Mitsukoshi, 1-7-4 Muromachi, Nihom-bashi, Chuo-ku, tel: (03) 3241-3311. Closed Mondays.

Printemps, 3-2-1 Ginza, Chuo-ku, tel: (03) 3567-0077.
10am to 7pm Closed Wednesdays.

Seibu (Main Store), 1-28-1 Minami Ikebukuro, Toshima-ku, tel: (03) 3981-0111. Closed Thursdays.

Sogo, 1-11-1 Yurakucho, Chiyoda-ku, tel: (03) 3284-6711. Closed Tuesdays.

Takashimaya, 2-4-1 Nihombashi, Chuo-ku, tel: (03) 3211-4111. Closed Wednesdays.

Tokyu, 2-24-1 Dogenzaka, Shibuya-ku, tel: (03) 3477-3111. Closed Thursdays.

FASHION BOUTIQUES

Bigi (By Inaba Yoshie), The **Shibuya Parco Part 2**, 5th Fl., 3-7 Udagawacho, Shibuya-ku, tel: (03) 3476-2077.

Hanae Mori, Hanae Mori Bldg, 3-6-1 Kita Aoyama, Minato-ku, tel: (03) 3400-3301.

Hiroko Koshino, Tokyo Creator Bldg, 3-51-10 Sendagaya, Shibuya-ku, tel: (03) 3475-5311. Closed Sundays.

Issey Miyake, Shibuya Parco Part 1, 1st Fl, tel: (03) 3464-6626 and **La Foret Harajuku,** 1st Fl, tel: (03) 3478-7698.

The Shirts (Hamilton Shirts), 3-2-5 Kita Aoyama, Minato-ku, tel: (03) 3475-1971. Closed Mondays.

Junko Koshino, 6-5-36 Minami Aoyama, Minato-ku, tel: (03) 3406-7370. Closed Saturdays.

Junko Shimada, Aobadai Terrace, 1-1-4 Aobadai, Meguro-ku, tel: (03) 3463-2346. Closed Mondays.

Kansai Yamamoto, 3-28-7 Jingumae, Shibuya-ku, tel: (03) 3478-1958.

Madame Hanai (By Hanai Yukiko), Roi Bldg, 2nd Fl., 5-5-1 Roppongi, Minato-ku, tel: (03) 3404-5791. Closed 3rd Thursday.

Madame Nicole (By Mitsuhiro Matsuda), Nicole Bldg, 1st Fl., 3-1-25 Jingumae, Shibuya-ku, tel: (03) 3478-0998
Note: In the same building is **Monsieur Nicole** by Kobayashi Yukio
Persons, 3-28-8 Jingumae, Shibuya-ku, tel: (03) 3401-5524.
Takeo Kikuchi, Vivre 21, 1st and 2nd Fl, 5-10-1 Jingumae, Shibuya-ku, tel: (03) 3498-2221.
Tokio Kumagai, Cedarstone Villa, B1, 15-5 Hachiyamacho, Shibuya-ku, tel: (03) 3477-2613. Closed Wednesdays.
Yuki Torii, 5-7-16 Ginza, Chuo-ku, tel: (03) 3574-8701.

"FASHION BULDINGS"

Neither department stores nor arcades, "fashion buildings" are uniquely Japanese. Mostly occupied by boutiques, many of them are very similar, so you may not want to spend much time visiting them all.

Axis, 5-17-1 Roppongi, Minato-ku, tel: (03) 3587-2781. Most close on Mondays.
Bell Commons, 2-14-6 Kita Aoyama, Minato-ku, tel: (03) 3475-8111.
International Arcade, 1-7-23 Uchisai-waicho, Chiyoda-ku, tel: (03) 3591-2764. Many of the shopkeepers speak a foreign language.
La Foret Harajuku, 1-11-6 Jingumae, Shibuya-ku, tel: (03) 3475-0411.
Lumine, Shinjuku Station South Exit, tel: (03) 3348-5211.
Parco, 15-1 Udagawacho, Shibuya-ku, tel: (03) 3464-5150.
Shimbashi Ginza 9, shopping center stretches a long way from Shimbashi Station under the train tracks. 9am to 9pm daily.
Spiral, 5-6-23 Minami Aoyama, Minato-ku, tel: (03) 3498-1171.
Seed, 21-1 Udagawacho, Shibuya-ku, tel: (03) 3462-0111. Closed Wednesdays.
Sukiyabashi Shopping Center, 5-1 Ginza, Chuo-ku, tel: (03) 3571-0487.
Wave, 6-2-27 Roppongi, Minato-ku, tel: (03) 3408-0111.
Wing Takanawa, 4-10-18 Takanawa, Shinagawa-ku; in front of Shinagawa Station.

JAPANESE PAPER (*WASHI*)

Haibara, 2-7-6 Nihombashi, Chuo-ku, tel: (03) 3272-3801. Closed Sundays and holidays.
Isetasu, 2-18-9 Yanaka, Taito-ku, tel: (03) 3823-1453.
Kurodaya, 1-2-11 Asakusa, Taito-ku, tel: (03) 3845-3830. Closed Mondays.
Kyækyodo, 5-7-4 Ginza, Chuo-ku, tel: (03) 3571-4429.
Ozu Shoten, 2-6-3 Nihombashi Honcho, Chuo-ku, tel: (03) 3663-8788. Closed on Sundays
Washikobo, 1-8-10 Nishi Azabu, Minato-ku, tel: (03) 3405-1841. Closed Sundays and public holidays.

GENERAL

Mikimoto, 4-5-5 Ginza, Chuo-ku, tel: (03) 3535-4611. Closed Wednesdays.
Uyeda Jeweler, Imperial Hotel, B1, 1-1-1 Uchisaiwaicho, Chiyoda-ku, tel: (03) 3503-2587.
Wako, 4-5-11 Ginza, Chuo-ku, tel: (03) 3562-2111. Closed Wednesdays.
Yamazaki, 1-7-7 Ginza, Chuo-ku, tel: (03) 3561-0491. Closed Wednesdays and holidays.

KIMONOS (ANTIQUE)

These shops specialize in antique *kimono, obi,* traditional blue and white textiles, *furoshiki, hanten,* etc. Prices from ¥1,000 up.

Flea markets (see list under FLEA MARKETS, next page) also sell them, and you can usually pick up very beautiful old *kimono* and *obi* in good condition.

Ayahata, 2-21-2 Akasaka, Minato-ku, tel: (03) 3582-9969. Closed Sundays and public holidays.
Hayashi Kimono, International Arcade, 1-7 Uchisaiwaicho, Chiyoda-ku, tel: (03) 3581-9826.
Ikeda, 5-22-11 Shiroganedai, Minato-ku, tel: (03) 3445-1269. Closed Sundays
Konjaku Nishimura, Hanae Mori Bldg, B1, 3-6-1 Kita Aoyama, Minato-ku, tel: (03) 3498-1759. Closed Thursdays.

LACQUERWARE (*SHIKKI*)

Bushi, Axis Bldg, B1 5-17-1 Roppongi, Minato-ku, tel: (03) 3587-0317. Closed Mondays.
Heiando, 3-10-11 Nihombashi, Chuo-ku, tel: (03) 3272-2871. Closed Sundays and public holidays.
Inachu Japan, 1-5-2 Akasaka, Minato-ku, tel: (03) 3582-4451.
Kuroeya, Kuroeya Kokubu Bldg, 2nd Fl., 1-2-6 Nihombashi, Chuo-ku, tel: (03) 3271-3356. Closed Saturdays, Sundays and public holidays.

MUSICAL INSTRUMENTS

Bachi Ei Gakkiten *(Shamisen)*, 2-10-11 Ningyocho, Nihombashi, Chuo-ku, tel: (03) 3666-7263. Closed Sundays and holidays.
Kikuya Shamisen Ten *(Shamisen)*, 3-45-11 Yushima, Bunkyo-ku, tel: (03) 3831-4733. Closed Sundays and holidays.
Tsurukawa Gakki Honten *(Koto)*, 1-12-11 Kyobashi, Chuo-ku, tel: (03) 3561-1872. Closed Sundays and holidays.
Ishida Biwa Ten *(Biwa)*, 3-8-4 Toranomon, Minato-ku, tel: (03) 3431-6548. Closed Sundays and holidays.
Chikuyusha *(Shakuhachi)*, 3 San-eicho, Shinjuku-ku, tel: (03) 3351-1270. Closed Sundays and public holidays.
Miyamoto Unosuke Shoten (drums), 6-1-15 Asakusa, Taito-ku, tel: (03) 3874-4131. Closed Sundays and public holidays.

PAPER LANTERNS

Hanato, 2-25-6 Asakusa, Taito-ku, tel: (03) 3841-6411. 10am to 9pm. Closed 2nd and 4th Tuesdays.
Kashiwaya, 2-3-13 Shintomi, Chuo-ku, tel: (03) 3551-1362. Closed Sundays.

UMBRELLAS (*KASA*)

Hasegawa Hakimonoten, 2-4-4 Ueno, Taito-ku, tel: (03) 3831-3933. Closed Sundays.
Iidaya, 1-31-1 Asakusa, Taito-ku, tel: (03) 3841-3644.

WOODBLOCK PRINT (*UKIYOE*)

Asakusa Okuramae Shobo, 3-10-12 Kuramae, Taito-ku, tel: (03) 3866-5894. Closed on Sundays, but will stay open for appointments. Specialist on books and prints on *Edo* and *sumo*.
Hara Shobo, 2-3 Jimbocho, Kanda, Chiyoda-ku, tel: (03) 3261-7444. All types of prints old and new, from the highest quality to a "bargain drawer." English is spoken here.
Matsushita Associates, Inc., 6-3-12 Minami Aoyama, Shibuya-ku, tel: (03) 3407-4966. Closed Sundays and public holidays.
Oya Shobo, 1-1 Kanda, Jimbocho, Chiyoda-ku, tel: (03) 3291-0062. Closed Sundays.
Sakai Kokodo Gallery, 1-2-14 Yura-kucho, Chiyoda-ku, tel: (03) 3591-4678.

FLEA MARKETS

Nomi no ichi are held almost every week in or around Tokyo. Normally held early in the morning till dusk, weather permitting, they are among the few shopping areas where bargaining is the rule. If you are looking for souvenirs, or something unique to decorate your home with, these flea markets are the places to look. Most of the dealers are rather old-fashioned junk dealers than genuine antique dealers. These are some of the major fairs:

Togo Shrine (Harajuku), nearest station Meiji Jingumae on the Chiyoda subway line, tel: (03) 3403-3591. Every first and fourth Sunday.
Arai Yakushi Temple (Nakano), nearest station Arai Yakushi-mae on the Seibu Shinjuku line, tel: (03) 3386-1355. Every first Sunday.
Nogi Shrine (Roppongi), nearest station Nogizaka on the Chiyoda subway line, tel: (03) 3402-2181. Every second Sunday.
Roppongi (on the steps of the Roi Bldg), nearest station Roppongi on the Hibiya subway line, tel: (03) 3583-2081. Every fourth Thursday and Friday.
Hanazono Shrine (Shinjuku-Sanchome), nearest station: Shinjuku Sanchome on the Marunouchi subway line, tel: (03) 3200-3093. Every second and third Sunday.

OUTSIDE TOKYO

WITHIN TOHOKU

• MATSUSHIMA
Shiogama Suisan Nakaoroshi Ichiban; morning market.
Owariya, in front of Suigen-ji; wind bells.

• AOMORI
Murata Kogei-sha, Shinmachi Dori; local crafts.

• MORIOKA
Kyabatake, near Minami Ohashi on the Kitagami River, daily from 5am; morning market.
Zaimoku-cho, every Saturday, April to November, 3pm to 9pm; night market offering colorful array of items for sale.
Iwachu, Nanbu Tekki; local iron crafts.

• IIZAKA SPA
Kodai Gangu, Nihonmatsu; local crafts.

ON HOKKAIDO

• HAKODATE
Chiaki-kan, in Horai-cho; handmade Japanese confections.

• NOBORIBETSU
Kagetsu Do, Hyotan Ame; Japanese candy, gifts and souvenirs.

• AKAN NATIONAL PARK
Rakan, on Route 240; local crafts.
Akan Kohan Visitor Center; local crafts.

WITHIN KANSAI

• ISE
Akafuku Honten, near Ise Naiguu; Japanese confections, souvenirs.

• NARA
Ikeda Gankohdo; Nara fans.
Somekawa Hakurokuen; Nara dolls.

• KYOTO
KAWARAMACHI, main north-south street:
Matsuya, Kawaramachi Dori; Kyoto dolls.

KIYAMACHI (parallels the Takase River, north-south):
Murakami Ju-honten, at the end of 4-jo Dori; Japanese pickles.
Tachibana Syokai; antiques.

TERAMACHI (downtown arcade):
Ippodo; tea and accessories.
Kyukyodo; high-class Japanese stationery.
Miyawaki Baisen-an; fans.

SHIJYO, main east-west street:
Erizen; kimono and accessories.
Ichihara Heibei Shoten; chopsticks.
Morita Washi; paper crafts.

ARASHIYAMA:
Ishikawa Taki no Mise; bamboo crafts.

• KOBE
Hon Takasagoya, Motomachi Dori 3-2-11; colorful gift items, souvenirs and Japanese confections.

IN SOUTHERN HONSHU

• HIMEJI
Azumadou, Kawahara Shoutengai; Japanese confections.

• HAGI
Ochadokoro, near Kikuya Yokocho; Japanese tea and confections.

ON SHIKOKU

• TOKUSHIMA
Fujiya; Japanese confections.
Aigura, Nishishinmachi Arcade; local crafts.

• KOCHI
Kitaura,Konyacho; dyed goods.
Tosa Mingei Ten; folk handicrafts.

ON KYUSHU

• NAGASAKI
Art Hata, in Kajiya-cho; original Nagasaki dolls.

• BEPPU SPA
Kishima; bamboo crafts.

• KAGOSHIMA
Satsuma Glass Kogei, near Shuseikan; local glass crafts.

ON OKINAWA

• NAHA
Hirugi, Keizairen Mingei Center 2F, Kokusai Dori; Ryukyuan dishes, dances; crafts for sale; in other words, a place to shop and eat.
Morita Sango no Mise, Kokusai Dori; Okinawan coral jewelry.

• OKINAWA CITY
Chuo Park Avenue, more than 100 shops and restaurants.

• ISHIGAKI
Mineya; fabrics.

• TAKETOMI
Tomokura; local crafts.

• IRIOMOTE
Shoutokuan; accessories.

LANGUAGE

The foreign visitor to Japan will rarely find himself in a situation where absolutely nobody is available to help out in communicating. Indeed, some Japanese will go to extraordinary lengths to help the bewildered tourist, using a curious blend of smiles, gestures and Japanese together with the odd recognizable word of English as a fairly effective means of communication. Simply looking helpless will often be enough to attract assistance.

In spite of the seemingly simple pronunciation of Japanese, a lot of foreigners manage to mangle the language into a form which is almost impossible for the native speaker to understand. It is mainly intonation that is responsible for this. It would be fallacious to claim that the Japanese language has no rise and fall in pitch – just listen to a group of schoolgirls conversing on the train to confirm this. It is important to avoid stressing syllables within words; whereas an English speaker would naturally stress either the second or third syllable of *Hiroshima,* for example, in Japanese the four syllables should be stressed equally.

The following list is designed simply to start you off in Japanese.

GREETINGS

Good morning	*Ohayogozaimasu* (usually only until about 10am)
Hello	*Konnichiwa*
Good evening	*Kombanwa*
Good night	*Oyasuminasai*
Goodbye	*Sayonara (Shitsure shimasu* for formal occasions)
How do you do?	*Hajime mashite?*
How are you?	*Ogenki desuka?*
It's good to see you again	*Shibaraku desu* (informally, *"Domo"* is enough.)
My name is…	*…to moshimasu*
I'm American	*Amerikajin desu*
I'm British	*Igirisujin desu*
I'm Australian	*Osturaraiajin desu*
I'm Canadian	*Kanadajin desu*

ASKING FOR DIRECTIONS

Excuse me, where is the **toilet**?	*Sumimasen.* **Toire** *wa doko desuka?*
Excuse me, is there a **post office** near here?	*Sumimasen. Kono chikaku ni,* **yubinkyoku** *wa arimasuka?*
Bakery	*Pan-ya*
Meat shop	*Niku-ya*
Fish market	*Sakana-ya*
Greengrocer's	*Yao-ya*
Stationery store	*Bumbogu-ya*
Pharmacy	*Kusuri-ya*
Shoe shop	*Kutsu-ya*
Barber shop	*Toko-ya*
Bookshop	*Hon-ya*
Cake shop	*Okashi-ya*
Toy shop	*Omocha-ya*
Supermarket	*Supa-Maketto*
Department store	*Depato*
Restaurant	*Restoran*
Hotel	*Hoteru*
Station	*Eki*
Taxi stand	*Takushii noriba*
Bank	*Ginko*
Hospital	*Byoin*
Police Station	*Koban*

OUT SHOPPING

This one	*Kore*
That one (near the other person)	*Sore*
That one (near neither of you)	*Are*
Do you have...?	*...(wa) arimasuka?*
Could you show me that one please?	*Sore o misete kudasai.*
How much is it?	*Ikura desuka?*
Don't you have anything cheaper?	*Mo sukoshi yasui no arimasenka?*
Can I try it on?	*Shichaku shite mo ii desuka?*
Do you accept (credit) cards?	*(Kurjitto) kado tsukaemasuka?*
I'll take this.	*Kore o kudasai.*
Three of these, please.	*Kore o mittsu kudasai.*

BOARDING THE TRAIN

Ticket (office)	*Kippu (uriba)*
A single ticket to Sendai, please.	*Sendai made, katamichi ichi-mae kudasai.*
Two returns to Nikko, please.	*Nikko made, ofuku ni-mae kudasai.*
Reserved seat	*Shitei seki*
Unreserved seat	*Jiyuseki*
First class car	*Guriin* (Green) *sha*
Which platform does the train for Nagoya leave from?	*Nagoya yuki wa namban sen desuka?*

Thank you (very much)	*(Domo) arigato gozaimasu* (informally, *"Domo"* is enough)
Thanks for the meal.	*Gochisosama deshita.*
Don't mention it.	*Doitashimashite*
Here you are.	*Dozo*
After you.	*Dozo*
Sure, go ahead.	*Dozo* (in answer to "May I...?")

DAYS/TIME

(On) Sunday	*Nichi-yobi (ni)*
(Next) Monday	*(Raishu no) Getsu-yobi*
(Last) Tuesday	*(Senshu no) Ka-yobi*
(Every) Wednesday	*(Maishu) Sui-yobi*
(This) Thursday	*(Konshu no) Moku-yobi*
Friday	*Kin-yobi*
Saturday	*Do-yobi*
Yesterday	*Kino*
Today	*Kyo*
This morning	*Kesa*
This evening	*Konya*
Tomorrow	*Ashita*
What time is it?	*Nan-ji desuka?*

IN THE RESTAURANT

Water	*Mizu*
Beef	*Gyuniku*
Pork	*Butaniku*
Chicken	*Toriniku*
Fish	*Sakana*
Beer	*Biiru*
Grilled	*Yaite*
Boiled	*Nite*
Fried	*Itamete*
Raw	*Nama*

NUMBERS

Counting is very complicated in Japanese! Counting up to ten on their fingers, the Japanese will go: *ichi, ni, san, shi (yon), go, roku, shichi* (or *nana*), *hachi, ku* (or *kyu*), *ju*. If they are counting bottles, they will go: *ip-pon, ni-hon, sam-bon, yon-hon, go-hon, rop-pon, nana-hon, hap-pon, kyu-hon, jup-pon*. Depending on what is being counted, the suffix will change. You will be fairly safe with numbers that don't need suffixes:

One	*Hitotsu*
Two	*Futatsu*
Three	*Mittsu*
Four	*Yottsu*
Five	*Itsutsu*
Six	*Muttsu*
Seven	*Nanatsu*
Eight	*Yattsu*
Nine	*Kokonotsu*
Ten	*To*

If you want five of something, simply point at it and say "Itsutsu kudasai."

STUDYING JAPANESE

As with most languages, the best way to learn Japanese is in context with the culture and society, and with native speakers as teachers. Those living in urban areas of Japan can take regularly-scheduled classes at their leisure – schools are everywhere in Tokyo, for example – mixing in their studies with work and play.

For those who don't live in Japan, but want to seriously study Japanese, there is a superb option, quite unique and worth considering.

The **Shibusawa International School** offers intensive (6 hours daily), live-in Japanese language studies at an elegant old estate in the town of Fukaya, outside of Tokyo. A student finishing a single three-month term will have a good foundation in conversational grammar, and some basic reading and writing skills. After six months, enough competence is obtained to do most anything, whether working in a Tokyo office or bumming around the country on tour.

There are four terms per calendar year. The full course is five terms, or 15 months. Many people come for six months or a year, then go on their way. Others come for three months at a time, returning again to continue the full course, or to brush up. Students come from all over the world, and at any one time, there are half a dozen nationalities represented among the 20–30 students attending. Classes are small, three to six per class.

The school has modern private rooms or group dormitory rooms, with laundry and, yes, western toilet and shower facilities. In addition to the language classes, there are aikido, calligraphy, and culture classes.

It is in the country, half an hour by bicycle (which the school provides) or ten minutes by taxi to the train station. From there, it's a little over an hour to downtown Tokyo. Some may find the isolation a bit too much, but it helps keep one's mind on the studies. The school has a television room and a cafeteria with a delicious menu of Japanese, Asian and western meals.

The school is part of the legacy of Shibusawa Eiichi, who was pivotal in bringing Japan into the modern economic and industrial world at the turn of the century. His great-granddaughter, Shibusawa Takako, started the school on a family estate in 1985.

Prices are actually on the economical side, considering the amount of language studies offered and the excellent facilities. Per month, fees include: tuition, ¥60,000; private room, ¥20,000; meals, 3/day, ¥54,000 or pro-rated depending on meals consumed. It's probably one of the best bargains in the country, and unquestionably time well spent.

Shibusawa International School, Tokyo Office
3-5-4 Shiba-koen, Minato-ku, Tokyo 105
tel: (03) 3433-5984, fax: (03) 3432-0561

USEFUL ADDRESSES

TOURIST INFORMATION

Tourists may write or contact any of the following organizations for assistance:

Japan National Tourist Organization (JNTO)
2-10-1, Yurakucho, Chiyoda-ku, Tokyo 100, Japan
tel: (03) 3216 1903, fax (03) 214 7680, telex: J24132 JNTOTYO

Tourist Information Centers (TIC):
Tokyo TIC, Kotani Bldg, 1-6-6 Yura-kucho, Chiyoda-ku, Tokyo 100, tel: (03) 3502-1461.
Narita TIC, Airport Terminal Bldg, Narita, Chiba Pref. 282, tel: (0476) 32-8711.
Kyoto TIC, Kyoto Tower Bldg, Higashi-Shiokojicho, Shimogyo-ku, Kyoto 600, tel: (075) 371-5649.

Japan Travel Phone is a nationwide toll-free service offering travel-related information and language assistance. It is operated by JNTO.

If within Tokyo or Kyoto, call the respective TIC offices. If outside Tokyo or Kyoto, dial 0120-222800 for information on eastern Japan and 0120-444800 on western Japan. You will be connected to an English-speaking travel officer. Service is available daily between 9am and 5pm.

Other useful numbers are:
KDD Information, international telephone information, in English: 0057 (toll free)
NTT Information, domestic telephone directory information, in English. 9am–5pm weekdays.
Tokyo, tel: (03) 5295-1010; Narita, tel: (0476) 28-1010; Yokohama, tel: (045) 322-1010; Osaka tel: (06) 313-1010; Hiroshima, tel: (082) 262-1010
Postal Information, in English, 9.30am–4.30pm weekdays, tel: (03) 5472-5851/2
JR Train Information, in English, information only, no reservations, 10am–6pm weekdays, tel: (03) 3423-0111
Japan Hotline, information and help about everything, in English, 10am–4pm weekdays, tel: (03) 3586-0110.

ART/PHOTO CREDITS

12/13, 59, 61, 102, 103R, 104, **Paul Van Riel**
106/107, 149L, 304, 326/327,
361, 362/363
180/181 **Pierre-Antoine Donnet/**
APA Photo Agency
14/15, 25, 75, 111, 142/143, 144, **Robert McLeod**
150R, 160, 164, 168, 197, 211L, 217,
219, 222, 238, 240, 241, 242, 243, 254,
297, 298, 299, 301R, 322, 355, 360
115 **Ron Kucera**
309 **Sam Davis**
153, 175, 211R, 212, 329 **Stuart Atkin**
165 **Tadashi Matsumoto**
116, 117 **Courtesy of Toho Video**
28/29, 30, 32, 33, 34, 35L, 35R, 36, **Tokyo National Museum**
37, 38, 39, 40, 41, 42, 43, 44, 45,
46L, 46R, 47, 92/93, 94, 95, 96, 97,
100, 103L
174 **Torin Boyd**
236 **'Wah'**
172, 177 **Wayne Graczyk**

Illustrations **Klaus Geisler**
Maps **Berndtson & Berndtson**
Visual Consulting **V. Barl**

INDEX

A

H

I

411

N

P

T

A
B
C
D
F
G
H
I
J
a
b
c
d
e
f
g
h
i
j
k

He'll take you to paradise and back for just 50 pesos.

Cash only, of course.